Hammer and Anvil

Hammer and Anvil

Nomad Rulers at the Forge of the Modern World

Pamela Kyle Crossley

ROWMAN & LITTLEFIELD
Lanham • Boulder • New York • London

The cover image has been adapted from the digitized Kitab-i bahriye (attributed to Piri Reis, c. 1554 and dedicted to Suleiman the Magnificent). It has been contributed by the Walters Art Museum to Creative Commons under the Attribution-ShareAlike 3.0 Unported License (CCBY-SA 3.0). Walters Ms. W.658, folio 23b, and is used here with permission of the Museum.

Published by Rowman & Littlefield
An imprint of The Rowman & Littlefield Publishing Group, Inc.
4501 Forbes Boulevard, Suite 200, Lanham, Maryland 20706
https://rowman.com

6 Tinworth Street, London SE11 5AL, United Kingdom

Copyright © 2019 by The Rowman & Littlefield Publishing Group, Inc.

All rights reserved. No part of this book may be reproduced in any form or by any electronic or mechanical means, including information storage and retrieval systems, without written permission from the publisher, except by a reviewer who may quote passages in a review.

British Library Cataloguing in Publication Information Available

Library of Congress Cataloging-in-Publication Data

Names: Crossley, Pamela Kyle, author.
Title: Hammer and anvil : nomad rulers at the forge of the modern world / Pamela Crossley.
Description: Lanham : Rowman & Littlefield, [2019] | Includes bibliographical references and index.
Identifiers: LCCN 2018031510 (print) | LCCN 2018035252 (ebook) | ISBN 9781442214453 (Electronic) | ISBN 9781442214439 (cloth : alk. paper)
Subjects: LCSH: Eurasia--History--To 1500. | Mongols--History. | Civilization, Turkic.
Classification: LCC DS33.5 (ebook) | LCC DS33.5 .C76 2019 (print) | DDC 950/.2--dc23
LC record available at https://lccn.loc.gov/2018031510

∞ ™ The paper used in this publication meets the minimum requirements of American National Standard for Information Sciences Permanence of Paper for Printed Library Materials, ANSI/NISO Z39.48-1992.

Printed in the United States of America

For Gene Garthwaite, who has encouraged the
several forms this manuscript has taken over thirty years

Contents

List of Maps	ix
Preface	xi
Acknowledgments	xv
Introduction	xvii

Part I: The Integrity of Eurasia

1 The Lost Continent	3
2 Light-Mindedness	23

Part II: Steppe Power in Settled Medieval Eurasia

3 The Turkic Tide	43
4 Belief and Blood	65
5 Sultans and Civilization	85

Part III: The Age of Far Conquest

6 The Predatory Enterprise	101
7 The Empires of the Toluids	133
8 Return of the Turks	167

Part IV: The Forge

9 Dissidence and Doubt	203
10 Intimations of Nationality	233
11 Ruling in Place	273

Epilogue	305
Index	319

List of Maps

Map 0.1. Reference map of Eurasian regions   xxi

Map 1.1. Early exchange core and trade road. Nomadic tracks through the Pamirs and Hindu Kush marked an early trade network linking the cities of Taxila and Peshawar and part of Transoxiana during and after decline of the Harappan networks of the Indus River valley, third and second millennia BCE.   7

Map 1.2. Major west and east extensions of the trade tracks and major cities of Eurasia, c. 1000 BCE to 1000 CE.   9

Map 1.3. Major overland trade roads of the Toluid period, c. 1200 to 1400 CE.   10

Map 3.1. Major political orders of Eurasia, c. 600 CE.   53

Map 4.1. Major political orders of the Abbasid–Tang era, c. 790 CE. *Note*: Contested areas are shaded.   76

Map 5.1. Major political orders of the Seljuk–Song era, c. 1000 CE.   97

Map 6.1. Major political orders at the beginning of Chinggis's long-distance campaigns, c. 1205.   102

Map 6.2. Chinggis-era campaigns in relation to the overland trade routes.   110

Map 6.3. Campaigns and overland transportation of the Mongol imperial era, 1229–1259.   121

List of Maps

Map 7.1. The Toluid era, c. 1250–1370.   149

Map 8.1. Turkic regimes and the Byzantine empire, c. 1300.   173

Map 8.2. Timurid-Ming Eurasia, c. 1400.   179

Map 8.3. Growth of the Ottomans, c. 1300. *Note*: Ottoman territories are crosshatched and contested areas are shaded.   186

Map 8.4. Growth of the Ottomans, c. 1400. *Note*: Ottoman territories are crosshatched and contested areas are shaded.   187

Map 8.5. Growth of the Ottomans, c. 1500. *Note*: Ottoman territories are crosshatched and contested areas are shaded.   188

Map 8.6. Growth of the Ottomans, c. 1600. *Note*: Ottoman territories are crosshatched and contested areas are shaded.   189

Map 10.1. The growth of markets for printed literature, c. 1480–1600. *Note*: Important early cities with printing industries are marked. Patterned regions are domestic markets for publications in regional vernaculars. Straight lines indicate the destinations (but not the transport routes) for works produced before 1600 in Hebrew and Arabic for diasporal communities and proselytizing missions.   261

Map 11.1. Ottoman-Ming Eurasia, c. 1500.   274

Preface

This book considers the impact of Turkic and Mongol regimes upon the densely agricultural regions they came to rule, particularly in the tumultuous period that marked the weakening of the cultural and political patterns of the "middle ages" across Eurasia. The rulers drew upon Central Asian traditions to promote vernacular languages, popular religions, and ideologies legitimating political authority independently from established religious hierarchies. The effect of these trends was to weaken the institutions of universalized language, scholastic religion, and theologically legitimated rulership that characterized the world we think of as "medieval." When transmitted to areas peripheral to Central Asian conquest, particularly Europe, they powered changes that, in retrospect, we see as "modern"—building the foundations of our criteria of identity, directing our science toward the fabric of reality, providing the tools for personal education and political enfranchisement.

This is not a research monograph. It is an extended essay on some sources of transformation from the late medieval to the early-modern period, written in and directed toward the allusive scope of readers of the English language. Its mile-wide and inch-deep conformation precludes the use of footnotes, which of necessity would overwhelm the text. Instead, each chapter concludes with reading notes that identify the sources of quotes, outline background reading, and suggest some specialized work that could be of interest.

Historians of thought are owed a preliminary apology for my cooptation and loose application of the term "idealism" to mean the ancient and ubiquitous concept of a noumenal reality that is able to be apprehended only by intuitive or ecstatic experience. This basic idea takes many different qualified and specific forms in Hinduism; Zoroastrianism; Buddhism; Platonism; gnosticism of the Christian, Jewish, and Islamic varieties; neo-Confucianism; and early Anabaptism, and I plead guilty to misusing "idealism" to link them together and contrast them to "rationalist" philosophies that have either affirmed the reality of the phenomenal world or insisted that it is best analyzed through an axiomatic mind/matter dichotomy. A similar but less grand apology is also due for my use of "dissident" to mean separatist and skeptical communities, whether best described as religious or philosophical. I hope that in context my terms are useful.

I must also apologize to specialists of the Islamic Middle East for using the term "Turkic" to refer to a range of languages, some more stable and durable than others, used across Eurasia in historical times. "Turkish" is used to refer to the modern language, and early modern standards such as Kipchak/Mamluk Turkish and Chaghatay Turkish are so named in the appropriate contexts. Persianists who generously read and commented on the manuscript have persuaded me to maintain their use of "Persian" to refer to a complex of cultural, literary, and historiographical developments across Central, South, and West Asia, sharing ancestry with and intertwining over the centuries with legacies that are also called "Iranian." So the text here tentatively consolidates "Turkic" matters and tentatively distills "Persian" from "Iranian"; in both cases, justification is found in academic custom, differing criteria in discernment of similarity and difference among historiographic traditions, and the best way of providing easy access to a variety of readers.

The strategy regarding proper names is to make them as wieldy and familiar as possible. Scholars will note that diacriticals and special characters are missing: Đại Việt is just Dai Viet, the dotless ı in Turkish is just an "i," and the Arabic *alif*, *hamza*, and *'ayn* are also left out (except for Shi'a, Shi'i, and Shi'ite, where they may help pronunciation), though they are not technically diacriticals. There is no consistency in the form chosen for names except to make each name distinct and easy to recognize when next encountered (though one hopes for similarity to the attested names, which often have many forms). For instance, there is not much justification for spelling the name of the last universally accepted Mongol khaghan as "Mongge" except that I am tired of hearing my students call him "Monkey." Place names are chosen with an eye to current geography whenever possible, which results in anachrony and looseness in terms such as "Byzantium," "Turkestan" ("East" and "West"), "Tibet," "China," "Manchuria," "India," "Palestine" or "Palestine/Syria," "Russia," "Iran/Iraq," and so on. The Pannonian Steppe, or Plain (or Carpathian Basin), is the Hungarian Steppe because it is a more wieldy name; the Kipchak/Western/Kazakh Steppe is just the Kipchak Steppe; the Taklamakan Desert is referred to in this book as the Tarim Basin, of which it is a part. Some places have a sort of world-history name (such as Taxila, Mecca, Tabriz, Chang'an, Turfan, Canton, Kaifeng) that may be used on maps instead of the chronologically correct name. Because of its etymological connections (via Arabic) with "Saracen" and "illumination," I have decided to use "the Levant" as a regional designation; this once-antiquated term has come back into fashion lately, so I would regard it as reasonable even without its meaningful (for this book) connotations. I can only ask readers to bear in mind the heuristic purposes behind the choices here and the premium put on common sense rather than close chronological or transliterative accuracy in place names.

Not only place names are occasionally anachronistic. As examples, I use *gazi* for periods that are too early, but in context I think it will make sense. I shouldn't say Japan had an "emperor," but I don't think readers need to be burdened with the unique *tennō*. I shouldn't use "Nevskii" as a family name, but it helps suggest relationships among individuals whose names readers may not need to see in the text.

A further deviation from precision is use of *mamluk* as a category of military slaves and also as the proper name (given by historians) to an empire based in Cairo; the italicized lowercase word applies to the social category and the unitalicized capitalized word ("Mamluk") means the state. The reverse applies with "Han," the name of a Chinese empire that later became a cultural identity name in China. Terms from Arabic, Persian, Turkic, and Mongolian are mostly not properly pluralized in the contexts in which they are clearly plural since readers do not need to know two foreign words when one will do. Specialists will also, I think, note the absence of terms (but not the descriptions) that often turn up in renditions of any part of Muslim history (e.g., *waqf, hajj, jizya, 'iqta, madrasa, qadi, hadith, madhab, 'arif, al-ishrāq, ghulam, dev şirme, halāl*), all of which for similar reasons have been left out of the text. The few foreign terms incorporated into the text are italicized on first use to indicate that they are not English (such as *millet*) and subsequently normalized by lack of italicization (except for *mamluk* and *han*, as indicated above).

While this lexical simplicity and familiarity is a high priority, I have also eschewed what I regard as baggage-laden constructions in the interest of having a narrative that is a bit more from the ground up. I have, as examples, avoided "Axial Age," "Silk Road(s)," "feudalism," "tanistry," and "Golden Horde" (or "Kipchak Horde" or "Desht-i-Kipchak").

Light coverage of the Mughals and the Safavids, as well as virtual omission of Romanovs and Qing is, I hope, explained by the fact that their chronologies are weighted well outside the period that is the focus of the book. But beyond those topics I must point out to those for whom this period is unfamiliar something that will be immediately obvious to those who are expert: the discussion here is selective (honestly, I hope), and many important topics have been left out. Part of this is strategic in order to keep topics to a minimum but demonstration sufficient. So the Xiongnu, Avars, Seljuks, and Mamluks get more attention, while Parthians, Skythians, and the Delhi sultanates get less. Topics already nicely covered by other authors—including the early Kara Kitai, Tibet, and Timurid-related topics—are handed off via the reading notes. There is also an obvious shorting of the Arabs (among the "other" pastoralists that the book is not about), who make necessary appearances but are not used for contrast to the degree that would be possible in a longer book.

As a postscript, I must apologize for alluding to titles by the following for some of my interior headings: William Wordsworth, Jerzy Kosinski, and Leslie Poles Hartley.

Acknowledgments

This book began many years ago as a study of the effects of the Mongol conquests on peripheral territories such as Japan, Myanmar, Thailand, Syria, Hungary, Poland, and the Baltic states. In the years since, many excellent new studies of the Mongol empires have appeared, while my interests gradually refocused on particular effects across Eurasia—both in the conquered and in the contiguous regions—of the spread of Turkic and Mongol military regimes. Small bits of the original book are still here, but most of it has disappeared, displaced by the developing discussion of the role of these regimes in accelerating continental change in the interval between what we retrospectively perceive as the "medieval" and the "early modern" worlds.

The ideas of the book go back to graduate student days, and I must first acknowledge the strong influence of Fred Donner and Dimitri Gutas, who helped me develop a minor field in Islamic history (and Arabic reading) at Yale, and by the expansive and restless imagination of my thesis adviser, Jonathan Spence. Subsequently, my interests were strongly reinforced and expanded by Joseph Fletcher, Albert Hourani, and Gene Garthwaite, the last of whose steady interest in the manuscript over 30 years has been a major inspiration. During the long period of working on the manuscript and investigating the problems associated with it, the gifts arriving via conversation, shared research, and correspondence have been innumerable, but I must note Sarah Allan, Chris Bayly, Peter Fibiger Bang, Michael Barany, Beatrice Bartlett, Ehud Benor, David Brophy, Michael Brose, Terry Burke, Paul Bushkovich, Ada Cohen, Nicola di Cosmo, James Cracraft, Stephen Dale, Ruth Dunnell, Dick Eaton, Dale Eickelman, Ben Elman, Tina Endicott-West, Carl Estabrook, Suraiya Faroqhi, M. Cecilia Gaposchkin, Richard von Glahn, Glenn Most, Valerie Hansen, Roger Hart, Jane Hathaway, Roland Higgins, Macabe Keliher, Metin Kunt, David Lagomarsino, Dominic Lieven,

Victor Mair, John R. McNeill, Victor Mair, Beatrice Manz, Sucheta Mazumdar, Jim Millward, R. I. Moore, David Morgan, Munkh-Erdene Lkhamsuren, James Nagy, Max Oidtmann, Peter Perdue, Evelyn Rawski, Mary Rossabi, Morris Rossabi, Jonathan Schlesinger, Walter Simons, Naomi Standen, Nancy Steinhardt, Lynn Struve, and C. Don Wyatt. I am also grateful for feedback on the manuscript and discussion on related research topics among my students Carter Brace, Anmol Ghavri, George Harvey, Alexandra Terrio, Nicole Tiao, and Billy Sandlund.

Many institutions have contributed funds or venues for encounter that have made the manuscript possible. They include the John Simon Guggenheim Foundation; National Endowment for the Humanities; Dartmouth College; Faculty Seminar in Race and Ethnicity, University of Texas, Austin; the Institute for Advanced Study; the Scheiber Lectureship at University of Binghamton; Department of History, University of Birmingham; Princeton Institute for International and Regional Studies; the China Colloquium at Yale University; the Institute for Chinese Studies, University of Ghent; Center for Early Modern History, University of Minnesota, Minneapolis; Modern China Seminar, Columbia University; Accademia di Danimarca, Rome; and Mansfield Freeman Center for East Asian Studies, Wesleyan University.

Nobody in our all-information age can produce a book like this by herself. All but a tiny corner of this manuscript has been produced by driving outside my lane—in fact, by careening across multiple lanes of a very expansive highway. Those who have generously acted as road guides, traffic cops, and repair and towing crews are much in my grateful thoughts: Morris Rossabi, Stephen Dale, Gene Garthwaite, Terry Burke, and above all, David Morgan and Peter Jackson, who each went well beyond the call of duty. Like guides, cops, and mechanics everywhere, they did not always find that their advice was followed, and I claim all stubbornly persisting errors of fact or interpretation.

Development of the early and middle versions of the manuscript has been aided by David Steinhardt's Massive Publishing Enterprise, not least for providing a steady sense of expectation and readership as well as sharp and determined editing. Final and very special thanks go to Susan McEachern, who has shown patience and faith far beyond what any editor owes her author.

Introduction

Our state of confident confusion about the definition of modernity is probably integral to the concept of modernity itself. We could establish—and many historians persuasively have established—all kinds of criteria to characterize the process of modernization or the condition of modernity. But what the first users of the term "modern" in fifth-century Europe referred to is what we most often mean by it today: The widespread consciousness of having crossed a threshold of discontinuities (in that first case, the spread of Christianity) that gives people of the present the sense that they are living very differently from people of the past. Each modernity begets a subsequent modernity.

Our current modernity is often noted as accompanied by, if not consisting of, the rise of universalisms such as rationalism and scientific objectivity, capitalism, international law and the affirmation of state sovereignty, nationalism, natural rights, democracy, technocracy—universalisms that give us the sense that whatever separates us from our contemporaries, the universalisms of modernity make us all closer to each other than any of us are to people of the past. The historical process of the emergence of these ostensible universalisms was indistinguishable from the attenuation of earlier universalisms. Those earlier universalisms of founded religious doctrines, continent-spanning religious hierarchies, widely unifying written languages of religion and commerce, and interlocking transregional dynasties were displaced by new institutions of locally defined identities overriding class, state mechanisms for regulating and historicizing those identities, and self-legitimating rulership. In their turn, these institutions provided the matrix in which new universalisms were generated and disseminated (in many cases through imperialist imposition) in the nineteenth and twentieth centuries. The role of the post-nomadic rulers in this process of dismantling medieval universalisms while releasing—indeed, actively promoting—new particularisms that would become universal and underwrite our current notions of "modernity" is the focus of this book.

Histories of states of nomadic origin are framed by deep assumptions relating to nomadism as a phenomenon. The Greek word *nomos*, which is the source of "nomad," was related to the idea of social divisions, technical specializations, or geographic allotments (and it shared ancestry with a word for partitioning and specialization that shows up in our suffix *onomy*). In this sense nomads were defined not only by what they did but also by where they did it since their spaces were compartmented on the margins of the agricultural, densely populated, self-styled "civilized" zones. For some twentieth-century social and cultural philosophers (see reading notes), nomadism became a trope for contemporary ways of living that transgressed or subverted the lines of order that define status and identity. For historians, nomadism is the history of marginality and ephemerality. Episodically, some nomads are recognized as having had dramatic impact. But in the long run, they were drowned in the comforts, the complexity, the permanence of settled life and structured space. Because of a lack of critical mass of population or endurance of their political orders, nomads were compelled over time to submit to the gravity of civilization and to be drawn from its edges to its center.

When we look to the period between about 500 and 1500, when peoples identifying themselves with traditions we would call "nomadic" came to control—and to govern for significant periods of time—great agricultural societies, we are left to ask a number of questions about their effect upon these societies. We have some clichés at hand. When their regimes were successful, the reasons lay in their acquired similarities to successful native regimes before them. When they were unsuccessful, the reasons were to be found in some stubborn adherence to nomadic customs or expectations. But the nomadic regimes themselves had been agents of large-scale cultural change, and these changes might long outlive the political regime that any originally nomadic group had imposed. This raises a question regarding our construction of nomadism as something real. In history, branchings and interaction of varieties of economic life produced a spectrum ranging—in theory—from exclusive nomadism to exclusive agriculturalism, with virtually nobody in Eurasia at the nomadic extreme except during military campaigns or environmental crises. Nomads can be designated more concretely as pastoralists—people at some moment in time depending primarily upon the care and processing of animals for a living, but always living and trading within a broader context of agricultural, urban economies. The romantic ascription of self-sufficient, freethinking, confinement-hating, rebellious qualities to "nomads" is a habit—if still interesting and in some ways a meaningful one—of agriculturally based elites. In light of the above, the use of "nomad" in this book will be provisional, hesitant, and sometimes schematic. It is a term of convenience.

The Turks may be regarded as the archetypical Eurasian nomads, yet the totality of what we know suggests that in their histories can be found the elements of political and cultural change that characterized the end of the medieval era. The justification of this claim lies partly in the looseness with which I use the term "Turkic." There are several excellent histories of the Turks (see Chapter 3 reading notes), and a new one (from me) is not needed. Turks were not always the originators of the institutions that interest me, and much that will be discussed in connection with one or another Turkic group here could easily be described as something other than "Turkic." The Turks were horse nomads, though certainly not the earliest. They perfected (if they did not invent) the formidable, mobile dwelling of the yurt, which provided not only astounding comfort in all seasons but also many of the fundamental political metaphors that would become ubiquitous throughout Eurasia. They were also important transmitters of the woven floor coverings we once called "oriental" carpets, which transformed later medieval interiors and provided opportunities for stupendous displays by monarchs all across Eurasia in the early modern period. Turks, in this frame of reference, refined and distributed vivid but flexible ideas of rulers legitimated through their direct favor by Blue Heaven. It was Turkic populations who provided the heft behind conquests we attribute to the Mongols and allowed the establishment of empires redrawing societies and political geographies. Their states, for similar reasons, favored making local vernaculars literary, making popular culture prestigious and profitable, and allowing folk religion a wide scope of influence over founded, hierarchical, established, or state religions. It was Turks who sustained and refined the academic and technological traditions that fostered the material tools of modern state power. And it was Turks who generated the ideologically aggressive and delicately centralized style of the Ottomans and Timurids and who challenged other empires to respond in kind.

But the characterization above does not cover all the critical uses of the term "Turkic" in this book. The word is used to refer to many peoples, languages, and institutions that in origin are not known to be Turkic—they may be on some Iranian linguistic spectrum, including Sarmatians, Alans, and Kurds; they may be Chinese, Skythian, Cimmerian, Tagbach, Xiongnu, Rouran, Goths, Slavs, Kitans, Jurchens, or something else. This book is not an exercise in linguistic or anthropological precision on this point—and in many cases, these particulars of some historical groups or regimes cannot be precisely determined. In this book, "Turkic" is first an invocation of the dichotomy drawn in many traditions between the ethical and esthetic institutions of large, agrarian states (civilization) and the threats from ostensibly restless groups whose economies are not fundamentally agricultural and who as a consequence are reputed to not respect law or reason (barbarians). In the historiographical traditions of the Islamic world, "Turk" became a representation of this role. The ancient Turan, who could not have been Turkic, were over time transmuted into a persisting Turkic menace at the periphery. But it is also a loose category of regimes between about 500 and 1500 playing the historical role of using institutions and values from outside major agrarian societies of Eurasia to rule those societies, often for long periods of time. They were not necessarily nomads nor Turks, but the arc of their military rise and rule of large societies presents a consolidated historical problem.

The discussion in this book takes empires ruled by lineages of Turkic, nomadic, or other non-agrarian origin as a contrasting proposition from nomadic economies or migrating populations in general. Not all regimes of nomadic origin insisted upon enduring identification of the rulership with anything overtly nomadic, even if their institutions and cultural tendencies are tempting to link to nomadic origins. "Post-nomadic" here describes the middle and late periods of the Mongol regimes and of the Ottomans, and it also encompasses later regimes, such as Ming China, Joseon Korea, and Muscovite Russia. Despite the fact of a strenuously anti-nomadic ideology in some of these regimes, the continuities of institutions and the cooptation of a post-nomadic framework of state and rulership makes them a necessary part of the sequence of understanding the impact of post-nomadic occupations across Eurasia.

Central Asia as a place and the early thirteenth century when the Mongols seemed (from our present perspective) to explode out of eastern Eurasia are fused in our historical view, but the relationship of that apparent disruption to continuities before and after can be elusive. From one perspective, the Mongol empire was the last great manifestation of the millennia of integrated contact across the land tracks of Eurasia, a period of continental integration during which differences between one region and another were discovered at the pace of a camel's tread or a horse cart's trundle; it was this frame of reference that was dying in the age of Niccolo Machiavelli (see epilogue). Looked at another way, the vast scope of the Mongol and Turkic empires permitted integration of knowledge, technologies, and ideas across Eurasia at an unprecedented pace. This was the prelude not to a new life of Eurasia as a single cultural or economic system, but to the split of Eurasia into "west" and "east"—experienced as shockingly disparate when travelers landed after months of looking at a featureless ocean. It was an age in which regional specialization and new ideologies of difference were generated by the accelerated pace of exchange.

In past decades, historians have explored in some detail the ways in which the period of the Mongol empires promoted cultural and technological exchanges that stimulated the emergence of new knowledge. My concern in this book is something related but different. Major local cultural changes under the nomadic rulers of populous agricultural societies across Eurasia ended many of the primary patterns that had characterized these societies for centuries. These changes were less the results of discrete encounters and exchanges and more the products of organic continental changes that had, in many ways, been accelerated or reinforced by the nomadic rulers of large, settled societies. The effects of nomad-derived government over populous societies led in some cases to the revival of earlier beliefs and political traditions, the discreditation of religiously legitimated rulership in various forms across Eurasia, and the rise of popularly derived notions of national identity. This book is not arguing that the nomadic rulers of great agricultural societies were the originators of Eurasian modernity, but that they played a distinct role in the catalyzation of changes we associate with the passage across the threshold to our own modernity—and that led to the destruction of post-nomadic regimes wherever they survived. (See Map 0.1.)

READING NOTES: INTRODUCTION

There will be occasion in later reading notes to point to the greater world of nomads in theory and in history, but at this point, I would single out a few: Katheryn M. Linduff and Karen S. Rubinson, *Are All the Warriors Male? Gender Roles on the Ancient Eurasian Steppe* (Rowman & Littlefield, 2008); Peter B. Golden, "Nomads and Their Sedentary Neighbors in Pre-Chinggisid Eurasia," *Archivum Eurasii Medii Aevi* 7 (1987–1991): 41–82, and *Nomads and Sedentary Societies in Medieval Eurasia* (American Historical Associa-

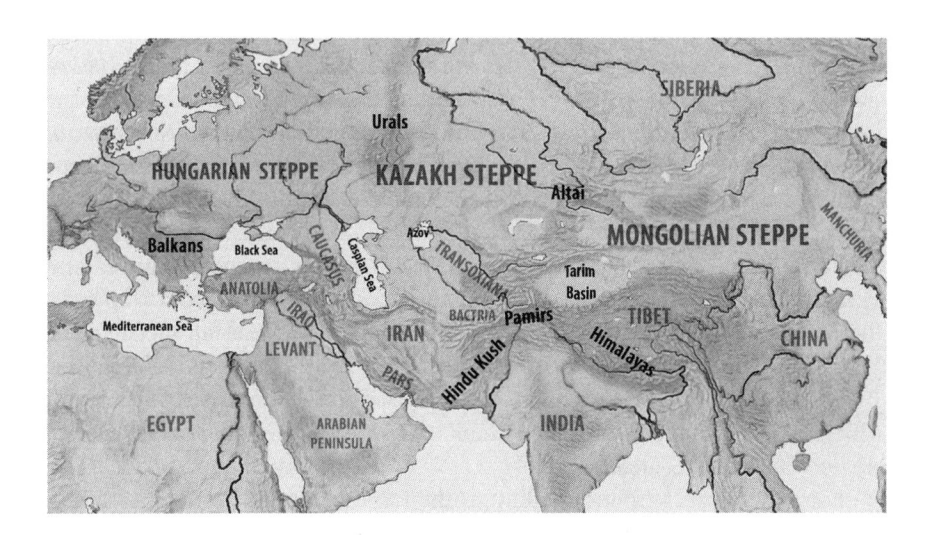

Map 0.1. Reference map of Eurasian regions

tion, 1999); S. S. Kalieva and V. N. Logvin, "On the Origins of Nomadism in the Asian Steppes," *Archeology, Ethnology and Anthropology of Eurasia* 39, no. 3 (Sept 2011): 85–93; David Sneath, "The Myth of the Kinship Society," in *The Headless State: Aristocratic Orders, Kinship Society and Misrepresentations of Nomadic Inner Asia* (Columbia UP, 2007), 39–65. "Nomadology" as a theoretical issue in cultural criticism comes from the work of Gilles Deleuze and Felix Guattari, as presented in earlier work, particularly *Mille plateaux* (1980), translated as *A Thousand Plateaus: Capitalism and Schizophrenia*, trans. Brian Massumi (U of Minnesota P, 1987).

Discussion of nomadism in anthropology and sociology is inexhaustible. For leading and representative works on comparative nomadism, particularly from an anthropological perspective, see Anatoly Khazanov's introduction to his 2001 edited volume (with André Wink), *Nomads in the Sedentary World* (Routledge, 2001). He suggested that for the most part nomads have not had a profound impact on the sedentary zones; contact between nomadic and settled has resulted in the nomadic undergoing most of the change. For samples of alternate views from historians, see Reuven Amitai and Michal Biran, eds., *Nomads as Agents of Cultural Change: The Mongols and Their Eurasian Predecessors* (U Hawaii P, 2015). Sneath, *The Headless State* (*op. cit.*), is an important contrarian discussion qualifying in some instances and repudiating in others the application of alterizing concepts ("tribe," "clan," "ethnos," and so on) to nomadic or ostensibly nomadic societies. On the debates surrounding the Sneath critique, see, as examples, Nicholas Kradin and Thomas J. Barfield, eds., *Nomadic Pathways in Social Evolution* (Oxford UP, 2003). Two influential, though not unchallenged, studies have put confrontations between the nomadic world and the sedentary world into context integrating history and anthropology. The earlier, by Rudi Paul Lindner, examined the origins of the Ottoman state: *Nomads and Ottomans in Medieval Anatolia* (Indiana UP, 1983). In the latter, Daniel T. Potts looks at the long, symbiotic relationship of Iran and Central Asia in *Nomadism in Iran: From Antiquity to the Modern Era* (Oxford UP, 2014), 157–186. The introductory chapter of each book offers excellent overviews of the scholarship on the relationships of nomads and agricultural regions in premodern Eurasia.

For a discussion of the use of "Turk" and "Turkic" to mean a broad and flexibly defined identity in Eurasian history, particularly in scholarship from the Muslim world, see Joo-Yup Lee, "The Historical Meaning of the Term 'Turk' and the Nature of the Turkic Identity of the Chinggisid and Timurid Elites in Post-Mongol Central Asia," *Central Asiatic Journal* 59, no. 1/2 (2016): 101–132 and Yehoshua Frenkel, *The Turkic Peoples in Medieval Arabic Writings* (Routledge, 2014).

For general background reading to the topics examined in this introduction, I would suggest Peter Golden, *An Introduction to the History of the Turkic Peoples* (Otto Harrassowitz, 1992); Carter Vaughn Findley, *The Turks in World History* (Oxford UP, 2004); Morris Rossabi, *The Mongols: A Very Short Introduction* (Oxford UP, 2012) and *A History of China* (Wiley-Blackwell, 2013); David O. Morgan, *The Mongols*, 2nd ed. (Blackwell's, 2007); Gene R. Garthwaite, *The Persians* (Wiley/Blackwell, 2006); Paul Bushkovitch, *A Concise History of Russia* (Cambridge UP, 2011); Thabit A. Abdullah, *A Short History of Iraq*, 2nd ed. (Routledge, 2011); James Forsyth, *The Caucasus: A History* (Cambridge UP, 2013); Stephen F. Dale, *The Muslim Empires of the Ottomans, Safavids, and Mughals* (Cambridge UP, 2010); Timothy May, *The Mongol Conquests in World History* (Reaktion, 2012); and Geoffrey Hosking, *Russian History: A Very Short Introduction* (Oxford UP, 2012).

I can also suggest these reference volumes for readers who want a more topical introduction or more detail on the subjects of this book or quick and reliable reference material: Yuri Bregel, *An Historical Atlas of Central Asia* (Brill, 2003); Paul Buell, *Historical Dictionary of the Mongolian World Empire* (Scarecrow, 2003); Christopher P. Atwood, *Encyclopedia of Mongolia and the Mongol Empire* (Facts on File, 2004); Gabor Agaston and Bruce Masters, *Encyclopedia of the Ottoman Empire* (Facts on File, 2009); and Timothy May, *The Mongol Empire: A Historical Encyclopedia*, 2 vols. (ABC-CLIO, 2016).

Part I

The Integrity of Eurasia

Chapter One

The Lost Continent

Eurasia is best thought of not as a continuous surface but as boundless multidirectional vectors of increasing speed over time, producing a historical theater that changes size and appearance as viewed from different perspectives. It is important that the topology of Eurasia is not really a doughnut, with "Central Asia" as a hole of attenuated population density, urbanization, trade, or contact. Instead, Central Asia was an early and continuous source of the integration of Eurasia as a whole, reduced to a frontier of cultural and historical study only in the early modern period. The alienization of Central Asia from European, Chinese, and South Asian familiarity thereafter is both a mark of our "modernity" and the point at which a sense of an integrated ecumene was lost.

TOPOGRAPHICAL EURASIA

Global historians regard the development of Eurasian history as a more objective research template than the parochial and, in many ways, illusory national histories that dominated the nineteenth and much of the twentieth centuries. But "Eurasia" is just another construction; we might as easily refer to the entire continent and its subcontinents as "Asia" (or any name at all). The contrived word "Eurasia" dates from the mid-nineteenth century, the beginning of a phase of grand academic and strategic thinking that integrated the eastern and western ends of the continent and delineated its supposed natural citadel, the steppe stretching from the Balkans (the name itself probably comes from a Turkic word for forested mountains) in the west to Mongolia in the east. The theorists of Eurasia have found its limits to be ambiguous. Originally—as in the writings of Halford Mackinder (1861–1947)—Africa was regarded as part of the root continent, connected not only by land but also the navigable waters of the Red Sea and the Mediterranean. The grounds for regarding Africa as integral to Eurasia are substantial. We know that before the sixteenth century the demographic and economic history of most of Africa conformed to the broad patterns of Eurasia.

But it is now the fashion, to which prominent writers such as Jared Diamond have subscribed, to define Eurasia by its east–west temperate zone axis, without Africa south of the Sahara. The grounds for this are also substantial. Here, I will use "Eurasia" in that east–west axis sense because it is familiar to most readers. An east–west temperate zone facilitated exchange of material and cultural influences from earliest times to the modern period. A few linguists propose a single origin for all the continent's major language groups. But many more agree that Eurasia has functioned as a weakly delimited *Sprachbund*, in which languages, whether related or unrelated in origin, have shared words that have traveled along with technology, social conventions, cultural ideas, and environmental change. Examples include English *mare*, Iranian *maal*, Mongolian *morin*, Chinese *ma*, all meaning horse; or German *hund*, Greek *kuon*, and Chinese *quan*, all meaning dog; or Russian *boyar*, Turkic *beg*, Uighur *beiluo*, and Manchu *beile* for a local headman or official. Current knowledge of the evolution of human haplogroups suggests that Eurasia is basically a community of human lineages postdating the emigrations from Africa, with contemporary lineages in Australia and descendant lineages in the Americas. The known genetic history corresponds in its basic outlines to hypotheses proposed earlier by linguistic historians, archaeologists, and historians of blood groups. Equally important, reconstruction of the genetic histories of apples, chickens, dogs, donkeys, grains, horses, and pigs shows that for them, too, temperate Eurasia was a coherent ecological zone.

CHRONOLOGICAL EURASIA

Extending terms such as "classical," "medieval," or "early modern" anywhere outside of Europe can appear to be patently Eurocentric. But it is possible to attach these chronological labels to broad patterns of change that are not primarily European in character, even if their first uses for periodization in English writing were in relation to European history. For instance, the "classical" period—the period when ancient Greece (800–300 BCE) and the Roman empire (27 BCE–476 CE) established some basic institutions of later European history—does not need to refer only to ancient Greece and Rome. The spread of ironworking, patterns of agricultural development, sea travel, the use of the horse for transport and war, urbanization, the emergence of dynastic government and written laws, differentiation of literate elites and priests from both aristocrats and the laboring population, and massive migration in search of land or safety were not exclusive to Europe but were characteristic of temperate Eurasia. They produced not only the Roman republic but also the Seleucid dynasty (312–64 BCE), the Mauryan (321–185 BCE), and the Han (203 BCE–220 CE). The end of the Han empire in 220 CE and the concentration of Roman administration and military struggles against the Sasanians in Iran in the fourth century suggests the transition to a different era. It was an age of new political structures resting on the networking of religious communities, some of which (as in the case of Buddhism and Christianity) originated in the classical period, some of which (as in the case of Islam) were native to this period. Heads of government—at times, but not always heads of state—were often militarists who were legitimated by the religious hierarchs. It was a period of consolidation of elites over wide spaces, linked by writing systems and classicized languages—foremost among them Sanskrit, Arabic, Greek, Latin, and classical Chinese—whose status was rooted in religious texts.

From the fifth to twelfth centuries, Eurasian government and law broadly spoke in two dialects. One was spiritual and moral—legitimating rulers, sanctifying war, and guiding education whether personal or mass. One was pecuniary and materialistic—quantifying damages; fixing access to land and water; obliging the rendering of tribute, tax, and corvée; and demanding the control of labor capacities, whether personal or mass. It was an age in which kings and emperors ruled with the endorsement of priests and elites made themselves recognizable by devout behaviors. Individuals tended to identify themselves by affiliation with a religious community (either local or universal), by recognized descent from an illustrious conquering ancestor, and by constraints of class. This was heuristic "medieval Eurasia." Those patterns were eventually overwhelmed by the effects of improved agriculture and the expansion of arable land; rising population and larger armies for the acquisition of more land or more defensible boundaries; much more efficient long-distance trade and travel; better medical knowledge, metallurgy, and observational astronomy; and cities increasingly enriched by imported money, investment, and credit. Empires on a new scale arose, emblemized by self-legitimating rulerships atop unitary states with impressive powers of secular coercion and indoctrination, partly thanks to rising urban literacy and the decreasing cost of printed materials. The rapid distribution of techniques improving farming, transportation, and hygiene contributed to rising populations and increasing urbanization. In this latter period, the ways in which people identified themselves changed fundamentally. Religion remained salient, but heritable class was fading or significantly revised. Both were now interwoven with regional identity, language, elements of popular culture such as cuisine, music, theater, long literary narratives, and early notions of race. It is what we commonly mean by the "early modern" period in Europe, but the trends were widespread across continental Eurasia. It was between these "medieval" and "early modern" periods—as Eurasian history, not European history—that the establishment of the nomad-derived courts of the Mongols and the Ottomans occurred. Their impact fostered or accelerated these trends not only in the lands under their direct domination but also over a much broader littoral with which they had friendly or hostile contact.

TRANSACTIONAL EURASIA

Eurasia consists of interlocking vectors—omnidirectional, frequently recursive, and of increasing speed over time—through which people disseminated material goods and cultural influences. These vectors have included the horse, Indo-European languages and migrations, Turkic languages and migrations, scripts, technologies, and ideologies. The early continental period marker for Eurasia may be the transition from the Bronze to the Iron Age. The beginning of the Bronze Age is unwise to date precisely because it varies with place and technology. Today, we tend to see the origins of the Bronze Age in the Ukrainian steppe and Anatolia by 3000 BCE, while 1200 BCE is a good marker for the earliest edge of the Iron Age—because the use of iron long predates the Iron Age and the use of bronze persisted after the end of the Bronze Age, the chronology is notional. It is perhaps bronze rather than iron that helps define Eurasia in light of the fact that there is no recognized Bronze Age outside of Eurasia (which includes North Africa). Central and Southern Africa, for instance, went straight to iron with no prelude in bronze except for transfers (material or informational) from the Mediterranean world. Metallurgy in North America appears limited to hammered copper, and in South America is found smelting and alloying for decorative and ritual objects. Australia had no metallurgy before contact with Europeans. Though the Eurasian transition to iron had various points of origination and came after hundreds—perhaps a thousand—years of working with proportions of iron mixed with tin, the general pattern reinforces the idea of the vicinage of Eurasia as a whole and suggests an early, inner knowledge core that fed the large agricultural zones at the continent's eastern and western extremes. The apparent chronology of introduction and adaptation of cultural technologies can be shown to conform broadly to the geographic relationship of a society to this exchange core—basically from the Himalayas north to the Russian steppe and between western China and eastern Iran.

Recent archaeology suggests that the passages for travel by foot, horse, and cart across Eurasia were not generated by a wish to get from one end to the other (say, from Egypt to China). It now appears more likely that travel over these tracks started from the center, or near the center, and radiated east, south, and west (see Map 1.1). Its earliest products were animals, wool, felt, minerals, ceramics, and slaves, and early tracks were determined by the best series of resting places within the core for moving nomads and their herds (primarily sheep). This so-called nomad algorithm (see reading notes) predicts the locations of Bronze and Iron Age sites now found within the core. It suggests that access eastward and westward was established by extension of these routes through mountains or across steppe and desert.

Areas at the convergence of early agricultural centers and the pastoral steppe, such as northern India or the eastern shores of the Black Sea, give evidence of steady ironworking as early as about 2000 BCE, and places more removed from the center, such as western Europe and northern China, are not regarded as part of the Iron Age until about 600 BCE. This suggests that the arrival and establishment of iron as part of local peace and war related less to the advancement of agriculture, or increasing population, or early state formation and more to something much simpler: proximity to well-traveled transport routes of Central Asia. This is not to say that the evidence today proves that this core area of Central Asia was the original home of iron manufacture. It is more likely that the sites with evidence of early iron technologies were stimulated by their proximity to the Central Asian exchange system that moved technological information and useful products

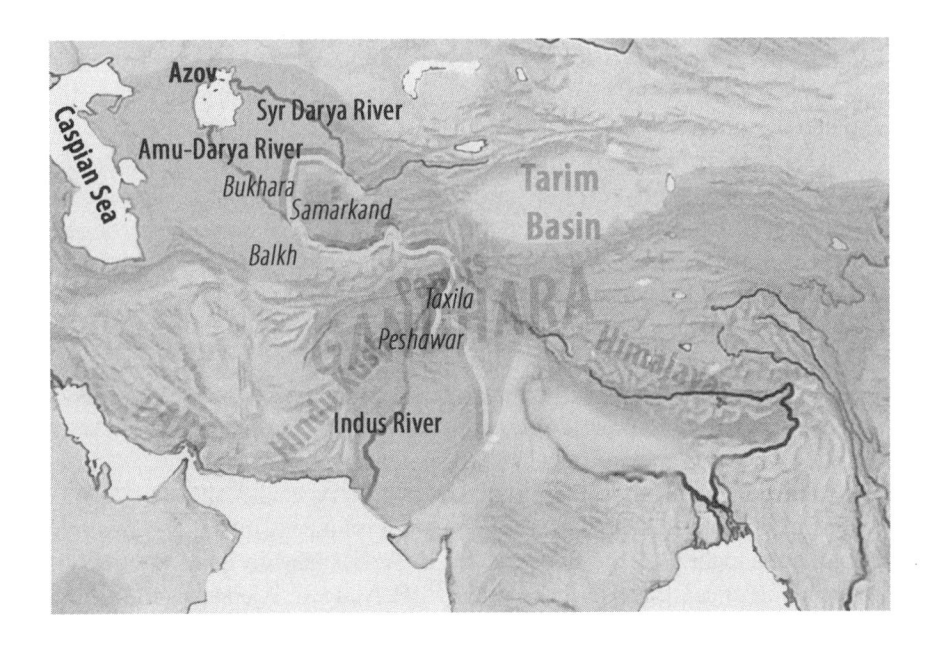

Map 1.1. Early exchange core and trade road. Nomadic tracks through the Pamirs and Hindu Kush marked an early trade network linking the cities of Taxila and Peshawar and part of Transoxiana during and after decline of the Harappan networks of the Indus River valley, third and second millennia BCE.

quickly. The same phenomenon may have been related to the role of Central Asian regions, such as Gandhara, in the last centuries BCE and early centuries CE as a center of accumulating Greek, Iranian, and Indian knowledge of mathematics, astronomy, pharmacology, and metallurgy. This exchange core continued to function until the later medieval period and is fundamental to understanding the dynamics of the Turkic and Mongol empires, all of which gravitated toward this core even if they originated to its east or west. Population distribution, technological and industrial specialization, routes of communication and conquest were all critically important to the accumulation of dynastic wealth and strategic domination. More relevant to this book, ideas and institutions could not be prevented from circulating rapidly and thoroughly through this space. The result was not only continual dialecticizing of languages and religions but also continual leakage of ideas and practices between the elite and the popular strata, contributing to the loss of traction by established elites in the age of the nomadic rulers.

RETICULATED EURASIA

The engine of Eurasian exchange in the historical period was a network of roads that in modern times is perceived as connecting the Caucasus and China. Explorers on the longest stretches of these paths in the nineteenth century knew the system was very old and hypothesized the ancient silk trade had been a controlling factor in its evolution (see reading notes). Famed explorer Ferdinand von Richthofen (1833–1905) called it the "Silk Road" (Seidenstrasse, evidently inspired by the medieval Germany's "Salt Road," Saltzstrasse, in its turn inspired by the Roman empire's Via Salaria). Silk certainly traveled over the network; its export from China was vigorous no later than about 1000 BCE, though it was not a legal export of a state based in China until 800 years later. But we now know that the system is much older than silk exchange and in its origins was not designed to transport any product from one end of Eurasia to the other.

The network was anchored by the cities of Bukhara and Samarkand (both in the enormously important region of Transoxiana between the Amu Darya and the Syr Darya rivers, roughly corresponding to modern-day Uzbekistan and a portion of south–central Kazakhstan), Herat and Kabul (in present Afghanistan), and Kashgar (now in Xinjiang Province, China). The westerly embarkation points of the network lay in Azerbaijan, by land, with short connections to sea trade farther westward at Antioch, Aleppo, and Tyre on the Mediterranean. It proceeded eastward south of the Caspian Sea. A northern route led to Samarkand and around the great Takla Makan desert (now in China's Xinjiang Province), and a southern route proceeded south of the Takla Makan. These two routes joined at Dunhuang, now in Gansu Province of China. From there, roads continued eastward to link with the Chinese capitals (before the tenth century located in the Wei River Valley in modern Shaanxi Province) and across southern China to Canton (Guangzhou), on the coast (see Map 1.2). The system also included South Asia—the greatest exporting region of the ancient world—and the Himalayas. In medieval times, sea routes brought the Indian Ocean and island Southeast Asia into the network. Communications between the coasts and the overland routes—primarily through the eastern Mediterranean and Iran, through India and Southeast Asia, and through China—were lively, and a vigorous sea trade brought parts of Africa, Australia, and the Pacific Islands into the exchange.

After the second millennium BCE, silk from China was carried to West Asia and to Europe by traders and was found in Europe by 500 BCE at the latest. In the Abbasid-Tang era (eighth to tenth centuries), the goods traveling to and fro included tea, silk, cotton, paper, fruits and vegetables (fresh and dried), ceramics, silver, gold, and glass. There was also plentiful human cargo—Buddhist missionaries beginning in the third century BCE but, in greater numbers, captives taken in one direction or the other to be sold as slaves. The estimates of enslaved or otherwise dependent populations across Eurasia in the ancient, classical, and medieval eras vary greatly, from a substantial minority to a majority. What can be said confidently is that regardless the society under discussion, dependent people were essential to the economy, a critical part of any military undertaking, and visible in the life of every independent or aristocratic household. In late classical and in medieval

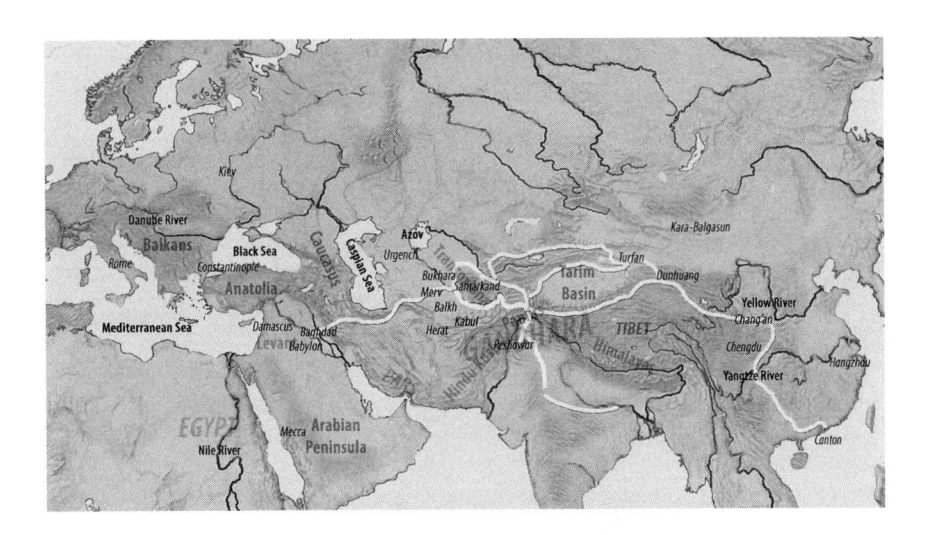

Map 1.2. Major west and east extensions of the trade tracks and major cities of Eurasia, c. 1000 BCE to 1000 CE.

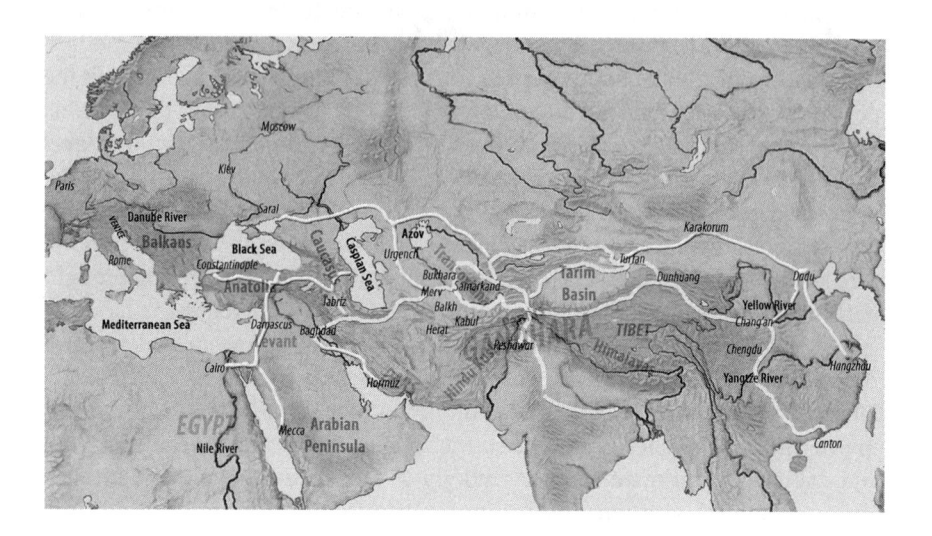

Map 1.3. Major overland trade roads of the Toluid period, c. 1200 to 1400 CE.

times, enslaved populations moving overland included Chinese, Koreans, Turks, Indians, Arabs, North Africans, Greeks, Franks, and Slavs. Cultural products went with them. Large urban markets in Iran/Iraq and China developed as a result of the trade, but Central Asia itself also underwent significant urbanization. The places and sizes of the cities were determined by their relationship to the movement of caravans and developing concentration of merchant wealth. In the desert, towns typically grew up around oases, where camels and horses watered. On the steppe, towns were located along the river valleys, which were frequented by nomadic bands. The great towns of Central Asia, including Marv, Bukhara, Tashkent, Samarkand, and Turfan, were all on the ancient transport system, all proximate to nomadic movement and influence. Many of these cities had secondary systems of markets and roads around them, and by this means western Mongolia was always connected to the continental trade through Turfan to Samarkand. In the thirteenth to fifteenth centuries, under the curatorship of the Mongol empires and particularly those of the Toluid dynasty, the system reached its maximum elaboration (compare Maps 1.2 and 1.3).

THE HORSE VECTOR

There is a reason why the use of horses in battle corresponds roughly to the beginning of written historical records. Together with the spread of iron technologies, horses were essential to the creation of large land empires in the classical age. But another aspect of horse history was equally transformative. Horses can go significant distances at roughly 10 times the speed of humans. The history of the domesticated horse is the history of the accelerating and deepening connections of historical Eurasia. Horses used for transport were late additions to the continental mechanisms of Eurasia. They took up roles in war and economy previously filled by donkeys, onagers, and oxen. The transfer of archery and lance fighting from the chariot to the back of a horse during the late first millennium BCE accelerated expanding overland conquest. Not least because they were both symbiotic with early agriculture and urbanization, pastoralism and the horse were intimately connected to the vitality of networked communications and trade. In Russia, West Asia, and East Asia (that is to say, on the expansive littoral of the exchange core), the skills necessary—including breeding, tacking, and military riding—were all spread by pastoralists, irrespective of where they had been invented. Like their largely Indo-European predecessors on the steppe, the Turks and Mongols were excellent riders, both in agility and endurance, and were adept at the special skill (for which there is a single word in all Central Asian languages) of shooting arrows from a moving horse.

Not only riding itself but the greatest supply of horses derived from the steppelands, making empires with a wide range of economic foundations reliant upon communication and trade with ostensibly nomadic zones. Early horse breeding may have been focused more on producing useful traits and less on producing large numbers of horses, and it long preceded the emergence of great empires. By 1000 BCE breeding centers across Central Asia offered horses of all colors and patterns. The Achaemenid empire of Iran—the model in so many ways for later large empires across Eurasia—was breeding warhorses as early as the fifth century BCE, when Xerxes imported Central Asian stallions to improve the speed of his horses. The Greeks quickly acquired these horses, replacing the small ponies they had previously used on the battlefield. Alexander (356–323 BCE) rode such a horse—Bucephalus—to defeat the Iranians in the fourth century BCE, after which he acquired their entire breeding program. In the third century BCE, the Han empire desired to breed their own horses. They imported the "Heavenly" horse—swift and tall with shining coats of the sort that today are seen in the Akhal-Teke breed—from Central Asia and forcibly acquired as many horses as they could from their Xiongnu enemies. The Tang empire of medieval China attempted to run a state breeding program but quickly became dependent on stallion exchanges with Tibet and Central Asia. Charlemagne wanted to control horse breeding for his empire but was dependent upon heavy horses from the Byzantine Empire and the Islamic world, particularly Spain and North Africa. Imperial control could be effective in producing type, but types could quickly be obscured in the constant search for large numbers of horses, which the agricultural empires could rarely produce.

But drawing too sharp a line between nomadic and sedentary horse types could be unwise. It was once thought stallions provided the traits to their offspring, but the genetic profiles of modern horses show there were no major breeding reservoirs of distinctly steppe or distinctly sedentary traits. Breeds were produced through the application of imported sires to local mare populations. When it comes to numbers, the contrasting roles of the steppe and the farming world are more clear-cut. Horses were plentiful and inexpensive on the steppe, but insufficient and precious in the agricultural world. Pastoralists in horse-friendly climates rarely refrained from selling horses to their sedentary enemies because the differential between the cost of a horse on the steppe and the price it could bring in the sedentary market was too great. The agriculturally based empires did not carelessly take their horses into hostile environments, and when the horses' limitations were reached they were withdrawn or the campaign abandoned. Alexander's exhaustion of 1,000 horses in pursuit of Darius pales beside the 120,000 horses reported lost by the Han empire in its campaigns against the Xiongnu (see Chapter 3) in the early second century BCE, but both episodes turn on one dramatic point: the supreme and exceptional sacrifice of precious resources to achieve a determined commander's goal.

Horse use was not only a technology but also a social institution. On the Eurasian littoral of Egypt or Shang-period China, horse teams and chariots demanded a select elite of warriors, wealthy enough to maintain their equipment and powerful enough to control grazing land and command supplies of grain. Horses had to be bred to be large enough to pull the chariots and trained to manage their loads with rather inefficient harnessing. Riders, particularly in war, were male, specialized in combat or sport, and were small in number. But in Central Asia, and particularly in regions where smaller grass-fed horses prevailed, riding was an ability all men in good health and many women possessed. It required only a formidably supportive saddle (see reading notes) and experience. The deployment of riders in warfare meant the difference between a riding herdsman (or hunter) and a riding soldier was not salient, and there was only light specialization of function along class lines. During the medieval period, Turkic warriors of the steppe developed chain mail, specialized fighting disciplines, and larger horses to carry armored men. First in Central Asia and then in the Middle East, Europe, and East Asia, the rise of new military elites empowered the skills and the material goods necessary to introduce new forms of cavalry that wrought similar changes to political and social structures across Eurasia. They built a platform for the establishment of Turkic military elites in the Balkans, North Africa, the Middle East, East Asia, and northern India whose influence would be transmitted to chivalric cults of Europe.

Wherever the horse was used in war across Eurasia, horse sacrifice was part of many transactions with a spiritual overlay. Horse themes in myth and religion spread widely across the continent, with the period of the Skythians (first millennium BCE) standing out for its seeding of animal and horse motifs in art and religion, from Scandinavia to China. The sacrifice of a horse or multiple horses was a widespread part of ceremonies commemorating political alliances, fealty relationships, and individual achievement or death. Evidence for this runs through the archaeology of all of Eurasia and is perhaps spectacularly illustrated in Bronze Age burials in what is now Mongolia featuring a tomb surrounded by 1,700 mounted horse skulls—for comparison, burials of grand persons from China at roughly the same time might have ostentatiously featured a few dozen to a maximum of a hundred sacrificed horses. Rulers all over Eurasia prized tribute presentations of horses suitable for sacrifice. Despite occasional conflicts with local tastes or religious principles, horse sacrifice remained an elemental part of imperial ceremonies through much of Eurasia until the eighteenth century.

In the medieval and early modern period, many languages of Eurasia used words (such as Italian *maneggiare*, English *manage*, or Turkic and Mongolian *darugha*, later transmitted throughout Eurasia) based on horse keeping, training, or riding to describe the governmental process itself—possibly because of the material importance of the horse in warfare and peacekeeping, more likely because methods of controlling the horse were natural analogies for small governments riding atop strong and willful societies. Closely connected to the idea of the horse and government was the continent-wide distribution of certain mythical motifs, many connecting Alexander and Bucephalus. The campaigns of Alexander at the interfaces of Iran, the Indus Valley, and Central Asia became an orienting moment in the establishment of Hellenic influence (mostly by merchants and academics, over centuries) in the cities of Central Asia, as well as in the commercial cultures that linked those cities together. In the "Alexandrias," or cities claiming to be established by Alexander, a residual Greek heritage was evident as a result of centuries of Seleucid dominance in Transoxiana, eastern Iran, and the Hindu Kush. This integrated Greek-Iranian heritage mingled comfortably with the later influences of Buddhism and Islam.

Greek knowledge of mathematics, astronomy, physiology, and architecture had been transmitted from these centers to northern India, and others had gone eastward into Central Asia. Literate men of Central Asia who read Greek in the third and fourth centuries CE changed, translated, illustrated, and elaborated upon the Alexander stories. Aesop's fables, Plato's ideas, the *authepsa* cauldron, artistic styles—including full-figure statuary in draped clothing, possibly reflected not only in Buddhist religious sculpture but in the "stone men" found from India to Korea—were inextricably woven into the fabric of Eurasia by the early centuries of the common era. By the time of the Mongols, the Alexander Romance—mythical narratives in many variations dealing with Alexander's attempts to defeat or elude Death—had been translated into or paraphrased in Old English, Irish, Middle High German, Norman French, Greek, Latin, Iranian, Bulgarian, Arabic, Ethiopian, Syrian Aramaic, Oguz Turkic, Mongolian, Tibetan, Chinese, and Korean. Its themes and imagery may be seen in literature as diverse as the Quran, the *Morte d'Arthur*, Marco Polo's *Il Milione* (see Chapter 10), and medieval accounts of Chinggis Khan. The *Romance* not only provided a unifying narrative for medieval Eurasia but also combined with other influences to generate a persisting representation of emperorship in which the horse was indispensable. It was only partly—but certainly at least in part—for his imperial role that Alexander became an authentic Eurasian culture hero. The iconography of Alexander and Bucephalus (seen in statuary, frescoes, and mosaic tiled floors) was a widespread representation of conquest and power.

NOMADS AND EURASIAN COHERENCE

The origins of pastoral nomadism are obscure, and it is possible that major nomadic complexes of Eurasia, Africa, and North America all had different sorts of beginnings. The nomads whom this book follows almost all originated in what is now the boundary between northern Mongolia and southern Siberia, near the source of the Onon and Selengge rivers in the Khentii mountains, probably beginning about three millennia ago. In their respective periods, they moved south to the Mongolian steppe and then on to North China and Central Asia. Unlike areas to its north, west, and south, the Mongolian steppe shows no evidence of agriculture before the last centuries BCE. Small populations apparently moved into Mongolia to raise sheep, goats, cattle, and horses to supply the needs of bordering agricultural areas with rising population density. Who was chosen for this task or whether the migrants were all volunteers is impossible to know. When Turks, Xiongnu, Rouran, or Mongols spoke of being born in the Onon-Selengge region, they were referring to the area that gave their ancestors their most recent identity. Where these populations lived before taking on their role as pastoralists is rarely part of the narrative.

Over time, many of these migrating communities became associated primarily with herding and its ancillary industries—skinning, tanning, felt making, and wool production, as examples. They seasonally shifted their locations to secure water and fodder, but their economies and originally their cultures and languages were continuous with agricultural areas. Though the steppe's human populations were moving with their herds, as groups they could rapidly change in size, from a few dozen to a few thousand people. They were stratified by ranks of aristocrats, commoners, and slaves. They moved in relation to fixed points—mines and ironworking installations, religious centers, caravan cities, and a small number of well-traveled trails—

and were rarely far out of reach of the market centers where they could sell their products of meat, wool, hide, felt, and iron. They were necessary to the agricultural sector not only for what they supplied directly but also because they often conveyed finished products from one region to another.

Nomadic groups' necessarily low rates of population density allowed them to occupy lands that would be exhausted by dense populations. But grazing can degrade the vegetation rapidly and require years for recovery, while the mineral content of the soil can be changed permanently. In their migrations, nomads frequently came into contact with other groups seeking the same land, water sources, or trading rights, and the results were typically warfare, alliance, or both. Competition was continual and could be intense, often exciting the formation of large-scale federations. Some groups made a specialization of providing protection and demanding tribute, including cash, silk, livestock, and humans. In times of unusual climate stress, conflicts increased, resulting in the extermination of small groups, growth of alliances, frequent emigration from groups that grew too large, and an increase in slavery—which some entered willingly as a way of avoiding starvation. Slaves were valuable not only for their direct contributions but also as currency. Weak groups secured land rights and protection from strong groups by providing them with slaves, livestock, weapons, silk, or cash. Some powerful groups found they could live almost entirely off tribute and so spent less time and resources on herding and more on military activities that would increase their tribute intake. Groups that perpetually engaged in warfare needed centralized, stable leadership. As each group grew, its political institutions became more complex. The institutions evolved in the medieval period to identify populations as by cultural attributes were the derivatives of early ways of marking slaves from the rest of the population.

When absolutely necessary, nomads could live briefly off meat (normally mutton), milk (from goats or mares), and blood products alone; for longer periods, that diet could be supplemented by roots, berries, and herbs. By the time of the rise of the Mongols at the end of the 1100s, the war diet had acquired prestige. Wealth and status tended to mean more fatty meat and alcohol and less vegetable matter of any kind, and there are a few examples of aristocrats adhering to the diet to the point of death. Through trade with sedentary cultures, nomads acquired cotton and cotton seed, silk (the favored dress of the Central Asian elites), vegetables, and grains. Many nomadic groups learned the value of having permanent settlements for the farming of grains and cotton and established their own villages—often dependent upon voluntary or enslaved migrants from the agricultural regions—at strategic points. The result was extensive frontier regions, particularly east of the Caspian Sea and in northern China, where nomadic peoples and agricultural peoples created pluralist economies in which farming, animal husbandry, ironworking, weaving, and long-distance trade were all elements. The agricultural societies depended upon nomads or travelers from the steppe to move products or to bring good breeding stock of horses or dogs.

Some permanent installations of the steppe were dedicated primarily to ironworking. Because it was used in bridles and stirrups, in the construction of wagons, and in weapons, iron was from earliest times a product associated with Central Asian peoples. The Turks, for instance, had been famous for their mines and ironworking stations south of Mount Altai. Throughout southern Siberia, Mongolia, and Central Asia, iron smithing was a deep and ubiquitous theme in folk stories and religious beliefs (see also Chapter 2). In addition to mining, nomads eagerly acquired iron implements in trade, then reworked them to their purposes. Many agricultural empires attempted to restrict the export of iron in any form to Central Asia, but none succeeded. Central Asians not only continued to work in iron but improved upon many of the sedentary technologies and then exported them back. The effects of this were evident in the fifth century, when Europeans picked up the iron stirrup from the Huns, and in the seventh century, when use of the rounded Turkic iron stirrup was transmitted throughout Eurasia by the nearly invincible Tang imperial cavalry. The Mongols retained the traditional Central Asian reverence for ironworking. Chinggis Khan's personal name, Temujin, meant blacksmith, and several of his prominent followers were sons of blacksmiths.

Eurasia as a historical proposition is distinguished not by its perimeters but by its mechanics of articulation—among them trade routes and product exchange, crop dissemination, languages, genes, technologies in textiles, ceramics and metals, and the many dimensions of horse keeping and use. The net effect of Eurasia's east–west continuities was to make Eurasia definable by its permeability. It was the range within which there were no secrets, making it no less a locality of time than of space.

READING NOTES: THE LOST CONTINENT

Eurasia is frequently (as here) the subject of definition, delimitation, and periodization, rendering varying results. For the foundation discussion from the nineteenth century, see Halford Mackinder, "The Geographical Pivot of History," *The Geographical Journal* 23, no. 4 (April 1904): 421–437. Jared Diamond's book, *Guns, Germs and Steel: The Fates of Human Societies* (Norton, 1997), examines the basic idea of an environmentally coherent, temperate-zone Eurasia that produced similar effects in its agricultural and densely populated regions over time—ideas explored much earlier by others, including H. G. Wells, *Outline of History* (George Newnes, 1919–1920) with some unfortunate extrapolations, Alfred Crosby, *The Columbian Exchange: Biological and Cultural Consequences of 1492* (Praeger, 1972, 2003) and

Germs, Seeds and Animals: Studies in Ecological History (M. E. Sharpe, 1994), and William McNeill, *Plagues and Peoples* (Anchor, 1976, 1998).

More recently, see discussion of Eurasia as a historical object by the following outstanding scholars: David Christian, *A History of Russia, Central Asia and Mongolia, Volume 1: Inner Eurasia from Prehistory to the Mongol Empire* (Wiley, 1998) and "Afro-Eurasia in Geological Time," *World History Connected* (U of Illinois), February 2008, http://worldhistoryconnected.press.illinois.edu/5.2/christian.html; David Anthony, *The Horse, the Wheel and Language: How Bronze Age Riders from the Eurasian Steppe Shaped the Modern World* (Princeton UP, 2010) and Christopher I. Beckwith, *Empires of the Silk Road* (Chapter 1 reading notes) . For a gemlike example of a specific historical phenomenon treated in a way that integrates Eurasia as a place, see Thomas T. Allsen, "Hunting Parks at the Core and on the Periphery," in *The Royal Hunt in Eurasian History* (U Pennsylvania P, 2006), 37–41.

The narration here of Eurasia as an ecumene is not meant to suggest to readers that the ecumenical narratives of smaller systems are not significant. The earliest of these conceptual histories in relation to the Mediterranean world were done by Henri Pirenne and Fernand Braudel. But for a more recent approach to the Arabic-using Mediterranean rim, see Mohamad Ballan, "Fraxinetum: An Islamic Frontier State in Tenth-Century Provence," *Comitatus* 41 (2010): 23–76 and "The Scribe of Alhambra: Lisan al-Din ibn al-Khatib, Sovereignty and History in Nasrid Granada" (PhD diss., U of Chicago, 2018). Northeast Asia has also been the subject of a developing ecumenical narrative; see Evelyn S. Rawski, *Early Modern China and Northeast Asia: Cross-Border Perspectives* (Cambridge UP, 2015); Nianshen Song, "Northeast Eurasia as Historical Center: Exploration of a Joint Frontier," *The Asia-Pacific Journal/Japan Focus* 13, no. 44 (Nov 2015): 1–19; and related to this, the innovative history by Walter McDougall, *Let the Sea Make a Noise: A History of the North Pacific from Magellan to MacArthur* (Basic Books, 1993).

The discussions of chronology in Eurasian and global history are innumerable. An interesting and frequently cited one is Victor Lieberman in his edited volume, *Beyond Binary Histories* (U of Michigan P, 1999), which lays out a general schema of development from a localized "medieval" world to a more integrated, standardized, centralized pattern in which commercialization, expansion of markets and resource acquisition, rapid population growth, and nationalism were likely. Thus, it might appear that much of Eurasia, at a minimum, could fit into a non-binary or world-historical paradigm right along with Europe; see particularly 242–301. For extended comment on this, see R. Bin Wong, *China Transformed: Historical Change and the Limits of European Experience* (Cornell UP, 1998), esp. 1–4; Lynn Struve, "Introduction," in *The Qing Formation in World-Historical Time*, ed. Lynn A. Struve

(Cambridge, MA: Harvard University Asia Center, 2004), 1–56; Jack A. Goldstone, "Neither Late Imperial nor Early Modern: Efflorescences and the Qing Formation in World History," in *The Qing Formation in World-Historical Time*, ed. Lynn A. Struve (Cambridge, MA: Harvard University Asia Center, 2004), 242–403; Lynn A. Struve, "Chimerical Early Modernity: The Case of 'Conquest Generation' Memoirs," in *The Qing Formation in World-Historical Time*, ed. Lynn A. Struve (Cambridge, MA: Harvard University Asia Center, 2004), 335–372; and the overview by Nicola di Cosmo, "State Formation and Periodization in Inner Asian History," *Journal of World History* 10, no. 1 (Spring 1999): 1–40.

On a nomad algorithm, see Michael Frachetti, C. Evan Smith, Cynthia M. Traub, and Tim Williams, "Nomad Ecology Shaped the Highland Geography of the Silk Roads," *Nature* 543, no. 7544 (March 2017): 193–198, https://www.nature.com/nature/journal/v543/n7644/pdf/nature21696.pdf. On the Bronze Age and what in this chapter has been called the "exchange core, " see Victor H. Mair and Jane Hickman, eds., *Reconfiguring the Silk Road: New Research on East-West Exchange in Antiquity* (U Pennsylvania P, 2014), particularly J. G. Manning, "Long-Distance Trade in the Time of Alexander the Great and the Hellenistic Kings," 5–14; Martina Unterländer et alia, "Ancestry and Demography and Descendants of Iron Age Nomads of the Eurasian Steppe," *Nature Communications*, Mar 3, 2017, https://www.nature.com/articles/ncomms14615.pdf; Edward G. Pulleyblank, "The People of the Steppe Frontier in Early Chinese Sources," *Migracijske teme* 15, no. 1–2 (1999): 35–61; Robert Drews, *The Coming of the Greeks: Indo-European Conquests in the Aegean and the Near East* (Princeton UP, 1988).

Historians such as S. A. M. Adshead (*Central Asia in World History*, Palgrave Macmillan, 1993) and Peter Golden (*Central Asia in World History*, Oxford UP, 2011) have repositioned Central Asia as basic to, not peripheral to, world or global history. There are many excellent books providing background on the history and cultures of Central Asia, though some are now outdated. Rene Grousset's *The Empire of the Steppes: A History of Central Asia* (Rutgers UP, 1970) is a classic text. It can be supplemented by selected chapters from Denis Sinor, ed., *The Cambridge History of Early Inner Asia* (Cambridge UP, 1990). On the transport technologies of early Central Asia, see also Richard Bulliet, *The Camel and the Wheel* (Harvard UP, 1975). More recently, see Beckwith, *Empires of the Silk Road* (Chapter 1 reading notes), and Peter Frankopan, *The Silk Roads: A New History of the World* (Vintage Books, 2015). On overland Eurasian trade, see Janet Abu-Lughod's study of the impact of Eurasian trade networks on thirteenth-century Europe: *Before European Hegemony: The World System A.D. 1250-1350* (Oxford UP, 1991). More recently, see James Millward, *The Silk Road: A Very Short Introduction* (Oxford UP, 2013).

In addition to the general works on nomadism cited in the reading notes for the introduction, see these particular discussions of Central Asian nomadism: "Bronze Age Herders of the Eurasian Steppes," Encyclopedia.com, 2004, http://www.encyclopedia.com/humanities/encyclopedias-almanacs-transcripts-and-maps/bronze-age-herders-eurasian-steppes; Daniel T. Potts, "The Coming of the Iranians," in *Nomadism in Iran: From Antiquity to the Modern Era* (Oxford UP, 2014). On the extremities of the Mongol diet (here suggested as applicable to all nomads), see John Masson Smith Jr., "Dietary Decadence and Dynastic Decline in the Mongol Empire," *Journal of Asian History* 34, no. 1 (2000): 35–52.

On the early empires of Eurasia, the following background is helpful: Matt Waters, *Ancient Persia: A Concise History of the Achaemenid Empire, 550-330 BC* (Cambridge UP, 2014); Romila Thapar, *The Penguin History of Early India: From the Origins to AD 1300* (Penguin, 2015); Nicola di Cosmo, *Ancient China and Its Enemies: The Rise of Nomadic Power in East Asian History* (Cambridge UP, 2004); John S. Major and Constance Cook, *Ancient China: A History* (Routledge, 2016); Richard N. Frye, *The History of Ancient Iran* (C. H. Beck, 1983, now available as a download at https://archive.org/details/TheHistoryOfAncientIran1983); Kamram Matin, "Uneven and Combined Development in World History: The International Relations of State-Formation in Premodern Iran," *European Journal of International Relations* 13 (2007): 3, http://journals.sagepub.com/doi/abs/10.1177/1354066107080132; Nicola di Cosmo and Michael Maas, eds., *Empires and Exchanges in Eurasian Late Antiquity* (Cambridge UP, 2017); Caspar Meyer, "Discovering Greco-Scythian Art," in *Greco-Scythian Art and the Birth of Eurasia: From Classical Antiquity to Russian Modernity*, ed. Caspar Mayer (Oxford UP, 2013), 1–38; Askold I. Ivantchik, "Early Eurasian Nomads and the Civilizations of the Ancient Near East (Eighth-Seventh Centuries BCE)," in *Mongols, Turks, and Others: Eurasian Nomads and the Sedentary World*, ed. Reuven Amitai and Michal Biran (Brill, 2005), 103–128.

The history of the horse is widely written, though some sources emphasize research particulars and some emphasize a more general and integrated approach. I have found the following helpful: my comments on horse-breeding ecologies on the steppe are heavily informed by Jos Gommans, "Warhorse and Post-Nomadic Empire in Asia, c. 1000-1800," *Journal of Global History* 2, no. 1 (2007): 1–21. On use of the horse in war, see Yaacov Lēv, ed., *War and Society in the Eastern Mediterranean: 7th-15th Centuries* (Brill, 1997). On horse sacrifice and burial in early Mongolia, see Francis Allard and Diimaajav Erdenebaatar, "Khirigsuurs, Ritual and Mobility in the Bronze Age of Mongolia," *Antiquity* 79 (2005): 547–563. On the origin of gaited or ambling horses, see as an introduction, Stephen Yin, "Vikings Possibly Spread Smooth-Riding Horses Around the World," *New York Times*, August 10, 2016, https://www.nytimes.com/2016/08/11/science/

horses-gaits-ambling-vikings.html. On the relative importance of the saddle in contrast to the stirrup and the relationship of the saddle to the social positioning of the horse, see Pamela Crossley, "Flank Contact, Social Contexts, and Riding Patterns in Eurasia, 500-1500, " in *How Mongolia Matters: War, Law and Society*, ed. Morris Rossabi (Brill's Inner Asian Library, vol. 36, Brill, 2017), 129–146. For horses relating to Central Asian nomads in particular, see Denis Sinor, "The Inner Asian Warriors," *Journal of the American Oriental Society* 101, no. 2 (Apr–Jun 1981): 133–144 ; and Morris Rossabi, "All the Khan's Horses," *Natural History* 103, no. 10 (Oct 1994): 48.

I have also consulted Anthony J. Spalinger, *War in Ancient Egypt: The New Kingdom* (Wiley, 2008); Wendy Doniger, "The Tale of the Indo-European Horse Sacrifices," *Incognita* (Leiden) 1 (1990): 1–15; Kristen Pearson, "Chasing the Shaman's Steed: The Horse in Myth from Central Asia to Scandinavia," *Sino-Platonic Papers* 269 (May 2017), http://sino-platonic.org/complete/spp269_horse_myths.pdf; David Anthony, "Let Them Eat Horses," *NEWSLETTER - Institute For Ancient Equestrian Studies*, no. 4/ Summer 1997, http://www.silk-road.com/artl/horsemyth.shtml; Robert Drews, *Early Riders: The Beginnings of Mounted Warfare in Asia and Europe* (Routledge, 2004); and Adam J. Silverstein, *Postal Systems in the Pre-Modern Islamic World* (Cambridge UP, 2007).

Studies of the Alexander Romance in literature and art are well developed. The following have been useful to me: J. A. Boyle, "The Alexander Romance in the East and West," *Bulletin of the John Rylands University Library of Manchester* 60 (1977): 19–20; Francis Woodman Cleaves, "An Early Mongolian Version of the Alexander Romance," *Harvard Journal of Asiatic Studies* 22 (1959): 1–99; Richard Stoneman, *Alexander the Great: A Life in Legend* (Yale UP, 2008); Z. David Zuwiyya, ed., *A Companion to Alexander Literature in the Middle Ages* (Brill, 2011); and Baohua and Oyun-Chimeg, "Comparative Study on Mongolian Version of Alexander Romance and Folktales about Alexander in Persian Language," *Sociology Study* 4, no. 12 (Dec 2014): 993–1000 (includes a retrospect of work by Poppe and Cleaves, with discussion of Alexander as the "horned one" in Quranic literature). For its specific impact on the primary traditional history of Chinggis, see "Alexander, Ja'a Gambo and the Origin of the Jamugha Figure in the *Secret History of the Mongols Proceedings of the International Conference on History and Culture of Central Asia* (Inner Mongolia People's Press, 2015), 161–176.

It seems to me that the representations of Bucephalus and Buddha's horse Kanthaka (which actually did help his owner escape death) may have been mutually influencing at least from the time of the narration of Kanthaka (whose name might have been inspired by a Greek loan-word) in the *Buddhacrita* in the second century BCE and the *Mahavastu* manuscripts of the c.

third century BCE. See discussion in Avaghosa (Edward Hamilton Johnston, trans. and ed.), *Acts of the Buddha* (Motilal Banarsidass, 1992), esp p. 61n3, and Reiko Ohnuma, *Unfortunate Destiny: Animals in the Indian Buddhist Imagination* (Oxford, 2017). See also Peilin Wu, "Aesop's Fables in Ancient China," *Central Asiatic Journal* 60, no. 1/2 (2017): 207–230. The assumption is long-standing that Greek styles in statuary influenced India, and if so, then the influence also spread throughout the Turkic world, Mongolia, and Korea. On the other hand, this could be another Eurasian phenomenon produced through frequent recursive contacts among all the continent's regions. The distribution of stone statuary throughout Eurasia has been recently discussed in Hayashi Toshio, *Skythian and Xiongnu Nomadic Civilization* [*Sukitai to Kyōdo yūboku no bunmei*] (Kodansha, 2007); a paraphrase of some of it is provided, with more extensive discussion of continuous patterns in ceramics and rock art, in Andrea di Benedittis, "A New Perspective on the Analysis of Koguryo Wall Paintings Iconography," *Journal of Northeast Asian History* 8, no. 1 (2011): 123–145.

Chapter Two

Light-Mindedness

The interpermeability of Eurasia is well demonstrated in the history of its ideologies, which rooted themselves widely and deeply and continued to penetrate the layers of religion and philosophy troweled over them by medieval institutions. The histories of Buddhism, Christianity, and Islam are imprinted with recurrent waves of influence from Central Asia, alloying the formal, founded religions with many of the ideas of much earlier ideologies linked to Hinduism, Zoroastrianism, and Manichaeanism. The role of Central Asia in these developments was less related to space and political control and more related to the syncretizing effects of frequent cultural exchange across the continent. Repeated colloquializing of religious doctrine was also reinforced by the fact that in their earliest forms the great religious ideologies of Eurasia shared basic concepts of time and causation and the interplay of perception and reality.

We vaguely see an ideological threshold at about 12,000 years ago, approximately at the end of the Ice Age, when suggestions of agriculture were evident in several parts of Eurasia. This was the age of the Gobekli Tepe cult site, the carving of the large Shigir wooden god found in Siberia in 1890 and evidently related to much earlier economic and cultural systems in the vicinity of Lake Baikal, and other archaeological evidence of that long era. The meanings of these sites and artifacts are not decipherable to us yet, but they may have been part of an early cosmological system in which the homes of gods and spirits (corresponding to what are called chthonic deities) were found in dark places—deep waters, underground chambers and tunnels, caves, or wells. Many of these themes are represented vestigially in known folklore, often associated with snakes or reptiles (and by extension, cave-dwelling dragons) who could talk or otherwise commune with humans. In this early thinking, life came from the dark. The recesses from which it flowed were reflected in, or continued in, the night sky, where the Milky Way was a road, or an island, or a river for conducting the dead and constellations, gods or heroes known to Paleolithic cultures.

FROM DARKNESS TO LIGHT

The evidence suggests that Paleolithic peoples of Eurasia—and most other places in the world—were shamanist, which is to say they believed that specific individuals were able to travel from the material to the spiritual world and back again, enlisting the help of the spirits of animals, trees, mountains, and waters to assure success in hunting, war, or healing illness. In many contexts there was also incorporation of ancestor worship, which would later entwine itself with the concept of dynastic rule. By the time that agriculture had become widespread across Eurasia—say, by 7000 to 5000 BCE—many spiritual systems were based on a notion of alternating light and dark. Darkness and shadow were associated with confusion, fear, deception, ignorance, and death. Light—including the sun, the dawn, the daytime sky, and fire—was knowledge, inspiration, divinity, and immortality. Mountains and trees were special. Each was rooted in the shadow-bound Earth but reached toward the sky and suggested ways for humans to get closer to the divine.

These religious systems were profoundly eschatological, insisting upon a final, catastrophic confrontation in which the only alternatives were the utter destruction of the phenomenal universe or the continued enslavement of humans to the forces of evil. Such generalized spiritual notions were joined, sometime in the Bronze Age, by a dualistic ideology that continued to grip cosmological thinking in Eurasia well into the modern period. Seasonal, annual, and biological rhythms were formalized into abstract representations of alternating opposites—weakness and strength, fertility and sterility, hot and cold, male and female, life and death. But the most pervasive and profound of the dualities was light and dark, from the earliest points represented as paralleling the struggle between truth and falsity, between knowledge and matter, between good and evil. In the Neolithic period—as agriculture emerged at various points and spread—the ideology of natural dualities became elements in the early infrastructures of Indo-European religion that preceded Jainism and Hinduism in South Asia. It was also strongly represented in the earliest Chinese ideation of *yang* (light) and *yin* (dark), which was ancestral to all Chinese philosophies of the first millennium BCE.

In historical times, the Vedic texts of India (the collection of revelatory narratives written in various forms during the second and first millennia BCE) suggest an early codification of the religion of light and dark. Fire worship was central to the rituals (aided by a drug not yet identified with certainty), which also included animal sacrifice, often of horses. The highest-ranking god, Agni, is fire and light personified. Around him floated a universe of lesser deities with ambiguous affiliations with the original light and ambiguous relationships with each other; in the evolution of Vedic tradition many lesser deities were eventually identified with specific values or social classes, and especially with the element of causation in human history. Foremost among them is Indra, a warrior, associated with blood and death. He is a force of creation and destruction, who generates the material world during his struggles with his enemies. He is not unequivocally an opponent of Agni, but he is an agitator in and a benefactor of the ongoing wars between the minor spirits—the original earth-spirit descendants, the *asuras*, and the newly rising spirits, the *devas*. His schemes and battles generate fear, confusion, hatred, lust, ambition, and violence, which animate human history. Elements of this early agrarian religion were later synthesized with diverse local myths and beliefs to form Hinduism.

In early Iran, similar myths and cosmological ideas were sorted and refined in Zoroastrianism, which eventually became rooted in Central Asia and continued to shape religious systems settling atop it. The dates of its founder Zoroaster or Zarathustra are open to question, but by the sixth century BCE the religion attributed to him had well-defined doctrines committed to literary form in the Avesta, which appeared a few centuries after monuments of the ancient Iranian empire give evidence that Zoroastrianism was part of the imperial cult. Light and dark are absolute values with separate origins and are in constant conflict in the world as perceived by humans. In the texts, the supreme spirit of light is usually called Ahura Mazda, which may have been an adaptation of divine names known earlier in Mesopotamia. He was creator of two twin spirits, Spenta Mainyu and Angra Mainyu. The former is a force for good and protector of light, but the latter is creator of the material world and an enemy of Ahura Mazda. This latter spirit, also known as Ahriman, is the source of suffering in the world and was the generator of history. In the war against Angra Mainyu, Ahura Mazda is aided not only by Spenta Mainyu but also by a population of lesser deities, including demons who work their will through the material world and are determined to destroy light in all its forms. The end of the conflict will result in the destruction of the material world—Angra Mainyu/Ahriman's world—and revelation of the true light of the universe. While the myths of Eurasia shared in the universal human tradition that water had flooded the world and created the conditions for human rebirth, they emphasized to a marked degree a common premonition of cosmic conflagration as the means of human liberation. Whether by water or fire, the Eurasian identification of destruction with liberation was persistent from the earliest to modern times.

The largest and most enduring of the Eurasian religions all qualified or suspended the relationship between irreconcilable light and dark. Nevertheless, as we will explore below, the older beliefs that light and dark could not mix, could not reconcile, were never completely eradicated. They reappeared in folk and heterodox religion, affecting all the major forms of hierarchical religious belief that spread across Eurasia in historical times. Beyond this fundamental concept of a struggle between goodness/truth (light) and evil/ deception (the material world), both systems are also characterized by a belief in a single original creator of the universe (even if there are multitudes of deities), who remains the leading force for good. In a number of the beliefs that were later derived from this cosmology, this creator of the universe is not actually the creator of the earth or of humanity. Instead, a demiurge—the Indric, Ahrimanic, Satanic, "lesser god" who controls humanity—is the instigator of the struggle between good and evil and an enemy from whom humans can be rescued only by their own appeal to the true creator and their longing for destruction of their earthly prison. Zoroastrianism also addressed the question of causation (communication, transformation) in the form of Mitra, the divine messenger. He is responsible for bringing to human affairs Ahura Mazda's insistence on truth, especially in the performance of contracts, friendship, and acts of fidelity to rulers and social superiors.

TEACHERS AND PROPHETS

One of the most successful revisions of the ancient light/dark cosmology occurred in northern India with the teachings of Siddhartha Gautama, whose traditional dates are c. 560 to c. 480 BCE. After his death, he is known as the "Buddha," or "Awakened One." Unlike Zoroaster, Siddhartha developed a highly abstract approach to Eurasian dualism. Instead of a creator spirit, Siddhartha addressed a supreme and undelimited consciousness (visually or verbally represented by light), the source of all truth. But like Zoroaster, Siddhartha regarded a belief in the reality of the material world as the source of human suffering. To end suffering, humans must choose to discipline their minds to achieve contact with the supreme consciousness, partly through meditation, and free themselves from the tyranny of delusion. The choice was whether to pursue such enlightenment or to remain credulously attached to the material world, and Siddhartha regarded the fate of individuals as being in their own hands. Instead of a personality such as Mitra, Siddhartha saw causation as an impersonal and uncommanded law (*dharma*). Those who fail to achieve enlightenment are doomed to repeated rebirths in the material world, a chain they cannot break until they set themselves to achieve their own salvation. Universal salvation, or freedom from the bonds of material suffering, cannot occur until the phenomenal universe is dissolved, an event the Buddhists assumed is in the distant future. In time, the sectarian teaching of Buddhism incorporated Hinduism's narrative of the struggle of the forces of light and dark. The *devas* returned as the warriors protecting Buddha and humans struggling for enlightenment, the *asuras* returned as the army of darkness, and the theme of a battle to the point of annihilation, in which the material world of deception is destroyed, became fundamental to many sects of Buddhism.

Even before it had spread from northern India into Central Asia and from there both eastward and westward, Buddhism had developed two different schools of thought. Theravada, the "way of the elders," reflected the earliest doctrinal agreements among the followers of the Buddha shortly after his death. It predicted not universal salvation but the enlightenment of only a predestined elite. It evinced a distinct religious style: ascetic, rigidly dualistic, highly oriented toward scripture (both in Sanskrit and in Pali) accompanied by secluded teaching. Though Theravada as a doctrinal system did not remain dominant, it bequeathed to Buddhism a tradition of ontological speculation about the nature of reality that had a widespread influence. Theravada was quickly challenged and ultimately superseded in India and Central Asia by Mahayana, "the greater vehicle." Mahayana's essential liberality provided a template for demotic religion across Eurasia, as it handily incorporated the worship of local deities and translation of scripture into local languages.

The Mahayana world—which at its height embraced all of Central Asia, South Asia, and East Asia, as well as parts of Iran and Iraq—was one in which the script of South Asia was known by a few, but a massive new religious literature in local languages (very often, written Chinese) was generated and widely disseminated. The permissiveness of Mahayana could extend to leaving scripture behind entirely and relying upon the compassion of the Buddha for instant enlightenment at the speaking of a phrase or even a single word. These popular sects of Buddhism transformed the cultures of Central Asia and East Asia, particularly in the period of Mongol domination. Mahayana's accommodation of local deities was largely accomplished through the medium of the *bodhisattva*, an enlightened soul which motivated by the great Buddhist virtue of compassion, declines to go on to salvation, instead remaining active in the salvation of others. The concept may have had an ancestor in the "beautiful spirits" (*amesha spenta*) of Zoroastrianism. Mahayana *bodhisattva*s had both benevolent and violent manifestations. The spirits of patience, for instance, had their resolve maintained by spirits of anger. Also, like Zoroastrianism, Buddhism's helping spirits, whether kindly or terrifying in their aspect, work always for the final destruction of the material world and the liberation of its captive souls. The concepts of spiritual protection performed by the *bodhisattva* were paralleled by a religious function of kings and emperors (modeled on the Mauryan emperor Ashoka, 304–232 BCE). The ruler as an agent of the Buddha would work to bring mankind into enlightenment. Mahayana priests claimed that protecting spirits aid the king in the governing of the state and prevent harm coming to the people living under him. State cults based upon this idea were powerful in the kingdoms of China after the fifth century CE. From there, they spread to Korea, and then on to the first unified government of Japan, in the seventh century. Well into the era of Turkic and Mongol domination of Eurasia, the tradition of Buddhist kingship continued to be elaborated and strengthened.

At the western end of Eurasia, many of the same themes of light and matter, good and evil were evident in Greek philosophy. A philosophical dualism came to a degree of codification with the career of Plato (c. 425–c. 347). The completeness of Plato's work—not whether some of the writing related to him was lost, which it certainly was, but how much of his actual teaching was committed to writing—is debated today. He may have reserved some teaching for an inner circle of initiates, which would have been consistent with the practices of Greek mystic and dissident cults that today are often associated with the mythical figure of Pythagoras. Plato was a dualist and idealist in the grand Eurasian style. He saw the material world as a fraud that existed in opposition to an abstract, immaterial world of truth. It was the obligation of the wise man to learn the means of apprehending the truth behind the illusion, primarily by engaging in critical, dialectical thinking in which he or his interlocutor/teacher constantly challenges his impressions and deductions, until the truth is revealed (even if it is unspeakable or unwritable). His belief in an immortal soul (*psyche*—almost the semantic equivalent of Zoroaster's *mainyu*, the elemental agencies behind events) suggests kinship with Indo-Iranian ideas.

The same broad currents that influenced Plato were also shaping religious cults throughout the Levant and Anatolia a few centuries later. Many religious sects were produced through the interactions of dualistic theories of the unreality of the material present, the representations of truth as metaphysical but intuitively attainable by human understanding, and the immortality that results from contact with the divine. A large number incorporated the idea of secret teachings, orally transmitted, as companions of their sacred texts. Among them was Christianity, which produced its first significant doctrinal communities in Anatolia in the latter half of the first century CE, with writings about a teacher who lived earlier, in Roman Palestine.

The teacher Jesus was, like Siddhartha, Socrates, and Confucius before him, not a writer. He was known through his reported teachings, and almost exactly like Plato he was reported to have told at least one of his students that he had no intention of publicly revealing the most serious of his doctrines. He taught the falsity of material life, the truth that is conveyed by images of light, the innate ability of humans to apprehend that truth through instruments of prayer and contemplation, and the psychic immortality resulting from apprehension of the divine. The conventional dates of Jesus' life make him a contemporary of the Jewish scriptural scholar Philo Judaeus (15 BCE–45 CE), whose commentaries showed influence from Greek idealist philosophy. Over the centuries, scholars of Jesus and Christianity have mused on the possible effects of Greek philosophy, Iranian religion, and Buddhism on the Christian doctrines, sometimes even fancifully attributing to Jesus a sojourn in India or Central Asia to absorb the ethos and the imagery of the earlier religions. More conservatively, it is hypothesized that Jesus was in contact with the ascetic, vegetarian, and egalitarian Essenes—and may have been affiliated with a closely related sect, the Nazarenes—who were influenced by the cosmologies of Iran and Central Asia, with a program for victory of the light mind over the corrupt body, in part by relying on meditation.

These direct connections, however, appear unnecessary as an explanation for the similarities of Christian tenets to the ubiquitous Eurasian ideologies of light and dark. The traits of Christianity that are easily connected to Greece or Iran or India do not have to be understood in narrow terms of encounter and exchange. They were all part of the general trends of Eurasian spiritual speculation since Neolithic times. It is less a question of whether Zoroaster or Siddhartha or Plato influenced Jesus (or the church founders whose writings made Jesus a teacher of millions) and more a question of their all being affected by the same or similar influences. In historical Eurasia, Zoroastrianism, Buddhism, Platonism, Daoism, Confucianism, and Christianity were local and dialectal to each other. When, in the fourth century CE, Christianity was coopted by the Roman emperor Constantine, these local qualities had already been wattled together with other popular religions of the Mediterranean world, including "Mithraism" (meaning here the fashionable cult among Roman soldiers that generated its own version of the ancient Indo-Iranian god of obligations, Mitra). The earliest Christian communities outside Anatolia and the Levant appear to have been in southeastern India (particularly Kerala), and constant commercial contact between that area and the Persian Gulf could have constituted a two-way conduit of early Christian influence eastward and residual Buddhist influence westward.

Similar and more extensive synthesis produced the movement of the Iranian religious leader Mani (216–276 CE). Like the older religions from which it was drawn, Mani's worship is directed toward light in the form of a supreme god. Mani declared himself to be the last in a long line of prophets, beginning with Adam and moving through Moses, Zoroaster, the Buddha, and Jesus. He affirmed the ultimate triumph of light in its struggle against darkness, insisting that the only hope for human salvation was complete transcendence of the deceitful material world. This was to be achieved through asceticism (including celibacy), abstinence (from meat, alcohol, and all physical pleasures), and withdrawal from society. True liberation comes, however, only with the achievement of enlightenment and death (Mani was in fact executed by the Zoroastrian orthodox authorities). Without enlightenment, death brings only rebirth and a continuation of sorrows. In ensuing centuries, the influence of Manichaeanism as an organized religion, in addition to its continuing influence upon some forms of Christianity and Islam, remained one of the hallmarks of Eurasian civilization. Despite the vivid similarities to the ideas of Buddhism, Mani regarded himself as a Zoroastrian first, while many of his followers (including for a time Augustine of Hippo, d. 430) regarded themselves as Christians. Certainly, by the time the Byzantine emperor Justinian I outlawed the Manichaeans as heretics in the early sixth century, their religion was regarded as a perversion of Christianity.

The most recent of the major religious traditions of Eurasia is Islam, with its deeply conflicted approach to the central concerns of early Eurasian religious cultures. It was in some ways a recognizable product of the Arabian peninsula—having strong kinship with Judaism—and not of Central Asia: Paradise (from an Iranian word for "garden," and probably dating back to Egyptian beliefs in the eternal home of faithful) was not in the sky. It was a multilayered garden, a perfection of earthly life to which the faithful would be admitted after resurrection of their bodies on the appointed day. But like the early religions throughout Eurasia, Islam posits an original, creating consciousness, overseeing the struggle between good and evil. The forces participating in this battle—causing things to happen—are, as in all the Eurasian traditions, derived from the creator itself. These secondary agents are not named spirits or minds, as in Zoroastrianism or Platonism, but are "messengers"—*al-malâ'ikah*. The same word (*mal'akim*) had been used for centuries in the Torah, and this specific sense of spiritual agents as messengers had earlier been imported into Greek and Latin (*angelos*). Some traditions of Islam, such as Sufism, recognize saints (*wali Allah*, "a friend of God")—who in their lifetimes were so exemplary in their faith that they could accomplish miracles. Though orthodox Islam does not prescribe prayer to any entity but God, some sects prescribe meditation on the virtues of the saints as a powerful tool for growing closer to God. And perhaps most strongly marking its connections to western Eurasia outside Arabia, Islam embraced the genealogy of prophecy codified by Mani, though its own prophet Muhammad was affirmed to be the last of the line and the revealer of definitive scripture in the Quran.

KNOWLEDGE AND SALVATION

In the time of Siddhartha and shortly after, Buddhism is believed to have had qualities that, much later, theologians and historians would describe as "gnostic." The word *gnosis*, from Greek "knowledge," became associated with forms of Christianity evident in the second and third centuries CE and revealed in the Nag Hammadi manuscript trove discovered in Egypt in 1945. Scholarly study relating to Christianity in the late nineteenth century established a strongly diffusionist model of gnostic-style beliefs, hypothesizing that the cosmology of Christian gnosticism must have specific origins in Zoroastrianism or even Buddhism. But the Nag Hammadi manuscripts revealed the development of Christian gnostic thinking as organically connected to the written and oral discourses within early Christian communities themselves. As a Eurasian belief system, early Christianity (or Christianities) had innumerable and ubiquitous sources of conceptualizing an absolute differentiation between darkness and light, the insistence that truth can be apprehended only through an intense experience of awakening, and a universal conflict between light and matter that would end in obliteration of the material world. The discovery of a documentary basis for gnostic discourse within Christianity seems, from the continental perspective, to have little significance beyond the illumination of gnostic refinement within a local context. There was probably never a serious reason to look for specific origins of elements of Christian gnostic elements in earlier belief systems. As later chapters will suggest, a return of gnostic concepts and gnostic intellectual techniques after undermining of the comprehensive authority of religious hierarchs by nomadic conquest regimes was a significant factor in the emergence of the early modern style.

In relation to early Buddhism, these gnostic-like qualities included religious communities that were overtly divided between those on the one hand who were regarded as adept, advanced, or elect (i.e., in possession of "knowledge") and those on the other hand who were regarded as students, seekers, or unselect (temporarily or permanently). Teaching among the elect was often secretly, perhaps orally, transmitted and kept separate from the lectures and writings presented to the auditors. The social division of the community was believed to reflect a supernatural hierarchy in which some individuals are destined for enlightenment and others are not. Predestination of this sort is connected to the omniscience of God; what God knows has already happened and cannot be altered. The role of saints of various kinds as benevolent rulers and teachers was characteristic of their Mitra-like divine agency in the world of men. Those so blessed were vessels of light and transcended matter. The earliest artistic traditions of Greece, Iran, and India frequently depicted halos, whether disks or clusters of rays, round their heads. Those not blessed are made of matter, deflect light, and dwell in darkness. Gnosticism in this style was widespread in western Eurasia in the last centuries BCE. Sects within Zoroastrianism, Buddhism, Platonism in Greece, and the religious movements of the Levant all evinced gnostic tendencies, and Christianity could not be expected to be immune.

Perhaps the most important of the gnostic influences in the religions of Eurasia was the fixation on questions of reality and doubt. As a consequence, the mind—the seat of perception and discrimination—was often objectified and analyzed in formal writings of gnostic schools of many religious networks. The inferiority and deceitfulness of matter in relation to light raised the question of whether the perception of matter is a projection of the mind or has a creator, a purpose, and a reality of its own. A general solution reached within Hinduism, Judaism, Platonism, some Christianities, and Islam was that the material world must have a source, or a generative intelligence, that is distinct from the source of light and truth: Indra, Ahriman, Satan, or the demiurge of Plato, roles also attributed to divine smiths such as Prometheus and Wayland. These generative—or crafting, sometimes literally, crafty—gods of the material world were either unalterably opposed, for one reason or another, to the greater god of the real universe or inadvertently came into conflict with it at some point.

The primary tool of such a world-coveting deity is ignorance—keeping humans subordinated through confusion or false loyalty. Gnostic influences were often seen in the established religions in the development of doctrines and rituals associated with conditioning the mind to perceive immaterial truth (to become literally "awakened" or "enlightened"), to establish lines of logic that would test received teachings, and to subvert orthodox authorities. Within a century of Siddhartha's death, Buddhist philosophers had developed complex but compelling hypotheses of how the mind generated the illusion of the material world and even proposed theories of reality in which the mind itself was seen as an original reality (see also Chapter 9). In the Christian tradition, the "doubting Thomas" figure is the archetypical champion of gnostic questioning, and the *Acts of Thomas* and *Gospel of Thomas* were excluded (under separate circumstances) from the Christian canon as it was shaped in the fourth and fifth centuries. Gnostics seem to have drawn the enmity of the Christian church leaders mostly because of their rejection of the idea that Jesus could have been both human and divine. They insisted that because light and dark are exclusive of each other in origin, nature, and destiny, Jesus could not have been both. Some proposed that he was the best of humanity but not divine. Others, following the logic of Manichaeanism, argued he was wholly divine and therefore could not in reality have suffered either crucifixion or resurrection. These groups, though numerous and widespread, were marginalized in the Roman doctrinal conferences of the fourth and fifth centuries, which eventually made orthodox the doctrines of Jesus as both divine and human, and of the holy "trinity" (which itself shared kinship with some ancient aspects of the Vedas and Avesta). Gnostics who questioned these teachings on the basis of the eternally exclusive relation of light to dark were pronounced heretics and afterward made their home in the regions marginal to or outside of Roman and then Byzantine dominance: Syria, Egypt, Iran, Afghanistan, northern India, the Central Asian steppe, and China.

Islam has also wrestled with the gnostic template. The Quran imports the gnostic rendition of Jesus' life in which he did not truly suffer crucifixion and resurrection. In a more general way, Islam had communities of belief that, like the Buddhists and Christians before, were animated by a conviction that intuitive faith could produce intimacy with God, bypassing the authority of the religious hierarchy. Sectarian differentiation within Islam produced communities with stronger gnostic influences than others (see Chapters 4 and 9). All schools of Islam have intensely debated the relationship of scripture and language to the reality of the supreme consciousness, the question of predestination, and the structure of the religious community. Like Theravada Buddhism, Islam has arrived at some of the most purely gnostic resolutions of these problems. It insists upon a congruence of the form of scripture with the thought of the creator, several orthodox schools affirm predestination, and its religious communities are rigidly stratified between the adepts and auditors. Islam also preserves the notion of an ultimate catastrophic clash between good and evil, but places the process in the present, rather than in a distant spiritual future.

Monasticism and eremitism inspired by abhorrence of the deceptions and corruptions of human society were continuing themes in gnostic beliefs and in some cases became a feature of conventional religious life, where self-segregation was a means of concentrating the energies of study and meditation or prayer. The idea that believers should insulate themselves against the world of matter and live in their own communities, independent of secular society, is first found in India, where Hindu and Jain monks were living in monasteries before the seventh century BCE. It had some impact in Greece, where monastic practices were attributed to Pythagorean communities in the sixth century BCE. In Buddhism, monasticism has been a fundamental feature of every sect since the fifth century BCE, at the latest. Both monasticism and eremitism were features of some sects of Judaism and Mithraism throughout the Levant at the time of the emergence of Christianity. For Mani and his followers, a life of physical denial and meditation would produce revelation that would lead to salvation and liberation from the clutches of the material world.

Apart from monasticism, the religious systems discussed here, with the qualified exception of Manichaeanism, all produced large clerical populations, often elaborately hierarchical and complexly financed. They all generated rich scholastic traditions, and they all developed doctrinal schisms between orthodox and heretical teachings. Much of their sectarian dynamism derived from the fact that they were not only all in constant contact with each other, but were, on the ground, in constant tension with the persisting popular religious ideas—largely dualistic and eschatological in character—that had been spread far and wide across the Eurasian networks before the first formal religions had emerged. Because of their origins in Central Asia and because of their attitudes toward religion and culture generally, the nomadic rulers of the late medieval period brought their own perspectives and policies to the worlds that centuries of rule by formal, hierarchical, scholastically oriented religion created.

THE STEPPE AND THE SKY

It is a notable characteristic of the Eurasian exchange core that it preserved folk beliefs that the founded religions militated effectively against, particularly in the more peripheral areas of Europe, the Middle East, and China. It also rapidly circulated new ideas, often precipitating syntheses of folk and formal beliefs. Among the earliest of these syntheses may have been the earth-rooted cosmologies and themes of light and daytime sky worship, united in widespread cults of the smith. Eastern Eurasian nomads, and particularly the groups who would later be denominated Turks, retained in their folk cultures their own origin myths of emerging from caves or mines. The veneration of iron mining and iron smithing in Siberia and Central Asia, and particularly in the areas settled or frequented by Turkic groups, remained a strong and unifying cultural theme from prehistoric to early modern times.

Mythology suggests that transformative fire, as in the smith's cauldron, was a persistent image among the prehistoric cultures of Siberia and northern Eurasia. Not only the earliest Turkic peoples but also the Ket/Yeniseian peoples (now known to be genetically and linguistically related to the Na-Dene peoples of America), the Samoyeds, and early Ugrian peoples as well as some of the Tungusic peoples associated ironworking with spiritual or prophetic powers, equating the shaman and the smith. The figure of the smith became associated with the demiurge—the force or intelligence that crafts the material world, often advocating for flawed humans against the judgments of a perfectionist god. The myths of Prometheus and of Wayland the Smith (who entered Scandinavian mythology from the Finno-Ugric peoples of the far north) translated to southern and northern Europe the same themes that pervaded the folk cultures and mythologies of central and northeastern Eurasia. The root word for iron, *tur*, in the sense of a thing hardened by a deliberate process, may have been related to the name "Turk," which probably had something to do with the idea of being forged by tradition; it took on meanings of strength, endurance, and things able to persist from ancient times into eternity. Through this connection, it is also possible that in pre-Achaemenian times the word may have inspired the name of the ancient and semi-mythical Iranian people, the Tur, for whom the imaginary region of Turan on the extreme eastern border of the Iranian world was named and whose association with Turks (likely by folk etymology) in the medieval period became a staple of Persian literature (see also Chapter 11).

In Central Asia, the light and dark cosmology in which smith figures played the role of agents or communicators between the two realms took additional vectors outside the founded religions. The earliest historical settlers of Central Asia were probably mostly Indo-Iranian speakers who brought their ideas of fire and sun worship with them. This may have included a rudimentary and not always consistent idea that spiritual entities lived in the sky or that human souls ascended to the sky upon death and/or salvation. But alongside it ran the earlier notion of a spiritual destination—a paradise—which was not necessarily in the sky but was a segregated place for the saved that could have been an island, a walled estate, something subterranean, or the future perfected Earth. The notion that paradise was up and that its antithesis (a shadowed world, or perhaps a place of torment) was down was old in both the Hebrew and the classical Greek traditions, but it was not unequivocal or universal. Certainly, the science of seeing the gods in the night sky as astrological formations and to see the sun as moving through the "houses" of deities was widespread from Egypt to China by the end of the second millennium BCE. In other cases, gods dwelled near the sky—on mountaintops such as Mount Olympus or Mount Otuken or Mount Meru. Humans seeking to approach the gods made pilgrimages to mountains all over the world, from prehistoric times to the present.

In the religions of ancient Egypt, the Hebrews, and the Canaanites, the dwelling place of God (where he might or might not be joined by souls awaiting a day of judgment) was not in the sky specifically; it was a place outside of the material world, beyond the canopy of the sky, beneath the deepest recesses of the earth—dark, peaceful, and sealed (quite a lot like the Greek *hades*). But there is evidence of sky-god conceptions before the Bronze Age in various parts of Eurasia. The pre–Greek inhabitants of Greece, for instance, appear to have had a sky-god who was later synthesized with Indo-European gods living on mountaintops and controlling the weather. But Central Asian populations of the historical period were consistent in their assertion that the daytime sky revealed either a supreme god or the favored phenomena by which the god could be known. By the time the earliest populations originating in Siberia made it to Central Asia (displacing or merging with the majority of Indo-Europeans already there), the tendency to see the sky—and not the earth, as in earlier times, or the waters—as the home of the spirits was fixed. The idea that God and the souls of the righteous live in a sky "heaven" divides the Christian New Testament from the "Old" Testament, not least because the interval between the two saw the permeation of the Levant by ideas from Iran, Central and South Asia, and Greece. Early shamanism reflected the importance of gods and souls in the sky with tales and rituals in which shamans were enabled by the companionship of birds to either be led or carried to the heavenly abode of the highest gods. Tales of culture heroes or spiritual figures riding birds, flying with birds, being protected by birds, or talking to birds may be connected to the importance of chicken-entrail and bird-migration divination in many Eurasian cultures. The complex of sky religion and flight was probably being alluded to in the New Testament of a dove descending from Heaven at Jesus' baptism. It is probably also alluded to in the Quranic episodes of Abraham affirming his faith by gathering doves, Solomon commanding an army of intermediate spirits (*djinn*) and birds, Jesus creating a living bird from mud, or of birds whispering into the ear of Muhammad. By extension, other divinatory animals—most eminently the horse—were also made to fly in myth and religious symbolism.

Words for "heaven" and "sky" remain at the center of many puzzles of Eurasian history. In early Turkic runes, we know the word as *tngr* or variations. A Greek inscription relating to the Bulgars referenced their god named *tangra*. In more recent Turkic languages, we know it as variations of *tengri* and in Mongolian, as *tenggeri*. It may originally have been the name of a deity or a comprehensive word for deities and later may have become associated with the sky through a consensus that the sky was either a deity in itself or a home of deities. The puzzle is deepened by the word *digir* (pronounced *dingir*) in ancient Sumerian, which meant a deity and was an ideographic component of the Sumerian word for "sky" (*an*—in the Gilgamesh, the Lord of Heaven). Of the western Eurasian traditions known today, Sumerian is perhaps the earliest to be consistent in associating the sky with a particular deity or locating the home of gods and souls in the sky. *Digir* is attested much earlier than the first reflections (in Chinese records) of a Central Asian use of the word *tngri*; the Sumerian word is written (as part of personal names at least) in the late third millennium BCE, but the earliest surviving reference to Central Asian *tngri* is a millennium or a millennium and a half later. This chronological gap corresponds roughly to the gap in the development of writing between Sumeria and China, so there is no compelling reason to think that the sequence of written attestation of the word is the same as the sequence of use. More interesting is that it also corresponds to the period in which the war chariot was transmitted from Sumeria to Central Asia and ultimately to East Asia while trade in tin and lapis lazuli provided continuous communications between Mesopotamia and modern-day Afghanistan.

There are other mysteries within this mystery. About the same time that Chinese records cite the use of the word *tngri* in Central Asia, the Chinese word *tian*—meaning "god," "nature," or "heaven"—was becoming secured in China as the reference to a supreme deity, creator, or judge. This was loosely but manifestly connected to the overthrow of the Shang dynasty and its displacement by the Zhou, which happened probably less than a century before 1000 BCE. The old Shang god, Di—whose name some scholars have speculated may be related to ancient Indo-European words reflected later in Latin *deus* and Hindu *deva* (from an Indo-Iranian source word that referred to the sky and to "shining")—was fading. It was displaced by Tian, the supreme god. The Zhou arose on the western edge of the old Shang world, which means the littoral of Central Asia, and several aspects of Zhou culture, politics, and technology (including the chariot) have been noted as showing the strong influence of Central Asia. Were *tian* and *tngri* the same word? Were they the same word as *digir*? And to make things even more intriguing, it is possible that Sanskrit *tan-* is connected. It means something like "overarching," "all pervading," or "limitless." That is for specialists to sort out. What is interesting here is that identification of "god" and "sky"—and especially "heaven" as simultaneously a physical phenomenon, a deity, and a spiritual place—was associated with Central Asian proximity. There is no need to associate it primarily with nomads, but there is good reason to associate it with the Central Asian territories that nomads navigated regularly and eventually ruled.

READING NOTES: LIGHT-MINDEDNESS

Much of what is discussed in this chapter relates to what is often called the "Axial Age," contributed by Karl Jaspers (1883–1969). For more on that, see S. N. Eisenstadt, ed., *The Origins and Diversity of Axial Age Civilizations* (SUNY Press, 1986) and Robert N. Bellah and Han Joas, *The Axial Age and Its Consequences* (Harvard UP, 2012).

On the association of some large, mythical ideas with Indo-Europeans, Iran, and India, see Fredrik T. Hiebert, *Origins of the Bronze Age Oasis Civilization in Central Asia* (Harvard University, 1994) and J. P. Mallory, *In Search of the Indo-Europeans: Language, Archaeology and Myth* (London, 1989). For more geographically specific discussions of the Bronze Age and early religious ideas, see Muhammad A. Dandamaev and Vladimir G. Lukonin, *The Culture and Social Institutions of Ancient Iran*, trans. Philip L. Kohl with D. J. Dadson (Cambridge UP, 2004) and Victor H. Mair, *The Bronze Age and Early Iron Age Peoples of Eastern Central Asia* (Institute for the Study of Man, 1998).

On ancient religions generally, there is an enormous scholarship, but the following have been helpful to me: Karen Armstrong, *The Great Transformation: The Beginning of Our Religious Traditions* (Knopf, 2006); Richard Foltz, *Religions of the Silk Road*, 2nd ed. (Palgrave Macmillan, 2010); Lawrence A. Kratz, "Geographic Origins of Religious Diversity in Eurasia," *Journal of Geography* 47, no. 6 (1948): 240–246; and Victor H. Mair and Jane Hickman, eds., *Reconfiguring the Silk Road: New Research on East-West Exchange in Antiquity* (U Pennsylvania P, 2014), particularly Michael Frachetti, "Seeds for the Soul: Ideology and Diffusion of Domestic Grains across Asia," 41–53. For a rather different approach, see Nicholas Baumard, Alexandre Hyafill, Ian Morris, and Pascal Boyer, "Increased Affluence Explains the Emergence of Ascetic Wisdoms and Moralizing Religions," *Current Biology* (2014), http://dx.doi.org/10.1016/j.cub.2014.10.063, and M. G. Levin and L. P. Potapov, eds., *The Peoples of Siberia* (U of Chicago P, 1964).

For background reading on the possible entanglement of *digir* and *tengri*, see Robert A. Di Vito, *Studies in Third Millennium Sumerian and Akkadian Personal Names: The Designation and Conception of a Personal God* (Gregorian Biblical Bookshop, 1993) and Arkadiusz Soł tysiak, "Physical Anthropology and the 'Sumerian Problem,'" *Studies in Historical Anthropology* 4 (2006): 145–158. For a vigorous discussion of the Di/Tian transition in the cosmological history of ancient China, see Sarah Allan, *The Shape of the Turtle: Myth, Art and Cosmos in Early China* (SUNY P, 1991) and "On the Identity of Shang Di and the Origin of the Concept of a Celestial Mandate (Tian Ming)," *Early China* 31 (2007): 1–46; and Chen Derong, "Di and Tian in Ancient Chinese Thought: A Critical Analysis of Hegel's Views," *Dao: A Journal of Comparative Philosophy* 8, no. 1 (2009): 13–27.

I assume that any reader can consult basic works of reference on shamanism, mythology, and world religion (and Bronze Age references from Chapter 1 may also be useful). The following works have been of special help to me: Wendy Doniger, especially in *The Implied Spider: Politics and Theology in Myth* (Columbia UP, 2010), and her student, David Gordon White, *Myths of the Dog-Man* (U Chicago P, 1991) followed much earlier scholars of Central Asia in tracing deep and early continuities of narrative and moral logic across the continent. See also Michael Witzel, *The Origins of the World's Mythologies* (Oxford UP, 2010).

On shamanism itself there is a mountain of scholarship; I point the reader to Mircea Eliade, Michael Taussig, and Michael Harner. The particular shamanism of interest here is what is more or less meant by "Siberian shamanism" (not the current fashionable one, the historical one). For definition of the field, see Manabu Waida, "Problems of Central Asian and Siberian Shamanism," *Numen* XXX, no. 2 (1983): 215–239, and for more recent work (after the period of Soviet scholarship), see Graham Harvey and Robert J. Wallis, eds., *Historical Dictionary of Shamanism* (Rowman & Littlefield, 2015). The following have also been helpful to me for this chapter: Julian Baldick, *Animal and Shaman: Ancient Religions of Central Asia* (New York University P, 2000); Caroline Humphrey and Urgunge Onon, *Shamans and Elders: Experience, Knowledge, and Power among the Daur Mongols* (Clarendon Press, 1996); Marjorie Mandelstam Balzer, *The Tenacity of Ethnicity: A Siberian Saga in Global Perspective* (Princeton UP, 1999); L. Karlson, "The Doe with the Golden Antlers: Representation of an Ancient Myth in Medieval Swedish Wrought Iron," *Acta Archaeologica* 51 (1980): 1–68; T. R. Viisto, "Early Metallurgy in Language: The History of Metal Names in Finnic," in *A Linguistic Map of Prehistoric Northern Europe*, ed. R. Grünthal and P. Kallio (*Mémoires de la Société Finno-Ougrienne*), 185–200; and Caroline Humphrey, "Shamanic Practices and the State in Northern Asia: Views from the Center and Periphery," in *Shamanism, History, and the State*, ed. Nicholas Thomas and Caroline Humphrey (U Michigan P, 1994). See also Walther Heissig, "New Material on East Mongolian Shamanism," *Asian Folklore Studies*, 49, no. 2 (1990): 223–233 and *The Religions of Mongolia*, trans. Geoffrey Samuels (Routledge Keegan Paul, 1980); Klaus Hesse, "A Note on the Transformation of White, Black and Yellow Shamanism in the History of the Mongols," *Studies in History* 2, no. 1 (1986): 17–30 and "On the History of Mongolian Shamanism in Anthropological Perspective," *Anthropos* 82, nos. 4–6 (1987): 403–413; and Giuseppe Tucci, *The Religions of Tibet*, trans. Geoffrey Samuels (U California P, 1988).

See also the remarks of Shagdar Bira, following Dorji Banzarov in hypothesizing that Hunnic shamanism represented an original form of Siberian shamanism, later filtered to Turkic and ultimately to the Mongol peoples: "Kizucheniyu istorii kul'ta Tngri u mongolov [A study of the history of the Tengri cult among the Mongols]," 3rd International Scientific and Practical Conference, "Tengrianism and the Epic Heritage of the Peoples of Eurasia: Origins and the Present" (July 2011), https://www.tuva.asia/journal/issue_2-3/3788-shagdar-bira.html. Presumably, the similar form of the name (*tangra*) suggests similar guesses could be extended to early Bulgar (see Chapter 3) shamanism.

On Zoroastrianism, see Matt Waters, *Ancient Persia: A Concise History of the Achaemenid Empire, 550-330 BC* (Cambridge UP, 2014); Mary Boyce, *Zoroastrians: Their Religious Beliefs and Practices* (Routledge, 2001); and Jenny Rose, *Zoroastrianism: An Introduction* (Routledge, 2011).

On Buddhism, see Donald S. Lopez Jr., *The Story of Buddhism: A Concise Guide to Its History and Teachings* (HarperCollins, 2001); Rupert Gethin, *The Foundations of Buddhism* (Oxford UP, 1998); Peter Harvey, *An Introduction to Buddhism: Teachings, History and Practices* (Cambridge UP, 2012); and the helpful website, "History of the Buddhist Canon," http://www.oxfordbibliographies.com/view/document/obo-9780195393521/obo-9780195393521-0036.xml. Especially important to this chapter (and to Chapter 9) is Siglinde Dietz, "Buddhism in Gandhara," in *The Spread of Buddhism*, ed. Ann Hierman and Stephan Peter Bumbacher (Brill, 2007), 47–74 and David Alan Scott, "The Iranian Face of Buddhism," *East and West* 40, no. 1/4 (1990): 43–77. My comments on Ashoka's views of his relation to religion are drawn from reading Romila Thapar, *A History of India*, vol. 1 (Penguin, 1990), esp. 70–75.

On Judaism, Platonism, and early Christianity (including Gnostic Christianity), see the classic by Han Jonas, *The Gnostic Religion: The Message of the Alien God and the Beginnings of Christianity*, first published in 1958 by Beacon Press (before extensive research on the Nag Hammadi trove) and now available in its third edition (2015); Daniel Boyarin, *The Partition of Judaeo-Christianity* (U Pennsylvania P, 2004); Lee I. Levine, *Judaism and Hellenism in Antiquity: Conflict or Confluence?* (U Washington P, 1998); Elaine Pagels, *The Gnostic Gospels* (Vintage Books, 1979); *Beyond Belief: The Secret Gospel of Thomas* (Vintage Books, 2003) and "'Gnostic' Is an Open Question: An Interview with Elaine Pagels," *Reality Sandwich*, 2011, http://realitysandwich.com/96150/gnostic_interview_elaine_pagels/. On Thomas as a theme in early modern art, see Glenn W. Most, *Doubting Thomas* (Harvard UP, 2005). On structuralist discussions of Gnostic layers in Eurasian myth and religion, see Ingvild Saelid Gilhus, "Gnosticism: A Study in Liminal Symbolism," *Numen* 31 (1984): 106–128. For Ioan Juliano's warnings against underestimating the spectrum of gnostic permeations of religious discourse, see his *Tree of Gnosis: Gnostic Mythology from Early Christianity to Modern Nihilism* (HarperCollins, 1992); see also Ehud Benor, *Ethical Monotheism: A Philosophy of Judaism* (Routledge, 2018), 12–13.

Part II

Steppe Power in Settled Medieval Eurasia

Chapter Three

The Turkic Tide

The adjectives used to describe the campaigns of Chinggis Khan in the thirteenth century often imply an unexpected fury of conquest bursting from Mongolia. But the rise of Chinggis's federation was in most ways consistent with the long history of federation and state-building by the Turkic-related populations across Eurasia, from the Balkans to China, from Siberia to northern India. It is a history not only of conquest, but of Turkic rule of large populations, both agricultural and urban, for hundreds of years before the rise of the Mongols or the Ottomans. The name "Turk" darts through various early documents in relation to peoples living in the band from the (now disappearing) Sea of Azov in the west to the modern Chinese province of Inner Mongolia. With generosity, the name can be traced to accounts in Latin of the first century CE, and with imagination, it can be seen in Chinese records of the late first millennium BCE or early Iranian narratives of roughly the same period. It appears unambiguously in Chinese documents only in the seventh century CE and is most explicit in runic inscriptions in relation to the empire historians refer to as "Gokturk." By the ninth century, Turkic peoples—mostly soldiers—had become part of the ruling castes of China, the empires of Central Asia, the Islamic Middle East, the Hungarian plain, and the Balkans. They did not share a single language, religion, or political system, but they played a role in generalizing some steppe traditions across Eurasian states and in some instances popular culture.

The homeland of the Turks was somewhere near the sources of the Onon and Kherlen rivers on the border between Mongolia and Siberia. Linguistics and genetics allow us to understand the history of Turkic groups back to the early first millennium BCE, a time when Mongolia was probably exclusively pastoral and connected to Central Asia and North China by trade. By the time the Turks became part of the historical record of China, they were already products of Central Asian synthesis. Genetic analysis not only of modern Turkic populations across Eurasia but also from recovered remains of the Xiongnu of third century Mongolia show that Turkic ancestors shared most genes with neighboring populations in Siberia and China. Their genetic profiles over time were shaped by the early settlement of the steppe by pastoralists, its later settlement by early Indo-European speakers, repopulations from Central and Eastern Europe, and later additions of waves of migrants with Siberian origins. By the middle centuries of the first millennium BCE the Turkic speakers had broken into a large number of independent bands. The ancestors of the Yakuts had moved into north and east Siberia. The ancestors of the Xiongnu were becoming dominant in Mongolia itself. Other groups such as the Dilie and Dingling (modern pronunciations of the names from Chinese records) were documented in what are now Gansu and Xinjiang provinces of western China. Many Turkic groups had already moved farther into Central Asia—away from the aridity of Mongolia and toward the more bountiful grasslands to the west. Some groups of Turks had begun the long migration that would eventually take them to Anatolia, the region we now call "Turkey."

EMERGENCE OF A STEPPE POLITICAL TRADITION

Turkic migrations left strong marks on emerging political organization across Eurasia. The first large federation connected to eastern Eurasian peoples was Xiongnu, which covered most of modern-day Mongolia, Inner Mongolia, and northern Gansu Province of China from the third century BCE to the end of the first century CE. Their movement east to west across Eurasia suggests that their early life—like that of the Indo-Europeans, who had earlier moved in the opposite direction across Central Asia—was inseparable from the horse. Early Chinese records retrospectively interpreted by the Han-period historian Sima Qian (c. 140–86 BCE) describe the Xiongnu and Turkic populations as nomads. Yet agriculture—specifically millet cultivation—can be surmised to have played a significant economic role, as the wide area of dispersal, linguistic influence, and haplogroup survival of Turkic populations indicates more robust population growth than exclusive pastoralism could have sustained.

The origins of the Xiongnu are disputed, as is the nature of their language. But their place in Turkic political history is secure. The campaigns that unified China twice between 221 BCE and 203 BCE also brought conflicts over the Gansu Corridor—the terminal eastern leg of the ancient overland trade network. In response to military losses to the Qin empire, the Xiongnu federation further centralized and increased the size of its armies, bequeathing to later steppe empires the "ten-thousand" (*tumen*) unit of military strength. Xiongnu forced the Han empire in China to agree to a treaty that required the regular payment of tribute as well as the occasional supply of women from the Han imperial lineage for marriage to the Xiongnu ruler or his sons. At the turn of the first century BCE, the rulers of the Han empire decided to throw off the dominance of Xiongnu. They undertook a new war with a larger and improved cavalry. The result was Han control of the Gansu Corridor, which was subsequently governed by most unified empires based in China. This established a firm southwesterly boundary to Xiongnu power and initiated a long decline in Xiongnu political coherence. By the time Han itself fell in 220 CE, divisions among the Xiongnu had all but eradicated the old federation. The southerly Xiongnu created small states in the style of the Han across northern China while the northerly populations stayed in Mongolia or moved westward.

Historians analyzing the patterns of Central Asian history have described a series of empires whose fates were controlled by a kind of geo-strategic dynamism with the great empires of the settled areas. In this model, because the Central Asian empires were nomadic, they were predominantly opportunistic and parasitical. Their populations were small and lived primarily off the wealth they could either pilfer or demand as organized tribute from the settled populations. Having no very complex income stream or fixed political geography of cities and capitals, the political organization was perpetually decentralized and unstable. As a consequence, steppe empires were ephemeral. When the settled empires could not muster the means for a sustained self-defense or expansion, the nomad empires might thrive, but when the settled empires grew strong again, the nomad empires had to recede.

It is hard to argue that the history of Xiongnu shows this general pattern. The Xiongnu federation was not short-lived. By the time of the Xiongnu split in the first century BCE, the federation was 200 years old, a duration that most dynastic regimes in China would not achieve. One source of longevity is indicated by the probable size of the population, which argues against a simple pastoral economy. The Xiongnu at the height of their war against the Han were reported to have fielded 300,000 horse-mounted soldiers, which suggests a minimum federation population of about 2 million (the modern population of Mongolia is about 2.5 million). The archaeology of the Xiongnu period also shows that there were substantial urban settlements. This required a steady supply of grain and most likely communities that specialized in production of iron implements for both peace and war along with wagons, ceramics, textiles (mostly based on wool), and decorative items of gold, iron, and bone. The Xiongnu *necropolii* discovered in the twenty-first century must have been the site of settlement also by caretakers, guards, craftsmen, and the farmers who fed them. Before the split of the Xiongnu federation in the first century BCE, there was a capital—at a spot venerated by subsequent Turkic states—in the Orkhon Valley in Mongolia (see Chapter 6). The stable capital meant roadways, food supplies, craftspeople, industries for mining, carpentry, brick making and stonework, and residences for the ruler and his high-ranking officials. The Xiongnu had a mixed economy with a substantial role for pastoralism and a style in warfare based on fighting or shooting from the saddle, but at the same time incorporating substantial agricultural and urban elements.

The apparent decentralization of government is insufficient reason to characterize the Xiongnu political organization as weak or unstable. Certainly, it was a contrast to the Qin and Han systems in China of an emperor—a single individual (or officials acting in his name) controlling all power and legitimating all law. But the imperial system in China was an innovation at the time. The Xiongnu political system shared some fundamental characteristics with the earlier political system of Zhou China, which had survived well over 700 years and may have been as influential as early Iran in the dissemination of political ideas and terms across Eurasia. The Zhou system was concentrically segmented, in which local rulers (*jun*) acknowledged a supreme ruler (*wang*) at their center. In Bronze Age Eurasia, this political scheme was widespread and is easily attested from China to Iran to Ireland. But at the Eurasian peripheries, such as Egypt, China, and southern Europe, the late transition to the Iron Age was often coterminous with displacement of these early political patterns by centralized rulership and administrative innovations reducing the sovereignty of local leaders. Central Asian empires tended to preserve and circulate the earlier political forms, with retention of aristocratic privilege, circumscribed rulership, and significant local autonomy of language and culture.

The Xiongnu supreme ruling figure (*shanyu*)—at least from second generation of the founding—was always a grown man, and the office passed to adult brothers of the former ruler if he had no son who was of age. He ordered the troops to war, and it was to the ruler that Chinese officials addressed their communications. Admission to the presence of the ruler was highly ritualized. Among his most important duties were the ceremonies propitiating minor spirits and venerating the supreme spirit of the sky. The ruler led with the aid of a council of high-ranking warriors, most of them his blood relatives. The government was segmented along territorial lines roughly corresponding to contours of this aristocracy, distributing responsibility for gathering tribute and organizing the military. The aristocrats supplied the candidates for the ruler, they legitimated him, and they did or did not consent to his decisions. Though it is impossible that the Xiongnu aristocracy did not have its own income from herds and farms, the Chinese accounts suggest that tribute from China was desired for the specific goal of distributing wealth to the aristocracy to reinforce the ruler's position. This is a succinct formulation of what would be a central and enduring feature of political consolidation among Turkic peoples.

The presence of a stable and systematic government does not mean that Xiongnu was a cultural identity. Before the rise of the Xiongnu federation, there was a wide variety of tribal and lineage identities throughout the region, all of which were to some degree "Turkic" and all of which to some degree were also Chinese or Iranian or Siberian. As Xiongnu expansion deleted these identities as political—that is, determining whom one recognized either as a supreme leader or to whom one reported for military action—they disappeared at least temporarily from the historical record. Some came back later, in various forms, and it is reasonable to assume that at a local level—at the level of marriage and family, if not employment and protection—many persisted. The Xiongnu political system was one that easily accommodated regional administrative segmentation and plural community identities, which also would remain an enduring characteristic of Turkic political orders.

As elsewhere in Eurasia, class was a far more definitive element in identity than language, dress, or religion. It is probable that an estate system—by which noblemen owned physical goods, animals, and people, but not always land—was already in place. It was an efficient way of administering everyday life, organizing and rendering tribute, and supplying men, horses, and equipment for war. The estates of the aristocrats were based upon slaves, whether abducted from China or taken during the wars of Xiongnu expansion in Siberia, Mongolia, and Central Asia. Slaves worked the fields and mines, they may have done menial work in the larger households, they cleaned the animal enclosures, and some were full-time soldiers. Slaves may have made up the largest segment of society, as war and the search for security drove increasing numbers of people into the apparent protection of slavery. Scholars of later periods of Central Asian state-building emphasize that servitude and dependency were rarely absolute conditions—as they could be in Rome or in Han China, for instance—but were performed in contexts of subordination to certain individuals. Those subordinated to high-ranking war leaders were likely to be of high status themselves within the military organizations, and those subordinated to a ruler were likely to be of high status in relation to the rest of the population. This quality of "slave" status in Central Asia was not unique but was widely distributed across Turkic military organizations, and the bonds it created between a lord and his dependents were strong enough to form the cores of civil and military administration in new federations. Sources as early as the Xiongnu suggest that institutions of servitude and political function were already linked, which may help explain the effectiveness and the longevity of the Xiongnu federation.

This era of Xiongnu rule in Mongolia roughly coincided with the domination of Central Asia by the Skythians. Corpses in what are now believed to be Skythian graves show a kind of genetic mirror image of those in Xiongnu graves; while the Xiongnu corpses are fundamentally eastern Eurasian with a strong western admixture, Skythian graves are fundamentally western Eurasian with a strong eastern admixture. Greek and Roman writers making reference to the Skythians appeared to be indicating any northern or eastern culture that was based on the horse, on pastoralism, and on frequent raids of settled areas. The earliest references to Skythians, as in Herodotus, seem to be clear references to horse nomads whose languages were some sort of Iranian. These groups were sometimes referred to by the name Saka, a version of which was probably also used in Han China to refer to Iranian (possibly Sogdian) nomads on their western borders. But late—that is, Roman period—references to Skythians imply they had an Asian origin. Like the Xiongnu, the Skythians were a true Eurasian population—but unlike the Xiongnu, the Skythians had no lasting confederation under a single leader, and under their own name, did not bequeath a state tradition to Central Asia.

From this perspective, the long debate over whether "Xiongnu" and "Hun" are the same name may be slightly specious. Both were the labels assumed by or given to elites within the federations, and even if the names were related, it predicts imperfectly the cultures of their followers. Contemporary comment made clear that the Huns were not a homogeneous population. Their armies were polyglot and included not only Turkic riders but also Skythians, Sarmatians, Alans, and Germanic-speaking Goths. As in the case of the Xiongnu, the ruling class of the Huns who swept into Europe in the fifth century may have had an identity of their own—the true Huns. Priscus's description of Attila was the description of a Central Asian, and the tents the Huns brought on wagons behind them were pretty clearly yurts. There is every possibility that among the Huns were some of direct Xiongnu descent and this may have been more pronounced among the rulers. Even without direct ancestry, these Hunnic leaders may well have wished to place themselves in succession to the Xiongnu and may have adopted some version of the name (though we do not know what the exact name of the Xiongnu, in their own language, was). In any event, the Hunnic "empire" is mostly notional. The Huns were more like a hierarchical booty network than an empire; the rulers subordinated groups of Central Asia, made them part of their gigantic raiding party, concocted various claims to territory and titles of the crumbling Roman Empire, and tried their luck at taking what they claimed. Soon after Attila died in 453, the mob disintegrated, and its constituent crews went their own way. The Huns are not part of the cumulative political history of Central Asia.

However, the Tagbach (Tuoba), Rouran, and the Hephthalites are. The Tagbach will be discussed below as founders of a particular elite culture in East Asia, but we are interested here in their possible role in a broader Turkic political style. They emerged in the aftermath of the Xiongnu demise and may have been from the verge of what is now the eastern Mongolian steppe and the mountain ranges of western Manchuria. We know something of their language from names and terms transcribed in Chinese records, and modern scholars refer to it as Sarbi (Xianbei). Sarbi language and culture may have characterized not only the Tagbach but other peoples with an origin at the Mongolia/Manchuria nexus. Linguists argue whether it is a Turkic, proto-Mongolic, or Tungusic language. With respect to political vocabulary, it may be a less important debate since these terms circulated quickly and there is no way to prove that any names or terms used by Sarbi speakers did not come from Xiongnu or earlier predecessors.

The Sarbi-speaking Tagbach may have been the first we know to use the term *khaghan* for a ruler, even though they did not continue to use this term after they founded a state (called by the Chinese name Wei and referred to historically as Northern Wei) in the fourth century. More intriguing, the common Central Asian terms for writing and for a scribe (*bidizhen* in modern Chinese transcription) occur in the history of the Northern Wei as part of a set of terms that flowed widely across Eurasia. In this case, the word was probably from an Indo-European root for carving or cutting that produced not only verbs for writing (e.g., Old Iranian and Turkic *bitig-*; Mongolian *bicig-*; Manchu *bithe-*; Iranian, Russian, and Slavonic *pis-* or *piš-*; old Chinese *prud* [writing instrument]; modern Chinese *bi*; and modern Korean *pil*) but also words that in English show up as "pick" and "paint." This suggests that from the Northern Wei at the latest, the role of written communications and record keeping—including but not limited to inscribed monuments—was always coterminous with state formation in Central Asia and Mongolia and that this history was acknowledged in the chains of inherited words for record-keeping activity. It also marks an early threshold of historicity for the collegial cabinet-style government evident in nearly all Turkic and Mongol regimes (see Chapter 6). The Northern Wei state was a landmark in the integration of Turkic political tradition and military organization with the literate appurtenances of state control of a large agricultural population. Its "Tagbach" name in various forms remained the definitive historical and geographic reference to "China" in the historiographical traditions of the Muslim and Turkic worlds for a millennium.

While the Northern Wei dominated north China, its client group of Rouran (330–555 CE) gradually gained control of a huge territory covering not only all of modern Mongolia and part of northern China but also the western part of Manchuria. The ruling caste may have included Sarbi speakers and certainly many who had been influenced by Tagbach culture; the Rouran language itself has remained a puzzle, and leading linguists consider it a possible isolate. Though Chinese records describe the early Rouran as nomads without settlements, the Rouran learned quickly from the Tagbach and in the last century of their federation evinced stable government and substantial literacy in either Chinese script or an adaptation of it to their own language. It appears that both *khaghan* and *khan*, which would become so central to Eurasian history, were used by the Rouran. The words' relationship and etymologies are debated, and it may be necessary to consider the vein of Iranian influence running through the Xiongnu to the Rouran to make sense of them. There is, for instance, a theory that *khan* may be derived, possibly during the Zhou period, from the Chinese term *guan*, for an official. If that is true, then *khaghan* has evidently been invented by inserting a syllabic break in the middle. This could have happened by emulation of Iranian *shahanshah*, "king of kings." That term, which was widespread across Eurasia as early as the Achaemenian empire, had in ancient Assyria described a political order of smaller rulers (and the term *shad*, a probable Turkic plural of *shah*, remained in use as a political rank in Turkic regimes for centuries) whose power revolved concentrically around a ruler of greater magnitude. There was therefore a shah over other shahs—a *shahanshah*—and in the Rouran confederacy, there was *khan* over other *khans*—a *khaghan*. On the other hand, *khaghan* is attested earlier than *khan*, suggesting that *khaghan* is not an augmentation of *khan*. In that case, the survival of both words must be explained. Unfortunately, the Rouran language may have taken with it the answer to the puzzle. Khaghan may have been picked up from the Tagbach, and Rouran semantics may have produced "khan" by some mechanism we do not know.

The Hephthalites enter the written record as subordinate to the Rouran and inhabiting their western frontiers. Since the fifth century when the Hephthalites began to harry western and southern Eurasia, they had sometimes been called the "White Huns," though the connection to the Huns was in the eyes of the beholders of northern India, the Mediterranean, and Byzantium. It is evident from the record that Hephthalite—or Hephthal, Eptal, Yipdal, Abdel, or something similar—was not the name for members of the group but was the dynastic name of their ruling family or ruling caste. The group itself (or their language) was called War or Var. By the middle fifth century, they had moved west and established a regime of their own in what is now Afghanistan, eventually expanding to present-day Pakistan, the western edge of Mongolia, and Xinjiang Province of China. Their leader was a khaghan; they had a capital city at "Gorgo," probably near Kubadiyan; they minted coins, developed significant urban settlements, encouraged the extension of agriculture, and maintained a large army both on foot and horseback with which they defeated attempted invasions by the last Sasanian kings of Iran and the Gupta rulers of northern India. The Hephthalites had a segmented political system that accommodated cultural plurality. Their ruling caste was organized into tight teams of leaders and subordinates, who as they died were buried together in large, round tumuli. They maintained a stable tribute collection and administrative system that relied not only on their own language but also upon the local Iranian dialect that had been the medium of government before they arrived. Their period saw a flourishing of statuary in the Greek and Indian styles, and their religious influences were various, including Zoroastrianism, Hinduism, Manichaeanism and in their late period, Christianity.

Historians debate, in relation to later orders of the Turks and Mongols, the significance of hereditary aristocrats and particularly the aristocratic estate system—in most of the Central Asian languages, called by some version of the word *ordo*—in both the coherence of ostensibly nomadic empires and their limitations of centralization. The role of hereditary elites is clear, and the likelihood that they had distinct identities is also clear. What is less clear is the degree to which political identities among the greater mass of commoners depended upon affiliation with the estates of aristocrats. In practice, it is evident that the *ordo* was the unit upon which large-scale military and political activity was based and it provided the framework by which commoners and slaves participated in and were rewarded for war and defense. For the Xiongnu and Rouran periods, we have little evidence of autonyms, and so the process of acquiring group names within lineages, lineage federations, or political unions is not well understood; whether group names defined followers in relation to leaders cannot be answered definitively. Any khan or khaghan was reliant upon those who commanded their own ordos and was required to reward them generously and consistently. Concentration of power in a single lineage or a single ruler may have appeared attractive to many nomadic leaders, but establishing such power would require dismantling of the *ordo* structures, which in itself would threaten the coherence of any empire that an ambitious khan was attempting to rule. This basic tension in Central Asian political tradition would determine the form and the fate of many empires of the medieval and early modern periods.

The Xiongnu and Hephthalite political traditions were continued and augmented by two large empires of the ensuing centuries: the Gokturk (sixth and seventh centuries) and the Uighur (744–940). A fundamental element of continuity was the political ideology of the Ashina imperial lineage, whose name may have been a reference to Xiongnu. In their mythical accounts of their history, they were the offspring of a wolf mother and a human father and were born in a mystical cave in what is now Mongolia. They ruled the Xiongnu and afterward were subject to the Rouran, but moved westward into Central Asia and declared themselves independent. Their regime prefix of Gok has been variously interpreted, though it is clearly a reference to a Turkic word that can mean blue, or the sky, or Heaven (whether deity or spiritual home), or the east. Gokturk might only have meant Turks who had migrated into Central Asia from the east. Or it could have been a specific invocation of sky/Heaven, a tempting interpretation because the Gokturks offer the first explicit political ideology of claimed universal rulership legitimated by the favor of the sky-spirit, manifested by success in war. The idea that the right to rule was made apparent only by Heaven's support of one side or another in a struggle was old in all parts of Eurasia but was becoming increasingly explicit in the rhetoric and rituals of the Xiongnu, Rouran, and Hephthalites before the Gokturks, who may have made it the basis of their imperial presentation through the device of their name.

The Gokturk empire, once it had displaced the last remnants of Rouran and Hephthalite regimes, brought the Ashina lineage to rule a territory on the same basic foundations as the Rouran and Tagbach before them (see Map 3.1). They had an impressive capital in the old Xiongnu capital region of the Orkhon Valley of Mongolia (see Chapter 6), and they had a patently segmented empire and a khaghan affirmed by an aristocratic council. They supported an official shamanism while accommodating a variety of religions that included Buddhism, Manichaeanism, and Christianity; establishments associated with these religions were frequently granted *darkhan*, the gift of freedom from tribute demands, which in earlier times was peculiar to the aristocracy. The oldest surviving monuments displaying Turkic in a runic script date from this era. Workers in iron, ceramics, textiles, painting, and music were, when needed, classified as specialists and made slaves in the khaghan's palace or associated facilities. Agricultural laborers were either transported to developing areas as slaves or left in place and given a special tax designation. The labeling of populations by their geographic or cultural origins was an early feature since it implicitly preserved the context in which the khaghan made gifts of these populations to his subordinates, kinsmen, and supporters.

A succession dispute in the late sixth century split the Gokturks into eastern and western segments. In the late seventh century, they reunited and began to challenge Tang China, the Abbasid caliphate, and Tibet for control of Central Asia. Iranian-speaking Sogdians became a major cultural and political influence in the reconstituted Gokturk empire. For centuries, the Sogdians had lived at the interface of northwestern Iran and Central Asia, and some of them were known as erudites who—by virtue of the script they had adapted from Syriac—had successively spread the influence of Greek, then Manichaean, and then Christian influence from Transoxiana to western China. The Turkic Uighurs were living in the western half of the empire, where they came under the cultural influence of the Sogdians. In 744, Uighurs captured the Gokturk capital in the Orkhon Valley, beheaded the last Gokturk ruler, and established a new khaghanate of their own.

Much of the Uighur style sprang from the crucible in which Sogdian West Asian scholastic and urban traditions were alloyed with Turkic ruling ideologies and administrative practices. The Uighurs renamed and occupied the old Gokturk capital and entered into an alliance with Tang China. They soon reunited the territories of the Xiongnu, controlling what is now Mongolia, Xinjiang Province of China, and the northern edge of Tibet. By the middle of the eighth century, Buddhism had been established in urban and a few rural sectors of Central Asia for centuries and in various degrees coexisted with shamanism among the Turkic populations. The Uighur court publicly converted to Manichaeanism due to influence of the Sogdians but permitted Buddhism and other religions among the population. In this period Central Asia's great cities of Bukhara, Samarkand, and Tashkent—all critical to the caravan trade—were characterized by a literate Buddhist culture with strong ties to Iranian and Greek traditions, to India, and to China. Uighur adaptation of the Sogdian phonetic script made possible several innovations in Uighur government, including the conversion from a tax in kind to a money tax and subsequently, more precise minting of coins. To imitate the prestigious monuments in Chinese that the Tang had erected in Mongolia, the Uighurs spun the Sogdian script 90 degrees so that it ran not right to left but top to bottom. The empire lasted about a century, but Uighur culture continued to influence urban life in Central Asia well into the period of Mongol domination.

"TURKS" RULING THE POPULOUS SOCIETIES OF THE EAST

After the split of the Xiongnu empire in the second century CE, the southerly tribes capitulated to the Han empire and entered into frequent economic and political contact with northern China. They sent envoys to the Han capital at Chang'an (modern Xi'an in Shaanxi Province) and helped the Han push northerly Xiongnu groups toward Central Asia. As the Han empire disinte-

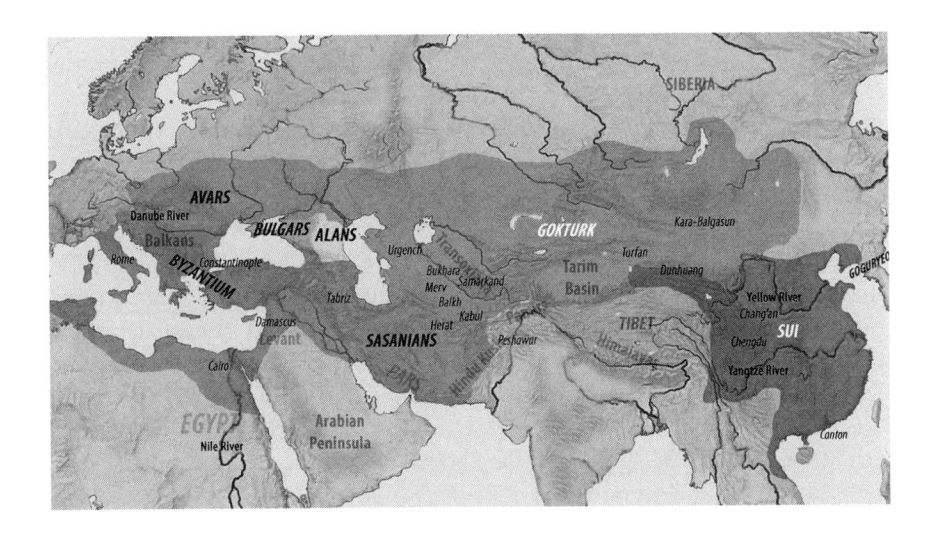

Map 3.1. Major political orders of Eurasia, c. 600 CE.

grated in the third century CE, southern Xiongnu leaders established their own states. In some of these states, the ruling lineage eventually took on Chinese surnames, and in more cases they emulated the ruling institutions of Han whatever they called themselves. The Chinese emperorship was of great interest. The Qin and Han empires had been strongly centralized, with all decisive power in the hands of one man, the emperor (*huangdi*). It was an innovation in China of the third century BCE, and only a century later may already have begun affecting the Xiongnu order, as war between Han and Xiongnu promoted an unprecedented degree of centralization in both empires. When Xiongnu headmen moved south of the Great Wall to establish their own states, they were quick to seek the technology of emperorship with all that went with it—a bureaucracy in the Chinese style, primogenitural transmission of the imperial office, a written law and knowledge of philosophy in the Chinese written language, rituals propitiating spirits of the environment and ancestors, and a court in a palace in Chinese style with emperors and courtiers dressed in Chinese silk robes.

In this age of many small states of Turkic origin scattered across north and central China, the degree to which the tension between the concentration of power in the hands of an emperor and his heir apparent and the traditions of corporate endorsement of a ruler may have created instability has been much examined. Certainly, the tension between court and aristocracy was real and affected particularly the early stage of political development of the states that ruled smaller or larger parts of southern Mongolia, western Manchuria, and northern China between about 300 CE and 600 CE. The founders of this imperial style were the Sarbi-speaking peoples and particularly the Tagbach, who established the Northern Wei state in the fourth century. In this case the emperor conspicuously alternated his worship and court style between Chinese and Tagbach modes. This did little to mitigate hostilities between nobles protecting the traditions of shared power and the Yuwen imperial lineage using the emperorship to keep power in their own hands. At one point the emperor moved his capital from the traditional territories to Luoyang in the old Han heartland, hoping to break the grip of the aristocracy.

In the short-lived successor states of the fifth and sixth centuries, a ruling caste emerged that gracefully melded the horse, falconry and archery skills, martial engagement, and clothing styles of the traditional north Asian aristocracy with education in Chinese literature, philosophy, and history. This elite consciously traced its ancestry to Tagbach elites of the Northern Wei era, and to Chinese officials of the period of disunion in North China. It was this aristocracy that, as the Sui dynasty, reunited China three centuries after the fall of the Han. After unification they began a series of conquests that for the first time made an empire based in China a true power in Central Asia. They remained the ruling class of the following Tang period. During transition from the first to the second Tang rulers in 626 and 627, the imperial lineage was riven by a violent struggle for succession and the determination of the winner—Li Shimin (598–649), after his accession to the throne known as Tang Taizong—to neutralize the threats from his brothers by any means. The result was a more centralized government, using written examinations to select officials for its bureaucracy—a measure intended to curb aristocratic influence in government by widening opportunities beyond their clientele. The Tang empire of the early eighth century competed successfully against the Gokturks for control of southern Mongolia and Central Asia, including what is now the Chinese province of Xinjiang. Tang expansion into Central Asia broke the Gokturk empire into an eastern portion recognizing the Tang emperor as khaghan and a western portion dominated by Sogdian cultural influence. The successes of Li Shimin in conquering not only his domestic rivals but also a string of enemies in Central Asia did not eradicate the lingering effects of steppe political and cultural tradition. Among the general populace, Tang dress—in which men wore trousers and women wore robes, the opposite of the earlier Chinese custom—became normal while Central Asian musical entertainments featuring stringed instruments and whirling dancers were enjoyed. Elite men played a form of polo—not strongly resembling our modern game but certainly featuring teams on horseback and camelback moving an object along a playing field. And Mahayana Buddhism (see Chapter 2) became widespread in China for the first time. At court, the high standing of elite women in comparison to women in earlier China often produced influential female political figures, most notorious of whom was the "woman emperor," Wu Zetian, who seized control after the death of her husband and ruled a court embracing Daoism and sectarian Buddhism—and rejecting Confucianism—from 690 to 705.

During this period a variety of Turkic groups cohered in the interstices between Uighur and Tang, the most important of whom were probably the Shatuo Turks, derived from the remnants of several earlier Turkic federations. Until the later eighth century, they were clients of the Tang empire, but after the peak of Tang power, most Shatuo transferred their allegiance to the Tibetan empire. Through their alliances with Tang and Tibet, the Shatuo retained or refined a degree of hierarchy and formal organization, particularly in the cavalries they provided to their patrons. The result was a continuous Turkic identity among them and a deep familiarity with Tang, Tibetan, and Central Asian military practices. Their influence increased in the last decades of Tang, putting them into position to continue to play an influential role in the two centuries before the rise of the Mongols. In 750, Tang attempted to take advantage of the Umayyad civil war that led to the establishment of the Abbasid caliphate, by pulling away the critical Kashgar region just west of the Tarim Basin. The Tibetan empire joined forces with the Abbasids to keep Tang out of Transoxiana. Tang strategy depended upon the Karluks, an eastern Turkic federation that was subject to the declining Gokturks. Unlike the

Tang, the Karluks had a local base and could not only field soldiers but also supply them. The Tang were hoping that the great numbers of their combined forces would win the day, but the Karluks surprised them by crossing to the Abbasid side. After the loss at the Talas River in 751 (see Map 3.1), about 20,000 Chinese soldiers and engineers were taken prisoner by the Abbasids. Tang expansion into Central Asia came to an end.

Tang and Uighur remained allies for some time. They contracted a number of imperial marriages, and the Tang emperors cordially accommodated Uighur preferences for worship in Manichaean temples during their sojourns at the Tang capital. In 755, a Tang general of probable Sogdian ancestry and another of probable Turkic ancestry rebelled. Their huge armies enjoyed rapid success, approached the primary capital at Chang'an, forced the flight of the Tang emperor, and declared their own dynasty—interestingly, the Yan dynasty, using the regional name for the present location of Beijing, later to be the dynastic capital of northern conquest regimes in China. But by 757, Uighur, Shatuo, and Abbasid troops had joined with Tang forces to crush the rebellion. In the aftermath of the civil war, relations between the Tang and Uighur courts continued to warm, as Uighur supplied Tang horses for its campaigns and facilitated trade between China and the Uighur territories in Mongolia. The alliance culminated in the marriage in 820 of a Tang princess to the Uighur khaghan, who presented 20,000 horses to the Tang to celebrate the engagement.

Thereafter, relations began to sour, apace with growing resentment among Chinese elites against the cosmopolitan culture that the Tang had fostered (see Chapter 4). The Uighurs were one of many targets of elite resentment. Even the Tang court felt that their cordiality toward Uighur had been presumed upon by oversized diplomatic entourages, inflated horse prices, and too many raids for booty and slaves across the Tang borders. The drain of silk, silver, and tea to the Uighur empire worried the court, as did the proliferation of Uighur moneylenders at the major points of trade. In rapid succession, the Tang shut down Uighur financial enterprises, restricted the importation of horses, and dissolved the Buddhist monasteries in 845. The Uighur government was already collapsing, and though there were succeeding Uighur khaghans, the empire never regained its former wealth or power. The same was true for Tang, which entered a period of disintegration through the rise to power of independent military governors—many of Turkic descent—along its northern and western borders. Tang ended formally in 906, and the last Uighur khaghan was deposed in 940. The two empires had constituted a Turkic spectrum of control of central and eastern Eurasia for nearly three centuries.

TURKS RULING THE POPULOUS SOCIETIES OF THE WEST

Middle Easterners and Europeans who encountered Huns, Avars, and Hephthalites were told or assumed that fiercer or better organized groups to the east had driven the invaders west. It is likely that environmental factors were more important, but in any case the evidence suggests that whole groups of Turkic speakers were not always the entities moving. Often, it was their ruling castes—for example, the Ashina with roots in Xiongnu times but later founding the Gokturk empire—who were in some cases not being driven west so much as seeking new political bases for themselves among less organized groups. Such opportunities tended to be found toward the west partly because the steppe lay in that direction, with its high proportion of pastoralists and low population density among the pre-Turkic settlers. The Iranian empire of the Sasanians (see Chapter 4) controlled the old homeland of the Sogdians; though the Hephthalites seized the eastern Sasanian lands, they were denied further conquests, which forced a kind of uneasy cooperation in management of overland trade. The Sasanians themselves—horse-mounted archers who had overthrown the Parthians in the third century—had enough credibility among the incoming Central Asians that they enlisted a good number of them in their cavalry and local government. This contributed to a resurgence of Sasanian power in the fifth century, when they gained control over the Levant and Egypt. Sasanian influence over Central Asia continued to be reflected in architecture, clothing, religious ideas, and literature for centuries. In significant ways the Sasanians shaped the complex of formal language and historical sensibility that distinguished residents of central and southern Iran from the Sogdians to the east as well as the Kurds and Sarmatians to the west: the Sasanian "Persians" associated themselves with the legacy of the ancient Pars province and forged a cultural style that would eventually mark all the great cities of Iran and Central Asia as well as the courts and high cultures of the Seljuk, Ilkhan, Ottoman, Timurid, and Mughal empires.

A more tangled net was encountered when immigrants from Central Asia reached the eastern marches of the Roman empire. The split of the empire into eastern and western parts led to the formation of a stable and coherent Roman military power based in Anatolia, contesting Sasanian control of the eastern Mediterranean. The boundaries were stabilized after Constantine moved his administrative headquarters to Byzantium in the fourth century. The presence of Central Asian mercenaries—including Huns, Alans, and Hephthalites—in wars involving Byzantium and the Sasanians suggests the ongoing search of the newcomers for land and status. By the end of the fifth century, a second front of arriving nomads had opened up in the Caucasus, particularly in Armenia. The most numerous among them were the Iranian-speaking Alans, who first harried the Sasanians and then became mercenary defenders of Sasanian lands against both the Byzantines and the Huns. This helped to inspire a charm offensive by the Byzantine empire, which hoped to lure the Alans to its own side. The importance of the Alans as a buffer with Central Asia is the background to the arrival of Turkic peoples by the late sixth century, when the record identifies not only the Avars and Hephthalites (who had some kind of kinship that is not precisely understood) but also the Onogurs, Oghurs, Sabirs, Bulgars, and the enigmatic Magyars, whose origins may have involved both Ugrian and Turkic sources. The Alans proved to be a diplomatic channel for Byzantine communications with some of the new arrivals and during the same period, fought alternately on the side of the Sasanians and on the side of Byzantium. The model of the Alans—as nomads entering the political and military systems of western Eurasia and then securing territory and a ruling title—is significant even though the Alans themselves had been, by the end of the seventh century, largely displaced as an independent force by the Turks entering the Caucasus and the Balkans.

The Avars became the first khaghans in Europe. In their federation, a Turkic language was originally dominant, but over time, a Slavic language became their standard, suggesting that any Turkic or Iranian descent among the Avars was limited to the ruling stratum. This may have been the source of debates at the time and since over whether the Avars of Europe were in fact the Avars who had been (and many continued to be) subjects of Gokturk. Early Avar successes gave them control of the lower Danube and the Hungarian steppe. Later, they exploited enmities among Gothic groups to move toward the Balkans. Slavs and Franks blocked them on the west, laying the foundation of a western frontier of a Central Asian cultural domain that would remain evident into the early modern period. The Avar khaghanate was an extension of the Turkic tide washing over Eurasia in this period, not an anomaly of steppe politics in the heart of Europe. The Byzantine empire tried for decades to dislodge the Avars. In the early 600s, the Avars, with and without allies, attacked Constantinople, and Byzantium promised enormous payments to Avar to avoid future war. Thereafter, the Avars found that their greatest problem was containing the ambitions of their confederalists—the Onogurs, Bulgars, and some Slavic groups in particular. Small chieftainships split off from the khaghanate, which was finally destroyed in campaigns by the Franks of the very late eighth century, part of Charlemagne's wars to make Europe Latinate Christian. The Slavic majority were distributed through the Byzantine empire, the emerging Slavic kingdoms, the rising Bulgar empire, and the Frankish Roman empire. The fate of the small number of Avar aristocrats is unclear, though they remained a presence in the noble genealogies of Hungary, Moravia, and Bulgaria.

In space and time, the Avars are closely connected to the large and long-lived Khazar empire, which controlled the Caucasus and what is now the

Russian steppe between the early seventh century and the middle eleventh century—almost concurrent with the founding of the Tang dynasty in China but lasting a century and a half longer (see Map 3.1). Unlike the Avars, the Khazars were unambiguously Turks, sharing some origins with the Uighurs as well as with the Onogurs and Bulgars. Their aristocracy could have included many descendants of the Ashina clan, which would have linked them with the Gokturks and, earlier, with the Xiongnu. When the western Gokturks disintegrated and the Uighurs and Sogdians headed east toward Mongolia and China, the Khazars emerged as one of the leading powers of the old western territories of Gokturk. They pushed both the Avars and the Bulgars farther west into Europe and became so critical to stabilization of the eastern boundaries of the Sasanian empire that the Sasanian court recognized Khazar on par with Byzantium and Tang. In the early eighth century, the Khazar aristocracy adopted Judaism as its religion, though there is evidence that many Khazar elites continued traditional Central Asian shamanism while Christianity, and after the early seventh century, Islam were also common. The general population of Khazar was diverse, with clear presence of Slavs and other Europeans, but its overall quotient of Turks and Iranians was high in comparison to Avar. Many of these were mercenaries hired by Khazar to protect itself against Byzantium and to participate in its ongoing wars against the Abbasid caliphate. Khazar was finally crushed by an alliance of Rus (see Chapter 4) and Oguz Turks (see Chapter 5) who seized control of the lower Volga in the early eleventh century.

Eastern European history has the same visibility problems as Central Asian history probably because the former is part of the latter. Not later than the time of Alexander, the Balkans and everything east of it is easily integrated into a Eurasian narrative but is not easily fit into a chronology dominated by England, France, or the Italian peninsula. As in Eastern Eurasia, the Avar-Bulgar-Khazar-Uighur continuum of the seventh and eighth centuries represented a spectrum of Turkic rule over urban and agricultural societies, allowing constant exchange of Central Asian and West Eurasian cultures. It facilitated the spread of Christianity in Central Asia and provided a persisting channel of Manichaean thought in Europe. It brought the khaghanate as a state form to the Balkans, the Hungarian plain, and Kiev. It promoted the hiring and integration of Turkic soldiers fresh from the steppe, initiating a pattern that would change the Middle East in later medieval times. And it gave early definition to a west Eurasian cultural province that would continue to influence Europe through medieval and early modern times. This foundational era in Turkic political history was marked by deepening experience with juggling centralized control over expanding armies with accommodating the status and power demands of aristocratic supporters; by increasingly overt objectification of cultural populations within the empires; by a tendency to insulate the rulership and close associates from excessive manipulation by aristocratic or bureaucratic factions by spreading patronage as widely as possible; and by a gradual state expertise in stabilizing and exploiting trade cities and agricultural zones.

READING NOTES: THE TURKIC TIDE

The following is of particular importance to this chapter: Florin Curta with Roman Kovalev, eds., *The Other Europe in the Middle Ages: Avars, Bulgars, Khazars and Cumans* (Brill, 2008).

Readers wishing for more detail regarding political dynasties or military histories of the states, regimes, or federations invoked can consult any of the exhaustive histories that have been produced over the past century. I can recommend none more highly than Peter Golden's *Central Asia in World History* (Chapter 1 reading notes), which was published just as this book went into final revisions. Its detail is graceful and will be found gratifying by many who feel the thematic and analytical focus in this book is inadequate. For background, see also books from earlier reading notes: Reuven Amitai and Michal Biran, *Mongols, Turks, and Others: Eurasian Nomads and the Sedentary World* (Brill, 2005); Beckwith, *Empires of the Silk Road* (Chapter 1 reading notes), "The Turk Empire," 112–139; David Sneath, *The Headless State: Aristocratic Orders, Kinship Society and Misrepresentations of Nomadic Inner Asia* (Columbia UP, 2007); Peter Golden, *An Introduction to the History of the Turkic Peoples* (Introduction reading notes). A useful companion text is Gerard Clauson, *An Etymological Dictionary of Pre-Thirteenth-Century Turkish* (Oxford UP, 1972). For a recent in-depth overview of scholarship on the relationships of federation names across Eurasia, see Penglin Wang, *The Mysteries of Ethnonyms in Inner Asia* (Lexington Books, 2018).

More will be said later of Turkic military servitude, but on the institutions and values generally, see Tatyana D. Skrynnikova, "Relations of Domination and Submission: Political Practice in the Mongol Empire of Chinggis Khan," in *Imperial Statecraft: Political Forms and Techniques of Governance in Inner Asia, Sixth-Twentieth Centuries*, ed. David Sneath (Western Washington U, 2006).

The most famous argument for the historical relationship between centralization and state formation in Central Asia on the one hand and centralization and expansion of agricultural states on the other is Thomas J. Barfield, *The Perilous Frontier: Nomadic Empires and China 221 BC to AD 1757* (Blackwell's, 1992). In recent work this has been denominated as the "dependency thesis" of Central Asian and Mongolian centralization; see Jean-Luc Houle, "Long-Term Occupation and Seasonal Mobility in Mongolia: A Comparative Analysis of Two Mobile Pastoralist Communities," in *Fitful Histories and Unruly Publics: The Archaeology of Eurasia from Past to Present*, ed. Kathryn Weber et alia (Oxford UP, 2016), which argues that even small-scale communities were stable for endogenous reasons; how such arguments scale up to states and empires will be debated indefinitely.

For discussion of Xiongnu and Sarbi uses of *shanyu/chanyu* for the ruler, see Wang, *Linguistic Mysteries* (*op. cit*); for debates over *khan/khaghan*, see the classic article by Lawrence Krader, "*Qan-Qayan* and the Beginnings of Mongol Kingship," *Central Asiatic Journal* 1 (1955): 17–35. On the early federations, from Xiongnu to Avars, see Nikolay N. Kradin, "From Tribal Confederation to Empire: The Evolution of the Rouran Society," *Acta Orientalia Academiae Scientiarum Hungaricae* 58, no. 2 (2006): 149–169; A. D. H. Bivar, "Hephthalites," *Encyclopedia Iranica* XII, no. 2 (Dec 2003): 198–201; Falko Daim, "Byzantine Belts and Avar Birds: Diplomacy, Trade and Cultural Transfer in the Eighth Century," in *The Transformation of Frontiers: From Late Antiquity to the Carolingians*, ed. Walter Pohl, Ian Wood, and Helmut Reimitz (Brill, 2001), 143–188; Agustí Alemany, "Sixth Century Alania: Between Byzantium, Sasanian Iran and the Turkic World," in *Ērān ud Anērān* (Webfestschrift Marshak, 2003), http://www.transoxiana.org/Eran/Articles/alemany.pdf; B. S. Bachrach, "A Picture of Avar-Frankish Warfare from a Carolingian Psalter of the Early Ninth Century in Light of the Strategicon," *Archivum Eurasiae Medii Aevi* IV (1984): 5–28.

On the etymology of the Eurasian word series for "write"—and whether it has a single origin in proto–Indo-European or an independent origin in the Turkic and Mongolian languages—see Peter Boodberg (drawing on "scattered" comments by Paul Pelliot), "The Language of the T'o-Pa Wei," *Harvard Journal of Asiatic Studies* 1, no. 2 (Jul 1936): 167–185; Gustaf John Ramstedt, *Einführung in de altaische Sprachwissenschaft* II (Suomalais-Ugrilainen Seura, 1952, 236); H[arry] Leeming, "Origins of Slavonic Literacy: The Lexical Evidence," *The Slavonic and East European Review* 49, no. 116 (Jul 1971): 327–338.

For background on Turkic migrations westward in this period, see Edward G. Pulleyblank, "The Chinese Name for the Turks," *Journal of the American Oriental Society* 85 (1965): 121–125 and "The 'High Carts': A Turkish Speaking People before the Türks," *Asia Major* 3: 21–26; Kürşat Yıldırım, "The Twelve Families of the Töles," *Central Asiatic Journal* 60, no. 1/2 (2017) 2: 265–272—like Pulleyblank, *op. cit.*, a study of the Gaoche/Dili/Dingling group; Daniel T. Potts, "From the Islamic Conquest to the Oghuz Infiltration," in *Nomadism in Iran: From Antiquity to the Modern Era* (Oxford UP, 2014); see also Peter Golden, "Oq and Ogur~Oguz," https://vdocuments.site/documents/oq-and-ogur-oguz-peter-b-golden.html; Osman Karatay with Umut Üren, "On the Earliest Mention of the Ethnonym 'oğ uz' in Western Turkestan," *Sixth International Conference on the Medieval History of the Eurasian Steppe* (2016); Colin MacKarras, *The Uighur Empire According to the T'ang Dynastic History: A Study in Sino-Uighur Relations*,

744-840 (U of South Carolina P, 1973); C. A. Macartney, *The Magyars in the Ninth Century* (Cambridge UP, 1969). On the Bulgars, see Panos Sophoulis, *Byzantium and Bulgaria, 775-831* (Brill, 2011); Charles J. Halperin, "Bulgars and Slavs in the First Bulgarian Empire: A Reconsideration of the Historiography," *Archivum Eurasiae Medii Aevi* III (1983): 183–200; James E. Montgomery, "Travelling Autopsies: Ibn Fadlān and the Bulghār," *Middle Eastern Literatures* 7, no. 1 (2004): 3–32. On the boundary struggle between Carolingians and Avars/Bulgars, see Pohl Waefer, Ian Wood, and Helmut Reiwiz, eds., *The Transformation of Frontiers: From Late Antiquity to the Carolingians* (Brill, 2001).

On China between about 300 and 1200, there is voluminous scholarship. Of special interest here, see Scott Pearce, "A Survey of Recent Research in Western Languages on the History of Early Medieval China," *Early Medieval China* 1, (1994): 128–149 and "The Way of the Warrior in Early Medieval China, Examined through the Northern Yuefu," *Early Medieval China*, 2 (2008): 87–113. Arthur Wright's *The Sui Dynasty* (Knopf, 1978) is a narrative of the reunification of China in the sixth century. For Tang, see Edward H. Schafer, *The Golden Peaches of Samarkand: A Study of Tang Exotics* (U California P, 1963); Jack Wei Chen, *The Poetics of Sovereignty: On Emperor Taizong of the Tang Dynasty* (Harvard East Asia, 2010); Mark Edward Lewis, *China's Cosmopolitan Empire: The Tang Dynasty* (Harvard Belknap P, 2009); and Frederick W. Mote, *Imperial China 900-1800* (Harvard UP, 2003).

On China's interconnections with Eurasia in this period, see Jonathan Karam Skaff, *Sui-Tang China and Its Turko-Mongol Neighbors: Culture, Power, and Connections, 580–800* (Oxford UP, 2012); Zhenping Wang, *Tang China in Multi-Polar Asia: A History of Diplomacy and War* (U Hawaii P, 2013); Dorothy C. Wong and Gustav Heidt, eds., *China and Beyond in the Medieval Period: Cultural Crossing and Inter-Regional Connections* (Manohar, 2014); and Patrick Wertmann, Mayke Wagner, and Pavel Tarasov, "Sogdian Careers and Families in Sixth- to Seventh-Century Northern China: A Case Study of the Shi Family Base on Archaeological Finds and Epitaph Inscriptions," *The History of the Family* 22, no. 1 (2017)1: 103–135. On the history of the Kara Kitai, see Michal Biran, *The Qara Khitai Empire in Eurasian History: Between China and the Islamic World* (Cambridge UP, 2005) and Marc Samuel Abramson, *Ethnic Identity in Tang China* (U Pennsylvania P, 2008). On the tensions between Turkic/Sarbi political traditions and Chinese emperorship in the early Tang and its reflections in contemporary historiography, see Isenbike Togan, "Court Historiography in Early Tang China: Assigning a Place to History and Historians at the Palace," in *Royal Courts in Dynastic States and Empire*, ed. Jeroen Duindam, Tülay Artan, and Metin Kunt (Brill, 2011).

For an introduction to medieval Tibet, see Rolf Stein, *Tibetan Civilization* (Stanford UP); Christopher Beckwith's important study, *The Tibetan Empire in Central Asia: A History of the Struggle for Great Power among Tibetans, Turks, Arabs, and Chinese during the early Middle Ages* (Princeton UP, 1987); and Elliott Sperling, "Tibet," in *Demystifying China: New Understandings of Chinese History*, ed. Naomi Standen (Rowman & Littlefield, 2012), 145–152.

Chapter Four

Belief and Blood

After the fall of the Roman, Han, and Mauryan empires, rulers from the steppe controlled larger and more diverse territories than rulers at any of Eurasia's peripheries. The subsequent rise of the great confessional conquest states, working on starkly contrasting principles, challenged these traditions and produced the adaptations that underwrote the remarkable revival of Turkic rule. The large patterns of a confessional age across Eurasia generated the medieval universalisms that by their coherence and then their decay frame the impact of the nomad rulers. After the fifth century and especially after the founding of Islam in the seventh century, the fusing of theology and conquest produced networks of standard written languages, new urban centers, and populations of clergy who could be enlisted as state functionaries, crystallizing formal religion doctrines, stable intellectual centers, and quickened networks of long-distance exchange. By the ninth century, a broad pattern of "two governments" or "two laws"—a consensus by which religious hierarchies legitimated secular rulers and administrators—could be found across the continent. It coexisted with less dyarchic, decentralized social states in which aristocracies controlled most of the power. This institutionalized segmentation created opportunities for a resurgence of steppe conquest, and ultimately steppe political orders, in the tenth and eleventh centuries.

ORIGINS OF THE CONFESSIONAL STATE

When Constantine won a civil war to remain emperor in 324, he took steps to shift the administrative center of the empire from Rome. He chose the Greek-speaking city of Byzantium, on the Bosphorus, as his new base close to his Christian mother's birthplace. Relocating to Byzantium put Constantine well inside the network of Christian churches spread over the empire's eastern reaches of Anatolia and the Levant. The creation of "New Rome"—which would soon be known as Constantinople—coincided with his conversion and efforts to standardize the doctrines of the complex and contentious Christian communities. Yet his policies suggested that his early career in the east—despite his strong and continuing connection with Britain and parts of the western empire—had given him ideas. He recentralized the emperorship and made it hereditary in his own line. He decreed accommodation for not only Christianity but also the old religions, including Roman Mithraism; indeed he pointedly participated in the rituals of these religions as his duties as caesar and pontifex maximus demanded. Consciously or unconsciously, he imitated Buddhist and Hindu traditions that had permeated Central Asia by building huge structures of worship on the sites of Christian miracles, starting with the Church of the Holy Sepulcher in Jerusalem. He granted Christian clerics the privilege of tax exemption, consistent with the Central Asian tradition of *darkhan*.

Constantine was long dead when the eastern Roman empire became a confessional state in 381, under Theodosius. War against the Huns had consolidated the administration at Constantinople and somewhat clarified the identity of the second "Rome." Religions other than Christianity were outlawed, and forms of Christianity not consistent with the prescriptions of the Council of Nicaea were increasingly deemed heretical. The emperor no longer assumed the title of pontifex or acted as head of the priesthood. Church authority was considered to be based in Rome (old Latin Rome), and they created the terms and institutions of the early papacy. But in Rome, disintegration of the empire in the west under pressure from the Ostrogoths created some chaos in church leadership. When in the sixth century Justinian reunited the empire from Constantinople and drove Gothic contenders out of Rome, he confirmed Italy as the center of papal authority, though his appointed popes tended to be from the eastern half of the empire. This unified empire—by which Constantinople ruled Rome and the popes by means of its mission office, the exarchate—survived until the middle eighth century, when Pope Stephen II turned away from Byzantine defense of Rome and instead relied upon the Franks. This began a few decades of development in which papal regimes became political states. The result was the creation of Charlemagne as Roman emperor in 800. It seems reasonable to refer to the Roman empire under Theodosius and the Frankish Roman empire under Charlemagne as confessional states, partly to distinguish them from theocracies.

From Theodosius to Justinian, the emperors at Constantinople gradually distinguished their rulerships from leadership of Christianity. This was partly because Christianity was not a single doctrinal community. Many theological issues, particularly relating to the exact role of divinity in Jesus' identity, had not been resolved. When resolved, as at the ecumenical councils dating from the time of Constantine, the resolutions were often not widely accepted. The Coptic Christians of Egypt had broken away before Justinian's time, and the widening network of Christians across Syria, Iran, and Central Asia were in perpetual tension with Constantinople, where they were regarded as heretics of the monophysite, Arian, or Nestorian varieties. While a central body of settled doctrine was emerging under the encouragement of the emperors at Constantinople, it was creating heterodox margins that were still ungovernable. This regional variation in religious doctrines was recognized as early as the late fourth century, when the patriarchate of Constantinople was put on an equal administrative and ceremonial basis with the papacy in Rome. The later Roman emperors claimed only temporal powers, a break from the Roman practices before Christianity, but it was their imperial mission to advance Christianity and ensure the safety of Christian communities within their borders. Their state was based upon endorsement and guidance of the religious authorities of Christianity for the purpose of advancing the earthly march of the religion. It was a confessional state.

But it was not the first confessional state of Eurasia. From earliest history, kings everywhere kept themselves favored in the eyes of spirits and gods and made themselves indispensable to the priestly class that ensured—or publicly affirmed, at any rate—solidarity between supreme spirits and the earthly ruler. Many of these kings left evidence of their conscientious gratitude to these deities in the aftermath of victories in war, and some claimed to actually be gods by virtue of divine descent or infusion of psyche. A confessional state, by contrast, not only legitimated itself in part through its mission to protect and advance a certain systematic and hierarchical religion, but its ruler was specifically legitimated in advance of and during his rule by approval of religious patriarchs consolidating the mission of the state and will of the divine. The relationship was not between the ruler and his deity but between the ruler and the leaders of a religious establishment. The model is traced to Ashoka, who ruled the Mauryan empire of northern India between 265 and 238 BCE. After a particularly destructive victory over a neighboring state, he converted to Buddhism. Before Ashoka's reign, Buddhist believers were gathered into a hierarchical and universalist community (*sangha*) that convened its own doctrinal councils. Ashoka built and sustained Buddhist monasteries and monuments at the sites connected to the life of the Buddha and granted stipends to luminaries of the Buddhist communities. He did not claim divinity himself or a special connection to Buddha. Instead, the religious establishment recognized him as the *chakravartin*, or "wheel-turning" ruler, who would move time forward by converting humanity to Buddhism. It does not appear that Ashoka considered this role to have made him an instrument of either Buddha or the religious leadership; it was an attribute of his rulership. The idea had roots in the older religion of Hinduism, which had prescribed specific temporal roles for kings. But under Ashoka emerged a systematic relationship of ruler to religious hierarchy in an empire of conquest. The Mauryan empire collapsed half a century after Ashoka's death, and his model of secular rule assisted by the endorsement of religious hierarchs disappeared from local view.

After the eighth century, Constantinople was at the center of a loose network of cultural, religious, and commercial connections encompassing the Balkans, the eastern Mediterranean and Greece, the Black Sea, Ukraine, and the western end of the overland transport network of Eurasia. For a time, the church and the empire retained Latin as an administrative language but eventually began to conduct governance in the local standard, Greek. The papacy became less relevant as the popes turned to the Franks for protection, though the "Roman" branch of the Catholic Church would not formally split from Constantinople until the eleventh century. For their part, the emperors at Constantinople were less concerned with the strategic changes of western and northern Europe and more concerned, as they had been since the time of the Avar khaghanate, with matters of the Balkans, the Danube basin, the Black Sea, and their longtime foes the Sasanians. And in the early seventh century, a new, vigorous confessional state with a great deal in common with the Byzantine empire became the greatest challenge of all.

CONFESSIONALISM AND CONQUEST IN WESTERN EURASIA

Before his death in 632, Muhammad ibn Abdulla of Mecca, near the Arabian coast of the Red Sea, had already amassed an army to seize major cities along the coast, protect his followers from assault by Arab tribal and town leaders, and wrest settlements away from the Byzantine empire. At his death, he had no successor as prophet. Instead, a caliph (*khalifa*) would act as patriarch of the community of believers. Disputes among the community over who should have been designated as caliph set up the rivalries that would later lead to the factional division of Islam between a Sunni majority—believing that Muhammad's father-in-law Abu Bakr had been properly chosen—and a Shi'i minority—supporting the rejected candidate, Muhammad's cousin Ali. Passing of the caliphate among a series of early contenders led, after disorder and bloodshed, to permanent alienation of the kin and supporters of Ali, the emergence and expulsion of smaller factions, and crystallization of power around the relatives of Abu Bakr's successors. During the rule of successive caliphs, an early conquest state was formed. In 661, its leadership was claimed by the Umayyad lineage of Mecca. To that time, fighting among the factions for control had occurred along the northern rim of the Arab world, close to Byzantine territories in Syria (see Map 4.1). The Umayyads established a capital at Damascus, virtually on the border with both Byzantium and the Sasanians. The long-term war between Byzantium and the Sasanians had weakened both sides. The Umayyads quickly destroyed the Sasanians, subsuming all of Iran and a good chunk of Central Asia. From the Byzantine empire, they seized the Levant, Iraq, and the eastern edge of Anatolia. In subsequent phases of conquest, their armies swept through North Africa, destroying the remnant Roman administration, then northward across Calpe—which they renamed Mountain of Tariq (Jabal al-Tariq, or Gibraltar) in honor of their commander—and into Spain and Portugal, which they took after destroying the Visigothic kingdom in the early eighth century.

Muhammad himself had used the title 'amir—emir—to describe his roles as administrator of the community and leader of the troops. The Umayyads gave this title to various of their field commanders who then undertook to administer and defend the territories as military governors. Because of the distance from Damascus (since they were posted from Spain to North Africa to Afghanistan), the emirs were independent in most military matters. Nevertheless, by law, the Umayyad caliphate was unitary, and the caliph retained temporal authority in civil and military matters. Despite this, the caliphate became Eurasia's most typical confessional state. In 750 the Umayyads were overthrown by the Abbasids—relatives of Muhammad who had once been Umayyad officials based in Iran. The center of the movement to displace the Umayyads had been in eastern Iran and Transoxiana, particularly the cities of Marv, Nishapur, and Herat. The Abbasids moved their capital from Damascus eastward to Baghdad, which was essentially a newly created city. Very soon, the Abbasids completed their control of Transoxiana, the Arabian peninsula, Egypt, Libya, and Tunisia. Umayyad successors, protected by emirs, remained in what is now Morocco, with a base at Fez, and in Spain (Andalusia), with their capital at Cordoba.

Abbasid administration was culturally and ideologically plural, as the caliphs struggled to maintain the coalition that had established the regime. Like the Umayyads before them, they made the accommodations with Christianity and Judaism that were mandated by the teachings of Muhammad as preserved in the Quran. Christians and Jews were occasionally high officials in the Umayyad territories of Syria, North Africa, and Iberia. After a period of ambiguity, the caliphate declared itself Sunni, or orthodox, in recognition of the original line of caliphs—an apparent contradiction of a major Shi'ite theme in their civil war against the Umayyads. For the first two centuries of Abbasid history, the court worked to balance patronage and cooperation with the religious hierarchy to accommodate not only Sunni but also Shi'i and other minority adherents. Abbasid conquests were accompanied by the demand that the conquered either convert or pay the tax required by Christians and Jews as "peoples of the book." In the Abbasid lands, traditional Arab polytheism virtually disappeared, traditional Persian Manichaeanism as a whole religious system was combatted with caliphal sponsorship and may have been defeated as an overt affiliation by the end of the tenth century, while Sunni influence gradually overshadowed Shi'i in both politics and court patronage of religious communities. To the extent that patronage of academies was effective in the mitigation of tensions, the precarious position of the Abbasid caliphate in relation to both Sunni and Shi'i elites promoted the development of scientific and technological knowledge for which the Abbasid period is famous (see also Chapter 9).

In both the Byzantine Empire and the Abbasid caliphate, historians have noted a tendency to rely upon the elites of the established religion for legitimacy yet to distance the ruler from the religious hierarchs—in space, in function, and in ceremony. This could be related to the doctrinal complexities that were afflicting both Christianity and Islam. In the case of Christianity, the growing estrangement between the Roman papacy and Orthodox Christianity was both theological and cultural. Reforms of the seventh century mandated by a sequence of Byzantine emperors of Armenian origin made Greek both the administrative language of the empire and the liturgical language of the church. Roman clergy not only adhered to Latin but appear to have neglected their skills in Greek, making communications with the patriarchate in Constantinople cumbersome. This speciation of the medieval church into Latin and Greek language venues had profound implications for Central Asia. The establishment of orthodoxy at the ecumenical councils of the fourth and fifth centuries had resulted in condemnation of the Syrian priest Nestorius (386–451) and his followers as heretics. Nestorius's approach to the tangled and increasingly risky question of exactly how and in what degree Christ was divine was to insist that the divine and the human in Christ were not comingled, indistillable, or preexisting; rather, they were distinguishable primarily through the role of Mary as mother of Jesus but not as Mother of God. In Central Asia, where the traditional cosmology of a world clearly divided between light and dark—which could not be comingled—was still ubiquitous, Nestorianism found a natural home. The Nestorian communities became the basis of what was, by the eighth century, a distinct church. It was modeled on the patriarchate in Constantinople, and it considered Greek-speaking Constantinople the worldwide center of Christianity. In Constantinople, the imperial court was aware that Central Asian Christians, over many of whom hovered some degree of heretical odor, looked to Constantinople for contact, affirmation, trade, and sometimes protection. Central Asians, the Balkan Slavs, and in later centuries the Kievan Rus, were all seen as part of a greater Christendom that acknowledged the centrality of Constantinople. But for the empire and the imperial court to remain central, it had to embrace the Christian mission without becoming captive of any particular Christian sect.

The Abbasids were struggling with the same balance of influence and patronage. Their subjects included the range of Iranian (including Persian) and Turkic-speaking peoples of Transoxiana; the Greek speakers of Central Asia, the Levant, and Egypt; the Arabs, the Copts, and the Berbers of North Africa; and smaller communities at the western end of the trade roads. Cultural and religious were intertwined. At least partly in recognition of the importance of the Iranian population in the caliphate, the Abbasids made increasing use of government organization, architecture, and personal goods (including clothing) in the Persian style of the Sasanians before them. This included the use of Persian court etiquette that objectified the caliph as an emperor—use of the prostration, use of architecture to create sacred precincts through which visitors passed before encountering the caliph himself, and use of a dais and throne. But the legacy of the Seleucids and Sasanians encompassed a Greek influence as well since Greek ideas, language, and sciences permeated the region of Central Asia from which early Abbasid support had come.

In both the Byzantine and Abbasid cases, the role of the religious mission as a legitimating principle was indispensable. Constantinople could afford to accommodate Roman doctrine and the Latin language, and it could afford to bring Jews, Muslims, Huns, Turks (including Kipchaks and the closely related Pechenegs), and Magyars into its armies; it could not afford to do without its confessional dedication to Christianity. In the same way, the Abbasid caliphate in Baghdad could afford to patronize Shi'i schools and charitable foundations or Christian and Jewish communities that provided needed expertise in science and finance; it could welcome Turks and Iranians of various cultures into its armies, but it could not afford to understate its dedication to Sunni orthodoxy or the mission of spreading Islam. The challenge for each of these empires was to use religion as a unifying force but avoid capture of the rulership by one or another doctrinal or cultural faction that could splinter the delicate imperial alliance.

The Abbasids proved more adept than contemporary European regimes at acquiring and extending ancient Greek science and philosophy. Refugees or apostates from Sasanian Iran could use Middle Persian (Pahlavi) to translate medical and mathematic treatises from Transoxiana and India. After the defeat of Tang forces at the Battle of Talas in 751, captive Chinese technicians and a developing alliance between Abbasid and Tang brought Chinese technologies of papermaking, ceramics, woodblock printing, silk production, and medicines to Abbasid lands. Christians in the caliphate—whether orthodox or Nestorian—who were good at Greek were often promoted to high academic rank because they could translate Greek classics into Arabic (see also Chapter 9). The need to keep the caliphate in good graces with not only competing Islamic sects but also merchants and ambassadors of many cultural backgrounds made the Abbasid caliphs receptive to international styles and knowledge. Abbasid technology became the most formidable in the world. Abbasid wealth and prestige were so widely known that in the eighth century several kings of Britain—at the farthest edge of the continent the Abbasids dominated—tried to duplicate their imprints, including their idea of Arabic script, on their gold coins.

The continental sway of the Abbasid realm can be summarized in proportions (see Map 4.1). At its height under caliph Harun al-Rashid (786–809), the empire was the largest in Eurasia, at about four million square miles (a little over 10 million square kilometers). Its capital at Baghdad was the largest and most populous city in the world. The Byzantine Empire—for many years the main Abbasid strategic opponent—was about an eighth the size and had about the same proportion of population. The territory of the Tang empire in China (in many ways the Abbasid alter ego in East Asia) was a little over half the Abbasid size, though its population was much greater—perhaps by as much as 30 percent. As for Charlemagne's empire, at its greatest extent, it did not exceed about 400,000 square miles (1 million square kilometers) and could not have reached a population of five million; it might have been about two-thirds the size of the Byzantine Empire in territory and population but was about a tenth the size of the Abbasid empire in both.

By the early years of the ninth century, the size, wealth, and military competence of the caliphate made clear to all possible challengers in Eurasia the need to keep friendly with it. After their confrontation at Talas (see Chapter 3), Abbasid and Tang became fast allies. Abbasid ambassadors visited the Tang court, and when a massive rebellion resulted in the sacking and occupation of major Tang cities in 755, Abbasid sent 4,000 troops to help defeat the rebels. In the reign of Harun al-Rashid, the Tang came to his support in a war with the Tibetan empire over control of what is now part of Afghanistan. The rising Uighur empire joined the Tang–Abbasid coalition against Tibet, and Tibetan expansion into Central Asia was thereafter contained. Abbasid, by using Tang and Tibet against each other at sequential moments, had taken the pressure off its eastern front. The caliphate also had new admirers from its west. Like the Tibetans, the Franks under Pepin the Short (714–768) saw an opportunity to forge a possible alliance with the new Abbasid caliphate—in their case, for purposes of destroying the Umayyad emirate at Cordoba. There was a friendly exchange of embassies, and the evidence is that there was vigorous trade from Frankish lands to the Abbasid—probably of raw materials, such as timber, wool, flax, and people to serve as slaves. A few decades later, soon after Charlemagne became the Frankish king, a few minor Muslim potentates in Spain encouraged him to initiate a reconquest of the Iberian Peninsula.

Though Charlemagne made excellent ideological use of his military clashes with Iberian Muslims, his battles overall were hardly directed against any Muslim regimes. Charlemagne's own confessional mission was the establishment of a Latinate Christian empire in central Europe, and an important strategy was the aggravation of small doctrinal differences within the Christian church into large ones. In the late 790s, he lobbied at Rome for sharper doctrinal opposition to Greek clerics, especially on the issue of whether the Latin liturgy should include language suggesting that Christ was a source of the Holy Spirit. In the meantime, he used his armies to force pagans to convert to Latin Christianity. At Roncesvalles in 778, he was fighting the Basques. He spent most of his military energies before 800 fighting eastern European pagans, many of them Turks. With his allies, he destroyed the Avar khaghanate in 804 and coerced the conversion of the population, drawing them from under the domination of the Bulgars.

An alliance with the Abbasids seems for a time to have been an important part of Charlemagne's strategy. The Abbasids were enemies of the Byzantines, as was Charlemagne, and the Abbasids were in occasional tension with the Umayyads of North Africa and Spain, as was Charlemagne. During the late eighth century, he was communicating fairly frequently (in eighth-century terms) with Harun Al-Rashid in Baghdad, and in 801 agents of both Charlemagne and Harun collaborated to get the elephant Abul Abbas to Aachen, with the Franks possibly under the impression that an elephant was of great military value. To their credit, the Franks managed to keep Abul Abbas alive for a decade. When Charlemagne had declared himself Roman emperor in 800 with the endorsement of Pope Leo III, the court at Constantinople brushed it off. Charlemagne declared war against the Byzantines, and his son Pepin led a naval campaign that captured the eastern Adriatic coast. From Baghdad, Harun al-Rashid urged Byzantine emperor Constantine VI to either submit to Charlemagne and convert to Roman Christianity or submit to Abbasid and pay the Muslim tax on Christians. Despite repeated exchange of ambassadors and the likely discussion of specifics of the plans, no military business between Charlemagne and Harun al-Rashid actually resulted, and Constantine VI was deposed and blinded by his mother in 797. In 813, a Byzantine embassy at Aachen greeted Charlemagne as an emperor (*basileus*), a decision probably facilitated by the fact that they could not make Harun al-Rashid an ally against the empire of the Franks.

Events among the Frankish, Byzantine, and Abbasid empires were bounded not only by the ambitions of these three courts but also by the dynamics of smaller states at their peripheries—most important the Khazars, Bulgars, and Rus. Even after Charlemagne's destruction of the Avar khaghanate in the early ninth century, eastern Europe remained under the control of Turkic and Finno-Ugric–speaking regimes. The Khazars still controlled the entire north coast of the Black Sea. The Bulgar khanate—soon to be the empire of the Bulgars, ruled by a caesar—was extending southward to control all the Balkans. The Bulgar ruling class had Turkic origins, but their population and some elites were Slavs. Their khan first wrung recognition from Constantinople in the middle seventh century and then nibbled away at

Byzantine territory in the Balkans until the eleventh century. They became Christians in the late seventh century, oriented toward the Patriarch of Constantinople, and thereafter were allies of Byzantium in the repeated wars against the Abbasids, when they were not fighting the empire itself for Balkan territory. The Bulgars contained the influx of Turkic Pechenegs and Ugric Magyars to the old Avar territories, but on their eastern march they faced a growing menace from the federation of the Kievan Rus, who since the ninth century had developed close political and cultural ties with Constantinople. Collapse of the Bulgar empire in the early eleventh century, primarily due to pressure from Rus, led to the absorption of their territories by Byzantium, which became a Balkan power again. The Frankish Roman empire may have taken the sudden enlargement of Byzantine territory as cause for alarm. In 1054, the pope excommunicated the Patriarch of Constantinople and his priests. From that point, neither the papacy nor the patriarchate recognized the authority of the other.

The schism between Rome and Constantinople was one of many eleventh-century developments suggesting that after centuries of expanding conquest supported by missionizing ideologies, processes of alienation and realignment were now limiting the size of confessional empires and opening wide spaces into which mobile, flexible mercenaries could create unusual new patterns of power. The distillation of the Frankish Roman empire into separate and competing regimes was a factor, but also important was the development of regional economies of war that made empires hungry for mercenaries to staff armies in response to rising defensive needs. The greater the fragmentation, the greater the need for mercenaries, and the greater the need for mercenaries, the greater the fragmentation. In Europe, the Normans had been confined to northwestern France since the tenth century. But in the eleventh century, they found a niche as mercenary bands fighting for the Latin Roman empire against the emirates of Iberia, and fighting for the Byzantines against the Abbasids and the small Turkic regimes growing up on the frontier between the empire and the caliphate. It was a prelude to the establishment of loosely related Norman regimes in France, England, Ireland, Scotland, Italy, Sicily, and North Africa.

The Normans were not unique; they were in some ways paralleled by the Varangians and Rus in the Byzantine world. According to their own history, the Rus were originally from Scandinavia, but migrated to the region of modern Ukraine and became rulers of Kiev and other cities, which they eventually confederated. If the self-account of the origins of the Rus is basically correct, then they share a general origin with the Normans and the Varangians who came from Scandinavia to be Byzantine mercenaries or to prey upon small farming and fishing communities by demanding tribute in return for protection. The riverine connections between Scandinavia and trading centers in Armenia and Syria are well-known from accounts of the

Abbasid lawyer and theologian Ibn Fadlan as well as from archaeology. Whatever the origins of the Rus, the Kievan federation was not a Scandinavian society. The area had already been well settled by Slavs and possibly some Magyar and Turkic Khazar groups before the arrival of the Rus. Like the Normans, and like their earlier Turkic counterparts in Eurasia, the Rus became a ruling class over the locals of Kiev, Suszdal, and later, Novgorod as well as smaller settlements. Rus aristocrats distributed the towns and surrounding countryside among themselves. In political organization, their federation more resembled their Central Asian than their eastern European neighbors: they had no monarch but only a grand prince—literally "great king" (*velikhii knyaz*) or king of kings—and the princes ("kings") collegially chose the grand prince as well as validating his policies.

Rus' supply of raw agricultural products as well as furs and slaves to the Black Sea trading system, which connected to the Silk Roads, made the princes rich. Their territories stretched north and south, virtually from the Baltic to the Black Sea. They fought the Khazars and the Byzantines for control of trade routes, but as the Khazar khaghanate unraveled in the eleventh century, the Rus came into conflict with the rising Pecheneg and Volga Bulgars. Differences with Byzantium were reconciled more or less. Despite a century and a half of sporadic warfare between the Byzantine empire and the Rus, Kiev had converted to Christianity and sought frequent instruction from the priests of the patriarchate in Constantinople. Slavic-speaking missionaries, some of whom were veterans of preaching among the Bulgars, were sent to Rus. In the crises of the eleventh century, the Kievan federation of Rus was not one of those states—such as Byzantium or Abbasid or the Bulgar empire—experiencing rising challenges from mobile forces (whether originating in Scandinavia or Central Asia). Its greatest threat, Khazar, collapsed in the middle eleventh century, and Rus proved to be one of the opportunistic states that expanded in this period. Its economy continued to grow, and its populations were enlarged by Khazar refugees while its decentralized political system remained stable for almost two centuries more.

EASTERN EURASIA IN THE CONFESSIONAL AGE

Though it would be difficult to argue that medieval China, Korea, and Japan were the bases of confessional empires, they showed clear traits of Eurasia's confessional age. In the eighth century, neither Korea nor Japan was an empire of conquest (excluding local consolidation), and so the criteria discussed above for the role of confessionalism would not suggest that they would show the deep marks of government dichotomized between the secular and the sacred, militarized aristocracy, and the establishment of language

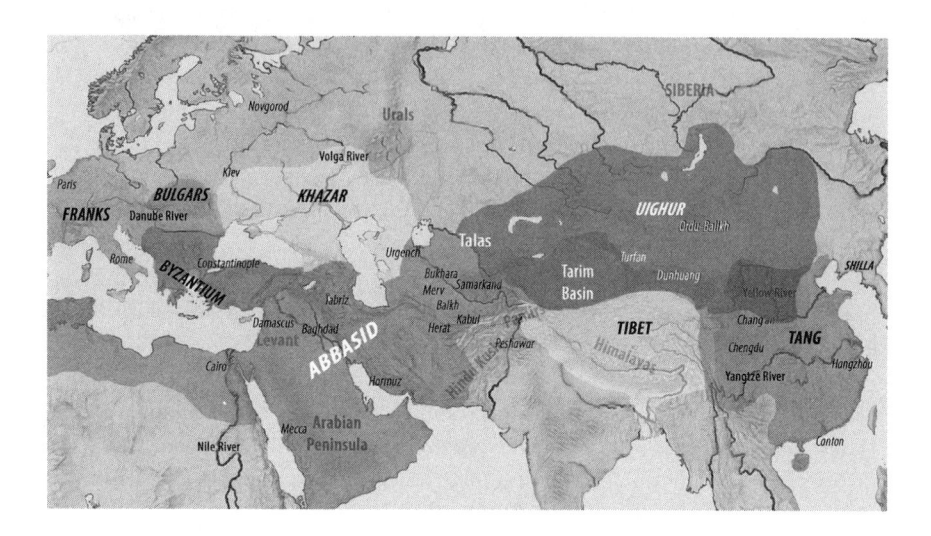

Map 4.1. Major political orders of the Abbasid–Tang era, c. 790 CE. *Note*: Contested areas are shaded.

use as a characteristic of confessional identity. It is possible that Buddhism was introduced into Japan by Gandharan or Sogdian monks in the fifth century, but much better attested are the many expeditions of monks and royal embassies to Japan from states of the Korean peninsula in the sixth century and later. Buddhism remained an integral part of royal ideology and ritual in medieval Korea, which was outstanding for Buddhist architecture and the printing of important Buddhist texts. Japan merged its identity as a state with Buddhism—represented by the installations, from the early seventh century, of a series of enormous statues of the Buddha and ceremonies connecting the statues to the political ambitions of regional dynasties. The legendary lawgiver of early Japan, Shotoku (574–622), was a patron of Buddhism and alloyed several Buddhist themes with the state ideology of his time. In the Heian period, beginning in the eighth century, indigenous Japanese folk religion—much later codified as Shinto—drove Buddhism out of the religious rituals of the imperial precincts, but Buddhism continued as a popular religion.

But for eastern Eurasia's most prominent conquest states of this era, traits cognate to state confessionalism took several forms. Tibet, Tang China—joined later by the state of Xixia—were vigorous conquest states of the eighth century, and all were in close contact with overtly confessional states to their west, foremost among them the Abbasid caliphate. In the early 600s, the kings of Tibet legitimated their rulership through partnership with Buddhist clergy. Because of Tibet's proximity to India and its suzerainty over

Nepal in the late seventh century, India was the primary source of Tibet's scholiasts and hierarchs. As Tibetan military power expanded in the seventh and eighth centuries, Tibetan authority reached into Central Asia and what is now southwestern China. Tibet's meddling in the troubles in Transoxiana in the early 700s was part of the background to the showdown at Talas, and a bit later Tibetan troops exploited the troubles in China to briefly occupy the Tang capital at Chang'an. By 779, Buddhism was the official state religion of Tibet, and the lamas ("teachers") became an essential element in investiture and public presentation of the monarch. A reaction by aristocrats championing local shamanism was thwarted in 842 when the king was assassinated and a new king—a supporter of the lamas—was installed. The court poured money into new monasteries and new study centers that attracted young monks from all over South Asia and the Himalayan zone. In the ensuing century, as Tibetan military power decayed, the hold of the religious hierarchy over the Tibetan kingship deepened. Kings aspired to the status not only of chakravartin but also of bodhisattva and depended upon the public acknowledgment of such status by the monks. For their part, the monks depended on the kings and aristocracy for land and money grants as well as political privileges and physical protection.

Particularly in the early years after its establishment in 618, Tang combined vigorous overland expansion with overt religious legitimation. The emperor had been a patron of Mahayana Buddhist clergy, who acknowledged him as an Ashoka-style conqueror (*chakravartin*) bringing enlightenment to humanity. Buddhist institutions were a prominent part of imperial life and of the urban populations in early Tang, and the prestige of Buddhism matched well the eminence of Tang as a commanding military and economic presence in eastern Eurasia. But the loss at Talas in 751 and a devastating civil war of 755–757 shattered the empire's reputation. The price of restoring peace was the establishment of independent military governors, many of them of Turkic background, whose power grew steadily to the end of the Tang period. These governors virtually assumed control of the country at the time of a large rebellion in 880.

The disasters of the ninth century contributed to a major cultural reorientation at the Tang court. As early as the late eighth century, some sectors among the Chinese scholar class were complaining of the effects of "foreign" religions in China. Buddhism, Manichaeanism, and Nestorian Christianity were all regarded to some degree as responsible for weakening of traditions of family governance, of exclusion of women from public discourse and property ownership, and of the loyalty of the imperial armies to the emperor. Islam was becoming known in China by the middle seventh century, brought by both the overland trade and the sea trade between the Indian Ocean and the south China coast. Like Christianity, it was associated with the arrival of merchants and soldiers from afar, invited or protected by Tang military organizations, and seeking to exploit China for wealth and status. But the religion with which the mid-Tang scholars were most impatient was Buddhism. The early and middle Tang periods had seen the rise of huge monastic institutions that recruited many hundreds of thousands of men and women, sometimes from high-ranking families. They not only siphoned off the wealth of their lineages through donations to the monasteries but when they joined the monasteries broke the procreative chain that would have allowed the wealth to be passed to future family members. In addition, the monasteries were tax exempt, depriving the recently impoverished state of needed revenue. Many had a history of involvement in the worst factional struggles of early Tang history, as princes competed to win the spiritual support of one sect or another. Buddhism was also blamed for elevating the status of women; it had been invoked by the woman emperor Wu Zetian (r. 680–705; see Chapter 3) as one of her legitimating ideologies during her period of rule, and the poet Bo Juyi (772–846) lamented that things had become so bad by the middle eighth century that families were celebrating the births of girls.

After the rebellion of 755, suspicion of Turks and Sogdians, worries over the Tang alliance with the rising Uighur empire, and exasperation over Buddhism's pervasive social and cultural influence moved Chinese literati to demand that the imperial court suppress the religion. In 845, the empire dissolved the monasteries, seized their gold and iron statuary, and sold the land. Cooks, gardeners, and launderers flooded the countryside seeking jobs; monks and nuns became ubiquitous as mendicants. All foreign religions were banned in the empire, and Daoism was driven underground. With imperial encouragement, champions of Confucian philosophy went to ideological war against not only Buddhism but also Daoism and the shoots of Islam. Leaders among the critics specifically proposed that the classical philosopher Mencius should be institutionalized as the source of political legitimacy and social values. The elite passion for Mencian hierarchies of men over women, civil over military, landowners over the poor, literate over the illiterate, aged over youth, and civilization (meaning the totality of these same hierarchies) over chaos (meaning folk cultures or nonagricultural economies) burned more brightly as the realities it prescribed became more unattainable.

After the middle ninth century, the Tang armies were increasingly in the hands of the governors of border provinces, many of them Turks, Sogdians, or Tibetans and all of them soldiers. Some of them were already in practice rulers of their own local dynasties by the late ninth century. It was only a matter of time before one of them would decide to overthrow the powerless Tang emperors at Luoyang. That happened in 906, when a former rebel turned powerful military governor concluded his years of terrorizing the Tang imperial family by deposing them. In the aftermath of the Tang, new states emerged and competed to inherit the legacy of the dissolved empire. The Shatuo Turks seized virtually all of north China and ruled it briefly.

Their northern territories were subverted and absorbed in stages by their former allies, the Kitans, who established their rule immediately after the overthrow of the last Tang emperor in 906.

For decades, historians described the Kitans as nomads speaking a language that shared a genetic relationship with Mongolian and inferred from this that the Kitans were close cousins of the Mongols. While this is possible, it is also possible that they—or at least the aristocrats among them—were descended from the elites of the Tagbach of the Northern Wei empire. Certainly, in the course of their empire the Kitan aristocracy was fortified by newcomers of Turkic and Chinese ancestry. At various points in their political history, they referred to their empire by the Chinese title of Liao (which refers to the qualities of iron). At about the time that the Kitans were establishing themselves in Mongolia, a combination of Shatuo Turks and Tibetan-related Minyak (Tanggut) people established a large empire (Tanggut, Xixia, or "Western" Xia) in what now encompasses parts of Gansu, Ningxia, and Qinghai provinces of China. It is possible that, as in the case of the Kitan empire, their ruling caste was descended in part from the Tagbach, which would have connected them to the rulers of Kitan and, earlier, Northern Wei and Tang. Kitan now had a new rival for control of north China, and in 980, a third emerged. An empire founded by a Chinese general who adopted the dynastic name Song had reunited most of the Tang territory in China, with the exception of the extreme north. Song entered into sporadic warfare with Kitan, attempting unsuccessfully to move as far north as the Great Wall, and in 1005 signed a treaty of peace (a costly one, for Song). In 1038, Song arrived at a truce with Xixia (see Map 5.1). The Kitan empire was destroyed by the Jurchens in 1115, and years of bitter warfare between the Jurchen empire of Jin and the Song followed, until Xixia, Jin, and Song were all destroyed by the invading Mongols in the thirteenth century (see Chapter 6).

Philosophical confessionalism in the late Tang style was characteristic of the empires in this set and corresponds in a general way to their propensity for conquest. In the case of Kitan, it was weak. The relatively powerless ruling family were personal patrons of Buddhist institutions but did not rely upon it greatly to legitimate their regime. Kitan's history of warfare against Song and the Korean empire of Goryeo gives it the aura of a conquest state, but our more recent knowledge of Kitan from archaeology suggests a regime far more interested in commerce and in supporting its expansive and powerful aristocracy than in conquest and occupation of neighbors. Their trade and diplomatic contacts with the Abbasid territories in eastern Iran and Afghanistan were frequent. They also traded with Tibet, China, Korea, and Japan as well as traditional and still stateless peoples of Manchuria and Siberia. They constructed a peculiar bifurcated government system that superficially echoed the old Northern Wei pattern of retaining and honoring the political traditions of both Manchuria/Mongolia and China. But in fact they merely distinguished between those areas of the empire to be indirectly administered through the aristocratic estate (*ordo*) system favored by the more nomadic among them and the areas to be directly controlled by the court through a Chinese-style civil bureaucracy.

The Kitan empire had a fascinating postscript. After they lost their primary capital in Mongolia in 1121, the imperial family went westward into Central Asia. There, they established a new empire, Kara Kitai. By the early 1140s, they had seized the capital of the local Turkic khanate, the Karakhans. The Kara Kitai polity amalgamated elite Confucian bureaucratic philosophy with a culture that was part Buddhist and part Islamic, with traces of Christianity and Manichaeanism. Among its anomalistic features was the fact that several of the Kara Kitai rulers were women. Religious alienation of the state from the majority of society was a vivid divergence from the confessionalist age of Eurasia, and it may have sparked the legends in Europe of "Prester John," a mysterious Asiatic Christian king whom Europeans hoped would fulfill their dreams for Central Asian Christianity and help them conquer religious sites in the Levant. It certainly laid the foundation for state building by the Mongols in particular, who in the early years of the thirteenth century would start their tenuous career of conquest and occupation on the ground where the Kara Kitai had preceded them.

In the case of Xixia, confessionalist qualities were much more obvious, a possible influence of Tibet. Buddhism was the state religion, and the court continuously invoked the mission of universal salvation in its legitimating iconography and edicts. Continuing what might have been a Northern Wei tradition, they represented their ruler as not only a bodhisattva but also as the Buddha himself, or his futurist avatar. The Xixia state was almost uniquely assertive in East Asia regarding religion. Texts and interpretation of Buddhism were under close state regulation and scrutiny, and inquisitions sought to root out shamanic practices, particularly among the ruling caste. On the other hand, the culture generally was cosmopolitan, showing strong evidence of Tibetan, Kitan, Chinese, and Turkic influences in language and dress and some traces of Islamic influence in culture. Xixia was most saliently a prodigious military power, which prevented encroachment by Kitan or Song and reaped hefty profits from its control of part of the overland road system.

In this age of confessional states, the relationships between religion and state expansion were direct. Eurasia was riven with imperial ideologies espousing "true" faiths—whether the Catholic doctrines of Christianity championed by the Franks, or the Orthodox Christianity of the Byzantines, or Sunni Islam of the Abbasids, or Judaism of the Khazars, or the Buddhisms of Tibet or Xixia, or the increasingly spiritual Confucianisms of late Tang and Song China. These faiths generated moral authorities in priests, teachers, and scholars who advised and legitimated the rulers, justified war and conquest, codified the marginalization of elites and commoners who remained loyal to traditional religions, and powered the development of long-distance communications in canonical languages that became transnational. Equally important, some states that in earlier times were limited in their administrative capacities could enlist clergy as administrators, rapidly thickening the presence of the state and improving its abilities of surveillance and military conscription. The age of the confessional empires spread the tools of literacy and a degree of popular education across Eurasia, making contracts, census taking, and tax collection—all the basis of the great empires of conquest—widely familiar. While in their periods of being strongly centralized the great empires of Byzantium and Abbasid offered to small and uncoordinated groups of mercenaries opportunities for employment and technology transfer, the decentralization of these empires in later times allowed the coalescence of these military populations into new forces of conquest and governance. At the same time, long-distance routes of commerce and proselytizing created large centers of wealth, some of them poorly governed or defended, which eventually excited the ambitions of nomadic federation leaders in need of resources to distribute.

READING NOTES: BELIEF AND BLOOD

A good deal of the background to this chapter is also given in the general sources suggested for Chapter 2, though the following should be added: Julia Ching, *Chinese Religions* (Macmillan, 1993); Jacques Gernet, *Buddhism in Chinese Society: An Economic History from the Fifth to the Tenth Centuries* (Columbia UP, 1995); Mark Edward Lewis, *China Between Empires: The Northern and Southern Dynasties* (Harvard UP, 2009); and Johan Elverskog, *Buddhism and Islam on the Silk Road* (U Pennsylvania P, 2011). For early Iran, see Gene R. Garthwaite, *The Persians* (Blackwell, 2005), 22–117. Early Byzantium is literally the hinge upon which much of the confessional age turns. See Cyril Mango, *Byzantium: The Empire of the New Rome* (Weidenfield and Nicholson, 1980) and Judith Herren, *Byzantium: The Surprising Life of a Medieval Empire* (Princeton UP, 2009). For those looking for more detail on the slow Byzantine divorce from Rome, Stephen Mitchell, *A History of the Later Roman Empire, AD 284-641: The Transformation of the Ancient World* (Wiley-Blackwell, 2006) is a sort of update of the great classic by J. B. Bury, *A History of the Later Roman Empire from the Death of Theodosius to the Death of Justinian* (1958), now available as a full download from several locations on the internet.

I would also underscore the importance of the following, which relate to the dynamics of changing religious affiliations and sharpening religious identities before about 1000 CE: H. A. Drake, Mu-chou Poo, and Lisa Raphals, eds., *Old Society, New Belief: Religious Transformation of China and Rome, ca. 1st-6th Centuries* (Oxford UP, 2017); Xinru Liu, *Silk and Religion: An Exploration of Material Life and the Thought of People, AD 600-1200* (Oxford UP, 1996); Richard Miles, *Constructing Identities in Late Antiquity* (Routledge, 1999); Isabella Sandwell, *Religious Identity in Late Antiquity: Greeks, Jews and Christians in Antioch* (Cambridge UP, 2007); Michal Biran, "The Liao and the Muslim World: Migrations, Diplomacy, Commerce, and Mutual Perceptions," *Journal of Song-Yuan Studies* 43 (2013): 221–251; Hyunhee Park, *Mapping the Chinese and Islamic Worlds Cross-Cultural Exchange in Pre-Modern Asia* (Cambridge UP, 2012); and Hyun Jim Kim, *The Huns, Rome and the Birth of Europe* (Cambridge UP, 2013).

In the fourth and fifth centuries, in particular the definition of Christianity and its spread through the Levant and Central Asia—two sides of one process—was critical in setting up the political dyarchies of the medieval period. In addition to general background, the provocative writings of Lev Gumilev (1912–1992) have long been an inspiration of sorts: His *Iz istorii Evrazii* (Nauka, 1993) is essential. There is apparently no English translation, though the dissertation by the historian Alexander Titov is very useful: "Lev Gumilev, Ethnogenesis and Eurasianism" (doctoral diss., London University (UCL), 2005—so far as I know, the only publication of Titov based on the dissertation is in Russian). Gumilev's defense of Central Asian Christianity as a church and a culture in its own right runs through several of his books (see also Chapter 7 of this book). The following have also been useful: Peter Frankopan, "The Road to a Christian East," in *The Silk Roads: A New History of the World* (Vintage Books, 2015), 45–61; Daniel Boyarin, "The Christian Invention of Judaism: The Theodosian Empire and the Rabbinic Refusal of Religion," *Representations* 85, no. 1 (2004)1: 21–57; Ian Gillman and Hans-Joachim Klimkeit, *Christians in Asia Before 1500* (U of Michigan P, 1999); Erica C. D. Hunter, "The Church of the East in Central Asia," *Bulletin of the John Rylands University Library of Manchester* 78, no. 3 (1996): 129–142; John Haldon, "Historical Development: The Rise of the Medieval East Roman World," in *The Palgrave Atlas of Byzantine History* (Palgrave Macmillan, 2005), 57–67; and Edward G. Pulleyblank, "A Sogdian Colony in Inner Mongolia," *T'oung Pao* 41: 319–352.

On the important relationships among Constantinople, the Balkans, and the Russian steppe, see Panos Sophoulis, *Byzantium and Bulgaria, 775-831* (Brill, 2011); Thomas S. Noonan, "The Khazar-Byzantine World of the Crimea in the Early Middle Ages: The Religious Dimension," *Archivum Eurasiae Medii Aevi 10* (1998–1999): 207–230 and "Volga Bulghāria's Tenth-Century Trade with Sāmānid Central Asia," *Archivum Eurasiae Medii Aevi 11* (2000–2001): 140–218; Stephen Nikolov, "The Pagan Bulgars and Byzantine Christianity in the Eighth and Ninth Centuries," *Journal of Historical Sociology* 13, no. 3 (Sept 2000): 325–364; and Mickail Kizilov and Diana Mikhaylova, "The Khazar Kaganate and the Khazars in European Nationalist

Ideologies and Scholarship," *Archivum Eurasiae Medii Aevi 14* (2005): 31–54.

The thesis of Khazar origins of the Kievan federation is venerable even if still provocative. Its locus classicus is Julius Brutzkus, "The Khazar Origin of Ancient Kiev," *Slavonic and East European Review* 3, no. 1 (May 1944): 108–124, with later development in Thomas S. Noonan, "The Khazar Qaghanate and Its Impact on the Early Rus' State: The translatio imperii from Itil to Kiev," in *Nomads in the Sedentary World*, ed. Anatoly Khazanov with André Wink (Routledge, 2001), 76–102). See also Thomas S. Noonan, "Byzantium and the Khazars: A Special Relationship?" in *Byzantine Diplomacy: Papers from the Twenty-Fourth Spring Symposium of Byzantine Studies*, ed. Jonathan Shepard and Simon Franklin (Cambridge UP, 1990), 109–132. On this, see also Peter B. Golden, "The Question of the Rus' Qağanate," *Archivum Eurasiae Medii Aevi II* (1982): 77–97 and "Khazaria and Judaism," *Eurasiae Medii Aevi* III (1983): 127–158. Additional sources include Boris Zhivkov, *Khazaria in the Ninth and Tenth Centuries* (Brill, 2015); Peter B. Golden, Haggai Ben-Shammai, and András Roná-Tas, eds., *The World of the Khazars: New Perspectives, Selected Papers from the 1999 Jerusalem International Khazar Colloquium* (Brill, 2007).

On the emergence of imperial ideology in the early Turkic empires, see Turan Osman, "The Ideal of World Domination among the Ancient Turks," *Studia Islamica 4* (1955): 77–90; Mori Masao, "The T'u-chüeh Concept of Sovereign," *Central Asiatic Journal 41* (1981): 47–75; Thomas Allsen, "Spiritual Geography and Political Legitimacy in the Eastern Steppe," in *Ideology and the Formation of Early States*, ed. Henri J. M. Claessen and Jarich Gerlof Oosten (Brill, 1996), 116–135; Peter B. Golden, "Imperial Ideology and the Sources of Political Unity among the Pre-Činggisid Nomads of Western Eurasia," *Archivum Eurasiae Medii Aevi II* 9, no. 2 (1982): 37–76; and Christopher I. Beckwith, "A Note on the Heavenly Kings of Ancient and Medieval Central Eurasia," *Archivum Eurasiae Medii Aevi* 17 (2010): 7–10.

For the Islamic world, material relating to the periods after the early Abbasids will be noted for Chapter 5, but the following have been helpful for this chapter: R. W. Bulliet, *The Patricians of Nishapur: A Study in Medieval Islamic Social History* (Harvard UP, 1972); Muhammad Qasim Zaman, *Religion and Politics Under the Early 'Abbāsids: The Emergence of the Proto-Sunnī Elite* (Brill, 1997); Anna Akasoy, Charles S. F. Burnett, and Ronit Yoeli-Tlalim, *Islam and Tibet: Interactions Along the Musk Routes* (Ashgate, 2011), 27; Michal Biran, "True to Their Ways: Why the Qara Khitai Did Not Convert to Islam," in *Mongols, Turks, and Others*, ed. Reuven Amitai and Michal Biran (Brill, 2005), 175–200; and Anatoly Khazanov, "Muhammad and Jenghiz Khan Compared: The Religious Factor in World Empire Building," *Comparative Studies in Society and History* 35, no. 3 (Jul 1993):

461–479. On the role of Al-Andalus in the forging of a European identity in the medieval period, see David Levering Lewis, *God's Crucible: Islam and the Making of Europe, 570-1215* (Norton, 2008). The history of Abul Abbas is known only from Frankish records and Einhard's biography of Charlemagne. It is possible that the large (12" x 6" x 5") ivory panel of the Virgin Mary from Aachen, now held in the Metropolitan Museum as a gift of J. P. Morgan, is made from a tusk of Abul Abbas (https://www.metmuseum.org/art/collection/search/464454). It was once thought that a preserved and incised tusk, trimmed with gold and jewels, kept in Aachen cathedral was a relic of Abul Abbas, but it is now believed to date from c. 1000 and be representative of the fashion for elephant tusk exchange with courts of the Islamic world. See Avinoam Shalem, *The Oliphant: Islamic Objects in Historical Context* (Brill, 2004), 94; see also Jon Mandaville, "An Elephant for Charlemagne," *Saudi Aramco World* 28, no. 2 (March/April 1977): 24–27.

Chapter Five

Sultans and Civilization

The confessionalist empire that was the Abbasid caliphate had in its administrative and legal apparatus distilled the spiritual from the secular functions of government. The application of power—*sultan*—was a defined aspect of sovereignty, and while the caliph was invested with it in his person, it could also be delegated to a separate individual, which happened in later Abbasid times. "Sultan" was eventually the title assumed by a majority of Turkic secular rulers within the Abbasid realm, all ostensibly protectors of the caliph and the religion. But in practice they were khans, and many used both titles in their lifetimes. They brought to the Islamic world the overt bifurcation of moral authority and secular power that was already pervasive across confessional Eurasia. They also initiated a style of rule that would lead the continent out of its medieval patterns by patronizing local languages, enfranchising commercial elites, and liberalizing the exchange of religious views and scientific knowledge. By the tenth century, Abbasid territories any distance from Baghdad were controlled by a patchwork of military magnates who had risen to power in the peripheries and established dynastic control over local trade and defense. The pattern was first seen in the western reaches of Abbasid domains in North Africa, where relatives of Muhammad set up a dynasty before the end of the eighth century. On the Central Asia facet of the caliphate, the earliest of such regimes were the Samanids and the Buyids, both of which were of local Persian origin. Their successors—the Karakhanids, Ghaznavids, Khwarazmians—were most often Turkic, all adherents of Sunni Islam, Persian speakers, or preferring Persian for written communications.

Militancy on behalf of Islam was at the heart of Turkic legitimation in the Abbasid world. Ottoman history later made *gazi* (from Arabic *ghazi*) the best-known term for those who participate in religious war, though the Ottomans themselves seem not to have used the term until the fourteenth century.

It was related to Arabic words for raiding or skirmishing outside a full battle, but in the Abbasid period it was irregularly applied to warriors for Islam, often used in the context of biography. The word occasionally was taken up by European soldiers of the Crusades to mean any soldier in a holy war, and via medieval French *razzia*, *gazi* is the source for the modern English word "raid." Turks coming into Abbasid service as mercenaries fulfilled the meaning of *gazi*. They were designated and accepted identification as "slaves" (*mamluk*) of the caliph, a clear cognate for them of the Turkic traditions of slavery—and of military slavery in particular. Even before the arrival of the European Crusaders after 1096, there was plenty for *mamluk* soldiers to do. Some of the small regional dynasties sprouting from the margins of the caliphate were not Sunni, but Shi'i. The influx of Turkic *gazi* stiffened the resistance of the Shi'ites in Iran and North Africa since enforcement of the hated orthodoxy was now associated with foreign incursion. Turkic mercenaries were able to demand increasing financial and military discretion from the caliphate; their dynasties eventually dominated Egypt, Syria, and northern India. The result was a faltering of Abbasid administration of the Levant, into which the Europeans sent their campaigns to establish their own Crusader kingdoms. But the *gazi* ideology (as it would later be identified) sustained the conceit that although Persian and Turkic military regimes were carving pieces out of the Abbasid territories, the caliphate remained intact.

EARLY KHANAL REGIMES AND THE PRIVILEGING OF THE VERNACULAR

The earliest history of the phenomenon of nomadic military castes conquering well-populated, agriculturally based societies and then governing them for any considerable period is not particularly clear. For medieval Eurasia, the relationship of the Bulgar khanate, which dominated the Balkans and Eastern Europe from the seventh to twelfth centuries, with the Byzantine empire drew Bulgar rulers into increasingly close contact with the native Slavic population. For a time it seems the khan and his military caste were mobile within their territories, traveling—in the style of any traditional Eurasian federation—from one military outpost to another to oversee occupation and exploitation of the area. By the eighth century, they had a permanent capital, fixed urban centers of trade, and methods of taxing the population. The most dramatic consolidation of the rulers and the ruled, however, probably came with the conversion—demanded by Byzantium in 865 while they were dominant in the relationship—of all classes in the Bulgar khanate to Orthodox Christianity. This closed a period in which the khans had flirted with Roman Christianity in order to enlist the Franks in their struggle against Byzantium. After 865, the Bulgar khans took Greek Christian names, increasingly used Greek as an administrative and diplomatic language, and built churches and palaces in the Greek style. With the encouragement of the khans and the acquiescence of the church in Constantinople, Byzantine missionaries who were sent into the Bulgar territories preached in the local Slavic language. The Bulgar khans became caesars and, when not taking advantage of intermittent opportunities to attack the Byzantines, were advancing the Byzantine—and the Orthodox Christian—cause against Avars, Magyars, and Khazars. The state reached its greatest stability and prosperity in the middle tenth century, when it was a junior partner of Byzantium. But the relationship led to eventual dissolution of the khanate, as Byzantium absorbed significant Bulgar territory and remnant territories maintained independence for only a century or so.

Beyond the institutionalization of a vernacular language, the khans were also indulgent toward the development of vernacular religious sects that the authorities in Constantinople considered heretical. Most significant among them was the Bogomils, whose religious doctrines drew together several diverse streams from eastern Christian heresies of the fourth and fifth centuries, most of them bound up with the residual effects of the Gnostic Christian (and pre-Christian) legacy. These previously condemned heresies were easily recognizable by their practices and tenets: the access of select people to God without the intercession of priests, the creation of the material world by a God-defying demiurge, the light-being of Christ and the impossibility that it was he (and not merely his physical representation) who had suffered crucifixion, and the requirement that believers remove themselves from the corrupting world to live as sinlessly as possible. The Bulgar rulers tolerated Bogomil beliefs, and Orthodox missionaries evidently did not succeed in eradicating them. The influence of these doctrines was amplified by the Byzantine policy of repeatedly settling captured Gnostic insurrectionists in Macedonia, at the southern edge of the Balkans. By the time that the Byzantine empire conquered the entire Bulgar khanate in 1018, the Bogomils were widely dispersed throughout the Balkans. With the split between Catholic and Orthodox Christianity in 1054, a small number of Bogomil congregations fell within the Catholic scope, primarily in Croatia, within easy reach of the Alps.

From one perspective, the Bulgar khanate followed the pattern that is conventionally assumed for later nomadic states occupying agricultural societies: the elites gave up their original language for another, apparently gave up nomadic migrations, looked after their settled bases, and intermarried with the local population. It could justifiably be said that they disappeared as a continuing community. But the effects of their rule were not ephemeral. First, the religion, architecture, and naming patterns adopted by the Bulgars were not those of the local population but those of the Byzantine empire, a sometimes patronizing and hostile neighbor. It would be rash to assume that

Byzantine culture was destined to dominate the Bulgar territories since the Franks were aggressively attempting to dislodge the Bulgars, which would have meant at least a temporary imposition of Roman religious culture on the majority of Balkan Slavs. In addition, the Bulgar khanate's contacts with the more patently Turkic regimes to their east suggests that maintaining their orientation toward Turkic language and shamanic religion was also a possible future. The Bulgars did not simply melt into the majority Slavic society, being changed by it and effecting negligible change themselves. The culture of the Slavs of the Bulgar territories was transformed by the Bulgar elites' choice of submitting to Byzantine dominance and adopting formal Byzantine culture, which they transmitted to the population generally.

Equally interesting is the fact that in the world of Orthodox missionaries, the Bulgar territories were distinct because of the use of Slavic as the language of preaching and evidently the primary language used by government representatives. Monasticism, an import from Central Asia, had a spectacular manifestation in the huge community at Rila, founded in the late tenth century. Today, the earliest surviving vernacular Bible (closely associated with the origins of Cyrillic script) is in the local Slavic language. It is the translation by Kyrill and Methodius in the ninth century, soon after the Bulgar khanate took its most independent (if not most successful) form. Hagiographies produced in Bulgarian in this period (evidently for teaching orthodox beliefs and fighting heretical local religious trends) later influenced the rise of hagiography as a genre across the medieval Christian and Muslim worlds.

MAMLUK REGIMES IN THE MUSLIM WORLD

Just as the background to the emergence of the Bulgar khanate was the fluctuating fortunes of the Byzantine empire, so the background to the medieval Persian and Turkic states that emerged in Iran and Central Asia was the weakening Abbasid government. The original base of independent regional power in the Abbasid system was landowning, and from the seventh to the tenth centuries, the powerful aristocratic Persian family, the Samanids, controlled virtually the entire eastern portion of the Abbasid empire. They actively promoted the use of Persian language (rather than the Abbasid standard, Arabic) for arts and governance and otherwise used the normal apparatus of the Abbasid caliphate to adjudicate disputes and impose taxes. It was under the Samanids that the lasting features of the Abbasid legacy were formed: Sunni (orthodox) Islam as the dominant doctrine and Persian language for both state and private uses. The Samanid regime attracted a large number of Turkic mercenaries, virtually all Sunni converts, and by the end of the tenth century, Turkic groups were dividing up the Samanid territories for themselves (see Map 5.1). As a result of these developments, the Ghaznavid sultanate was established in Afghanistan in the late tenth century. They—and to a greater extent the Karakhans to their north—showed a trait that would become a feature of nomadic rule over settled zones: they noted that the script could be used to write any language, not only Arabic and Persian. There is evidence that they might have commissioned work in their own vernacular that is now lost. Surviving documents and epigraphic samples show the inclusion of Turkic vocabulary, reflecting local practice. This tendency to accommodate local languages and customs, even in as severely Sunni a regime as the Ghaznavids, would become an enduring feature of sultan government.

As the Abbasid central order weakened, Turkic *mamluk* mercenaries in the Ghaznavid style were able to establish several regimes of their own on the Abbasid fringe. They were ostensibly loyal to the Abbasid caliph and tended not to refer to themselves as khan—their traditional sovereign term—but as sultan, making them functionaries of the caliph. Among these new regimes, the *mamluk* tradition of warriors of Islam suggested the sultan specifically as the leader of warriors. The Ghaznavids perpetuated the Samanid combination of Sunni state religion and civil administration by Persians in the Persian language. They added the Turkic tradition of military leadership of the sultan and military identity for all male Turkic elites. Ghaznavid *mamluks* made raids into India, and in the early thirteenth century, *mamluk* groups controlled the Ganges and Indus river basins for most of the thirteenth century. These regimes benefited from the fact that the political center of India was well to the south and the main obstacles to *mamluk* power in northern India were the small regimes run by the *rajputs*—federated Hindu kings who may themselves have had a distant Central Asian origin in the Hephthalites. The *mamluks* in northern India found the Hindu *rajputs* to be determined enemies of Islamic influence. But the *mamluks* won the struggle for domination of most of the region and created the foundations for the Delhi Sultanate, which distinguished itself not only for martial prowess but also for sponsorship of architecture, science, and philosophy. South Asian historiography would, in commemoration of their *mamluk* origins, label the Delhi sultanates the "slave" (*ghulam*) dynasties.

Over the Gokturk and Uighur periods, the Turkic Oguz migrated to the western side of Central Asia so that, by the end of the Uighur Khaghanate in the ninth century, they were part of the western Turkic populations that had been affected by Sogdian culture, Buddhism, Judaism (thanks to Khazar influence), Nestorian Christianity (see Chapters 4 and 6), and Islam. During the Ghaznavid period, a large population of Oguz began to flow across Ghaznavid territory toward Abbasid. By the end of the tenth century, one of these Oguz leaders, Seljuk, had moved to the banks of the Syr Darya River in Transoxiana. He converted to Islam but seems to have never became a *mamluk*. In the middle eleventh century, his grandsons destroyed Ghaznavid control over the eastern provinces. The caliphate granted the Seljuks collectively the title of sultan and invited them to Baghdad to pry the city from the grasp of the Persian Buyids, which the Seljuks succeeded in doing in 1055. Soon, another Seljuk aristocrat was put in charge of suppressing nascent, independent Christian kingdoms in Armenia and Georgia, and another was sent to make war against the Byzantine empire. The Seljuk sultan Alp Arslan captured the Byzantine emperor at the battle of Manzikert in 1071, setting off a reaction in Europe that helped initiate the Crusades in the Levant before the end of the century. The result was that the Byzantine empire lost Anatolia—virtually their homeland—not to the Abbasid caliphate but to the Seljuks, who established a cadet regime, the Sultanate of Rum (that is, Rome), there. By the last decades of the eleventh century that had been so disastrous for both Byzantium and the caliphate, the Seljuks were in de facto control of not only Anatolia but also the Levant, eastern Iraq, virtually all of Iran, and Central Asia as far as modern-day Kazakhstan.

In their earlier period, the Seljuks used a segmented state form. The sultan parceled out domains to members of his aristocratic lineage, and the aristocrats as a group endorsed the selection of the sultan and enactment of his policies, a virtual replication of Turkic political tradition. In their own domains, each collected his own taxes and enforced his own laws so long as they did not conflict with the Islamic law of the caliphate. As the largest and most influential of the *gazi* states of the tenth and eleventh centuries, the Seljuks developed a political ideology that would have lasting later influence. The Abbasid caliph still lived in Baghdad, and the Seljuk rulers—originally also based at Baghdad—could not separate their material authority from his spiritual authority. Particularly after the branch of the Seljuk empire was established in Anatolia, the sultans saw a continuous world that included themselves, the Abbasid religious authorities, and militarily independent regimes—mostly but not exclusively *mamluk*—in Central Asia, northern India, and North Africa.

Like the Ghaznavids before them, the Seljuks relied upon the juridical school of the Hanafites, followers of an eighth-century scholar who had argued for liberal interpretation of the law (i.e., interpretations not coming literally from the Quran). The Hanafites were encouraged in most Turkic sultanates, not least because oral tradition suggested that their founder Abu Hanifa (699–767) had been killed for claiming that Turks could be Muslims as pious as the Arabs. But it was also important that the Hanafites provided a strong argument reconciling the—ostensibly temporary—rule of non-Muslims over Muslims, so long as the non-Muslim regimes were pluralist enough to allow Muslims access to Islamic judges.

The Hanafites were associated with the developing concept of *dar al-islam*, or the "house" of Islam. It was the expanding world of Islam militant against the *dar al-Harb*, the "house" of war—everywhere that Islam was not the primary or a recognized religion—where the *gazi* were still struggling to extend Islamic rule. *Dar al-islam* was an ideal of a Muslim world that could be spiritually unified even if geographically discontinuous and culturally diverse. It would include not only Sunni but also Shi'i and all divergent sects. It would embrace Arabs along with Persians, Turks, Indians, Africans, Berbers, Spaniards, and Sicilians. In their view, *dar al-islam* extended to any society in which Muslims and the sanctioned groups ("the peoples of the book"—Jews, Christians, and other groups recognized in Islamic legal discourse) lived safely and with access to their own laws, whether or not the ruler was a Muslim. This was an enormous advantage in the culturally diverse span of the Muslim territories in Abbasid times and would be an even stronger asset to later empires of Turks and Mongols. For the Seljuks, *dar al-islam* also conditioned their position with respect to orthodox Sunni Islam. They considered themselves the enemies of heterodox sects within the Abbasid sphere, but in practice their ideological position was much more ambiguous. From an early point, the main court of the Seljuks tended not to sponsor orthodox legal schools in their palace cities, and they clearly did not select their own officials on the basis of Sunni affiliation. Their most famous counselor, Nizam al-Mulk (1018–1092), always advised that securing the loyalty of the Turkic military population and consolidating relations with Muslim state leaders of all sects were far higher priorities than religious purity. In Anatolia especially, the Seljuks' cultural and spiritual lives were complex. They had a continuous cultural exchange with Constantinople, and after 1071 frequently received Christian, Greek-speaking wives from the Byzantine ruling family—with the result that late Seljuk Anatolian sultans were often partly Greek by ancestry and cosmopolitan in education.

The Seljuks stand out for their contribution to the sultanate tradition. They appear to have been a larger population than the Ghaznavids had been, and both the soldiers and the sultans were inclined to preserve more of Turkic tradition than the Ghaznavids had done. Their administrative language was Persian, and the language of religious instruction was Arabic. But in some Seljuk areas, Oguz Turkic remained the vernacular of the aristocracy and the military while Greek was commonly spoken throughout Anatolia. The sultans were casual enough about their relationship with the Abbasid caliphs that they began to revive an old Iranian term to describe themselves—the *padishah*, meaning the "elevated ruler." It had strong connections to the ancient Iranian title *shahanshah* (king of kings). It also recalled the khanal tradition of collegial rule, since there must be many *shahs* before there is a *padishah*. More significantly, it suggested a ruler who did not need to be endorsed by a caliph. In this period of holy war and confessional states, the Seljuk approach was an unusual one.

Maintaining control of their large domain (see Map 5.1) was challenging in an era of local military dynasties emerging from the Abbasid political recession. Khwarazm, south of the Aral Sea, was an area of ancient settlement by Indo-Iranian speakers. It had been an intersecting point of Iranian and Greek civilization, though subjected to repeated incursions by groups of Skythians. It was also at the crossroads of Zoroastrianism, Central Asian Mithraism, and Buddhism for centuries. After the fall of the Seleucids, it was independently ruled until its conquest and conversion to Islam by the Umayyads in the seventh century. In the middle Abbasid period, border dynasties skirmished for control. Khwarazm was dominated by one or another of them until the rise of its own dynasty of sultans in the early eleventh century. In the middle twelfth century, revolts among Seljuk soldiers on the Central Asia front opened an opportunity for the Khwarazmians to extend their independence to a large area from western Iran to central Afghanistan. This was the beginning of the brief but impressive Khwarazmian empire, one of the last and largest of the Central Asian sultanates (though its ruling title was *shah*). By 1200, Khwarazm controlled all Iran and most of Afghanistan. Any power wishing to reach Baghdad from Central Asia would have to go through it.

SULTANAL ECONOMICS

The sultanates linked their legitimacy to specific achievements in material culture. This was partly connected to their roles as patrons of both the Sunni communities and agreeable Muslim dissident communities. Grants for mosques and schools, charitable foundations, travel on the pilgrimage to Mecca, and monuments to the distinguished dead were constant calls on the sultan's purse. He had to remain credible to the leaders of the religious congregations within his borders since losing the allegiance of clerics would create opportunities for challenges from within the lineage or from sultans of neighboring territories. On the other hand, the sultans—like their predecessors among Turkic khans—were wary of becoming captive to any doctrinal sect and avoided it by spreading their patronage as widely as possible. The overall effect was that the sultan had to be a sponsor not only of a wide array of cultural institutions but also of architects, engineers, building contractors, and technicians, and he influenced the style of everything they created. There was a certain lingering influence of the legacy of Baghdad. In the middle Abbasid period it was likely the world's largest city and was certainly graced by the world's most impressive public monuments. Palaces, courtyards, stable yards, paved open spaces for markets, special platforms for public address, tombs of dead sultans, and, whenever possible, gigantic mosques connected to the sultan's lineage were required for the all sultans to continue the Abbasid legacy, wherever their own capitals might be. Building was often interrupted by inadequate funds, wars, or periods of public mourning, but there was no escaping the expectation that it would resume.

State wealth—which had been not easily separated either in terminology or in concept from the khan's personal wealth in Turkic tradition—was an urgent issue with the sultanates, the primary reason they directed their conquest efforts against large cities and the most productive agricultural areas. The greatest expenses were the army—soldiers and families, horses, grain to feed soldiers and horses, weapons, uniforms, road repairs, and housing—and the sultan's household. This usually included multiple wives, many children, servants and tutors, bodyguards, cooks, housekeepers, and scribes. Like the khans, the sultans were required to maintain a constant flow of rewards toward aristocrats and common soldiers to keep their armies together. The priority was to combine constant rewards with novel limitations on the freedom of the warrior bands. The strategies were numerous. When he could, the sultan would enslave technicians (particularly workers in iron, brass, glass, paper, and ceramics) captured in war or conquest, creating new channels of technological transfer and novel design motifs. The armies underwent various degrees of bureaucratization, dividing them into units—often delimited in decimal steps of hundreds, thousands, and the ubiquitous ten thousand (*tumen*; see Chapter 3), which did not resemble their traditional groupings—and breaking up the old patterns of loyalty and solidarity. They were sometimes tied to the land as settled occupiers and peacekeepers and given small land grants that over time could convert their progeny to tax-paying landowners or farmers. In rhetoric, as well as in law and administrative institutions, military slavery became idealized as a perpetuation of the original *mamluk* status that had brought Turks into the caliphate in the first place.

The money for all this came from various sources. The oldest, for the Turkic warriors, was booty—the quick seizure of massive amounts of goods in warfare. For pacifying the aristocrats and the putative military slaves, land or horses could often be substituted for cash. Sultans could elaborate upon the population classifications of their khanal predecessors in such a way as to marginally increase the visibility of sultanal gifting. In addition to designating captured technicians as slaves and labeling dependent populations by the geographic or cultural context in which they were acquired, the sultans could now make a point of distinguishing Muslim adherents and their communities from others, and all designations had implications for tax liability. The "peoples of the book" paid a special tax that Muslims avoided, and the inclusion of many non-Muslim populations increased as the sultanal conquests moved into Anatolia and Central Asia. But most of the wealth was provided by agricultural households. Taxes in grain or textiles—or either one converted to silver or gold—fed the sultan's treasury. To collect the grain, he needed a bureaucracy to keep track of and assess the value of both people and land, collect the designated amount at the designated time, divide it between local officials and the sultan if required, and keep track of how much was being spent by the sultanal household and the bureaucracy once it was in his capital. These were not tasks done by Muslim clerics. They were done by scholars and officials well versed in Persian language and literature, sometimes educated at prominent schools across the Abbasid world. The techniques of Abbasid accounting were rapidly adopted and remained conventional in the Turkic sultanates until the eighteenth century. To keep expenses low, the sultans employed as few officials as possible. Unlike some other imperial systems across Eurasia, the sultans had only specific responsibilities in lawgiving. Aristocrats and soldiers could come under traditional Turkic law in some matters, and most disputes were handled by Muslim clerics within their congregations or judges recognized by the state. Crimes by high-ranking aristocrats or appeals of the most severe verdicts were normally referred to the sultan and he always had a few legal experts on hand, perhaps part-time, to advise him. Education was administered through community schools, with the sultan expected to make occasional grants as a sign of goodwill. The poor were supported by charitable foundations funded by leading families.

The Seljuk sultans were, like their Ghaznavid predecessors, attracted by and subsequently anchored by the wealth of developed agriculture and prosperous cities. The Ghaznavids themselves controlled large portions of the trading routes, including the nodal cities of Transoxiana, Afghanistan, and eastern Iran. Many of these cities were larger than any in Christian Europe at the time and were connected to the long-distance trade routes that not only stimulated the economies but also supported the formation of early corporations financing the caravan trade and providing credit to merchants engaged in it. The sultanates invested in these enterprises and protected the trade by securing the routes. Because they tended to not have histories of long-term landownership and management, they emphasized the importance of cities and commerce. For similar reasons, they tended to permit weakening of the privileges of landed elites and to promote the status and economic opportunities of merchants. No sultan, however, found a perfect method of balancing finances. Warfare to expand the booty base always created higher demands for rewards and, as a result, more warfare. At the same time, keeping civil government small by outsourcing tax management to "tax farmers"—who undertook to collect a certain amount in taxes and to keep the rest as profit— over the long term led to crushing tax demands and uprisings that had to be quelled at great expense and at risk of government credibility.

SULTANS AND LIBERALITY

The fact that few sultanates achieved a high degree of centralization was not a failure of state building, but a long-tested state pattern that accommodated both Turkic practices of shared political power and Islamic values of a monolithic moral authority. Patronage of Sunni Islam reinforced the tenuous stability of these early sultanates. The sultans on the eastern marches of the caliphate took it as their special mission to eradicate paganism, which included Manichaeanism and Buddhism. They also claimed as their mandate the subordination (sometimes the outright elimination) of dissident Islamic sects. This allowed the sultan to enhance his powers of military command and civil administration of occupied areas, making his supremacy in the sultanate even more clear, despite continuing his dependence upon the endorsement of Turkic tribal leaders. By the time that the *mamluks* of northern India won their power struggle against the *rajputs* and the Seljuks of Rum settled comfortably at the interface of Byzantium and the caliphate, the role of Turkic sultans in the defense and encouragement of civilization was firm. They were no longer only the military adjutants of the caliphs; they were rulers in their own right, protectors of the caliph and the religious community and masters of their own armies and bureaucracies. In practice, the sultans acted as their linguistic counterparts, the emperors of Christendom. They could do everything except bestow divine approval on themselves.

Decentralization of political authority usually meant local discretion in religious patronage. The networks the sultans created nurtured worlds of scholarship in which they had varying personal interest but which they sponsored for reasons of prestige. The sultans of Delhi sheltered outstanding mathematicians, astronomers, and engineers. The Seljuks hosted philosophers, physicians, mathematicians, and astronomers who revived the work of classical Greece. In other ways they continued the trends of the Abbasids that had produced unprecedented fluidity of knowledge, among mathematicians in particular; the great Seljuk-era poet and mathematician Omar Khayyam (1048–1129) is often cited as an exemplar of the cosmopolitan, expressive, flexible intellectual world of the Seljuks (but see also Chapter 9 on the complexities of his environment). As important as their standards and networks were to the transmission of knowledge across Eurasia, equally important features of the early period of the sultanates were the discontinuities, the contrasts, and the diversifications. Their official devotion to Sunni Islam did not prevent them from tolerating divergent Muslim sects and some pagan religious legacies, including their own shamanism (see reading notes). They were particularly sympathetic to folk religion and popular pastimes.

The Seljuk period saw the rise in influence of the Islamic teachings we call "Sufi" as cultural and legal influences. At the time, *sufi* (from a term that probably described the dress of the adherents) referred to the ideal of making faith in and personal connection with God integral to individual identity. It was not restricted to either Sunni or Shi'ite sects, nor was "sufism" a doctrine itself (see also Chapter 9). Because of its pursuit of an intuitive communion with God, Sufism diverged from the rationalist religious schools that had dominated the earlier Abbasid period. This communion was facilitated by induction of a mild trance through dancing and singing or, in some cases, the use of drugs. Many historians of religion have noted some similarities between the Sufists and the Christian Gnostics (see Chapter 2), who also pursued an intensely personal, intuitive relationship with God, often through experiences of ecstasy. While the conservative religious establishments—whether Christian or Muslim—were increasingly preoccupied with scriptural scholarship and legal commentary, Gnostic-inspired Christian sects and the Sufis based their knowledge on verbal transmission, often in secret, of doctrines that passed from revered teachers to their students in closed groups that saw themselves as separated from society at large.

For the Seljuks and many other Turkic leaders, the Sufis may have had an additional appeal. Some of their practices looked like shamanism, and some historians have speculated that the Seljuk rulers in Anatolia made Sufis a prominent part of their investiture ceremonies because they believed that they were shamanic variants, but because of a perceived parallel in spiritual access, allowing the Sufis to transmit supernatural power to the ruler (see the reading notes). Under the Seljuks, Sufi practitioners and their congregations practiced freely, were influential, and established their niche in the Muslim world permanently. In Seljuk Anatolia, they played the roles that community leaders, Sunni teachers, and other orthodox Sunni religious authorities assumed in the central Seljuk/Abbasid capitals of Baghdad and Isfahan. The Seljuk period, in part as a result of direct court patronage, is remembered as the seminal period in the development of popular Sufism and particularly the development of major centers of Sufist learning in Transoxiana and Central Asia. Sufist culture at all levels is remembered as a hallmark of the Seljuk period. The comic folk hero, Nasruddin, was by legend a Seljuk-era Sufi adept. Sufis were important personal and political advisers at the sultan's court in Anatolia, and the best-known Sufi poet—Jalal al-Din Rumi (1207–1273, "Rumi" being a reference to Anatolia)—was the son of a Transoxianan legal scholar.

The cultural impact of the early sultans of the tenth through twelfth centuries is best understood by remembering that they were by definition masters of the frontiers. First, they were at a geo-cultural frontier. They were not at first at the center of the Abbasid caliphate but were at interfaces with North Africa, with the Balkans—where Orthodox Christianity was consolidating its dominance—and with Central Asia—where Islam was still struggling to become the enduring majority religion. Their cultural impact was—as in the case of the Bulgar khans and the Ghaznavid sultans—transformative. They imported, imposed, and gave prestige to a religion that was not native and within a surprisingly short time—roughly a century—transformed Central Asia from a mix of various religious traditions to a dominant network of

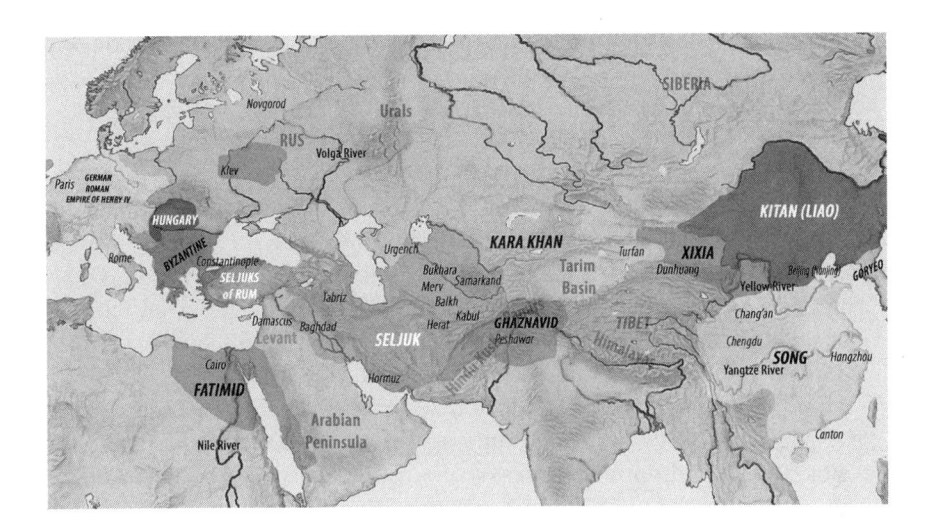

Map 5.1. Major political orders of the Seljuk–Song era, c. 1000 CE.

Sunni Islamic congregations, plentifully interspersed with Sufi practitioners. In the process, they introduced a written medium (Arabic script) that displaced all others, making it a universal and accessible tool not only for religious education but also for mathematics and bookkeeping, diary writing, and long-distance communication. Persian written in an adapted Arabic script became a lingua franca, allowing merchants and scholars alike to pursue their business across political and linguistic boundaries. Second, they were at a time frontier, fueled by the ideologies and conquest missions of the confessional age, while opening a new era of commercially keen, scientifically encouraging, and religiously ambivalent rulership.

READING NOTES: SULTANS AND CIVILIZATION

For the Bulgars, see Chapters 3 and 4 reading notes. For additional background related to this chapter, see J. A. Boyle, ed., *The Cambridge History of Iran, Volume 5: The Saljuq and Mongol Periods* (Cambridge UP, 1968); Stephen F. Dale, "India, Iran, and Anatolia from the Tenth to the Sixteenth Century," in *The Muslim Empires of the Ottomans, Safavids, and Mughals* (Introduction reading notes), 10–47; Reuven Amitai and Michal Biran, eds., *Mongols, Turks, and Others: Eurasian Nomads and the Sedentary World* (Brill, 2004); Peter B. Golden, *An Introduction to the History of the Turkic Peoples* (Introduction reading notes); and Christopher I. Beckwith, "Aspects of the Early History of the Central-Asian Guard Corps in Islam," *Archivum Eurasiae Medii Aevi* IV (1984): 29–44.

For background on the Karakhanids, see Michal Biran, "Ilak-khanids (or Qarakhanids)," *Encyclopaedia Iranica* online, http://www.iranicaonline.org/articles/ilak-khanids and R. N. Frye, ed., *The Cambridge History of Iran, Volume 4: From the Arab Invasion to the Saljuqs* (Cambridge UP, 2008).

For early Turkic imperial ideology, see Chapter 3 reading notes.

For the Bogomils, see Chapter 9 reading notes.

The indispensable author for the Ghaznavids is Clifford Edmund Bosworth. His Ghaznavid studies were collected in *Medieval History of Iran, Afghanistan and Central Asia*, vols. 10–18 (Variorum, 1977). In addition, his "The Early Ghaznavids," in Frye, *op. cit.*, 162–197 and "Notes on the Pre-Ghaznavid History of Eastern Afghanistan," *Islamic Culture* 9 (1965), 16–21 have been important for this chapter. See also Ali Anooshahr, *The Ghazi Sultans and the Frontiers of Islam: A Comparative Study of the Late Medieval and Early Modern Periods* (Routledge, 2008).

For background on the Seljuks, see A. C. S. Peacock, *The Great Seljuk Empire* (Edinburgh UP, 2015) and with Sara Nur Yıldız, eds., *The Seljuks of Anatolia: Court and Society in the Medieval Middle East* (I. B. Tauris, 2013); Osman Aziz Başan, *The Great Seljuqs: A History* (Routledge, 2014); Richard Foltz, "The Turks: Empire-Builders and Champions of Persian Culture (1027–1722)," in *Iran in World History* (Oxford UP, 2016); H. Moayyad, "Omar Khayyam," in *Iranian Literature*, ed. E. Yarshater (SUNY Press, 1988), 147–160; Reem Saud Al Rudainy, "The Role of Women in the Būyid and Saljūq Periods of the Abbasid Caliphate (339–447/950–1055 to 447–547/1055–1152): The Case of Iraq" (PhD diss., University of Exeter, 2014); and Alexander Daniel Beihammer, *Byzantium and the Emergence of Muslim-Turkish Anatolia, ca. 1040–1130* (Routledge, 2017). As a footnote to the influence of the Oguz Turks (and possibly the Seljuks particularly), see the study of the Turkic origins of a word for *wonder* or *miracle* in Armenian (and the context of the exchange): E. Schütz, "Tangsux in Armenia," *Acta Orientalia Academiae Scientiarum Hungaricae* 17, no. 1 (1964): 105–112.

The degree to which the Seljuks (and the Ilkhans, Timurids, and Ottomans after them) were attracted to Sufism because of some kind of resemblance to their traditional shamanism—and because of that particular attraction were accepting of Islam generally as a system of belief and social organization—was once assumed to be significant (and tends to be associated with the work of M. F. Köprülü) but has been qualified and to some degree discredited by later studies of Devin Deweese, Reuven Amitai, Peter Jackson, and others. For an overview, see Reuven Amitai, "Sufis and Shamans: Some Remarks on the Islamization of the Mongols in the Ilkhanate," *Journal of the Economic and Social History of the Orient* 24, no. 1 (1999): 27–46, in which the author points out that the Seljuks and Ilkhans were less attracted to the extreme ecstatic practitioners and more attracted to centrist Sufi groups. See also Chapter 9 of this book.

Part III

The Age of Far Conquest

Chapter Six

The Predatory Enterprise

When the Seljuks were consolidating control of Anatolia, at the eastern end of Eurasia a leader emerged who has become a legend in world history—Temujin, after 1206 titled Chinggis Khan. It was not long after his death that propagandists for his descendants called him "the world conqueror." Today, China, Kazakhstan, and Mongolia all compete to have him recognized as their national hero. Geneticists trace to him a Y-chromosome marker that is believed to be present in about 16 million men (or about 1 man in every 250) today. Modern writers see him as the adumbration of the psychologically acute, strategically innovative, personally ruthless model for corporate executives and a few heads of state today. But in his own time, Chinggis intentionally conquered nowhere outside Mongolia and only a few locations by accident—despite wreaking a huge amount of destruction against humans, architecture, and the natural environment. He covered a great deal of ground and wounded or finished off a number of sagging states but hardly merited the title of "world conqueror." It was his successors—men who ruled wealthy, agriculturally based societies—who made fundamental contributions to transformation of the medieval world. It was they who built on both the historical memory and the narrative traditions of wider Eurasia to start the myth of the world-straddling Chinggis and his empire, to glorify themselves and legitimate their positions in the Mongol and Turkic political worlds.

THE EASTERN STEPPE BETWEEN CITIES

The eastern part of the Eurasian steppe that we today call Mongolia was not, historically, a void or even much of a frontier. It was more like the nexus point of eastern Siberia, western Manchuria, and northern China, all of which

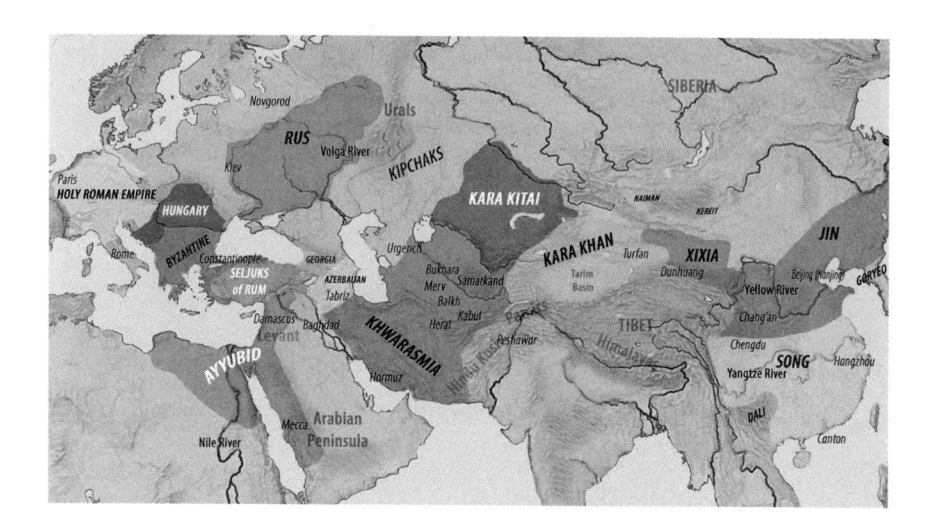

Map 6.1. Major political orders at the beginning of Chinggis's long-distance campaigns, c. 1205.

were populated and cultivated, with vigorous long-distance economic networks. Mountain ranges—particularly on Mongolia's northern boundary with Siberia—generate several large rivers and numerous tributaries, spreading over the steppe's relatively flat expanses, supplying herds with not only water but also grass, flowers, and herbs. This elevated water-source area was dominated by nomadic populations from Neolithic times. Mongolia and its connected westward steppe was a fluid world of Turkic, Mongolian, Chinese, Siberian, and some very old Iranian influences. The Gobi Desert demarcated the steppe lands to the north and west from a much more populated, arable stretch that runs along the north side of China's Great Wall.

These wide and varied nomadic zones were tangential to a persisting urban and political center in the Orkhon Valley, which marks the center of present-day Mongolia. The Orkhon River originates in the Khangai Mountains at the western end of this valley and flows eastward toward the location of what is today the Mongolian capital, Ulan Batur. The length of the valley was inhabited from Paleolithic times. In the Xiongnu and Gokturk periods, the center of settlement was at the western end. Statuary in the steppe style—with buried feet and features etched into broad, full figures above—and the famous Orkhon stelae were placed there by the Gokturk rulers in the eighth century. The Xiongnu, and later the Gokturks, established capitals there. The Uighurs appropriated the capital after they destroyed their Gokturk overlords in the middle eighth century. They referred to it as Ordu-Balikh—capital of the khan's estate. Monuments of the period, still extant near the Khangai

Mountains, advised the local Turkic peoples to avoid both the allure of China's material goods and the attraction of competing Turkic and Iranian chiefs across Central Asia. They praised the natural gifts of the waters, forests, and mountains of the Orkhon Valley and advise Turks to live peacefully off its resources. The blessings of the locality were attributed to the sacred power to rule believed to be granted to Turkic supreme khans by spirits—both natural and ancestral—concentrated in the Khangai Mountains.

Ordu-Balikh was typical of what archaeologists and historians now understand as the small city of the steppe. These are typically characterized by rectangular walls of stone or rammed earth. Inside may remain little evidence of permanent structures, but it is hard to define what "permanent" might mean in this context. The walls were permanent, certainly, and the interior precincts were left open, likely to accommodate the erection of family tents, or yurts. These were not always considered temporary or casual dwellings. They were heavy, often expensive, and once put up it was a chore to take them down. The yurts of aristocrats could have elaborate carved roof beams or entryways. Heat was provided by a central hearth (often lined with heavy stones), sometimes featuring a large ceramic or iron stove. The yurts were better insulated against the winter cold, wind, and snow than a wooden or brick structure might be and designed with side openings to allow the breezes of summer to cool the shaded interior. Often, they were mounted on carts, giving them a permanent wooden floor and perhaps an iron hearth, and transported from location to location without being dismantled and reassembled. The absence of evidence today of wooden, stone, or brick structures within the expansive walls of the steppe cities does not mean that they were intended as rest stops or their populations were mostly transient. They could have been crammed with semi-permanent or permanent structures of wood and felt and occupied in all seasons.

The monuments of the Ordu-Balikh ruins speak of grand prosperity, a time when "slaves had slaves." The city was actually the northeastern-most point of the Central Asia trade and communications network, and it was the articulation point between the eastern steppe and urban, literate, settled Eurasia. It was not on a direct road but was connected to Turfan (or Turpan, now in Xinjiang Province of China), which was a major overland trade entrepôt. When Ordu-Balikh was captured by Kirghiz Turks in 840, the Uighur elites fled to Turfan and from there dispersed to other trade network cities; in many of these localities (including Turfan) Ordu-Balikh refugees eventually became rulers. From the Orkhon Valley to the farmlands of southern Mongolia, the urban, agricultural, and pastoral sectors of the steppe were widely spaced but nevertheless tightly bound in economic and political relationships. A ninth-century description from a Samanid visitor described the experience of riding over the wide and apparently uninhabited grasslands, which gave way to fields (likely millet) and the villages of the farmers. His first hint of the city of Ordu-Balikh as he approached over the plain was the crown of the golden yurt that rose a hundred feet above the wall of the imperial compound. Inside, he found the city populous and bustling with commerce.

In the tenth century, the Kitans (see Chapter 4) shifted steppe urbanization eastward. They maintained three capitals in eastern Mongolia, one in Manchuria, and one in northern China. They also built at least one massive cemetery complex and many walled compounds for tens of thousands of dependent populations they had resettled by force from Manchuria and China. The smaller nomadic populations of Kitans, Uighurs, and Shatuo Turks were registered in military rolls of the estates (see Chapter 3). How much free roaming they did and how much they continued to rely upon a pastoral economy while the empire was intact is unclear. What is clearer is that the Kitan shift of urban settlements eastward and massive resettlements of dependent populations created the economic and geographic infrastructure for the emergence of the Mongols on the eastern edge of the Mongolian plateau.

The Jurchens, who named their empire Jin (Gold or Golden), took control of Manchuria, southern Mongolia, and a considerable part of North China after 1121. The Jurchens were not nomads, and partly as a product of their relatively settled economy, their population in comparison to the Kitans was large. Their government was more centralized than Kitan and much closer in structure, staffing, and law to the Song empire in China. They constructed rammed-earth fortifications, dividing their strip of southern Mongolia from the rest of the steppe (anticipating today's division between the Inner Mongolia province of China and the Republic of Mongolia). Occasionally they used bribes or propaganda to keep the leading federations of the steppe hostile to each other. A decade or two before Chinggis's birth, the Jin encouraged the Tatars to capture the Mongol leader, and when he was presented to Jin authorities, they nailed him to a wooden mule. Mongol hatred of both the Tatars and the Jin was sealed from that point forward.

THE CONTEST TO CONTROL MONGOLIA

The twelfth century appears to have been a time of climate change almost everywhere in temperate Eurasia except for northwestern Europe. Regions that had accumulated wealth and population in the previous couple of centuries—the leader among them, the Abbasid lands that had enjoyed a boom in cotton production—experienced difficulties due a derangement of normal rain patterns. In Turkestan and Mongolia, herds could grow larger, population could increase, the season for warfare and competition became longer. Iran and Iraq became drier, choking agricultural production, and the steppe became warmer and wetter. These unusual conditions marked the early years of the thirteenth century and appear to coincide with the emergence of the Mongol federation led by Chinggis Khan.

By that time, the Mongolian steppe was population-heavy on its western side, fairly well structured by travel and trade among its widely scattered urban points, and cosmopolitan due to its connections to the Central Asian caravan networks. But destruction of Kitan left Mongolia without formal governance, and the Jin empire of the Jurchens did not attempt to make up the deficit. The militarization of the Mongolian steppe in Kitan times combined with this subsequent lack of government to create a theater in which extended lineages and federations based upon them controlled most economic life. There is evidence of federation-building on a significant scale at several points in the twelfth century, often accompanied by the Turkic and steppe custom of systematic elimination of not only rivals for political (and economic) power but also their entire families (often including women). Once formed, federations were used to occasionally battling each other for local access rights or political dominance. Abduction, wife-nabbing, ransom, assassination, and the occasional massacre were often part of the conflict. Families changed their cultural character easily, sometimes from generation to generation, depending upon the linguistic, economic, or religious influences to which they were exposed.

There were many dozens of federations whose names are mentioned in oral or written histories, but three were dominant and played critical roles in the rise of Chinggis Khan (see Map 6.1). The Merkit controlled most of the Orkhon Valley north of the city of Ordu-Balikh (by then all but abandoned). They showed the influence of the Orkhon Valley's long connections to the overland trade networks. Buddhism, Manichaeanism, and Nestorian Christianity—all legacies of the Uighur empire—were well entrenched among them. Considerably west of the Merkit, the Naimans spent most of the twelfth century subordinated to Kara Kitai, though by 1200 they emerged as a local power. To the south of the Merkit, based in the vicinity of Ordu-Balikh, were the Kereit. They were more obviously Turkic and known, then and now, for the extent of Nestorian Christianity among their elites. South of the Gobi were a variety of groups known collectively as the Onggut, who dominated the southern Mongolian region on the Jin frontier. Like the general population of Mongolia, they were largely Turkic in origin; in Tang times, they had been the Shatuo Turks, and after the Tang demise they established a few small kingdoms of their own and merged into the populations of the Kitan and Xixia empires. By the late twelfth century, they showed a Chinese influence (and probably had many of Chinese descent among them). They were subordinates of the Jin Jurchens for a time, and as a sign of approval, the Jin allowed their khans to call themselves by the Chinese title *wang*, which put into Turkic and made plural, is *onggut*. They showed the common range of religions of twelfth-century Mongolia and may have been affected to a greater degree by Islam than others of the federations at this time.

Small groups of people with the name "Mongol" or something similar were mentioned in Tang records as early as the ninth century along with other minor groups such as the Mongol enemies, the Tatars (a widely dispersed name in Mongolia and western Manchuria, attested in both Turkic inscriptions and Tang records from the eighth century onward). Chinggis's immediate male ancestors were all chiefs over the Mongols. They were members of the Borjigin lineage, part of the aristocratic stratum of eastern Mongolia that included the chiefs of several federations, including the Kazakh and Kirghiz Turks. In the mid-twelfth century, the Mongols' leader Yesugei was poisoned by agents of the Tatars. His son, Temujin (born sometime between 1155 and 1167, with historians generally settling on "1162"), was spirited away to safety by his mother. For years, the family lived in exile and poverty under protection of the Kereits, until Temujin was old enough to return to the Mongols and claim his hereditary status as a chieftain. He attracted to his side talented and ambitious men as sworn brothers, or *anda*, and together they worked to consolidate their power.

The Mongolian source on this period (see reading notes) credits Temujin's early survival, and then success of his campaigns, to help from his childhood friend and sworn brother, Jamukha. The latter was a vicious fighter, a good strategist, and often a cruel victor, which made him a danger to Chinggis once an estrangement arose between them. The history suggests that the hostility may have represented a larger hostility between a group within the federation who wished to live pastorally, making their living from the expansion of their herds and pastures, and a group of elites living on the exaction of tribute from weaker or conquered peoples. Jamukha describes himself as lower in birth and, at one point, urges Chinggis to pause in his campaigns to allow grazing of sheep and cattle. Chinggis takes this as a disturbing declaration of intentions and quickly parts company with his sworn brother, who he feels is an enemy of Chinggis's class of tribute collectors. Once Chinggis finally defeats Jamukha and tracks him down in Kara Kitai territory, this narrative has Jamukha insisting that Chinggis kill him, however unwillingly, to preserve the new unity of the Mongols (indeed Jamukha swears to support Chinggis's cause from the afterlife). The death of Jamukha and the acclamation of Temujin as Chinggis Khan were structurally one event in political myth. It is a necessary legitimating moment in the transition from traditional segmented, decentralized political life in Mongolia to unified rule under a supreme leader.

Muslim sources are less dramatic in their depiction of the rivalry between Jamukha and Chinggis. They make it clear that the vacuum left on the steppe by Jin policies induced many contemporary campaigns of unification, one of them led by Chinggis and one of them led by Jamukha. In these sources,

Jamukha was not of particularly lowly birth, even if he was not wealthy—his lineage claimed to be part of the Borjigins, meaning he was a natural-born aristocrat and a distant kinsman of Chinggis. He also must have been as good as Chinggis at gaining and distributing booty because by 1201 he was recognized by the Merkit and Kereit as the *gürkhan*, the title for a supreme khan widely used in these decades (most notably by the Kara Kitai to whom Naimans had previously been subject). When Kereit aristocrats destroyed Chinggis's fighting force in 1203, he quickly reorganized and delivered them a devastating defeat. Jamukha rode west to join the Naimans. His ultimate defeat, capture, and execution (in this version, not by Chinggis but by a cousin of Chinggis to whom Jamukha was rendered) was central to the story of Mongol expansion across the northern steppe toward Transoxiana.

It was in these campaigns of the first years of the thirteenth century that the seeds of both a Mongol state and a Mongol occupation strategy were formed. The small group recognized as Mongols in, say, 1180 would never have had a hope of victories on the scale that Chinggis had achieved by 1206. In the early phase of small-scale subordination of neighboring federations, Chinggis relied upon personal and family relationships to enlist followers. He was able to effect significant political changes in small groups by carefully targeted murders of rivals and extermination of any members of their families to prevent the kind of political claims that Chinggis himself had made as a young man after he and his brothers had escaped a mass murder by the killers of his father. Eventually, Chinggis accrued enough fighters—probably under 10,000—to challenge powerful groups like the Merkit and Kereit. This meant that well before 1204, when Chinggis mounted his great campaigns against the Naimans, his followers were overwhelmingly Turkic, which is the reason that many of the names of Mongol institutions—for example the law (*yasa*), the tax system (*yasak*), or the family tent (*yurt*)—occur in the histories in Turkic form and not in Mongolian (which would be *jasa*, *jasakh*, and *ger*, respectively). Like steppe powers back to the Xiongnu, we call the Mongols by the name of their ruling caste, not by a name that would reflect the cultural features of the population associated with it.

Chinggis built on the Kitan policy of cultural identification of his subject population. Studies of political vocabulary from Chinggis's time and shortly after (see reading notes) suggest something of how the Mongol regime was organized before and after 1206. Among commoners, consanguinity seems unconnected or only loosely connected with political affiliation. Words that today are often associated with familial relationships had earlier meanings of being grouped together, for whatever reason (often security or labor). Words that today mean tribe or lineage federations referred in Chinggis's time to subdivisions of some larger unit, with both territory and people attached. Among the most commonly used words to place individuals within Chinggis's consolidating organization was *ulus* (clearly, cognate to if not borrowed from Turkic *uluš*), which in modern Mongolian is the word for "nation." But in Chinggis's time, *ulus* was the Mongolian word that loosely corresponded to *ordo*. It designated not only an estate but a patrimony—an estate that would remain attached to a certain household or the heirs of a certain person. It was simultaneously a reference to the hereditary elites who controlled the *ulus* and to the people who were subordinate to it. Modern readers often see it as equivalent to state, and there is certainly a sense in which medieval Mongols used it to designate the historical states of China or India as well as contemporary states like Song China—not because they were designating them as states in our terms, but because they saw them as cognate to the patrimonial *ulus*. They also used it to refer to their own regime—the "Great" Mongol Ulus, *yeke mongghol ulus*—and they used it to refer to the Mongol elites (and by extension their followers) who made consolidation possible.

The word *irgen* appears in the thirteenth- and fourteenth-century documents more often than *ulus*. It is a word that refers to population groups. The importance of the term is a reminder of Chinggis's urgent need for a substantial population to fuel his fortune and conquests, and his keen attention to securing the loyalty of these masses. The way *irgen* is used, for instance, in the Mongolian history represents the process of conquest and consolidation under Chinggis. The Kereit, Merkit, and Naimans were *ulus* before 1206 and afterward were *irgen*. The term *irgen* is also used to designate culturally or linguistically discrete populations without sovereignty. The Kereit, Merkit, and Naimans were reduced from *ulus*—sovereign peoples—to *irgen*, as were the Tatars, Uriangkhad, and the Onggut. Commoners appropriated from territories that were under attack or who had submitted were also each an *irgen*—this would eventually extend to Chinese, Koreans, Jurchens, Tibetans, Persians, Russians, and Franks.

Manipulating the relationships between *irgen* and their leaders was essential to Chinggis's campaigns of unification. In the Mongolian sources, he mentions at several points that some groups—outstanding among the Merkit and Naimans—had been privileged to retain their previous ranks and command over their forces that they had enjoyed before the unification. But their perfidy was justification for reorganization of their military forces into a decimal hierarchy topped by the *tumen*, a group of 10,000 whose captain reported directly to the *khaghan* or his council. It is likely that Chinggis would have done this anyway. Decimal organization of the military was ubiquitous across northern Eurasia, from Rome and Byzantium to China, and for essentially the same reasons that it had a long history in Central Asia: to break up traditional band loyalty and allow quick estimation of troop strength and logistical needs. This reorganization of the military was one facet of the essential and increasingly complex tasks of collection and redistribution that were Chinggis's campaigns. The Mongolian history states that he selected 80 men to serve as his security force "from the sons and younger brothers of commanders of a thousand and of a hundred, as well as from the sons and younger brothers of mere ordinary people, choosing and recruiting those who were able and of good appearance." He also ordered the creation of duty rosters for this group, with day and night shifts and three-and-a-half-day rotations, and insisted that when off duty, the security force would be quartered in a pattern encircling the Chinggis's sleeping quarters.

The passage establishes a level of complexity that could not have been achieved without substantial aid from a chancellery, probably one writing Mongolian in a script adapted from the Uighurs. The development of an inchoate bureaucracy, and the role of Uighur and Persian men in it, is difficult to reconstruct partly due to the indifference of the Mongolian history toward any aspect of Chinggis's career that touches on the urban, the cosmopolitan, and the commercial. But Muslim sources are clearer on this for the obverse reason—they prize the role of Muslim literati in the Mongol story. It is, for instance, likely that following his defeat by the Kereit in 1203, Chinggis withdrew to the fastnesses of northeastern Mongolia, lost a large part of his Mongol force, and reconstituted his armies with new allies from the Khingan mountain region. Muslim sources say he was aided in this restructuring by at least a few Muslim merchants as well as bureaucrats of Uighur and Kitan descent. These men are named in Muslim sources, but most are ignored in the Mongolian history, which narrates the Mongol conquests as the work of a small number of fanatically devoted Mongol horsemen.

EXPANDING THE PENUMBRA OF PREDATION

Continuous internal tribute for redistribution was an important resource for the expansive Mongol regime, and Chinggis had to refine the science of predation. To his east, in Manchuria, were scattered groups of mixed Tungusic, Mongolian, and Turkic background who were easily brought under the Mongol aegis. To the south, Xixia was in economic decline, and weak leadership had permitted factionalism to paralyze the government. To the southeast, the hated Jin empire of Manchuria and northern China had had a difficult last half of the twelfth century, as its elites were afflicted by factional struggles. Military expenses resulting from its intermittent wars with Song left Jin weakened and focused on continued fortification of its southern, not its northern, borders. To the southwest, the decentralized Karakhanid regime was delicately poised over the substantial populations of Transoxiana. To Chinggis's west, Kara Kitai had been destabilized by seizure of the rulership by the Naiman leader Kuchluk (see Map 6.1).

The first of these weakened states to attract Chinggis's military attention was Xixia. The society was wealthy. It controlled the Gansu corridor, through which ran the western terminus of the Eurasian overland trade net-

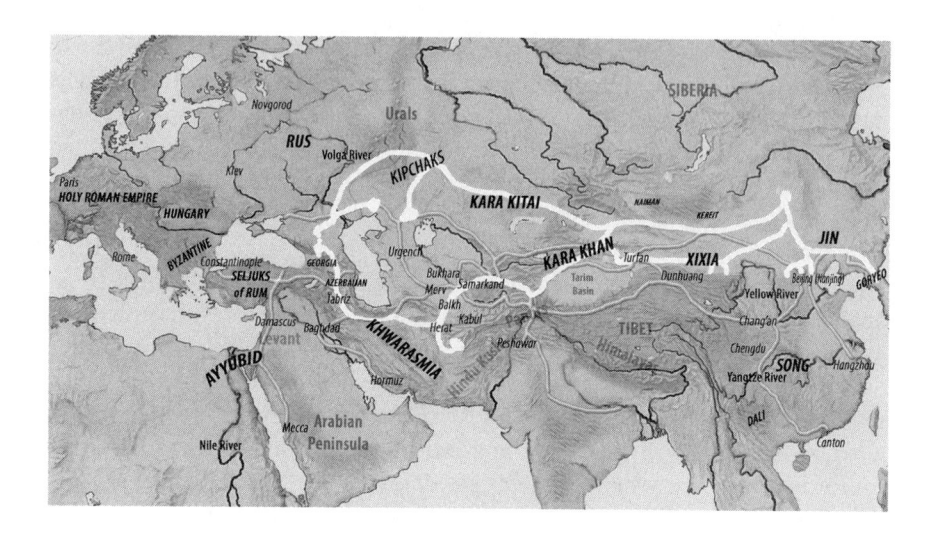

Map 6.2. Chinggis-era campaigns in relation to the overland trade routes.

work as well as what was renowned at the time as the best grazing land in the world. It also encompassed critical iron-mining areas, and its agriculture—primarily barley, sorghum, and millet, the common crops of both Mongolia and northern China—was well developed. Its legal code changed over time, but in a general way (and similar to the practices of the Kitans), applied Tanggut law to pastoral populations and Tang-derived Chinese law to the large Chinese-speaking farming populations. The royal family and Buddhist temple complexes owned a large part of the land and collected tribute from the farmers working it. They also monopolized iron, jade, salt, steel, and porcelain production. At the same time, the substantial minority of traditional pastoralists in Xixia were perhaps the most successful in eastern Eurasia. They supplied Xixia's primary exports of wool, felt, leather, camels, and horses. They were also the foundation of Xixia's formidable military, allowing the Tanggut ruling family to successfully declare independence from Song China and to resist incursions from Kitan, Jin, and Tibet. But by the opening of the thirteenth century, Xixia had been weakened by factionalism at court and repeated foreign incursions, including by the Kereits. In 1209, Chinggis's troops attacked the capital (modern Yinchuan, in Ningxia Province of China). His attempts to actually destroy the capital by diverting the Yellow River to flood the city were failures, but the Xixia emperor agreed to become a regular contributor to Chinggis's booty business, supplying a Tanggut princess as a hostage bride. Xixia faithfully paid its tribute and allied itself with Chinggis in what would prove a long war against Jin, but it refused to help Chinggis attack Kara Kitai.

From 1214 to 1216, Chinggis was able to mount simultaneous tribute-demanding campaigns against Jin and Kara Kitai. In the campaigns against Jin, he was frustrated by the walls around the capital (which was part of modern-day Beijing) and camped outside them until the population would surrender rather than starve to death. As in the case of Xixia, Chinggis continued to demand slaves, cash, silk, and a hostage bride as a show of good faith. Rather than comply, the Jin imperial family abandoned Beijing and went south to their second capital, at what is now the city of Kaifeng. Jin administration north of the Yellow River was shattered, and consequently, there was no authority to collect the tribute and deliver it to Chinggis. Mongol troops occasionally conducted raiding parties across the countryside, exacting their payment in whatever way occurred to them.

Something new happened in the case of Kara Kitai and the contiguous territory of the Karakhans. In the very early 1200s, the Naiman leader Kuchluk, after seizing rulership of Kara Kitai, made the mistake of persecuting the Muslim majority (ostensibly for the purpose of advancing Buddhism), at the same time trying to start a war with wealthy and populous Khwarazm (see Chapter 5) to the south. A Mongol force of 20,000 arrived at Kuchluk's capital (Balasagun, in modern-day Kirghizstan) to demand the customary tribute and hostage-bride arrangement, but they discovered that the government and army had collapsed, making extraction impossible. Kuchluk was eventually given by locals to a Mongol general, who took his head as a trophy and returned to Mongolia. Chinggis's lieutenant in Kara Kitai realized that he could win over the local population by promising to allow the free practice of Islam. The remaining problem was how to mine wealth from a territory in which the state had been destroyed. For the first time, the Mongols had to supply their own. They left a Mongol governor, supported by Mongol military commanders and Muslim clerks, to manage the levy of tribute.

Chinggis led as many attacks as possible and left the others to a small number of trusted lieutenants. In the campaigning months of late spring, summer, and early autumn, subordinates found him, his armies (numbering somewhere between 20,000 and 100,000 depending on the campaign), and his domestic entourage en route to or from operations and carried out their business of strategic consultation and booty distribution. Winter sheltering, organizational requirements, and the need to reaffirm relationships by worshipping, sacrificing, and feasting together nevertheless made some kind of gathering place a requirement. The evidence suggests that it was in Chinggis's ancestral territories, in eastern Mongolia; it was very possibly the modern site Awarga on the Kherlen River.

To Chinggis's west was the complex frontier of Turkic khanates, from nearby Kirghiz to the Kipchak-Cumans farther west. The western steppe was a competitive neighborhood. Strife, overgrazing, trading, and tribute rights had in the past driven the Oguz Turks south into Abbasid territory (the beginnings of the Seljuk story; see Chapter 5), and a segment of Kipchak *mamluk* had gone south to join Turkic regimes from India to Egypt. The Mongols had first clashed with the Kipchaks repeatedly during their attacks on Kara Kitai. This time, Chinggis ordered a sustained campaign against them. Pursuit of the Kipchaks took the Mongols not only west toward Rus and also through the Caucasus kingdom of Georgia. In 1223, the Mongol forces defeated combined Kipchak and Rus armies at the lengthy battle at the Kalka River in present-day Ukraine, and afterward executed the grand prince of Kiev. The subsequent challenges of stabilizing a western boundary and dealing with shaky administrative innovations in former Kara Kitai and Karakhanid lands made Khwarazm a worry for Chinggis. In comparison to the partly nomadic steppe lands of Kara Kitai and Karakhan, Khwarazm was densely agricultural and heavily populated. Like other parts of the Abbasid world, its economy was suffering from decline in cotton production due to effects of climate change. Nevertheless, it was militarily formidable and had just doubled its territory by swallowing up the western territories of the Ghurid sultanate based in northern India, giving Khwarazm sway from the Caspian Sea to the Pamir Mountains, including Transoxiana and most of what is now Iran.

CHINGGIS CONFRONTS THE SARTIC WORLD

A Mongolian stele of 1224 invokes Chinggis's victory over "Sartaghul," which meant Khwarazm—to the Mongols, the densely populated, settled, significantly urban Muslim world. The origin of the word (and variants *sartak*, *sertek*, and so on) is unclear, and its development had been meandering. Scholars have speculated that it may be derived from Sanskrit, Turkic, or Mongolian words of various meanings, without an authoritative conclusion. It is clear enough that, whatever its origins, it became widespread in the Turkic world as a way of referring to Persian-speaking inhabitants of towns (of Bukhara and Kashgar particularly). That meaning of "Sart" would continue to have a long career of use at the courts of the Ottoman and Mughal empires in reference to inhabitants of the cities of Central Asia. The Sartic world was one of cities linked by caravan culture and economy. In the thirteenth century, it was overwhelmingly Muslim but with pockets of Christianity, Zoroastrianism, Manichaeanism, and Buddhism. It was Persian in its book culture, many speech realms, dress, cuisine, and architecture but was also heir to the Sogdians and the Uighurs as a demographic, linguistic, and cultural integration of Iranian and Turkic elements.

In 1218, Chinggis sent an ambassador to the Khwarazm shah requesting a trade agreement and tacit recognition of Mongol control over Kara Kitai and

Karakhanid. A local governor seized the ambassador and killed him. The next year, Chinggis sent another ambassador with Persian interpreters who reached the Khwarazm capital at Urgench (not the city in Uzbekistan with this name, but "Konye-Urgench" in modern-day Turkmenistan), demanding reparations and the death of the governor who had killed the previous ambassador. This time, the shah personally ordered the execution of the Mongol emissary and sent Chinggis's Muslim interpreters, beardless, back to him. Realizing that Khwarazm would never take a neutral position on Mongol domination of its northern borders, Chinggis personally led his forces into Khwarazm to avenge the insult of his ambassadors' deaths.

The Khwarazmian campaigns were something new for Chinggis (now well into his 50s and perhaps past 60). This time his advanced planning included careful organization and provisioning of his armies, which with his enlistment from allied or defeated regimes included not only Mongol and Turkic horsemen but also large numbers of infantry. His recruits from the merchants and bureaucrats of Kara Kitai provided not only better capacities for logistical planning but also important information, which he carefully sifted. More important, he now led regiments of engineers—Arabs, Persians, and Chinese—who built and maintained catapults, huge crossbows, naphtha-fueled fire lances, and exploding canisters capable of breaching huge city fortifications. Khwarazm was the crucible in which the Mongol forces became oriented toward the terrain and the strategic features of the agricultural world, and their results were mixed. Chinggis never succeeded in avenging himself on the shah, who died of disease on an island defended by his son, Jalal al-Din, who had escaped to India.

Much of the imagery of the conquests comes from this period and from the Khwarazmian campaigns in particular, including the suppression of a few large rebellions that took the lives of Mongol occupation governors. But what is true, what is likely, and what is untrue are insoluble problems. The number of combatants is an imposing mystery. The Khwarazmians certainly had a large force—usually agreed to be at least 400,000—at their disposal, which they distributed among their cities. A later Mongol-sponsored Persian history suggests that Chinggis had a total of about 120,000 warriors at this time (which would possibly be smaller than the forces Chinggis took into Xixia). Even with catapults, battering rams, and exploding canisters (none of which operate themselves), it is impossible to believe that within the space of a year Chinggis defeated the Khwarazmians with a force ratio of 1:4 or 1:5. Other Muslim sources appear a bit more credible, even suggesting that Chinggis's army was in fact larger than the combined Khwarazmian defenders. Part of the answer to the question of the conquest force might be that all overland conquests until well into the early modern period depended upon convincing a critical mass of inhabitants to conquer themselves. Before the campaigns against Khwarazm, Chinggis had acquired a large Turkic following in the territories of western Mongolia, Kara Kitai, Karakhan, and Kirghiz, and was gaining Chinese-speaking defectors (many of them partly Kitan or Jurchen descent) constantly in the wars against Jin and tensions with Xixia, and all outnumbered Mongols by a tall ratio. It is likely that the campaigns in Khwarazm and elsewhere in the Sartic world brought in a significant number of fighters from the defending armies, particularly from the former Ghurid territories that had been so recently conquered by the shah. The conquest of Khwarazm argues a Chinggis force that was probably equal to the Khwarazmians, with the advantage of choosing its targets and concentrating or dividing its numbers to the best advantage in each case.

From the Khwarazmian cities of Balkh, Herat, Samarkand, Bukhara, and most especially Urgench, came the reports of horrifying Mongol atrocities that, for many, encapsulate the entire meaning of "world conqueror." There is no doubt that Chinggis was deliberately brutal toward enemies and their families, and this had been his style from the time he had a handful of companions fighting somebody else's handful of companions. Killing all candidates for leadership among a defeated population was a convention. Executing survivors rather than taking them prisoner would also be a necessary tactic in winter, drought, or desert conditions, and there is evidence of drought in Khwarazm at this time. Moreover, terrifying a population into surrendering rather than fighting was always Chinggis's preference, and it continued to be the preference of his successors. Even the most sadistic anecdotes are persuasive. The question of episodic brutality of the conquests is distinct from the question of numbers slaughtered. In the early thirteenth century there were a few cities across Eurasia with populations of a million or more—the largest was probably Angkor in modern-day Cambodia, but Cordoba, Constantinople, Baghdad, Chang'an, and Kaifeng were also at or near the million mark. But too many times the Mongols from Chinggis forward were reported to have killed "a million" people in cities that could not really have had anywhere near a million people in or near them. It may in some cases have been deduced by arithmetic: The Muslim records say that after the fall of Urgench, each Mongol (i.e., member of the Mongol forces) was required to kill 24 of the inhabitants; if the Mongol forces numbered, say, 50,000 (probably often the range of a siege force), that would be 1.2 million. If the order reported for Urgench became generalized by historians to all Mongol campaigns, then regularly multiplying estimates of Mongol forces by 24 would probably result in the numbers similar to those reported in histories written in the fourteenth century and later. The most likely scenario is that in the worst cases, the total executed may have been in the tens of thousands but carried out in ways so gruesome—beheading and piles of heads, boiling alive, bodily orifices filled with molten metal, disemboweling, horse trampling—that tens of thousands had the effect of millions and millions. Executions are not easy work with swords or arrows (or even mass burnings), and it is unlikely that the Mongols expended the time and effort to kill hundreds of thousands or millions of people who would be useful as slaves. Chinggis, in fact, perpetuated the Turkic tradition of capturing, enslaving, and transporting to his own encampment technicians of every kind: ironworkers, gold and silver jewelers, painters, architects, engineers, doctors, and prognosticators. Equally important, only survivors tell the tale, and the Mongols were eager to have the tales of their horrific conquests told.

By 1220, the war had concluded and Chinggis appeared to have suddenly acquired a densely agricultural territory dotted with wealthy commercial cities, a rich network of religious schools and mosques, and an accomplished bureaucracy. Before the arrival of the Mongols, the territories of Kara Kitai, Karakhan, and Khwarazm had been ruled by khanal regimes in which the tradition of Turkic segmented and collegial government had been overlaid to some degree by Persian bureaucratization, by Uighur urban mercantile culture and bureaucratic expertise, and by Abbasid legacies of religious and legal advisers. They all provided Chinggis the literate manpower to manage and distribute his resources effectively. This growing class of civil helpers were his interface with the expansive Sartic world of commerce and accounting. Khwarazm also confronted Chinggis with the problem of dealing with large Muslim populations. He had emerged in the culturally diverse and fluid environment of eastern Mongolia and from his earliest campaigns, probably had Turkic Muslim followers. He and his associates soon identified Muslims—whether Turkic or Persian—as peoples with specific uses in financial management, record keeping, good relations with wealthy merchants, and the machines of war. But moving through Kara Kitai toward Khwarazm, the human landscape changed dramatically. In Khwarazm, Muslims were not people with distinctive attributes; they were virtually all of the population. More important, their rulers were legitimated not by Blue Heaven but by a caliph sitting in Baghdad and speaking on authority of the revealed word of God.

THE OGEDEID TRANSITION

After 1222, Chinggis sent his sons and generals eastward again, determined to force the submission of Jurchen Jin. He ordered a force exceeding 100,000 to attack the new Jin capital at Kaifeng, which proved difficult, not least because Xixia troops who were pledged to aid in the destruction of Jin deserted. In 1226, Chinggis led a revenge expedition against Xixia that destroyed major towns and cities, delegating to his lieutenants the task of attacking Jin. But he fell ill—the cause may never be known and is speculated to have been alcoholism, or poison, or a fall from a horse, though he could have died of any disease of old age. On his deathbed, he received news that the Xixia capital had been taken and the ruling family exterminated. The Jin empire survived, as did the regimes of Korea, Song China, the Central Abbasid lands and the Caucasus, and the Kievan federation of Rus.

In the aftermath of Chinggis's death, it was reported that his body was taken back to Mongolia and buried with appropriate sacrifices, human and animal. The specific location is unknown. A tradition has it buried in the Khentii Mountains, his ancestral home. Common sense suggests that the body was buried in northwest China, where he probably died. Chinggis's spirit became the focus of a shamanic cult, its implements guarded by men from the family of two brothers who had been his leading generals, residing at his winter camp on the Kherlen River. The idea of worshipping Chinggis, either at this location or a few others that took on prestige in the coming centuries, was indispensable to generating new standards of legitimacy in the federation.

Chinggis's children were probably innumerable, but four of his adult sons were recognized as legitimate (all children of Chinggis's primary wife, Borte) and expected to provide his successors: Jochi (1181–1227), Chaghatay (1183–1242), Ogedei (1186–1241), and Tolui (1192–1232). Rivalries among these brothers had emerged in the conquest of Khwarazm, where each demanded territory and tribute of his own and disputed the apportionment to others. Who would lead the federation, and what form the alliance would take, was unknown at Chinggis's death. Mongol rules regarding the continuation or distribution of Chinggis's estate were complex, and the fate of the new rulership among the Mongols was unclear. This was partly because Chinggis's *ulus* was regarded as personal property and was presumed to stay within his direct lineage. Those particulars combined with the political imperative to find a collegially endorsed leader of that *ulus*, with or without direct rights of ownership. In practice, the period of consultation and disputation that followed Chinggis's death distilled the rulership as a political object from the questions of personal ownership of Chinggis's property.

This was partly facilitated by the fact that Chinggis's war command was more cohesive and tested over a much longer time than had been the case with any previous companion group in the Mongolian steppe. Even as early as 1204, it is clear that around Chinggis himself had developed an elaborate organization of bodyguards, domestics, doctors, secretaries, harem women, and caretakers of his children. From among his sworn brothers (*anda*) and trusted generals, a sort of cabinet government had evolved—the *keshig*. The name came from Turkic *kezig*, which denoted the day and night shifts of bodyguards, but long before Chinggis an inner command structure had emerged from this group. Turkic khans (and the Kitans) had long relied upon a trusted and privileged group of soldiers (and later, some bureaucrats) to look after their personal security, convey their secret communications, and manage their most urgent affairs. Among the Kitans, there is some detail on the way that collective advisory rule worked, often including high-ranking civil officials, sometimes men of partly Chinese descent. In its earliest form, the *keshig* was attached to the leader's estate and, as a consequence, did not succeed to the next leader; instead, a deceased leader's *keshig* became managers and protectors of his property, wives, and children.

In Chinggis's case, the *keshig* accompanied him in shamanic rituals, planned and executed military campaigns, and in some cases carried his messages between campaign theaters. The flexibility of their duties was an important aspect of Chinggis's attitude toward organization: it should be small, tightly bound by loyalty, easily surveilled, convertible between peace and war, and focused relentlessly on the priorities of wealth extraction from the conquered and distribution to the military caste. The *keshig* became increasingly critical in the security and occupation of territory in Chinggis's time, and his successor broke tradition by accepting a portion of his late father's *keshig* as his own. Even without Chinggis's leadership, the federation was superficially united under a set of institutions beyond the *keshig*. First was the *khuriltai* (borrowed from Turkic *kurultay*), or congress, the gathering of lineage and federation leaders for all weighty decisions. Second was the legal code, the *Yasa* (*Jasakh*), which evolved from a set of customary laws—and there is some question whether it took written form much before the end of the thirteenth century. Among other provisions, the code banned theft and murder; established a rudimentary judicial system; and prescribed methods of food preparation, especially butchering, that were considered clean by shamanic standards. Third was the Mongol style of taxation (and tax exemption, the *darkhan*), which was derived from the nomadic tribute customs of Central Asia. Taxation was, in comparison to warfare and raiding, an efficient method of extraction, and the Mongols both adopted and transformed (sometimes repeatedly) the taxation systems of the regions they conquered. Fourth was the institution of decimal military organization, which allowed centralization of command and flexibility in deployment.

Most materially, the empire was united by the *yam*, or post network, which reduced from months to weeks the time for delivery of communications from the capital to the outlying regions. It was most proximately an adaptation from the old Tang system of post routes through Central Asia (which may itself have been adapted from a system established by the early Iranian Achaemenian empire). It was based upon a series of post stations, each about 25 miles from the next along the major road and each keeping a group of about 400 horses. A single courier was entrusted with the message at his point of departure and exchanged his mount at every station until he reached his destination. Couriers rode without stopping between stations, strapping themselves in the saddle so that they would not collapse from fatigue. The foundation of the system was the phenomenal riding capacities of the couriers, aided by the advanced metallurgical skills of the Chinese, who knew how to cast the large iron bells that were rung as the riders departed their stations to alert the next station to saddle and provision a horse. At a top speed of 125 miles a day, the system surpassed the 100-mile daily maximum of the Roman postal system. With its closely spaced and well-provisioned stations, it fostered the improvement and policing of the Eurasian trade routes, which facilitated the travel of people and goods throughout Eurasia during the Mongol period.

By the end of Chinggis's life, rudimentary occupation forces were also deployed in northern China, Transoxiana, and parts of Iran. The collapses of Kara Kitai and Karakhanid, and abandonment of much of north China by the Jin under pressure of Mongol tribute-demanding campaigns, created problems of security and extraction that diverted military energies and gradually slowed the rate of predation. This made more urgent the requirement to establish at least thin occupation regimes and defend new frontiers that would previously have been abandoned in a return to camps in Mongolia. In northern China and Transoxiana, garrisons had been left behind to prevent incursions from competitors and to provide adequate camping spaces for the Mongol forces and grazing spaces for their herds. The resident units had originally been called "scout" troops—*tamma*, from a Chinese term for mounted scout—because of their positions at the forward fringes of campaigns. *Tamma* later became associated with being stationed in foreign or frontier places. Agents of Chinggis—whether they were Mongols, Turks, Chinese, or Persians—were installed as governors to oversee the work of local bureaucrats (who in most cases had worked for the demised regime) in census taking and tax collection. The English term might sound grander than the Mongolian—the evidence is that they were middle and high-middle military commanders. Gradually, the jurisdictions of governors were formalized as "circuits" (*colge*—inspired by the Tang empire administrative term *dao*, for a road or route, but designated as an administrative district).

For Chinggis and his successors, the Xixia and Jin (and before them, the Kitans) provided a model of plural systems of law, using one set of institutions—census registration, taxation, marriage and property registration, dispute resolution, and military obligations—for their densely populated agricultural spheres and another for their sparsely populated nomadic spheres. Something roughly parallel had existed in Khwarazm, inspired by Abbasid practices of formally designated confessional identities by population. The Mongol application of plural registration and juridical communities to the Muslim world was gradual, with Kara Kitai as a transition point. There, the Mongol occupiers found that the Muslim majority was used to being bullied by the Buddhist government of Kuchluk, and agreeing to let Muslims live as Muslims while the Mongol forces lived under their own rules was fairly simple. In Khwarazm, however, the shahs, though of Turkic origin, had been Muslims—and self-described *gazi*—for generations. They ruled over a large population of the same religion, and they all acknowledged the authority of the caliph. Neither Chinggis nor his collection of advisers and grown sons were inclined to arouse the Khwarazmian population to rebel, whether for religious reasons or in opposition to oppressive extraction of tribute. Though Chinggis did not repeat Kuchluk's mistakes, he also did not allow high-ranking Muslim generals or advisers to grow overconfident. Like his early generals occupying Kara Kitai, he simply expressed no religious interest at all. He asked no recognition from the caliph, and he declared no privileged religion in any of the occupied territories. He left the minimal number of occupation troops possible, kept his governor in the background and the native local officials (overwhelmingly Sunni Muslims) in the forefront, and carried on with his business.

Some historians suggest that rivalries and enmities among Chinggis's four sons had been sharp and early, and were excited by disputes over the division of spoils from Khwarazm. But the evidence that the four sons were irreconcilably divided in their own lifetimes is ambiguous. It is a mainstay of Mongol historical lore that Jochi was suspected to be illegitimate since he might have been conceived during a period—extremely early in Temujin's career—when Borte was held hostage at an enemy camp. Nothing much suggests any kind of coldness of Chinggis toward Jochi. It was Jochi himself who took offense in 1222 when Chaghatay publicly suggested that Jochi was illegitimate and therefore could not succeed Chinggis. The claim was quickly and sternly contradicted by Chinggis. But Jochi set up a camp on the Russian steppe and never returned to Mongolia. He predeceased Chinggis by a short period of time (or so all evidence suggests) and so was not a factor in the succession discussions after 1227. Chaghatay is often depicted as becoming an enemy of Jochi after disputes over whether the major cities of Khwarazm should be swiftly and brutally destroyed (Chaghatay's position) or persuaded to surrender (the position of Jochi, who expected to receive revenue rights over them).

Chinggis's unwillingness to spark further conflicts between Jochi and Chaghatay was apparently a factor in his increasing reliance upon Ogedei for management of family financial and military affairs. Ogedei was confirmed as the new ruler in 1229 and reigned until his death in 1241. We may know what he looked like, thanks to his well-known portrait (painted about a hundred years after his death), showing him as stocky in the same way as Chinggis, red bearded, hazel eyed, and well prepared for drafty northern interiors with his domed, fur-trimmed winter helmet. As a teenager, he had joined his father's campaigns, experiencing the defeats in 1203 and later becoming prominent in the destruction of the Merkit. He was named to the *keshig* in 1206, leading his own units in the wars against Jin in the 1210s and joining his older brothers Jochi and Chaghatay in some of the worst mass slaughters of the Khwarazmian campaign. With the confidence of the war council and the full support of his living adult brothers, Ogedei's reign was not seriously troubled by challenges from within the federation. He established the institutions of empire among the Mongols, with a proper capital and a new title of khaghan—the supreme ruler of rulers—which he assumed in 1229 and had retrospectively inserted into documents (instead of "khan") in written references to Chinggis.

Chaghatay, the oldest surviving of Chinggis's sons, did not interfere with imperial affairs in the reign of Ogedei. He set up a capital in what is now Xinjiang Province of China, close enough to Mongolia for his troops to remain in contact with their families but also close to his territories—which for a time encompassed most of the Sartic world in Transoxiana, Turfan, and eastern Iran. Overall, Ogedei proved adept at blunting tensions within the lineages. He made few demands on Chaghatay. He honored Jochi's son Batu and severely chastised family members—including his own son Guyuk—who quarreled with Batu over the wars in the west. He adopted his younger brother Tolui's first son, Mongge, and even tried, after Tolui's death in 1232, to arrange a marriage between his son Guyuk and Tolui's widow (she declined). Ogedei relied upon his brothers and nephews to continue to secure, expand, and exploit the territories they had so improbably gained. His departure from the traditions of mass extermination of rivals was significant, not least because it produced a new political class: the Chinggisids, separate from the broad Borjigin lineage from which Chinggis had come. It would influence Mongol and Turkic empires for centuries.

When working well, the new imperial apparatus allowed Ogedei an overview of the campaigns in China and Korea, Iran, Iraq, the Caucasus, and the Kazakh steppe (see Map 6.3). In 1233, with encouragement of the Song empire to the south, Mongol forces seized the Jin city of Kaifeng, and the next year, the fleeing Jin emperor committed suicide. The former Jin lands became not only a source of impressive new revenue but also a staging point for dealing with Korea. A Mongol expedition into Korea in 1219 had resulted in what Chinggis thought was an agreement by the Korea court to pay tribute. But Korea reneged in 1225, and Chinggis never succeeded in punishing it. Ogedei sent a series of raids during the 1230s, but all were unsuccessful. Intermittent warfare against Korea continued to the end of Ogedei's life. Meanwhile, in western Iran and the Caucasus, Jalal al-Din—the fugitive son of the late shah of Khwarazm—had returned from India and was attempting to create a new sultanate to resist Mongol movement west of the Caspian Sea. Unfortunately for him, this required defeating sitting rulers across Armenia and Georgia as well as the remnant Seljuk state in Anatolia. Before he could succeed at that, Jalal al-Din was attacked by a newly arrived Mongol force, after which he was killed by locals. The Mongols set up their own governors for collection of tribute and levied troops from the region to harry the Seljuk forces to their west. The Seljuk sultanate of Rum was still a

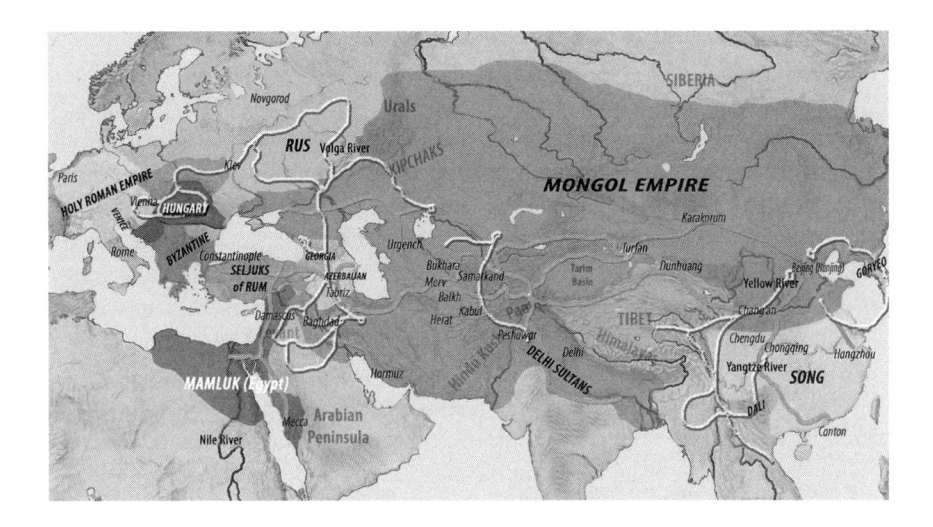

Map 6.3. Campaigns and overland transportation of the Mongol imperial era, 1229–1259.

militarily competent state and—still in early stages of occupying Khwarazm—the Mongols were more inclined to strike a truce and carry on crushing the small and weak rather than confronting any formidable competitors. They were also attracted by the idea of a functioning state that could gather and deliver tribute. They demanded hostages from Seljuk, a personal visit by the sultan to pay respects to Ogedei, and a Mongol governor to oversee tribute obligations. The Seljuks demurred, and at the time of Ogedei's death, intermittent Mongol raids against Seljuk were inconclusive.

Following the path of least resistance, the Mongols moved north in 1238 (see Map 6.3). Mongol and Kipchak forces roving west across the steppe were able to join with the expedition coming from the south, and they began delivering ultimatums to the cities of the Kievan federation. The decentralized and increasingly disorganized leadership of Kiev provided no prince to do any negotiating (perhaps because the last Kievan prince to fall into Mongol hands was executed in 1223). In 1240, the Mongols destroyed Kiev and moved toward Hungary. There they found a substantial amalgamated army of Kipchaks and Kievans who had escaped westward and allied themselves with a Hungarian force. But the alliance did not hold, and the Mongol armies moved into Hungary as the Hungarian leadership fled into Central Europe and the Balkans. In Poland and Bohemia, the Mongols fought and defeated hastily convened local militia, and in December 1241, they rode across the frozen Danube toward Vienna. But once on the other side, they received word that Ogedei had died; they turned around and headed east to join the funeral ceremonies and the ensuing consultations.

At his death at age 55 or 56, Ogedei was estranged from his eldest son, Guyuk, and perhaps also from his adopted son, Mongge. He designated a grandson as his successor, but it soon became clear that the Chinggisid congress would not accept this choice. Debates and negotiations continued for five years. In 1246, the congress convened and selected Guyuk the new khaghan. He perpetuated the pragmatic approach to Sartic culture and religion that had characterized the style of Chinggis and Ogedei. He promoted Persian-speaking Muslim officials as their skills and service merited and balanced their numbers whenever possible with Uighurs and Chinese—but made no accommodations for Muslim religious authorities. Guyuk ruled for only two years, but they were critical years. He stepped into a maze of campaigns, both military and administrative, to intimidate, or conquer, or occupy a huge area from Korea in the east to Kiev in the west.

Guyuk was the first Mongol khaghan to have a voice in European letters, and it is the voice of a universal conqueror, who dictated a letter (via John of Plano Carpini, see below) to Innocent IV rejecting the pope's demand that the Mongols convert to Christianity. Guyuk responded by admonishing the pope to show true piety by submitting himself to the khaghan, whose conquests were clear evidence of Heaven's endorsement. Guyuk not only demanded submission of the papacy but also of the Abbasid caliph still sitting in Baghdad, who refused. Guyuk assigned commanders and funds toward carefully organized campaigns against both Baghdad and the heterodox Ismailis who had headquarters in the mountains south of the Caspian Sea. He renewed campaigns against Korea and the military behemoth, the Song empire in China. He interfered in succession struggles among the Seljuks and dictated the division of Georgia into two kingdoms. Armenia pledged as a feudatory. Andrei Nevskii showed up in the Mongol capital in 1247 to submit and be recognized grand prince of the Kievan Rus federation, with his brother Alexander as prince of the city of Kiev itself. And Guyuk's universalism may have extended to the Mongol aristocracy; when he died of an unknown illness in 1249, he may have been in the process of attempting to tame the independence of Batu.

After Guyuk's death, the scene was fairly orderly because of the extraordinary prestige and long experience of Mongge. As a grandson of Chinggis and the adopted son of Ogedei, Mongge was endowed with high standing, which he had augmented by his leadership of Mongol armies in the campaigns in the west. He had accompanied legendary Mongol war leaders in the victories across Ukraine, Hungary, Poland, and the Balkans and had ridden with them across the Danube. After Guyuk's death, Jochi's son Batu was nominated as khaghan on his outstanding battle record, but he declined and supported Mongge. It took only about two and a half years (considering the logistics, a quick resolution) for the congress to proclaim Mongge—aged about 40—as the new khaghan in 1251. It was the beginning of a transformational era of rule over huge agricultural economies by the sons of Tolui and brothers of Mongge (see Chapter 7).

UNIVERSALIST KARAKORUM

The transition to an administrative state—if a thin and still highly personalized one—under Ogedei had demanded a capital for the khaghan. Chinggis's style of leading as many campaigns as possible and using his personal prestige to enforce decrees was in the past. Ongoing wars in China, western Iran, the Caucasus, and the Kazakh steppe along with a new war against Korea in the 1230s required a physical base where revenue, receipt, and distribution could be centralized and written communications in the necessary languages could be managed. Ogedei looked well west of his ancestral lands, toward the revered Orkhon Valley. Chinggis had had corrals and storage sheds built near the ruins of Ordu-Balikh to use as a staging area for his Khwarazmian campaigns. The area was still surrounded by good farmland, and it was connected indirectly to the Eurasian trade system. Straightened finances resulting from the simultaneous campaigns meant that not much happened by way of major building at Karakorum until the late 1230s, when Ogedei ordered construction of a wall and a palace. As the Turkic khaghans had done with nearby Ordu-Balikh, Karakorum was designed by engineers from China and the Islamic world and was decorated by craftsmen captured and indentured during the campaigns across Central Asia. Ogedei's two successors as undisputed khaghan developed Karakorum as a cosmopolitan and reasonably attractive city. When Guyuk was installed in 1246, there was an international elite in attendance. A Franciscan friar represented the good wishes of the pope, a Kievan grand duke represented the Rus nobility, an ambassador brought greetings from the king of Armenia, both claimants of the kingships of Georgia were there, and a Seljuk sultan and a member of the sultanal family of Egypt represented the diplomatic interests of the Turkic elites of West Asia.

Karakorum's general organization showed the clear legacy of Ordu-Balikh, with separate precincts for aristocrats, soldiers, and artisans. The city was bifurcated by a broad north–south avenue comfortable for horse troops and caravans, and hosteling foreign visitors was a brisk business. The khaghan's palace had a figurative view over the rest of the city. Most famous among its many reported adornments was a tree fashioned entirely of silver. Its grounds also included a Chinese-style green stele (still standing today) mounted atop the figure of a tortoise. Modern excavations suggest brick and rammed-earth buildings heated by hypocausts (often adding Chinese-style heated brick beds), extensive foundries for smelting iron and copper, smithing in various metals, and glass production. The extent and depth of its trade are suggested by caches of coins from across Eurasia. A leading historian of Mongolia notes, "Chinese roof tiles, roof ridge ornaments, a gold bracelet and ceramics, silver coins and cenotaphs with Arabic inscriptions, Indo-Nepalese Buddhist figures, and a silver drinking fountain built by a Frenchman" (see reading notes) among the finds. The continental span of Karakorum artifacts suggests that long-distance trade and communications were the essence of its character.

European visitors of the fourteenth century also noted the separate walled religious parishes—for Muslims, Buddhists, Daoists, Confucianists, and Christians, all equipped with the appropriate worship centers, libraries, and monuments. It is not likely to be a coincidence that the first formal Jewish ghetto in Europe appeared in Venice—the European city with the closest ties to the overland trade and to Karakorum itself—in the early sixteenth century. Europeans came as merchants and missionaries. John of Plano Carpini (Giovanni da Pian del Carpine, 1185–1252) is the best known among them today, and he may have been the most courageous. He was probably in Saxony when the Mongols terrified Europe with their approach to Vienna in 1241 but, within a short period, accepted a commission from Innocent IV to take himself—then over the age of 60—directly to the Mongol court and make the case for Roman Christianity. His party first visited Batu's camp north of the Black Sea and waited there until they had permission to proceed to Karakorum. Their journey of about 3,000 miles from Rome to the vicinity of Karakorum appears to have taken about three and a half months (including the sojourn with Batu), a testament to the speed (and extreme rigors) of the overland system. His party was held at a compound outside Karakorum and witnessed the investiture of Guyuk on August 24, 1246; Plano Carpini was dispatched from there, Guyuk's letter in hand, in November and traveled back to Kiev through the winter.

But William Rubruck (fl. 1253–1255; see reading notes) made the most famous observation of Karakorum when he said that the palace did not quite compare to the village of St. Denis (now part of Paris) and that the khaghan's palace was not "a tenth" of the monastery at St. Denis. William's comment is enigmatic to us today. We think of St. Denis as a pokey medieval hamlet, and if we take William seriously, we think it means that Karakorum (or at least the palace) was unimposing in the extreme. But William, as a Franciscan, knew that St. Denis was a wealthy district of royal tombs and that its cathedral/monastery complex was among the most magnificent anywhere in Eurasia. The village itself was also known for its dense population, filthy streets, and shady commerce. A a loyal churchman, William was eager to assure the pope (who suffered Guyuk's insults in 1247) that the khaghan's great capital had nothing on St. Denis, much less on Paris or Rome. But exactly what

William meant can probably never be clear to us today—we cannot even be sure whether his "one-tenth" comment referred to size or to grandeur of the palace. We can infer that he considered the khaghanal palace nothing wonderful—and if he was looking for spires, rosettes, and cobbled courtyards, we can be sure he was disappointed. It would be nice to know what William was thinking by this comparison because we now believe that at the time he visited Karakorum—a decade after John of Plano Carpini—the population had grown to a point of outstripping the available agricultural resources and perhaps even its supply of clean water. It is difficult to believe that its population ever got much above 12,000—possibly the most diverse 12,000 anywhere in the continent at the time—though defining residency and distinguishing part-time from full-time inhabitants would be a challenge. Whatever the exact numbers, by the time that Guyuk's successor Mongge became khaghan in 1251, Karakorum was past its zenith, and its location was becoming a problem as the limits of its local agriculture were strained, the shape of the war fronts changed, and the empire began to collapse from within.

The fortunes of Karakorum under Ogedei and Guyuk were controlled by the successes and failures of the regime in collecting and controlling wealth. The days of using war booty and tribute from subordinates to provide family members and close allies with their share of the takings were over. The large population of North China—probably 25 to 30 million people, mostly farmers—produced a steady flow of cash and grain. Ogedei had been dispensing it westward—partly to reward his generals in the campaigns in western Iran, the Caucasus, and Russia and partly to provide generous grants to politically influential Muslim schools, mosques, and clerics. Ogedei grasped that the war fronts and the management of large populations in North China, Transoxiana, and Iran were so complex that they could not be accomplished without reliance upon a class of full-time governors and bureaucrats, even if it meant increased spending on salaries. At the same time, alienating the Chinggisids and the Mongol nobility by canceling their own rights—nearly all of which dated to decrees by Chinggis—to collect tribute would have been fatal to the unity of the enterprise. Ogedei was so careful of Chinggisid opinion that he tolerated their skimming of tribute and pilfering of horses and supplies from the courier system.

The initial solution was to mandate revenue sharing. The towns, lands, and populations that were the direct inheritance of the khaghan were assessed based on population. Income was expected to work out at the same ratio in relation to population, with a minor share going to the khaghan and the major share staying with the local holder. In most localities the khaghan appointed the tax collectors—who made the apportionments of cash, grain and herd animals—while the holder could appoint his own governors and local officials. The principle nicely merged the traditional booty principles of Chinggis with the Karakorum empire's eagerness to systematically collect wealth from the staggeringly endowed (compared to Mongolia and the Turkic steppe) cities of Central Asia and farmlands of China and Iran. The Ogedeid state sought, implemented, modified, canceled, and revised tax practices in search of an effective system that would not displease Mongol aristocrats or arouse significant resentment among the conquered populations. Two tax systems were readily at hand. The Chinese tradition of census and tax by full-time, professional bureaucrats had been tested and improved over about 1,500 years. On the other hand, the Muslim world's practices of tax farming, which had major variations in late Abbasid times, had about 500 years of success. In earlier Abbasid times, landowners had collected the stipulated taxes from their tenants, but later, across Transoxiana in particular, local merchant partnerships bid on contracts to provide a stipulated tax and keep the rest as profit. This commercial tax farming had the appeal of low costs to the khaghan's court. As an initial step, Ogedei ordered that North China and the Sartic world each be assessed and taxed according to the methods familiar to it and be managed by local civil officials who would be loyal servants of the khaghan.

Ogedei was delighted with the level of cash, silk, and grain arriving from his province of farmers in the former Jin territories. Partly as a way of assuring Chinggisid control over territories that had informally come under the command of the generals who had led the North China campaigns, he assigned his nephew Kublai to take charge. Ogedei authorized the organization of the territories into multilevel administrations, with Turkic or Mongol officers assigned to administrative circuits that, as the Jin domain was being whittled away, multiplied across southern Manchuria, northern and northwestern China, and Shandong province. Tax administration was run overwhelmingly by officials of Chinese descent, most of whom had lately been Jin employees. They collected taxes even in lands that had been functioning as small grants to leading Mongol military families. This made the Chinese tax system, which was already expensive because of the number of salaried officials employed, unpopular among the Mongol aristocrats. When Ogedei's military campaigns forced a retrenchment in spending, Sartic-style revenue farming—mostly managed by Sarts—was imposed upon North China. Officials of Chinese descent became less visible in the new government. Not only Mongol governors but also judges proliferated in the new province accelerating the displacement of Mongol and Turkic tribal war leaders and their high-ranking followers. By the time of the final collapse of Jin in 1234 and absorption of their remaining territories, the old patterns of informal tribal conquest and exploitation of occupied territory had been superseded by the fundamentals of formal government. Nevertheless, complaints to the new khaghan Guyuk from Mongol aristocrats in North China were persistent enough that he canceled the tax-farming system and, for good measure, executed the Muslim officials operating it. He was himself surrounded by Christians, and partly to diminish disproportionate Muslim influence, he insisted that the khaghanate show no official sponsorship of any religion or cultural tradition. It was one of many ways in which both economic and political requirements of the Mongol regimes were tied to cultural and social policy.

Though Batu's support of Mongge was an important element in the relatively swift and peaceful transition of 1251, the installation of Mongge marked a dynastic change at Karakorum that permanently severed access of the Jochid, Chaghataid, and Ogedeid lineages to the khaghanship. Mongge's younger brother, Kublai, was already piling up successes in North China and Korea and gathering more resources for war against Song China. Another younger brother, Hulagu, was becoming more prominent in the campaigns against the Abbasid caliph and against the Ismailis. Their cousins on the western steppe and Central Asia controlled vast expanses of land and a few pockets of substantial wealth. But Kublai and Hulagu were in virtual possession of densely populated, agricultural economies whose potential for generating wealth and military force greatly outweighed the wealth commanded by the other Chinggisid lineages. When it became necessary to fight their Chinggisid relatives in a civil war, they had the financial and human resources to end the empire and a found new regime that uniquely and profoundly changed Eurasia.

READING NOTES:
THE PREDATORY ENTERPRISE

A good deal of background reading relevant to this chapter has been cited in previous chapters.

On the background to the rise of the Mongols, see Joseph F. Fletcher Jr., "The Mongols: Ecology and Social Perspectives," *Harvard Journal of Asiatic Studies* 46, no. 1 (Jun 1986): 11–50; Neil Pederson, Amy E. Hessl, Nachin Baatarbileg, Kevin J. Anchukaitis, and Nicola Di Cosmo, "Pluvials, Droughts, the Mongol Empire, and Modern Mongolia," *Proceedings of the National Academy of Sciences* 111, no. 12 (Mar 2014): 4375–4379; Bat-Ochir Bold, *Mongolian Nomadic Society: A Reconstruction of the 'Medieval' History of Mongolia* (Routledge, 2013). For sources for my comments on *irgen*, see Bold, *op. cit.*, 113, and especially Lkhamsuren Munkh-Erdene, "Where Did the Mongol Empire Come From? Medieval Mongol Ideas of People, State and Empire," *Inner Asia* 13, no. 2 (2011): 211–237, esp. 213–215. See also Kam-sing Tak, "The Term *Mongγol* Revisited," *Central Asiatic Journal* 60, no. 1/2 (2017): 183–206.

A small number of contemporary documents relate to the rise of Chinggis Khan, and a modest number of histories were written within a hundred years of his death in 1227. They can be roughly divided between the Muslim sources (largely in Persian) and Mongolian-language sources, though there are also important chronicles in a few other languages. The Mongolian sources include the enigmatic *Secret History of the Mongols* (*Mongghol-un nighuca tobciyan*), clearly based on oral traditional relating to Chinggis and his campaigns (see also Chapters 10 and 11). See also Muhammad Nabeel Musharraf, "An Overview of the Historical Sources of Mongol History," *The Scholar* (Jun-Dec 2016): 1–22.

Leading Mongol specialists have differing views on the precise dating of the *Secret History* (and many have felt that 1228 is authoritative); for an overview (and a conclusion that 1252 is the likely date), see Christopher P. Atwood, "The Date of the 'Secret History of the Mongols' Reconsidered," *Journal of Song-Yuan Studies* 37 (2007): 1–48. The relative obscurity of the *Secret History* after the Ming period was due to the fact that no original in Mongolian script has been found, though there are indications in other records that a Uighur-script Mongolian original was written, perhaps immediately after the death of Chinggis. On the orders of Kublai, the saga in spoken Mongolian was rendered into Chinese characters on the basis of their sounds (see Chapters 10 and 11). It could not have been very accessible to either Mongolian or Chinese readers at the time it was written (leaving historians to speculate reasonably that a Mongolian original has been lost, even if it survived into the early modern period) and after the fifteenth century, was accessible to almost nobody. In the nineteenth century, the manuscript was discovered by a Russian churchman in Beijing, and European linguists interested in both medieval Mongolian and medieval Chinese were able to reconstruct a sensible Mongolian text, consonant with oral traditions that have survived in some parts of Mongolia. It has been translated into English several times; see most recently (from the original), Urgungge Onon, *The History and the Life of Chinggis Khan (The Secret History of the Mongols)* (Brill, 1990). The translation by Igor de Rachewiltz, *The Secret History of the Mongols: A Mongolian Epic Chronicle of the Thirteenth Century* (Brill, 2013, 2014) is now available in its entirely (re-edited by John C. Street) via Open Access from Western Washington University (2015). See its introduction for a history of the text (pp. x–xi), which points out that the first attestation of "khaghan" in relation to the Mongol rulers occurs in 1229 in reference to Ogedei. See also academic translations by Ernst Haenisch (1937) and Francis Cleaves (1982).

On the resonances of *The Secret History of the Mongols* with earlier narratives across Eurasia, see Larry W. Moses, "Epic Themes in the Secret History of the Mongols," *Folklore* 99 no. 2 (1988): 170–173 and a remarkable essay by Christopher P. Atwood, "Alexander, Ja'a Gambo and the Origin of the Jamugha Figure in the *Secret History of the Mongols*" (Chapter 1 reading notes). For inherent interest, see Larry Moses, "Triplicated Triplets:

The Number Nine in the *Secret History of the Mongols*," *Asian Folklore Studies* 45, no. 2 (1986): 287–294.

The only surviving Chinggis-era text that invokes the Sart (*sartaghul*)— and is inspiration for my discussion here of a "Sartic world"—is the so-called Chinggis stele. It is described in two short essays by Gongor Lhagvasuren, "What Is the Script on the Chinggis Khan's Stele About?" Asian Traditional Archery Research Network, 2009, http://www.atarn.org/mongolian/mongol_1.htm, and the second, "The Stele of Genghis Khan," *Olympic Review* XXVI (1997): 13, http://library.la84.org/OlympicInformationCenter/OlympicReview/1997/oreXXVI13/oreXXVI13j.pdf. The former references the term and suggests that the purpose of the stele might have been to provide a platform for the relatively new Mongolian Uighur script.

For Chinggis himself, there are too many biographies to enumerate. A fresh recent text is Ruth Dunnell, *Chinggis Khan: World Conqueror* (Pearson, 2009). A good collection of accessible essays by researchers is William W. Fitzhugh and William Honeychurch, eds., *Genghis Khan and the Mongol Empire* (Odyssey Books and Maps, 2013). Leo de Hartog's *Genghis Khan, Conqueror of the World* (1989) has been re-issued by Tauris Parke Paperbacks (2004). J. A. Boyle's translation of Juvayni's *The History of the World Conqueror* (see Chapter 11), with an introduction by David O. Morgan, was re-issued by University of Washington Press in 1997.

On the Chinggis campaigns, see these specialized studies in addition to well-known narratives: On the Uighurs: Thomas Allsen, "The Yüan Dynasty and the Uighurs of Turfan in the 13th Century," in *China Among Equals: The Middle Kingdom and Its Neighbors, 10th to 14th Centuries*, ed. Morris Rossabi (U California P, 1983), 243–280; the late Joseph Connor Bell, *The Uyghur Transformation in Medieval Inner Asia: From Nomadic Turkic Tradition to Cultured Mongol Administrators* (U of Louisville, 2008); Michael C. Brose, *Subjects and Masters: Uyghurs in the Mongol Empire* (Western Washington UP, 2007).

On other rivals or enemies: İsenbike Togan, *Flexibility and Limitation in Steppe Formations: The Kerait Khanate and Chinggis Khan* (Brill, 1998); Michal Biran, *The Qara Khitai Empire in Eurasian History: Between China and the Islamic World* (Cambridge UP, 2005); Peter Lorge, *The Reunification of China: Peace through War under the Song Dynasty* (Cambridge UP, 2015); Zhu Ruixin et alia, *The Social History of Middle-Period China* (Cambridge UP, 2017); James Chambers, *The Devil's Horsemen: The Mongol Invasion of Europe* (Atheneum, 1979); and Peter Jackson, *The Mongols and the West, 1221-1410*, 2nd ed. (Routledge, 2018); and *The Mongols and the Islamic World: From Conquest to Conversion* (Yale UP, 2017).

There being no Chinese imperial history of Xixia (see Chapter 11), much of our information on the history comes from a cache of documents discovered at Kharakoto (now in Inner Mongolia, China) in the early twentieth century; the history of the documents and the documents themselves are now available in the "Digital Silk Road" collection mounted by Toyo Bunko Rare Books department, Toyko—see http://dsr.nii.ac.jp/rarebook/08/index.html. en. On religious government in Xixia see Ruth W. Dunnell, *The Great State of White and High: Buddhism and State Formation in 11th-Century Xia* (U Hawaii P, 1996) and Chapter 4 of this book.

On the transition to occupation after conquest, see John W. Dardess, "From Mongol Empire to Yuan Dynasty: Changing Forms of Imperial Rule in Mongolia and Central Asia" *Monumenta Serica* 30 (1973/1972): 117–165; Michal Biran, "Central Asia from the Conquest of Chinggis Khan to the Rise of Tamerlane: The Ögodeied and Chaghadaid Realms," in *The Cambridge History of Inner Asia, Volume 2: The Chinggisid Age*, ed. Peter B. Golden, Nicola Di Cosmo, and Allan Frank (Cambridge UP, 2009), 46–66 and "The Mongol Transformation: From the Steppe to Eurasian Empire," in *Eurasian Transformations Tenth to Thirteenth Centuries: Crystallizations, Divergences, Renaissances*, ed. Johan P. Arnason and Björn Wittrock (Brill, 2004); David Morgan, "The 'Great Yasa of Chinggis Khan' Revisited," in *Mongols, Turks, and Others: Eurasian Nomads and the Sedentary World*, ed. Reuven Amitai and Michal Biran (Brill, 2005); and as an illuminating local study, Paul D. Buell, "The Sino-Kitan Administration in Mongol Bukhara," *Journal of Asian History* 13, no. 2 (1979): 121–151. On the history and importance of Urgench, see Muhammed Mamedov and Ruslan Muradov (il Punto, 2001); additional Russian scholarship is summarized in *Kunya-Urgench, Turkmenistan: Nomination of the Ancient Town of Kunya-Urgench for Inclusion on the World Heritage List by the Government of Turkmenistan* (2005), http://whc.unesco.org/uploads/nominations/1199.pdf.

On encounters forced or facilitated by the Mongol conquests, see Christopher Dawson, *The Mongol Mission: Narratives and Letters of the Franciscan Missionaries in Mongolia and China in the Thirteenth and Fourteenth Centuries* (Sheed and Ward, 1955, reprinted in 1966 as *Mission to Asia: Narratives and Letters of the Franciscan Missionaries in Mongolia and China in the Thirteenth and Fourteenth Centuries* by Harper & Row, and in 1980 as *Mission to Asia* by the Medieval Academy of America)—the classic source text for the visits of European clerics to the Mongol courts. Rubruck's account has been retranslated by Peter Jackson, with an introduction by the author and David Morgan, as *The Mission of Friar William of Rubruck: His Journey to the Court of the Great Khan Möngke* (Hackett Publishing Company, 2009). See also Hyunhee Park, *Mapping the Chinese and Islamic Worlds: Cross-Cultural Exchange in Pre-Modern Asia* (Cambridge UP, 2012); Michal Biran, "Encounters Among Enemies: Preliminary Remarks on Captives in Mongol Eurasia," *Archivum Eurasiae Medii Aevi* 21 (2015): 27–42 and "Kitan Migrations in Inner Asia," *Central Eurasian Studies* 3 (2012), 85–108.

On the history and accounts of Ordu-Balikh and Karakorum, Takashi Osawa, "Revisiting the Ongi Inscription of Mongolia from the Second Turkic Qaγanate on the Basis of Rubbings by G. J. Ramstedt," *SUSA/JSFOu* (*Journal de la Société Finno-Ougrienne*) 93 (2011): 147–203, provides a concrete exploration. Equally engaging on that level is Eva Becker, "Karakorum: Fragen auf Stadt-plan," *Zentralasiatische Studien des Seminars für Sprach- und Kulturwissenschaft Zentralasiens der Universität Bonn* 37, no. 5 (2008): 9–32, which has been translated into English and is available at https://www.academia.edu/12174481/Karakorum_-_Questions_about_the_city_layout. For my reference to the content of the Orkhon inscriptions, see E. Denison Ross and Vilhelm Thomsen, "The Orkhon Inscriptions: Being a Translation of Professor Vilhelm Thomsen's Final Danish Rendering," *Bulletin of the School of Oriental Studies* 5, no. 4 (1930): 861–876. See also James Pringle, "Lost City's New Horizon: Capital Founded by Genghis Khan Rediscovers Its Past," *Far Eastern Economic Review* 145 (1989): 50. For the quoted description of Karakorum material riches, see Rossabi, *The Mongols: A Very Short Introduction* (introduction reading notes), 47.

As Peter Jackson pointed out in "William of Rubruck" (*Encylopaedia Iranica*, http://www.iranicaonline.org/articles/william-of-rubruck), Rubruck's dates of birth and death are unknown, leaving his age during his journey as unknown. See also *The Mission of Friar William of Rubruck* (*op. cit.*); his translation of Rubruck's account regarding the comparison of Karakorum and St. Denis reads "discounting the (khan's) palace (Karakorum) is not as fine as the town of St. Denis, and the monastery of St. Denis is worth ten of the palace" (221). For context of the comparison (St. Denis was for some time the base of Peter Abelard; see Chapter 9), see William Chester Jordan, *A Tale of Two Monasteries: Westminster and Saint-Denis in the Thirteenth Century* (Princeton UP, 2009). The existence of the silver fountain is mentioned only by William and is not corroborated by known physical evidence, and there is some suspicion that William may have invented or enhanced his description as a favor to Guillaume Bouchlier, who was a silversmith in Karakorum and may have provided his son to William as translator. For an excursion in search of the fountain in literature and art history, see Sarolta Tatár, "The Iconography of the Karakorum Fountain," https://www.academia.edu/2914023/The_Iconography_of_the_Karakorum_Fountain.

On the history of the Venice ghetto, see Joanne M. Ferraro, *Venice: History of the Floating City* (Cambridge UP, 2012) and Elisabeth Crouzet-Pavan (trans. Sharon Neeman), "Venice between Jerusalem, Byzantium and Divine Retribution: The Origins of the Ghetto," *Mediterranean Historical Review* 6 (1991): 163–179. On the reinforcement of urban segregation by another conquest-era phenomenon—plague—see Sheldon Watts, *Epidemics and History: Disease, Power and Imperialism* (Yale UP, 1999).

Chapter Seven

The Empires of the Toluids

Once securely in power, Mongge initiated a purge that was novel in Chinggisid politics to that point: he executed a large number—perhaps hundreds—of high-ranking Ogedeid sympathizers in the armies and the bureaucracy. But most Ogedeid kinsmen—all sons, grandsons, or great-grandsons of Chinggis—were permitted to retire with their lands, slaves, and herds. When the purges concluded, Mongge was more firmly in charge than, perhaps, any previous khaghan. He also had on his side his surviving adult full brothers, the sons of Tolui—Kublai, Hulagu, and Ariboka—who together with their cousins were still expanding the range of Mongol tribute collection east and west. Mongge's period as khaghan (1251–1259) saw widened control over the wealthiest societies of Eurasia between the Urals and the Pacific, between the Arctic and the Himalayas. There were two large strategic problems before Mongge. In the southwest, it was Transoxiana, Central Asia, and eastern Iran (including former Khwarazm). There was harassment and murder of Mongol officials and governors, and in the middle 1250s came news that the Ismaili sect in Iran was planning to assassinate the khaghan. Mongge's younger brother, Hulagu, was put at the head of a force sent to wipe out the Ismailis. In 1258, his forces seized Baghdad. In the east, the remaining challenge was the Song empire. It was centralized, militarily competent, and hugely populated (not less than 70 million people, perhaps substantially more). Getting Song to agree to tribute and a lack of hostilities would assure time for the Mongol regime to consolidate its control over North China, Korea, and Tibet. It would also provide a steady influx of wealth. Guyuk had had a general plan to attack Song in pursuit of a tribute agreement, but it was not an easy target. Kublai succeeded after a few years in forcing the kingdom of Dali—in modern-day Yunnan Province of China—into submission, which gave him a new staging area for the campaign against Song from the west.

In 1258, the royal court of Korea was surrounded and captured, providing a new platform for attacking Song from the east. In 1259, Mongge led his troops into China, but at the height of the siege of Chongqing, he was taken ill by some infectious disease, possibly cholera, and died. As at the death of Ogedei, the Mongols suspended or attenuated their campaigns everywhere, and the commanders took Mongge's body to Karakorum. The congress to select the next emperor was convened at Kublai's new city of Shangdu—near the location of present-day Duolun, in Inner Mongolia—in 1260, but rejection in some quarters of Kublai's bid to succeed Mongge led to the civil war that ended the empire. During the war, Kublai fought both hostile Mongol forces and Song China. After 1265, he made a site within the present city of Beijing his new base—Khan-balikh, City of the Khaghan, in Chinese called Dadu, the "great capital." In 1270, he declared a new dynasty (a Chinese concept) for himself with the Chinese name of Yuan (the origin). Enmity of Central Asian Mongols to Kublai would be generalized to the empire he founded in China. He continued the war against Song—who conducted the longest and in many ways the fiercest resistance of any Eurasian state.

From the turmoil of a civil war, the two Toluid brothers Kublai and Hulagu forged a federated regime that, because of its control over two of Eurasia's wealthiest and most populous regions, overshadowed other Mongol empires in power and immediate influence. Like their Turkic predecessors, they reconfigured the elites and the court cultures of their domains. They encouraged new dimensions of popular cultural expression through poetry, theater, and formal histories, as well as facilitated the transmission across Eurasia of an increasing volume of scientific knowledge. But within decades, each regime acknowledged the damage that war and predation had inflicted upon the countryside. They pursued new taxation and development policies intended to restore a predictable income from agriculture. Neither succeeded, but they foreshadowed early modern theories of management and social hierarchy.

WAR AND THE BIRTH OF EMPIRE IN CHINA AND IRAN

In reaction to Kublai's declaration of himself as khaghan in 1260, a substantial portion of the Chinggisid aristocracy immediately declared that Kublai's youngest brother, Ariboka, should succeed as khaghan instead. His father Tolui had, after all, been Chinggis's youngest son and heir to the khaghan's estate, and Ariboka was Tolui's youngest son. Ariboka was given Mongge's great seal and installed in the palace at Karakorum. He was able to use the seal on official documents to command preparations across the empire to resist a campaign from Kublai. Batu had died in 1255 and his brother Berke sent word from the Kazakh steppe that he supported Ariboka, as did Chaghatay's grandson Alghu in Transoxiana, who had only just assumed the khanship there. The situation was overall weighted against Kublai, but events proved that his base in China gave him an insuperable advantage. He cut off grain supplies from China to Karakorum in the summer of 1260, which eventually forced Ariboka to find agriculturally independent sanctuaries in Siberia. With Ariboka's abandonment of Karakorum, the fate of the empire was largely in the hands of Mongge's sons. When things looked most dire for Kublai, quarrels among the Chinggisid princes fractured Ariboka's coalition. At least one of Mongge's sons defected with the khaghan's seal, which he turned over to Kublai. At the end of summer 1264, Ariboka and his commanders surrendered. The non-Chinggisids on Ariboka's side were executed, while the Chinggisids were apparently given amnesty. Ariboka died two years later at age 47.

The empire was over. Karakorum was ended as a place of any political significance and was rapidly depleted of population. It would suffer repeated depredations in the late thirteenth century as Kublai and Chaghatay descendants fought over it and would finally be obliterated by troops of Ming China in the early fifteenth century. Today, the location is dominated by the ruins of the Erdene Zuu monastery, built in the sixteenth century. The demise of the Mongol empire left a clear dichotomy between the Toluids on the one hand, who controlled immense wealth and solidly defensible territories in China and Iran, and the remaining Chinggisid lineages on the other, who still depended upon partly nomadic populations in raggedly configured—if strategically critical—regimes of the steppes. Hulagu spent the early years of the civil war fighting with his Jochid cousins over control of the Caucasus. That local war as well as the long-term conflict that he and his successors had entered against the Mamluks based in Egypt (see Chapter 8) helped in some ways to centralize, stabilize, and define his government in Iran. In Kublai's case, the war against Ariboka that destroyed the Mongol empire had been pursued while he was holding his southern border against the Song empire. When the Mongolian war was concluded, Kublai was free to concentrate his full force against Song.

During the reigns of Ogedei and Guyuk, demands sent from Karakorum to the caliph's court in Baghdad had succeeded in extracting substantial tribute (including captive humans, among them European Crusaders), a few ceremonial appearances of Abbasid ambassadors at Karakorum, and fairly good assurances that the caliph accepted Mongol control of Transoxiana and Central Asia. However, the caliph (like the pope in Rome) ignored Guyuk's summons to come to Karakorum and grovel before the khaghan in person. Eastern Iran, which had been under Mongol control for decades, was an easy staging point for campaigns to harry the Abbasids. Ostensibly to punish the Ismailis for threatening Mongge, Hulagu demolished the Ismaili headquarters in the Alburz Mountains in 1256 and then issued his ultimatum to the caliph. The last remnants of the Abbasid caliphate resembled other fractured, depleted, or precariously balanced regimes that the Mongols had specialized in targeting. Independent sultanates had diverted to themselves most of what had been Abbasid revenue. The caliphal government cut expenditures for the military, leaving it unable to successfully quell sectarian riots that plagued Baghdad through the 1240s and 1250s. The government also failed to repair city walls and water systems after a serious flood. The caliph made no orderly attempt to provision the capital or communicate with neighboring (and not altogether friendly) Muslim governments to request aid. The result was that Hulagu—whose forces were probably invigorated to be in latitudes where winter campaigning was possible—at the end of January 1258 built the trench works and trebuchet ramps needed to smash the city walls. His Persian and Chinese engineers were so central to his strategies that Hulagu did not bother to respond to an Abbasid cavalry charge with Mongol horsemen—instead, he had his engineers flood the ground by destroying dikes along the Tigris.

Almost three weeks later, Hulagu was in possession of Baghdad. The enormous city was the jewel of Muslim civilization and had been the economic engine for the development of much of Central Asia from the eighth century on, bringing great prestige to the Abbasids and the Seljuks. Its architectural styles had influenced virtually all the cities of the Caucasus, Transoxiana, and Khwarazm. Its libraries and generations of mathematicians, astronomers, engineers, and historians had collected not only their own knowledge but the residual knowledge of ancient Greece, India, and China; via Constantinople, Delhi, and Turfan, the knowledge had been disseminated to Europe, North Africa, Kiev, Central Asia, South Asia, and East Asia. Hulagu's armies destroyed it. The libraries were burned, the treasuries looted, the palaces sacked. Not only the city but also the countryside—which had suffered 30 years of Mongol attacks—was destroyed. The historian Ata-Malek Juvayni (1226–1283), who later worked under the sponsorship of the Ilkhans (see Chapter 11), wrote of areas left "as featureless as the palm of the hand." A contemporary quoted eyewitnesses as saying "neither people, nor grain, nor food, nor clothing" could be found in the entire province of Khurasan (eastern Iran and western Afghanistan) and that, over a huge expanse of land, "people ate only human flesh, dogs and cats for a whole year." The human toll from the loss of Baghdad has defied meaningful estimate—hypotheses range from about 100,000 to about one million. It is realistic to assume that one-third to one-half of the population was exterminated and, within reason, to consider a higher proportion. Victims included the Abbasid caliph and all male members of his family. They did not die in the fighting but were held for more than a week while Hulagu considered their fate. In the end, he decided that the prudent course was to eliminate all possible contenders for what he clearly considered a rulership. The most reliable narratives of the caliph's death describe him as being wrapped in a carpet and trampled by the horses of Mongol soldiers—perhaps an honorable death, perhaps merely an attempt to protect his killers from being polluted by his blood. His son was taken captive and sent to Mongolia, where he (and his descendants) lived permanently.

Kublai was not only attempting to consolidate his control over the Karakorum empire but was also fighting in Korea to mop up resistance after the surrender of the king in 1258. He was determined to continue the long-running campaign against the Song empire in central and southern China. Song was a sternly militaristic and expansionist state, which for its entire existence had been at war with imposing neighbors on its north and northwestern boundaries. The expense had been ruinous, even though the advances in military technology were marvelous. Song innovations included the use of what is now called "gun powder"—sulfur, charcoal, and saltpeter (potassium nitrate)—for explosives to destroy enemy defense works; mass-produced iron body armor in three standard sizes; exploding grenades filled with sharpened iron shrapnel; huge mechanized crossbows and elevating trebuchets, often propelling burning missiles; and fireproof cast-iron bridges and watchtowers. It also commanded a formidable navy. All the weapons of land were successfully adapted to be used aboard their ironclad warships, many of which could be driven by paddle wheels when the wind weakened or died. In the early thirteenth century, the standing Song army—including cavalry units equipped with Mongolian and Central Asian horses—probably enrolled a million and a quarter men, and the navy may have used 100,000 men and a few thousand ships of various configurations. Song is estimated to have spent 80 percent of its annual budget on war.

On the western side of Song China was Tibet, which had no large-scale state organization at this time. Kublai and a cousin who had been on the ground in Tibet since 1240 rightly guessed that allying with the religious hierarchy there—particularly the head of the Sakya sect of Tibetan Buddhism and his young nephew, Phags-pa—would advance Toluid interests. In 1249, they recognized the leader of the Sakya sect as governor of Tibet, and he instructed community leaders in Tibet to acknowledge Mongol overlordship. Phags-pa later became effectively the governor of Tibet as well as a high-ranking adviser and spiritual legitimator of Kublai. In 1253, Kublai used the position in Tibet to make his strike against a new target, the Dali kingdom (in modern Yunnan Province of China), run by Buddhists speaking a Thai language. It controlled a lucrative trade route between northeastern India and southern China and would provide advantageous staging for attacking Song from the west. After attempts to arrange submission and tribute were frustrated by local Chinese commercial magnates dominating the Dali court, Kublai arrived at the head of a new expedition, and the ruler of Dali rushed to surrender. He accepted a governor and tribute obligations but retained his rulership in name. An attempt to use Dali as a base for a Mongol attack on Dai Viet shortly (see Map 7.1) afterward was stymied by terrain and supply problems.

In 1259, Mongge ordered an exploratory expedition into Song's Sichuan Province from Yunnan, with an army of several hundred thousand. When Mongge died during the campaign, Kublai assumed command of the forces. He was presented with a novel challenge: much of the war against Song would have to be fought on the Yangtze River, the many substantial lakes of central China, and the Pacific coast. Korea became an important naval station and source of marines for Kublai's coastal forays. The campaign was slow and carefully provisioned, relying heavily upon Chinese engineers from the former Jin territories. Hulagu helped by sending Persian engineers. Supply lines were threaded over land and water, bridges were built to accommodate cavalry and siege engines, and villages were razed to allow the war horses area to graze. With trebuchet and rocket destruction of fortifications, Kublai gained ground in small increments. It was not until 1276 that his forces reached the Song capital at Hangzhou. A few members of the Song imperial family, with the infant emperor in tow, managed to keep up a rather feeble resistance movement until 1279, when imminent capture led to their annihilation by a spate of murder and suicide. Kublai was ready to take his place not only as khaghan of the Mongols but also as emperor of China.

THE ILKHANS AND THE END OF RELIGIOUS GOVERNMENT IN MEDIEVAL IRAN/IRAQ

At some point during his command of the campaigns in Iran and the Caucasus, Hulagu took on the title *il-khan*—possibly meaning subordinate khan, possibly meaning sovereign khan—used at least occasionally among the successors of Chinggis's sons, but at some earlier point used by Hulagu to characterize his relationship to Mongge. After Mongge died in 1259, Hulagu purged all his Jochid cousins from his service in Iran and Iraq, rejected Berke's complaints from the Kazakh steppe about execution of the caliph, and began to dispute Berke's right to control the Caucasus. In effect, this second civil war among the Mongols of the early 1260s (which would continue on and off until nearly the end of the Ilkhanate in the 1330s) formed a new dynasty based in Iran/Iraq: the Ilkhans. When Hulagu died in 1265, Kublai—who was concluding the war against Ariboka—lost his most stalwart ally. But Hulagu's successors recognized Kublai as khaghan until his death in 1294 and extended that to the Yuan dynasty that he founded in China. Rulers of the Ilkhanate regarded themselves as part of a single enterprise—an empire founded on Toluid guardianship of Chinggis's legacy.

After Hulagu died, his own immediate subordinates in Iran/Iraq selected his eldest son as his successor, and the young khanate was immediately engulfed in renewed war both against Berke and against Chaghatay cousins attempting to seize the richest cities in Transoxiana and Turfan for themselves. Before the end of the thirteenth century, the Ilkhans had also gone to war repeatedly against the Mamluks in Egypt over control of Syria. In the meantime, the Ilkhanate was pursuing political, financial, and military conflicts with the many small regimes across Iran/Iraq, the Caucasus, and Anatolia that had accepted vassal status in the 1260s and 1270s. Steadily, these states were diminished to provinces of the Ilkhanate, a process that ended the remnants of the Seljuk sultanate and was complete by the early fourteenth century. Outside the imperial estates and the central administrative regions around the Ilkhan capitals in Azerbaijan, local landed gentry who had sworn allegiance to the Ilkhans handled administration and peacekeeping under the surveillance of their governors—who were often descendants of the sultanal and royal families of the Seljuks, Kara Kitai, Georgians, and Armenians.

The political order of the Ilkhans was a combination of the traditions of the Ghaznavids before them; the political traditions of the Turkic states, particularly the Seljuks; Persian Muslim bureaucracy based on Abbasid institutions; and Mongol practice. The Ghaznavids had synthesized the early Abbasid traditions of bureaucratic government with an integration of Persian and Indian influences. The result was a system of centralized rule under a sultan (which the Ilkhans came to use as a normal title for their ruler in the fourteenth century) and his prime minister, or *vizier*, in which leading bureaucrats had an influential role. Abbasid viziers, via their civil bureaucracy, the *diwan*, had comprehensive duties and, in some cases, private armies. Influenced by such a model, Hulagu made use of the vizier as a pillar of administration, but he was wary of the potential of the vizierate to become an independent power base. He limited the role of the vizier to the duties of tax collection and keeping a count of the population. He also split the functions of the vizier into two offices, promoting rivalry between the holders—a strategy used at many levels of the civil government. Viziers were not powerful again under the Ilkhans until the time of Rashid al-Din at the turn of the fourteenth century (see Chapter 10). They were before and even after that overshadowed by Hulagu's *keshig* (see Chapter 6), which may have numbered 10,000 men, and made clear that the military was in control in the Ilkhan state. In the same way that the Mongols had utilized Muslim frustration in their conquest of cities in Central Asia, so, too, did they utilize Christian frustration in their seizure of Iran, often appointing Christians to high rank in the bureaucracy. In some cities in Iran, Iraq, and Syria, Hulagu forced the conversion of mosques to churches.

The Seljuks before the Ilkhans had declared themselves passionate warriors for Islam and servants of the caliphs (whom they in fact tended to ignore).

The Ilkhans considered Muslim an identity, one that they were reconciled to incorporating into the empire but apparently did not intend to assume. Hulagu and his immediate successors were public adherents of Buddhism. For a half century, they did not encourage Mongols to convert. They were cautious of the history of sectarian conflict among Muslims and were also deterred by the perceived incompatibilities between the doctrines of Islam and the Mongol way of life. Certain of the early Ilkhans showed favoritism toward less orthodox Muslim groups. Hulagu, for instance, was inclined to give privileges to the Shi'ite sect to which his most trusted adviser, Nasir al-Din Tusi (see Chapter 9), belonged. It was decades before the Ilkhans made the crucial decision to support Sunni and not Shi'i Islam, but they were not completely consistent; the Ilkhans Gazan and his brother Uljeitu were baptized Christians while they were still children, and Uljeitu temporarily reversed the dynastic policy and supported Shi'ism instead of Sunnism.

Not only many Mongol aristocrats across Eurasia but also observers in Europe were surprised when Hulagu's great-grandson Gazan declared himself a Sunni Muslim when he seized the rulership in 1295. The conversion was part of a bargain to enlist local military support for the coup, but when Gazan's emboldened Muslim supporters attempted to initiate persecution of Buddhists, Christians, and other non-Muslims, Gazan suppressed the campaigns (and ultimately executed the instigator), strengthened the Christian patriarchate in Iran, and excused Christians from the tax on non-Muslims. The Ilkhans were open to Shi'ite and Sufist influences and maintained friendly institutional and personal relationships with Christian hierarchs while continuing to revere the Ilkhanate's early fidelity to Buddhism even after the rulers had converted to Islam. After Gazan's death in 1304, his brother Uljeitu continued his dual policies of establishing Islam and protecting Christians. Among the Ilkhan Mongols as a group, Islam was spreading steadily before 1258 and, after 1295, spread rapidly; in the early fourteenth century conversion became a legal requirement.

Gradual acclimation to and eventual conversion to Islam at the Ilkhan court was a major factor in the empire's relations with neighboring regimes. The Jochid Mongols of the Russian steppe used the death of the caliph in 1258 as a rallying point in their war with the Ilkhanate over control of the Caucasus. The Mamluks, who prior to 1258 were no particular friends of the caliph, welcomed a scion of the Abbasid lineage to Cairo and installed him as the new caliph, after which they attempted to persuade other Sunni communities to accept him. The Ilkhans wanted to consolidate their control over Damascus and went into Syria against the Mamluks just as the news of Mongge's death arrived; most of the army withdrew, leaving a smaller force to fight and be defeated by the Mamluks at the battle of 'Ayn Jalut in 1260. The Ilkhan regime continued an intermittent war against the Mamluks in Syria for a half century—about the same period of time they continued their war against the Jochid Mongols in the Caucasus—with inconclusive results. At several points, an alliance of the Mamluks and the Jochids against the Ilkhanate appeared a possibility, but it was never realized.

In mid-thirteenth-century Europe, myths of "Prester John," the mysterious Asian Christian king who was always on his way to free the Holy Land from Muslim control, were long-standing. The legend was occasionally fanned by deliberate hoaxes and sometimes by hopeful misunderstandings. Some Crusaders inspired by the legend did individually enlist in the Ilkhan effort against the Mamluks, and some were later excommunicated by the popes for it. The most famous advocate for an Ilkhan alliance was probably Louis IX (1214–1270) of France, who at the low point of his campaigns in the Levant received Mongol ambassadors suggesting an alliance to defeat the Mamluks; no alliance was realized before Louis's death. Shortly, Henry III (1212–1272) of England attempted to engage the Ilkhans in joint campaigning. The Mamluks successfully blocked the plans, after which Europeans were beginning to lose interest in the Levantine Crusades. The Ilkhans, however, maintained contact with the thrones of France and England and sent missions to Rome (including the famous embassy of the Turkic Christian cleric, Rabban Sauma; see Chapter 9). Though later popes remained enthusiastic about the idea of converting the Mongols, improved information may have impressed upon them that the Ilkhans were junior partners of the khaghans in China. Converting the khaghan in Dadu would convert the Ilkhans, but the opposite was not obviously true.

After Gazan, the Ilkhans experienced a slow decline, which in character was like the decline of the Mongol regimes elsewhere. The extraction of revenues from the population for the support of the Mongol military elite caused widespread popular unrest and elite resentment. The Mongol nobles themselves became fiercely competitive for the decreasing revenues, and fighting among Mongol factions destabilized the government. As the power of the Ilkhans frayed, the expansive ambitions of their cousins to the north, the Jochids on the Russian steppe, were aroused. In the middle fourteenth century, the Jochids began to come down through the Caucasus into the western regions of the Ilkhan empire and soon into their central territory, Azerbaijan. They aided in the dismemberment of the Ilkhan empire and briefly occupied its capital and some major cities before being displaced by the Timurids (see Chapter 8).

THE YUAN EMPIRE AND UNIFICATION OF CHINA

When Song was defeated in 1279, Kublai's empire combined all of historical China (and added, for the first time, Yunnan) with what we would now call Manchuria, lower Siberia, Mongolia, and some parts of modern Xinjiang

Province. North and South China were reintegrated after an interval of about 280 years. The opportunity to reconstruct China's administration, its political geography, and its elite culture were all presented to Kublai. It is thanks to the *History of the Yuan*—written by the inimical successors of the Yuan, the Ming (see reading notes)—that a vivid historical figure, Yelu Chucai (1190–1244), is credited with alerting Chinggis and Ogedei to the virtues of civil law and government. Yelu carried the Kitan imperial family name and was regarded as a descendant of the Kitan emperors, but in his own life was a Jin official who surrendered to the Mongols around 1215. He was known to them as "Long Beard" (Urtu Saghal), may be the last-known person to be fluent and literate in the Kitan language, and became one of the leading native officials in the Mongol occupation of North China. Yelu Chucai's instruction of Chinggis is captured in pithy exchanges in the *History*. When Chinggis taunted Chucai about being useless as a warrior, Chucai retorted that the bowyer is more important than the archer. Chinggis mused that his generals proposed razing the buildings and clearing the farms to create pastures for their horses. Yelu argued that the economic benefits of taxing the land and commerce could yield 500,000 ounces of silver, 80,000 bolts of silk, more than 120,000 bushels of millet—enough to supply many campaigns. Chinggis allowed Chucai to enlist officials to collect the taxes as an experiment, and on the basis of its success, agreed to make the system permanent. A census also proposed by Chucai, and first conducted in 1235, became the basis of a household tax and a new infantry based on the Chinese-speaking population of North China. In a separate episode, Chucai convinces Chinggis to listen to the advice of a talking chimera of some kind (deer-like but green, with a horse tail and a single horn), who advised him to go home and stop killing people.

The dialogues are likely apocryphal and were written by officials eager to attribute Mongol success in China to the interventions of a Confucian scholar (parallel to Persian historical accounts crediting Muslims with similar interventions). A comparison of contemporary documents shows that Chucai was indeed a member of the *keshig* but was a scribe (*bicigci*), the lowest rank. There is no evidence that he exercised sustained command duties outside of China. And when it came to the designs of Kublai's capitals at Shangdu and Beijing, or the name of the Yuan dynasty, or the legal structures of the Yuan, it appears that the former Jin official Liu Bingzhong was more influential than Yelu Chucai. Nevertheless Chucai was a pivotal conceptual figure. Some of his ascribed ideas had an effect on the Mongol leadership, and he was clearly a favorite of Chinggis and Ogedei. Even his fanciful ideas were often indulged—as when Ogedei permitted him to create an examination system, even though it produced a minuscule number of graduates who moved into marginal or menial offices. Chucai was also an important cultural guide for Chinggis and Ogedei. His biographers in the Ming, staunch Confucians all, took particular note of Yelu's attempts to reverse the rising tide of Daoist influence.

Yelu Chucai, among other figures noted in the Yuan history, represented the fact of northern Chinese domination over southern China, and the northern lead in reconstruction of the empire's administration and communications networks, features that would mark China's political history into the ninteenth century. Kublai intended to remain where he had been living since the 1230s, at the old Kitan and Jin southern palace compound within what is today Beijing. To bring the capital and its new population of conquerors rice, silk, cash, and whatever else was desired, the Grand Canal was reinvented. In the seventh century, the Sui empire (Chapter 3) had dug the Grand Canal to bring products from the newly developing agricultural sphere in the Yangtze Delta to the Sui capital near modern-day Xi'an, Shaanxi Province, creating an east–west axis of trade and travel. Song later destroyed the canal, fearing that it would be used by Xixia or Jin to invade. Kublai commanded that a new Grand Canal run the 1,100 miles from the same Yangtze Delta heartland north to Beijing, constructing a north–south axis in eastern China that dominates the country today.

The traditional marking of China into more than a hundred small circuits under the Tang and Song required a relatively large number of civil servants. It is probable that the Song empire at various periods was supporting a minimum of about 20,000–25,000 full-time centrally appointed officials (including governors, county magistrates, and full-time inspectors as well as a large central bureaucracy), who were paid well enough that Song may have enjoyed a relatively low level of corruption. When the Mongols first moved into North China in the time of Ogedei, their administrative circuits, each with its own enfeoffed governor and judges, were of irregular size and reporting obligations but tended to be much smaller than the Tang circuits, requiring even more officials.

In Ogedei's time, Chinese bureaucrats had used the term *zhong shusheng*—"central scribal department"—to refer to his chancellery, among whose high priorities after 1215 was consolidation of smaller units into larger, more efficient ones. Kublai's officials continued this practice and referred to the outlying administrative units as *xing zhongshusheng* (in modern Chinese, its contraction *xingsheng* is the word for "province"), meaning, roughly, "subsidiary replications of the central scribal department." The 10 provinces imposed upon the former territories of Jin and Song were clearly the direct source of the provincial boundaries of present-day China. As the name suggests, the method of expanding government was simply to replicate elements of the central bureaucracy on a small scale in each province. This replicative structure was intended to keep the government light by delegating as much responsibility as possible away from the khaghan to his aristocrats and governors in the provinces, but to allow central surveillance by standardizing offices and duties. The provinces of North China were under more direct control by the khaghan's government than the provinces of South China. But the new administrative scheme was not intended to loosen the grip on income. A special province encompassing all Mongolia and part of Siberia was treated as the khaghan's personal patrimony. Like Ogedei, Kublai insisted that wealth come to him (hence the importance of the Grand Canal) and that he would distribute salaries, stipends, and grants to those receiving them; enfeoffed aristocrats (of which there were many) were to forward grain and in-kind tribute on the traditional ratio. Kublai followed the example of his predecessors in relying heavily upon Sart officials to oversee the treasury.

Yelu Chucai, Liu Bingzhong, and a dozen other figures associated with civil government in the Yuan empire represent a characteristic aspect of Toluid government in both China and Iran. The Toluids weakened the grip of the existing elites on government by identifying and rearranging the social and cultural segments already present, to the disadvantage of the previously privileged group. In Iran/Iraq, Hulagu and his successors had leaned toward Christians and Jews and away from Sunni Muslims. In China, Kublai leaned away from the influential families of central and southern China and toward literati from the north—men who under the Song regime would have had little chance of rising to the top of the bureaucracy. This was not a matter of significant upward mobility or the creation of meaningful new opportunities for those who formerly enjoyed little or no social and cultural leverage. It was a matter of restricting the total size of government appointments and giving significant advantage in the available appointments to those who were most likely to realize their good fortune and credit it to some degree to their Toluid ruler. They were in their persons both agents and embodiments of the tendency in most Turkic regimes of the middle ages to wend toward moderation and popularization in their effects upon government as well as society and culture.

In both Toluid empires, the bureaucracy outside the census and tax system and outside the management of the imperial household was sparse or nonexistent. The traditional government functions of historiography, law, inspecting and reporting on local conditions, and hortatory rhetoric were truncated or abandoned in the interest of keeping the state small, inexpensive, and easier to manage. Kublai delegated most conflict resolution and complaints to the landed elites in the provinces and sent inspectors from time to time to assure that abuses were not sparking uprisings. He was at first unenthusiastic about anything that would give what he considered undue importance to Chinese officials—most especially, officials from southern China. He refused the examination system, whose purpose had been to supply officials that he had little need of. Yet he eventually incorporated Chinese rituals and music into his court protocols and relied upon Chinese doctors and diviners. He agreed to greater representation of Chinese philosophy in the education of his sons and began to learn the expressions of the Chinese political tradition, including "benevolent government"—which meant, in practice, not crushing farmers under the weight of the tax system. Most interesting, he agreed to restore the censorate—the panel of officials charged with observing and criticizing the emperor's behavior, which had strong parallels with Turkic collegial traditions—and the basic elements of Song civil bureaucratic structure.

Apart from the directly taxed provinces, there were external provinces, sometimes of unique political character. Korea was put under a special "conquest province" regime (see below), and Dai Viet and Champa (respectively north and south of modern-day Vietnam) were "contingent provinces" (in practice, feudatory states). Tibet was under the control of the Sakya religious sect, which reported to the khaghan through a special communications bureau (*xuanzheng yuan*). But beyond this, administrative frontier stability was never established. Even at the time of his death in 1294, Kublai was still plotting a new sea invasion of Japan (which had already failed twice) and Java (which failed in 1293). The empire was constantly challenged on the west by the Chaghatay khans of Central Asia and periodically afflicted with uprisings by unhappy farmers and local elites. The Bagan empire (in modern-day Myanmar) was a constant problem. Kublai intermittently invaded, then extracted promises of tribute, then invaded some more, and then signed a formal treaty of Bagan's submission. By the end of Kublai's life, Bagan had collapsed, but the Yuan forces had not tried very hard to set up an occupation of their own, resulting in constant, low-grade disorder along the border.

Kublai's one success at extraterritorial administration was Korea. Neither Chinggis nor Ogedei had been able to force submission of the Goryeo court, but in 1258, the decades of warfare had resulted in a devastating split in the Korean government and isolation of the king, who surrendered. The cultural losses in the war were severe, and agriculture was heavily damaged. Afterward, the relationship of the Korean court to the Kublai's court was cemented by the repeated intermarriage. By the middle fourteenth century, the Goryeo kings were mostly Mongol by descent and comfortable with the Mongolian language, dress, and custom. Many resided at Dadu, and the travel of the kings and princes and their families and entourages between China and Korea was regular. The connections provided an outlet for Korean products—most particularly cotton, which the Mongols demanded for their military uniforms and the Chinese sought as an alternative to silk, wool, or their own, more expensive cotton. Opportunities created in Korea by the Mongol occupation opened new avenues for advancement to scholars who were willing to learn and translate Mongolian, landowners who were willing to open their lands to falconry and grazing, and merchants who capitalized upon the new royal traffic to Dadu. In this and other ways, the Mongols encouraged the rise of a new, landed, educated power class in Korea.

While the Yuan khaghans viewed China, Korea, Yunnan, and Vietnam as discrete parts of their domain, they had a schematic way of viewing outside societies—as either supplicants or enemies. Immediately to their west were the descendants of Chaghatay and Ogedei, who had rejected Kublai and his successor's claims to the khaghanship and opposed the subsidiary Toluid empire in Iran. The Jochids of the Kazakh steppe were not any more pleased with the Yuan and frequently reinforced Chaghatay troops in their campaigns to drive Yuan armies out of Central Asia. The non-Toluid Chinggisids attempted to disrupt not only travel and communications between the Toluid empires but also captured in transit a good deal of cash and goods. In the early fourteenth century, the Yuan emperors hoped to call a truce in the war with Chaghatay, but this was on the cusp of the decade that saw the fragmentation of both the Yuan and Ilkhan empires, and no significant restructuring of relations between Yuan and the Chaghatay or Jochid regimes ensued.

European visitors came to Yuan China with a new variety of interests. The end of the Christian campaigns in the Levant shifted the attention of Rome away from the Ilkhans and toward the khaghans seated at Dadu. The small tradition of European churchmen sojourning in Karakorum resumed, this time with Dadu as the destination. The evidence suggests, however, that the first Europeans to successfully reach Dadu may have been merchants—the leading merchants of Venice, the Polo brothers, Maffeo and Niccolo (whose life dates are both estimated to be c. 1230–c. 1294). Their nephew Marco (1254–1324) most likely accompanied them and stayed for years in the Yuan empire, even if there are details of his lucrative written account (see Chapter 10) that appear to have been made up. The churchmen coming after were better documented: Odoric of Pordenone (1286–1331), who provided a vivid description of thirteenth-century Hangzhou; John of Monte Corvino (1247–1328), who had a long career at Dadu and was made archbishop there by the popes in the early fourteenth century once they found out he was still alive; John of Margnolli (1290–1360), whose journey through Byzantium, the Jochid territories, the Chaghatay khanate, Yuan China (where he presented the last Yuan emperor with a gigantic black horse), and Southeast Asia was only one chapter of his remarkable life. Historians consider his visit to Dadu as marking the height of the period of overland integration in Eurasia—the integration that was the mark of the Toluid period.

When the Yuan empire ended in the late fourteenth century and was succeeded by Ming, waves of Mongols migrated north from China back to Mongolia, to continue the Yuan dynasty. But Mongols long resident on the Mongolian steppe did not acknowledge the leadership of this "Later Yuan" empire, and Mongolia was divided east and west. War between these groups was frequent through the late fourteenth and fifteenth centuries. Overland trade was somewhat impeded by the continuing disorder but remained an important economic resource for the western Mongols (the Oyirods), in particular. There was also mounting trouble for the Ming empire in China, which hoped to bring all the Mongols under its domination and to convince them to render tribute (see Chapter 11). Various Mongol and Turkic groups did mount embassies to China to the extent that it made it easy for them to trade with the Chinese. They were otherwise hostile, and Ming attempts to suppress a resurgence of Mongol power led to the disastrous war of the middle fifteenth century in which the Ming emperor was captured by the Mongols and the Chinese capital at Beijing briefly attacked.

CITIES AND TERRITORIAL DEFINITION

Both the Yuan and the Ilkhan rulers built their own capitals and redefined their realms as distinct territorial entities. At its height, the Abbasid caliphate had stretched from Afghanistan in the east to Morocco in the west, and the city network around Baghdad—including Damascus, Kufa, and Basra—had been a natural strategic and cultural center. The Ilkhans were stopped at Syria by the Mamluks (see Chapter 8); they eventually controlled some of the old Seljuk territories of Anatolia but went no farther west. They preferred to establish a capital east and north of Baghdad and settled on Maragha in Azerbaijan, at the southern end of the Caucasus, though Baghdad continued as a kind of second capital. After Hulagu's death in 1265, however, his successors transferred the palace to nearby Tabriz (see Map 7.1). Its facilities were in place since the town had surrendered to Hulagu and escaped destruction. In the early fourteenth century, the Ilkhans attempted a Karakorum-like project at Sultaniyya—close to both Maragha and Tabriz—which thrived for almost two centuries but today is recognized almost solely for the tomb of Uljeitu. The Ilkhan cities became noted throughout Eurasia for their architecture, including mosques and churches built under sultanal patronage. They used the same practices that went back to the design and decoration of Ordu-Balikh: Chinese and Persian architects worked together to design the palace and city fortifications, using Chinese-style wall murals, roof figurines and flying corners, and Persian-style tiles and gardens.

Like Ordu-Balikh and Karakorum, the cities were divided into precincts by religion and social status. Outside the imperial complex, the larger city was composed of walled precincts, and outside of these were estates, gardens, and sometimes whole towns owned by aristocrats and high officials. The most famous belonged to Gazan's adviser Rashid al-Din (see Chapters 10 and 11), who claimed that his holding included 30,000 families; a couple dozen caravan stations; many hundreds of foundries; factories for papermaking, grain milling, and textile production; a mint; religious schools; and medical academies and hospitals run by doctors from Syria, Egypt, India, and China. The locations of the Ilkhan capitals were fundamental to the emerging historical distinction between Iran and Iraq. They established that the political heart of Iran lay at the southern end of the Caspian. The Safavids would use Tabriz as their capital beginning in the sixteenth century, and the Turkic Qajars would use nearby Tehran as their capital in the eighteenth century. The location oriented Persian culture less toward Syria and the Arabian Peninsula and more toward its older connections to Anatolia, Central Asia, and India.

In his capital of Dadu (see Map 7.1), Kublai set himself atop an imperial complex that had been used by the Kitan and the Jin. Much earlier cities in more or less the same space had been significant—and the Central Asian military rebels against the Tang had attempted to establish their own dynastic capital there in the mid-eighth century—but the political center of China had been a thousand miles to the west. During both Kitan and Jin, the palace complex had been rather small, concentrated in the area of present-day Beihai Lake and the White Pagoda in the Forbidden City. A portion of the Mongols' old palace grounds is still closed off for the use of the mysterious and powerful at Zhongnanhai. Beginning in 1266, Kublai expanded the palace complex with the help of Chinese and Persian architects and engineers. A hammered earthen wall (small portions of which can still be seen) separated it from the rest of the city. Like Karakorum, the city was transected by wide north–south avenues suitable for horse troops and caravan stations. Buildings resembled earlier Chinese capitals, and Kublai underscored its Chinese elements by including a new temple to Confucius, as well as Heaven, earth, and moon. But the imperial city was given a Mongol touch by decorative furs and wide spaces where Kublai, his comrades, and sons lived in yurts for weeks at a time. He was reported to have brought grass from Mongolia to be planted in his palace grounds in Dadu. With its permanent artery, the Grand Canal, linking it to the developing agricultural and commercial center in the Yangtze River delta, the site of Dadu would—with only brief interruptions—remain the imperial capital, Beijing, until the twentieth century and continue as the national capital thereafter.

Kublai did not neglect his earlier capital at Shangdu (the Xanadu of Marco Polo, who probably visited it in 1275). It was a still a tiny complex about a square mile in size, inside which was the walled palace compound. Kublai lavished resources on Shangdu to the extent that development of his capital at Dadu may have been impeded, which is symbolic of his view of himself as owner of Mongolia and khaghan of the (now ghostly) Great Mongol ulus. Like Dadu, Shangdu was defined and protected by hammered earthen walls. Outside the city was a hunting park—Coleridge's "stately pleasure dome"—where Kublai and his courtiers practiced the traditional skills of riding and shooting.

THE TOLUID EXCHANGE

Dadu and Tabriz/Maragha anchored the far ends of a system of material and intellectual exchange that rewrote everyday life, culture, science, and technology not only in parts of China and Iran but also in the cities that were continually influenced by the Eurasian trends of the Toluid period, particularly Delhi, Moscow, Constantinople, Baghdad, and Damascus. The fact of travel between Iran and China was not new. The trade network had been in operation for centuries, and its traffic had burgeoned in Abbasid–Tang times. But the Toluid exchanges were faster and richer than previous (see Maps 1.3 and 7.1). Dadu had its large sector inhabited by Sart merchants, scholars, technicians, and soldiers, and a number of cities across Azerbaijan had Chinese quarters, with a few rural towns being virtually entirely composed of Chinese residents. The overland system was enhanced by a certain amount of standardization in security, fees, currency, and formats for hosteling and resupply. The commercial tax, because it involved a stamped endorsement, was simply called the "stamp" (*tamgha*—stamp, seal, medal, brand, or a flag with a seal image upon it) by the Mongols and eventually became a feature of trade throughout Eurasia. Tokens of endorsement (sometimes seen by historians as ancestors of the passport) were issued by Yuan and Ilkhan governments to assure safe passage of legal travelers, and garrisons of Yuan or Ilkhan soldiers oversaw as much as they could of the roads. The postal system (see Chapter 6) provided an infrastructure of regular stations, services and security that grew and expanded their facilities for storage, public hostel-

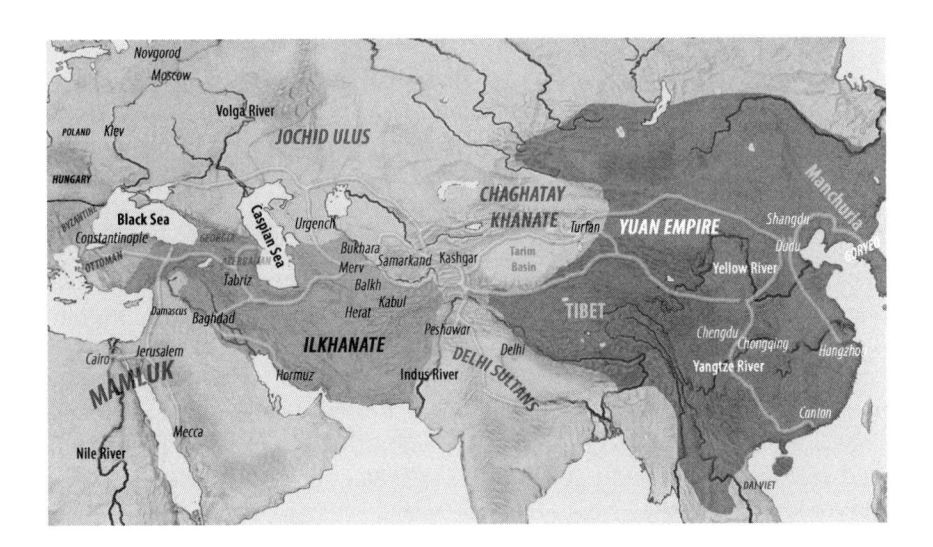

Map 7.1. The Toluid era, c. 1250–1370.

ing, horse markets, and entertainments (most lucrative among them, prostitution). Corporations—in some instances based upon long-distance lineage connections—in China and Iran provided credit to merchants sending goods over the roads. Towns along the Persian Gulf grew as transit points for North African goods joining the caravans in Azerbaijan and Iran. Tabriz itself increased hugely in size, and today is still the largest city in northwestern Iran. In a similar way, towns along the South China coast—Guangzhou (Canton), Quanzhou (Xiamen), and Huizhou perhaps most prominently—prospered as Southeast Asian goods arrived by sea to connect to the eastern end of the trade road network.

The exchanges in material goods brought intertwining influences on clothing design, decorative motifs, musical styles and instruments, and cuisine. Painting in both Iran and China was discernibly influenced. Chinese dumplings and rice dishes became popular in Iran, and Persian melons and spices became part of Chinese cuisine. Cotton produced in Transoxiana and Korea found ready markets in China and Iran. Paper, ink, and woodblock mass-printed contracts as well as popular and religious literature (see Chapter 10) moved east and west across the network. Bookkeeping techniques were shared, and the Muslim abacus arrived in China. But perhaps the most profound impact came from the sharing of scientific and technological knowledge. Messengers between Maragha/Tabriz and Dadu carried books and scientific instruments across the continent. Hulagu established a new observatory and research academy at Maragha and brought together the leading astronomers and mathematicians from the Islamic and the Chinese world. It may have been partly inspired by the Ismaili headquarters at Mount Alamut in the Alburz Mountains, which he had destroyed in 1256.

Certainly, Hulagu's adviser Nasir al-Din Tusi (1201–1274; see Chapter 9), who had been recruited or captured at Mount Alamut, was a leading influence on the design and construction at Maragha. Hulagu knew something of Tusi's reputation as a mathematician and put him in charge of a number of critical financial affairs. He also knew of Tusi's fame as an observational astronomer and relied upon him to predict eclipses and identify auspicious dates. Finally, Hulagu relied upon Tusi as an astrologer, and may have initiated his campaigns against Baghdad when Tusi's readings indicated the time was right. As both a manager and an intellectual, Tusi was perhaps the most important Persian figure of the Toluid period. The academy he created produced astronomical tables and mathematical formulae that continued to be influential for centuries afterward. Christian colleagues at Maragha translated the academy's mathematical and astronomical work into Greek, and the translations found an audience in Constantinople, where scholars had followed Seljuk-period work of Islamic mathematicians and philosophers for a century. There was particular interest in the close critiques of Ptolemy's views of the solar system. Tusi himself speculated upon the relationships of spheres of unequal size circling each other within a scheme of epicycles, attempting a better explanation for retrograde motion of the planets. Historians of astronomy now believe that Copernicus (who made clear that he knew something of the work of Persian and Iraqi astronomers of the Seljuk period) saw translations of Tusi's notebooks at some point, most likely transmitted from Constantinople to Rome.

The influence of Maragha in Dadu is also remarkable. Hulagu had promised to send Tusi to Mongolia to construct an observatory for Mongge, but after Mongge's death such ambitions shifted to Dadu, where Kublai established a Maragha-style academy that included an imposing observatory and a large library. Maragha had been built on a natural mesa, but Kublai had none available on the relatively flat plain around Dadu. Instead, he had an elevated observatory dating to the Jin era that Ogedei had restored. On the site, Kublai had an enormous new artificial platform built, the predecessor of the great observatory (elaborated in Ming times) that now stands on East Chang'an Street in Beijing. The Chinese had a long tradition in observational astronomy, and Kublai ordered that a replica of a famous Song-period celestial clock—basically a huge mechanized armillary sphere—be built at the new observatory. The foremost Chinese mathematician, Guo Shoujing (1231–1316), was appointed head astronomer, and Sart Bukharan mathematician Jamal al-Din (f. 1255–1291) was dispatched from Hulagu with designs and metallurgical specifications for armillary spheres of the precision used at Maragha, as well as the first globe known in China. The Turkic and Mongol fascination with the sky as both a spiritual and a navigational resource rapidly recalibrated itself from folk wisdom to science.

Acknowledging two academic traditions as well as two languages, Kublai established two separate academies, and one of their shared missions was to improve demarcations of the summer and winter solstices. The double legacies in mathematics and astronomy, combined with the use of vertical indicators for observing solar movement—gnomons—across the huge expanse of the Yuan empire led to much better calculations as well as acknowledgment of both a solar (which Guo Shoujing calculated to 365.25 days) and a lunar year. The groups, led by Guo, also contributed to major engineering and water-conservancy projects around Dadu. In these exchanges, the Chinese contributed to West Asian mathematics the concept of decimal fractions, and West Asians coming to China brought along their development of algebra, trigonometry, and cartography. The astronomical and mathematical exchanges between Maragha and Dadu were perhaps the most spectacular and today the best-known achievements of Toluid science, but they were only part of a complex that included pharmacology, anatomy, agronomy, botany, and clinical medicine. Turkic rulers before the Mongols had usually kept a Chinese doctor in residence, and Kublai—who may have suffered from gout—was no different. The dynastic history details his attempts to supplement the medical staff with Indians, Persians, Koreans, and Uighurs, although the medical schools he ordered founded in the provinces were overwhelmingly staffed with Chinese who might in other times have had civil service careers. Both the Ilkhans and the Yuan had a keen interest in the most exact possible representation of their large and complex territories. In the Islamic world, experiments to build on Greek concepts of cartography had gone on for a few hundred years, attempting to represent and precisely place geographic features on a convex global surface. Some had coordinated space and time, using astronomical tables to check distances on land and sea, suggesting good knowledge of longitude, which Europeans would not master until the eighteenth century. In 1267, Jamal al-Din presented Kublai with a colored grid map based upon these centuries of Abbasid science. From Kublai's court, grid-based cartography spread to Korea, where this style of large-scale mapping became better rooted than in late medieval China. For at least two centuries, the Muslim world would be regarded in China as the source of cartographic knowledge.

A direct effect of the Mongol occupation of China was the development of destructive gunpowder and practical weapons. China is often given credit for the invention of gunpowder, but anecdotal evidence in the Chinese records traces its source to a Sogdian Buddhist monk of the sixth century, which suggests that it was a Central Asian knowledge. The combination of charcoal and saltpeter was described by the monk as having wondrous powers for alchemical transformation of elements, and in this connection he mentioned sulfur as well. Evidence from painting and poetry indicates that when Byzantine artisans in the seventh century learned to use naphtha in an instrument that functioned like a flamethrower, the Chinese quickly learned it too. This may also have been a Central Asian skill, for some of the earliest devices for distilling naphtha have been found in the Gandhara region. By the eleventh century the Chinese made and used flamethrowers based on the slow igniting of naphtha or gunpowder in a long tube. The weapons were used not only to intimidate and injure foot soldiers and horses but also to ignite thatched roofs in hostile villages and, occasionally, to set fire to enemy ships and riggings. The Song learned to enrich the saltpeter to increase nitrate in the mixture and, in this way, produced percussive explosions. Launched from catapults, canisters filled with the explosives could rupture fortifications or inflict mass casualties. Ships could be set afire from a distance. It appears that the Song were also the first to experiment with the construction of barrels from which to project gunpowder explosions. Their earliest devices were broad and squat, carried on special wagons to their emplacements. From the mouths of the barrels projected the gunpowder mixed with scattershot minerals that would in turn be ignited by the firing of the gun. The Chinese also learned to use gunpowder to fire masses of burning arrows over enemy fortifications.

But it was the Mongols who used Song expertise to develop cannons, and the likelihood is that a Toluid exchange of Chinese chemistry and West Asian metallurgy was the crucible. Indeed, in 1280, in the immediate aftermath of the conquest of Song, the Yuan were creating their first weapon featuring a projectile that completely filled the mouth of the gun, concentrating the explosive force. They used cast bronze for the barrel and iron for the ball. The new weapon could be aimed better and shot farther than the earlier devices of the Song. At the same time, its ability to tear through brick, wood, and flesh without suffering destruction itself was unprecedented. Knowledge of the cannon and ball flashed westward across Eurasia. By the end of the century, more accurate and mobile cannons were being produced in the Ilkhanate, and no later than 1327, the small, squat cannons, called "bombards," were being produced in Europe. The ideas of lengthening the barrels for accuracy and making the cannons smaller and more portable probably arose independently in eastern and western Eurasia. The fourteenth century saw the emergence of a great variety of guns, from enormous cannons pulled by teams of horses to small mortar launchers that could be carried by individual soldiers. As cannons became more powerful, the philosophy behind the construction of fortifications changed. Castles built around residential complexes were now vulnerable to bombardment over their walls, and the functional construction of walled towns and residences declined after the fourteenth century across Eurasia—an exception was Japan, where cannon technology was poorly developed. The discovery and improvement of guns and cannons under the Mongols is only one side of the application of gunpowder science. Chemists in China used knowledge of formulae related to gunpowder to construct noxious gas pellets that would not only paralyze enemies but also expel evil spirits and reduce the populations of disease-carrying insects. Gunpowder was used for mining excavations, canal building, and irrigation. From Tang times gunpowder was also used in China or fireworks displays on ceremonial occasions, which delighted European visitors to Karakorum and Dadu who saw such things for the first time.

The Ilkhans frequently relied upon the information exchange network to solicit political and strategic advice from Kublai. At his end, these communications were often handled by Bolad Chingsang (Bolad Aqa, d. 1313), a Mongol aristocrat whose family had been affiliated with Chinggis Khan's household. Bolad was educated with the Chinggisid princes, served successfully in the military, and showed an early talent for translation from Chinese to Mongolian. He was an extraordinarily capable and often ruthless individual, equally effective on the battlefield and in the interrogation chamber. By the 1260s, he was one of Kublai's most trusted advisers and was ordered to work with Chinese officials to select traditional Chinese institutions and rituals to be employed at the Yuan court. He was also a valued addition to Kublai's creation of an imperial library and development of the observatory academy. Bolad was by all appearances Kublai's indispensable man—leading military projects for occupation and policing of Song territories, reforming the military appointment practices, and consulting on convergence of Mongolian and Chinese law and bureaucracy at Dadu. Perhaps his most dramatic demonstration of importance came after the 1282 murder of Kublai's Sart treasurer Ahmad Fanakati, who was accused of cruelty and corruption by Chinese officials. Bolad investigated the case and executed the apparent assassins but provided Kublai proof that Ahmad had indeed been as criminal as his opponents had charged; an infuriated Kublai ordered Ahmad's body desecrated and his male relatives executed.

Not long afterward, Kublai made the decision to send Bolad to the Ilkhan court (then presided over by Hulagu's grandson Arghun). It was intended as a temporary mission of communications and aid, but when Bolad and his assistant (named "Jesus"—Isa) tried to return to China, they were intercepted by a Chaghatay army; in the fray they were separated, and Bolad returned to Tabriz while Isa managed to get back to Dadu. Bolad was received as a permanent adviser sent by the khaghan to the Ilkhanate. He quickly became a powerful and feared figure at Tabriz as he had been in Dadu. He showed some skill at negotiating between rival Mongol factions and was of some use to the Ilkhans in staving off fatal fissures in the ruling military class. But his primary policy influence came with Gazan's seizure of the throne in 1295. This was when he formed his partnership with Gazan's primary adviser (and vizier) Rashid al-Din (1247–1318)—a partnership sometimes seen as the dual embodiment of the cross-continental Toluid exchange. From Bolad, Rashid al-Din learned and recorded a great many details of Yuan government and technology, including the traditional Chinese practice of using inked fingerprints to verify signers of documents, the functions of the censorate, and the collection and management of imperial archives. More profound was the access to a new historiographical vision that Bolad's collaboration afforded Rashid al-Din. The two streams of Mongol and Muslim narratives on the early history of the Mongols merged, and Rashid al-Din asserted that it was only because of the God-endorsed conquests of the descendants of Chinggis Khan that a new awareness of the breadth and pluralities of human experience was possible (see Chapter 10).

There were also great dangers to the exchange. The Europe from which Rubruck, da Pian del Carpini, and the Polos traveled had been free of plague for nearly five centuries. The West Asian world of Ibn Battuta had seen no plague since about the year 1200. Song China had contained plague by use of building codes and urban hygiene, but the bacillus had lingered in the highlands of the Dali kingdom of Yunnan. After the conquest of Dali, military and supply traffic provided the means for carrying plague from Yunnan to central China, northwestern China, and across Central Asia. Along the routes, rats, marmots, and other desert rodents were massively infected and passed the disease on to dogs and people, who passed it among themselves. The caravan traffic across both the deserts and the steppes of Central Asia infected the caravan towns. In the 1330s, communities of Turkic Uzbeks involved in the caravans were devastated by plague. In 1338, a Nestorian town near Issyk Kul was nearly depopulated. The Jochid Mongols were incapacitated by the plague during their assault on Kaffa, in Crimea, in 1346. A single account (written by a man most likely not present) of Mongols catapulting diseased corpses over the city walls might be true. Crimea was permanently infiltrated by plague. From there, both Europe and Egypt would be repeatedly infected by fleas from rats, cats, and sailors aboard ships bound across the Mediterranean. Exactly what the "Black Death" was is still sometimes debated, but bubonic plague was clearly one of the diseases at work, weakening the resistance of urban populations in particular and unleashing new waves of latent illness. Typhus, influenza, and smallpox traveled with the plague, constituting the great pandemic of 1347–1352. The human and cultural damage that resulted was perhaps greater than any of the direct consequences of the military conquests of Chinggis or his heirs. Though it is tempting to associate the social disorder of conquest with the plague as twin illnesses, it was not the Mongol invaders themselves who brought the disease but the trade made possible by Mongol assurance of the safety and order of the Eurasian trade routes. Peace and profit, in this case, were the channels by which pandemic illness ravaged Eurasia in the middle fourteenth century.

TOLUID PHYSIOCRACY

Across the range of Mongol empires of the thirteenth and fourteenth centuries, merchants rose in society and often to high political influence. Since the time of Chinggis, the income of Mongol elites had depended not only on taxing a thriving overland trade but also in investing, together with Sartic partners, in corporations financing and managing caravans. This elevation of merchants was a novelty in China, where merchants were by convention regarded as parasites on society whose greed had to be restrained by severe government surveillance and intervention. This was a rhetorical convention only since, during the Song period in particular, many landholding families had begun to invest heavily in transportation and sales of manufactured goods, finance, and urban entertainment. But the muting of official disapproval of merchants was a change for urban life. Many of the great families of the Song period who had spent much of their fortunes on the education of their sons for competition in the examinations and entry into government service had to find other uses for their money. Most commercial activities, from financing of caravans to tax farming to loaning money to the Mongol aristocracy, were managed through Sart financial partnerships, often originally based in the Ilkhan territories. In Yuan China, the corporations were first made up of Sartic immigrants, but the Chinese later purchased places in them. The result was a brilliant urban life in many parts of the Toluid world. It was financially enriched by the overland trade and its domestic tendrils as well as building projects at Dadu and the entire expanse of the Grand Canal. It was culturally enriched by the flow of money into urban entertainments (including theater, which was strongly nurtured by the imperial court and the Mongol elites; see Chapter 10). In Iran, Iraq, and Azerbaijan, well-connected cities, especially those producing goods for export, also showed evidence of economic and cultural rebound. Whether in the Ilkhan or the Yuan territories, whether on land or in the Persian Gulf or the China coast, important trade cities had a similar experience, with rises in wealth and population.

The countryside was another story. Some rural areas with strong market connections to thriving cities began to recover quickly. Silk-producing areas of China or carpet-producing towns in Iran, for instance, prospered once the terrors of the conquests had passed. It appears that cottage industries connected to the urban economies and overland trade continued to advance under the Toluids. The cultivation of mulberry trees and cotton fields and the construction of irrigation systems (encouraged by the Toluids, who had a great interest in irrigation systems and favored those of West Asia), dams, and water wheels were all common features of village technology. The production and dissemination of handbooks describing techniques for farming, harvesting, threshing, and butchering thrived. Villagers also continued to worship technological innovators as local gods. In China, one of the most interesting of these cults, the worship of Huang Dao Po, who brought her special knowledge of cotton growing, spinning, and weaving from her native Hainan island to the fertile Yangtze River Delta, began under the Yuan. But more remote areas often lingered for long periods with abandoned fields, wells poisoned by unrecovered human and animal corpses, ruined irrigation systems, and broken roads and bridges. In some areas, Mongol and Turkic nomads moved into the countryside and took the best land, often damaging adjacent land with their livestock or horses. Poorly supervised soldiers and even Buddhist monks under the protection of the Yuan court raided villages to take what they wanted. Taxes, excessive extraction by tax farmers, and forced tribute continued to crush much of the rural economy. The discretion permitted not only to tax collectors but also to land grantees (almost all Mongols or high-ranking Sart officials) was a huge problem in both China and Iran, diminishing returns to the imperial treasury and inciting disorders among desperate farmers. Refugees from intolerable rural conditions, migrants in search of work, or farmers fleeing oppressive tax collection created a continual stream of transient populations into less settled or regulated regions.

Rural conditions are assumed to be part of the explanation for sharp drops in population in China and Iran during the Toluid period. Many historians in the early twentieth century believed that, on the basis of figures reported for the slaughters of the conquests and, later, plague, the two regions might have lost as much as 90 percent of their populations. More recently, historians have estimated a possible drop in China from about 110 million at the end of the Song to 60 or 70 million at the end of the Yuan. Historians of Iran still sometimes quote a "90 percent" figure, but it is difficult to estimate the losses when averaged across regions. Documentary evidence shows rural localities in northern China losing as much as five-sixths of their populations over the entire thirteenth and early fourteenth centuries. Though it is commonly assumed that the 25 to 30 percent of European population killed by the Black Death were overwhelmingly urban, in both Iran and China, plague ravaged both the cities and the countryside (where farmers, truckers, and merchants often lived closely together in village compounds). What is now known of bubonic plague suggests that it is airborne only in its last stage and, in its early stages (when the carrier was most likely to encounter a significant number of people), could be contracted only by contact with skin pustules. Rural communities in both China and Iran could be densely packed even if widely spaced. This could have been a factor in wider dissemination of disease than in Europe. Or the descriptions of Black Death as primarily an urban affliction could be overdone.

Yet demographic history—and particularly the effects of trauma and policy upon it—is always tentative. Census figures in China have never been truly exact (since they have always focused on tax payers and men eligible for military service), and passages of apparent drop in population are hard to attribute with any specificity to violent death, indirect deaths from disease, suppressed birth rates, or displacement of living populations from census records. In Iran, war with the Mongols was continuous from the 1220s to 1260. In China, there was continuous warfare between 1215 and 1279. China's sharper population losses in the north may have been due to the massive southward movement of people attempting to flee before the Mongols' advance, and it is clear that the fall of Song also precipitated migrations to Southeast Asia. Any or all of these could be factors in the dramatic diminution of population suggested in the records.

Surviving records are not the only indicators of demographic distortion. Scientists today note a gross change in environmental conditions of the period of Toluid domination of the major population centers of temperate Eurasia. Specifically, they document a prolonged decline in carbon dioxide levels, of the sort that only a few periods of history evince. A reasonable hypothesis is the concatenation of changes associated with war, random violence, disease, and economic mismanagement in the populous Yuan empire particularly. Overall, it seems reasonable to assume that China's population losses through death, non-birth, and migration may well have amounted to 40 percent, and there is every reason to believe that Iran's proportional losses were at least equal or greater. Nevertheless, neither of these populations could have been reduced by 90 percent, or even 60 percent. The genetic history of China suggests no bottleneck or major displacements corresponding to this period. Iran's story may be slightly different. Today's female-line genomes show long and intimate connections to Iraq and the Persian Gulf, probably dating to the early Iranian empire's colonization of the Arab world. But male-line genetics suggest a distinct (though not majority) influx of Central Asian markers, most likely the effect of the continuous arrival of nomadic warriors, primarily Turks, from Sasanian times on and continuing in greater volume through the Ilkhan and subsequent periods of Turkic domination.

Population reduction of some significant degree can nevertheless be assumed for both China and Iran, and in itself would have had a marked effect on tax revenue. But collection practices were additional problems. Tax farmers acting within the law arrived in villages with armed enforcers who dealt harshly with residents reluctant to surrender the demanded amount in grain, textiles, or cash. Neither Toluid regime provided sufficient inspectors to compel tax farmers or civil tax officials to obey the law—many tax farmers were more like heads of protection rackets who demanded any amount of money they thought they could extract. The exorbitant rates to which the countryside was subjected drove many landowners into debt and servitude and prevented the reinvestment necessary to maintain productivity. Many taxes were collected in kind; this confiscation of staples together with the drop in production arising from war damage and population dislocation caused the price of grains to rise so much that it became difficult for the governments to procure supplies for the soldiers' granaries. Both governments appropriated land to acquire grain directly or expand grazing for army horses. This could avoid the effects (for the imperial treasury) of market fluctuations, but it rapidly shrank the tax base further. The result was that near the end of the thirteenth century, agriculture in both regimes was depressed, rural populations were in flight, and revenues intended to support the army and the bureaucracy were reduced to a trickle. At the same time, Mongols who had been settled as *tamma* soldiers were sometimes, decades later, unemployed and selling themselves into slavery to survive.

By the later thirteenth centuries, the Yuan and Ilkhan rulers noticed what historians notice today: their rural sectors were in decline, yielding far too little in tax revenue, and failing to support the urban sectors adequately. They became, at least in their pronouncements, confirmed physiocrats. They intended to protect both the productivity of the countryside and, as a corollary of that, the welfare of the farmers. Land and taxation were handled on roughly the same scheme by the two Toluid regimes. In the earliest phases, land that had previously belonged to Song or Abbasid aristocrats was appropriated by the conquerors for themselves. Some of the land was distributed as *ulus* to Chinggisid kinsmen or high-ranking generals, and a major portion was retained for the ruler to cover the costs of himself and his household. In accord with Turkic tradition, these lands included as a matter of course all the farmers and technicians resident on them, all managed by a special office. Remaining land was either retained by landed gentry who capitulated or were given to favored officials as private property; in Iran, some land was already entailed as the property of religious foundations, which the Ilkhans tended to respect. The establishment of the military and noble estates profoundly affected Mongol life. Common Mongols were permanently settled in their locations, and nomadism among the Toluid Mongols went into a decline. The noble estates came to depend less on pastoralism and more on agriculture.

After the exposure of Ahmad Fanakati's corruption of the tax system in 1282, Kublai was convinced that, although pillaging the Chinese countryside was an effective way to conduct a raiding economy, great wealth was a matter of long-term cultivation. The *History of the Yuan* credits Bolad with the advice that heralded a new policy: "Agriculture and sericulture is the source of clothing and food; if one does not devote attention to the source, the people will not have sufficient clothing and food, culture cannot flourish, and kingly government, for this reason, will not come to the fore here. You should be willing to consider this." It was in response to this advice that Kublai ordered creation of the new bureaucratic office (supervised by Bolad) to rebuild the rural infrastructure, revitalize its markets, and educate farmers. The connection between agricultural reform in the Yuan and the Ilkhanate is incarnate in the person of Bolad, who after immigrating to Iran, shared with Arghun and then Gazan, the principles of long-term rural curatorship.

Rashid al-Din, urging the Muslim principles of compassion and economic community, pressed the same message. Gazan agreed and admonished his aristocrats, "If you wish to be certain of collecting grain and food for your tables in the future, I must be harsh with you. You must be taught reason. If you insult the farmers, take their oxen and seed, and trample their crops into the ground, what will you do in the future?" Gazan ordered an updated land assessment and stipulated precise sums to be levied in each locality. He provided cash grants to enslaved Mongols so that they could buy their freedom, and many were later enrolled in a new military unit commanded by Bolad. Gazan's accountants adopted the Abbasid methods of daily bookkeeping, using hierarchies of space and time to accumulate both the recording of real income and the estimation of future revenue. Tax rates were lowered not only on agricultural produce but also on the transport of goods. Farmers were no longer required to provide housing, food, or draft animals to soldiers on demand; physical abuse of farmers by landholders was forbidden; and the values of silver currency were stipulated and standardized across the realm. Paper money modeled on Kublai's notes had been introduced a few years before Gazan seized the throne, and soon after his succession Gazan ordered the notes seized and destroyed. The reasons for his eradication of paper money are not clear, but it is likely to have been related to the failure of the paper currency to either replenish the silver stores in the Ilkhanate coffers, or gain the confidence of Iran's populace.

The Toluid focus on the principles of appreciating and protecting agriculture began to show some effects in both China and Iran/Iraq by the turn of the fourteenth century. While all Chinggisid regimes across Eurasia (see Chapter 8) continued to privilege soldiers, merchants, and some spiritual leaders, the Toluids also were careful to foster improvements in agriculture and revere the native institutions of rural landholding. It would be too much to say that in either case an appreciation of the actual cultivators resulted—the "peasants" were not respected in law or in imperial edict. What each regime did recognize, however, was the way in which traditional values of Islam and Confucianism protected agricultural productivity, the stability of grain markets, and the status of landholding gentry and aristocrats. As a consequence, both the Yuan and the Ilkhans earned the respect, however grudging, of literate elites.

The acceptance, however, seems never to have become broadly rooted in the rural population. By the middle fourteenth century, both the Yuan empire and the Ilkhanate were regularly afflicted by rural uprisings objecting to the lighter-but-still-heavy tax burdens, the lesser-but-still-occurring predations by aristocrats and rogue troops, and what were perceived as unjust decisions by Toluid governors or overseers. These objections combined with tensions among the Mongol aristocrats in both regimes and repeated incursions from Chaghatay or the Jochids to pile crushing pressures on the two slender governments. The Yuan empire was split by civil war among the Mongol elites; weakened by floods, epidemics, and inflated grain prices; and then overwhelmed by a huge rural uprising in 1368. The leader of the rebellion declared himself the emperor of the new Ming dynasty. In the Ilkhanate, officials at the court of Abu Sa'id accused Rashid al-Din of still being a Jew who had falsely claimed to have converted to Islam, and implicated him in the death of Gazan's brother (and successor as sultan) Uljeitu. Rashid al-Din was beheaded in 1318. After Abu Sa'id death in 1335 with no designated heir, Ilkhan leaders were unable to find a political solution to the succession; they quickly split the regime and attempted a disunited defense against rural uprisings as well as invasions from the Jochid khanate on the northeast and from the Mamluks on the west. The Ilkhanate dissolved in stages, ending with the death of the last recognized ruler, Togha-Temur, in 1353. In the countryside, landowners returned to the unrestrained exploitation of Hulagu's time. Though neither succeeded in establishing a lasting economic base they foreshadowed early modern theories of management and social hierarchy, and sparked cultural that would continue for centuries.

READING NOTES: EMPIRES OF THE TOLUIDS

For general background on this period, see the classic text, John Andrew Boyle, *The Successors of Genghis Khan* (Columbia UP, 1971), a partial translation of Rashid al-Din's history (see Chapters 10 and 11). Also indispensable is Boyle's edited *The Cambridge History of Iran, Volume 5: The Saljuq and Mongol Periods* (Cambridge UP, 1968). Thomas Allsen is the main source of the discussion here of Bolad Chingsang (the latter a title used for a high-ranking minister, a *darughaci*, or a director of the *keshig*); see Kai-lung Ho, "The Office and Noble Titles of the Mongols from the 14th to the 16th Century, and the Study of the 'White History' *Cayan Teüke*," *Central Asiatic Journal* 59, no. 1/2 (2016): 133–177; see Thomas Allsen, *Mongol Imperialism: The Policies of the Grand Qan Möngke in China, Russia and the Islamic Lands, 1251-1259* (U California P, 1987) and *Culture and Conquest in Mongol Eurasia* (Cambridge UP, 2001). See also Michal Biran, "Central Asia from the Conquest of Chinggis Khan to the Rise of Tamerlane: The Ögodeied and Chaghadaid Realms," in *The Cambridge History of Inner Asia, Volume 2*, ed. Golden, di Cosmo, Frank (Chapter 6 reading notes); Frederick W. Mote, *Imperial China 900-1800* (Harvard UP, 2003) and David M. Robinson, *Empire's Twilight: Northeast Asia under the Mongols* (Harvard East Asia, 2009). David Morgan's classic essay, "Who Ran the Mongol Empire?" *Journal of the Royal Asiatic Society of Great Britain and Ireland* 1 (1982): 124–136 is now regarded by its author as wrong; see his "Mongol or Persian? The Government of Ilkhanid Iran," *Harvard Middle Eastern and Islamic Review* 3, (1996): 62–76; Morgan's revisionist approach to Ilkhan imperial dissolution is found in "The Decline and Fall of the Mongol Empire," *Journal of the Royal Asiatic Society* 19, no. 4 (2009): 427–437, where he explains his skepticism regarding the factionalism hypothesis as the cause of Ilkhan disintegration.

In addition to the relevant chapters of David Morgan's *The Mongols*, see also "The Mongols in Iran: A Reappraisal," *Iran* 42 (2004): 131–136—which is an overview of scholarship from Ann K. S. Lambton to Charles Melville—and "The 'Great *Yasa* of Chingiz Khan' and Mongol Law in the Ilkhanate," in *Muslims, Mongols and Crusaders*, ed. Gerald Hawting (Routledge, 2012). See also Allsen's remarkable chapter, "Historiography," in *Commodity and Exchange in the Mongol Empire: A Cultural History of Islamic Textiles* (Cambridge UP, 1997). From Michal Biran, see primarily "The Mongol Conquest of Baghdad Revisited: Violence and Restoration According to Contemporaneous Biographical Sources," in *Chinggis Khan and Globalization*, ed. T. S. Tserendorj and N. Khishigt (Mongolian Academy of Science, 2014), 321–327; "The Islamization of Hülegü: Imaginary Conversion in the Ilkhanate," *Journal of the Royal Asiatic Society* 6, no. 1-2 (2016): 79–88 and "Music in the Conquest of Baghdad: Safi al-Din Urmawi and the Ilkhanids Circle of Musicians," in *The Mongols in the Middle East*, ed. Bruno De Nicola and Charles Melville (Brill, 2016), 33–154.

Though Il-khan as "subordinate" khan fits much of the career of Hulagu (and also its few uses by the Jochids), it is possible to read it differently, as "sovereign" khan (remembering that this was not an age in which sovereignty and subordinacy were read as seriously dichotomous as they are today). See the discussion of this in Peter Jackson, *The Mongols and the Islamic World* (Chapter 6 reading notes), 139. If "sovereign khan" was the intended meaning of "il-khan"—and the fact that it did not appear on Hulagu's coins until Mongge was dead—then it would neatly parallel the Ilkhans's use of "padishah" as title of the ruler. On use of *il-khan* as a generic term, see Reuven Amitai, "Evidence for Early Use of the Title *ilkhan* among the Mongols," *Journal of the Royal Asiatic Society* 301 (1991): 353–362 and Michael Hope, "Some Remarks about the Use of the Term *īlkhān* in the Historical Sources and in Modern Historiography," *Central Asiatic Journal* 60, no. 1/2 (2017): 273–299.

On economic and financial aspects of the Toluid period, see Joel Mokyr, *The Lever of Riches: Technological Creativity and Economic Progress* (Oxford UP, 1990) and John Butcher and Howard Dick, *The Rise and Fall of Revenue Farming: Business Elites and the Emergence of the Modern State* (St. Martin's P, 1993). For Allsen's translation of Kublai's instruction to the Mongols to change attitudes toward farmers, see *Culture and Conquest*, 67; compare to Gazan's instructions on the same point from I. P. Petrushevsky, "The Socio-Economic Conditions of Iran under the Ilkhans," in *The Cambridge History of Iran, Volume 5: The Saljuq and Mongol Periods*, ed. J. A. Boyle (Cambridge UP, 1968), 494.

More recent background texts on the Ilkhans are Michael Hope, *Power, Politics and Tradition in the Mongol Empire and the Ilkhanate of Iran* (Oxford UP, 2016); George E. Lane, *Early Mongol Rule in Thirteenth-Century Iran: A Persian Renaissance* (Routledge, 2003); Judith Kolbas, *The Mongols in Iran: Chingiz Khan to Uljaytu 1220-1309* (Routledge, 2006); and Julian Raby and Teresa Fitzherbert, eds., *The Court of the Il-khans, 1290-1340* (Oxford UP, 1996). See also George E. Lane, "The Mongols in Iran," in *The Oxford Handbook of Iranian History*, ed. Tourai Daryaee (Oxford UP, 2012), 243–270 and John Andrew Boyle, "Some Thoughts on the Sources for the Il-Khanid Period of Persian History," *Iran* 12 (1974): 185–188.

Other sources that have been helpful for this chapter include Muhammad al-Faruque, "The Mongol Conquest of Baghdad: Medieval Accounts and Their Modern Assessments," *Islamic Quarterly* 32 (1988): 194–206; Charles

Melville, "The Keshig in Iran," in *Beyond the Legacy of Genghis Khan*, ed. Linda Komaroff (Brill, 2006), 135–164; George Lane, "Arghun Aqa: Mongol Bureaucrat," *Iranian Studies* 32, no. 4 (Autumn, 1999): 459–482; I. P. Petrushevsky, "The Socio-Economic Condition of Iran Under the Il-khans," in *The Cambridge History of Iran, Volume 5: The Saljuq and Mongol Periods*, ed. J. A. Boyle (Cambridge UP, 1968), 483–537; M. Minovi and V. Minorsky, "Naṣīr al-Din Tūsī on Finance," *Bulletin of the School of Oriental and African Studies* 10, no. 3 (1940): 755–789; John Masson Smith Jr., "Mongol Manpower and Persian Population," *Journal of the Economic and Social History of the Orient* 18, no. 3 (1975): 271–299; and A. Bausani, "Religion Under the Mongols," in *The Cambridge History of Iran, Volume 5: The Saljuq and Mongol Periods*, ed. J. A. Boyle, (Cambridge UP, 1968), 538–549 (covers the conversion of Gazan).

On Ilkhan struggles and accommodations with other states see, Reuven Amitai, *Mongols and Mamluks: The Mamluk–Ilkhanid War, 1260–1281* (Cambridge UP, 1995); Marshal G. S. Hodgson, "The Isma'ili State," in *The Cambridge History of Iran, Volume 5: The Saljuq and Mongol Periods*, ed. J. A. Boyle (Cambridge UP, 1968), 422 –482; John Andrew Boyle, "The Ilkhans of Persia and the Princes of Europe," *Central Asiatic Journal* 20, no. 1/2 (1976): 25–40; Samuel M. Grupper, "The Buddhist Sanctuary of Labnasagut and the Il-Qan Hülegü: An Overview of Il-Qanid Buddhism and Related Matters," *Archivum Eurasiae Medii Aevi* 13 (2004): 5–78; Elliot Sperling, "Hülegü and Tibet," *Acta Orientalia Academiae Scientiarum Hungaricae* XLIV, no. 1-2 (1990): 145–157; Laurence Lockhart, "The Relations between Edward I and Edward II of England and the Mongol Īl-Khāns of Persia," *Iran* 6 (1968): 23–31; and Reuven Amitai, "The Impact of the Mongols on the History of Syria," in *Nomads as Agents of Cultural Change : The Mongols and Their Eurasian Predecessors*, ed. Reuven Amitai and Michal Biran (U Hawaii P, 2015).

For background on the Yuan empire, see Morris Rossabi, *Kublai Khan: His Life and Times* (U California P, 1988); John W. Dardess, *Conquerors and Confucians: Aspects of Political Change in Late Yüan China* (Columbia UP, 1973); Ch'i-ch'ing Hsiao, *The Military Establishment of the Yüan Dynasty* (Harvard East Asia, 1977); John D. Langlois, ed., *China under Mongol Rule* (Princeton UP, 1981); Elizabeth Endicott-West, *Mongolian Rule in China: Local Administration in the Yuan Dynasty* (Harvard East Asia, 1989); David Farquhar, *The Government of China under Mongolian Rule: A Reference Guide* (Steiner, 1990); Thomas Allsen, "The Rise of the Mongolian Empire and the Mongolian rule in North China," in *The Cambridge History of China, Volume 6: Alien Regimes and Border States: 907-1368*, ed. Herbert Franke and Denis C. Twitchett (Cambridge UP, 1994), 321–413; David M. Robinson, ed., *Culture, Courtiers and Competition: The Ming Court (1368-1644)* (Harvard East Asia, 2008); Timothy Brook, *The Troubled Empire:*

China in the Yuan and Ming Dynasties (Belknap Harvard, 2010); and John W. Dardess, *Ming China, 1368-1644: A Concise History of a Resilient Empire* (Rowman & Littlefield, 2012). For Yuan foreign relations, see Morris Rossabi, ed., *China Among Equals* (Chapter 6 reading notes). For economic history of the period, see Herbert Franz Schurmann, *Economic Structure of the Yüan Dynasty: Translation of Chapters 93 and 94 of the 'Yüan Shih'* (Harvard UP, 1956) and Richard von Glahn, *Fountain of Fortune: Money and Monetary Policy in China, 1000-1700* (U California P, 1996).

The following have also been significant sources for this chapter: David Farquhar, "Structure and Function in the Yuan Imperial Government," in *China under Mongol Rule*, ed. John D. Langlois (Princeton UP, 1981), 25–55 and from the same volume, Morris Rossabi, "The Muslims in the Early Yüan Dynasty," 257–295; Paul Heng-Chao Ch'en, *Chinese Legal Tradition under the Mongols: The Code of 1291 as Reconstructed* (Princeton UP, 1979); David Farquhar, "Chinese Legal Tradition under the Mongols: The Code of 1291 as Reconstructed," *Ming Studies* 15, no. 1 (Fall 1982): 7–9; John Masson Smith, "From Pasture to Manger: The Evolution of Mongol Cavalry Logistics in Yuan China and Its Consequences," in *Horses in Asia: History, Trade, and Culture*, ed. Bert G. Fragner, Ralph Kauz, and Angela Schottenhammer (Osterreichische Akademie der Wissenschaften, 2008); Bettine Birge, *Marriage and the Law in the Age of Khubilai Khan: Cases from the Yuan Dianzhang* (Harvard UP, 2017). See the biographies of Yelu Chucai, Liu Bingzhong, and Ahmad Fanakati in Igor de Rachewiltz et alia, eds., *In the Service of the Khan: Eminent Personalities of the Early Mongol-Yüan Period* (Harrossowitz, 1993); see also Christopher P. Atwood, "Ahmad Fanakati," in *Encyclopedia of Mongolia and the Mongol Empire* (Facts on File, 2004).

For Yuan relations with contiguous societies, see Herbert Franke, "Tibetans in Yuan China," in *China under Mongol Rule*, ed. John D. Langlois (Princeton UP, 1981), 25–55; Jayeeta Gangopadhyay, "Tibetan Scholars in the Yuan Court of China," *Bulletin of Tibetology* 2 (1992): 16–22; Luciano Petech, "Tibetan Relations with Sung China and with the Mongols," in *China Among Equals* (Chapter 6 reading notes), 172–203; Elliott Sperling, "The Ho Clan of Ho-chou: A Tibetan Family in Service to the Yüan and Ming Dynasties," in *Indo-Sino-Tibetica. Studi in onore di Luciano Petech*, ed. Paolo Daffina (Bardi, 1990), 359–377; Charles Backus, *The Nan-chao Kingdom and T'ang China's Southwestern Frontier* (Cambridge UP, 1981); George Lane, "The Dali Stele," in *Horizons of the World: Festschrift for Isenbike Togan / Hududü'l-Alem: İsenbike Togan'a Armağan*, ed. Nurten Kilic-Schubel and Evrim Binbash (Ithaki Press, 2011); and William E. Henthorn, *Korea: The Mongol Invasions* (Brill, 1963). On the talking beast Chucai and Chinggis encountered on the way to India, Chucai actually later identified the animal as a rhinoceros (i.e., he identified it in relation to a loan word from Sanskrit that can mean "rhinoceros"), from his study of an earlier Chinese dynasty, where the animal was described as understanding four languages. Readers will not be surprised to learn that it resembles (particularly in its eloquence) a beast disastrously encountered by Alexander (in the *Shahnameh*; see Chapters 10 and 11 of this book). See the fascinating discussion in Abolala Souvadar, "The Han-Lin Academy and the Persian Royal Library-Atelier," in *History and Historiography of Post-Mongol Central Asia and the Middle East: Studies in Honor of John E. Woods* (Otto Harrassowitz, 2006), 467–484, esp. 476–478.

On overland encounters of the period, the foundation source in English is Christopher Dawson, ed., *Mission to Asia* (Chapter 6 reading notes). See also Paul D. Buell, "Food, Medicine and the Silk Road: The Mongol-era Exchanges," *The Silk Road* 5, no. 1 (Summer 2007): 22–35; Richard Smith, "Expanding Webs of Exchange and Conflict, 500 CE-1500 CE," in *The Cambridge World History, Volume 5: Expanding Webs of Exchange and Conflict, 500 CE-1500 CE*, ed. Benjamin Z. Kedar and Merry E. Wiesner-Hanks (Cambridge UP, 2015), 233–256; Hyunhee Park, *Mapping the Chinese and Islamic Worlds: Cross-Cultural Exchange in Pre-Modern Asia* (Cambridge UP, 2012); Da-Sheng Chen, "Chinese-Iranian Relations VII.: Persian Settlements in Southeastern China during the T'ang, Sung, and Yuan Dynasties," in *Encyclopaedia Iranica* V, no. 4 (1991): 443–446; H. A. R. Gibb (trans.), *Ibn Battuta: Travels in Asia and Africa 1325-1354* (Darf Publishers, 1983); C. F. Beckingham, "The Achievements of Prester John," in *Between Islam and Christendom*, ed. C. F. Beckingham (Variorum, 1983), 3–24; Lev Gumilev's 1970 essay on Prester John was translated by R[obert]EF Smith as *Searches for an Imaginary Kingdom: The Legend of the Kingdom of Prester John* (Cambridge UP, 1988 and 2009); Denise Aigle, *The Mongol Empire: Between Myth and Reality* (Brill, 2014); Peter Jackson, *The Mongols and the West, 1221-1410* (Chapter 6 reading notes); and Rosamund Allen, ed., *Eastward Bound: Travel and Travellers, 1050-1550* (Manchester UP, 2004). A fairly recent assessment of the account of the Black Death being catapulted into Kaffa is Mark Wheelis, "Biological Warfare at the 1346 Siege of Caffa," *Emerging Infectious Disease* 8, no. 9 (Sep 2002): 971–975; Emil Bretschneider's *Mediæval Researches from Eastern Asiatic Sources: Fragments toward the Knowledge of the Geography and History of Central and Western Asia from the 13th to the 17th Century*, vol. 2, a publication from 1888, is now in the public domain in the United States.

On the Toluid exchange, see first, Thomas Allsen, "Overview of the Relationship," in *Culture and Conquest in Mongol Eurasia* (Chapter 7 reading notes) and the lecture text, "Technician Transfers in the Mongolian Empire," published by University of Indiana in 2002. For science and technology in particular, see Judith Pfeiffer, ed., *Politics, Patronage, and the Transmission of Knowledge in 13th-15th Century Tabriz* (Brill, 2014) and Roxann

Prazniak, "Siena on the Silk Roads: Ambrogio Lorenzetti and the Mongol Global Century, 1250-1350," *Journal of World History* 21, no. 2 (June 2010): 177–217. For gunpowder and firearms, see Joseph Needham et alia, eds., *Science and Civilisation in China, Volume 5, Part 7: Military Technology: The Gunpowder Epic* (Cambridge UP, 1986); J. R. Partington, *A History of Greek Fire and Gunpowder* (Johns Hopkins UP, 1998); and Kenneth Warren Chase, *Firearms: A Global History to 1700* (Cambridge UP, 2003).

For Chinese astronomical knowledge before Song, see Edward H. Shafer, *Pacing the Void: T'ang Approaches to the Stars* (U California P, 1977). For the exchanges with Maragha, see P. A. L. Chapman-Rietschi, "The Beijing Ancient Observatory and Intercultural Contacts," *Journal of the Royal Astronomical Society of Canada* 88, no. 1 (Feb 24, 1994): 24–38; George Saliba, "The Role of Maragha in the Development of Islamic Astronomy: A Scientific Revolution before the Renaissance," *Revue de Synthèse* 108 (1987): 61–373 and "Horoscopes and Planetary Theory: Ilkhanid Patronage of Astronomers," in *Beyond the Legacy of Genghis Khan*, ed. Linda Komaroff (Brill, 2006). On the question of Nasir al-Din Tusi and Copernicus, see Ute Ballay, "The Astronomical Manuscripts of Naṣīr al-Dīn Ṭūsī," *Arabica* 37 (1990): 389–392 and I. N. Veselovsky, "Copernicus and Nasir al-Din al-Tusi," *Journal for the History of Astronomy* 4 (1973): 128–130. Jerzy Dobrzycki and Richard Lynn Kremer demonstrated that Europeans before Copernicus were not already working with the mathematical models used at Maragha; see "Peurbach and Marāgha Astronomy? The Ephemerides of Johannes Angelus and Their Implications," *Journal for the History of Astronomy* 27, no. 3 (2016): 87–237. See also Willy Hartner, "The Islamic Astronomical Background to Nicholas Copernicus," *Ossolineum, Colloquia Copernica* III (1975): 7–16 (reprinted in Hartner, *Oriens-Occidens: Ausgewählte Schriften zur Wissenschafts-und Kulturgeschichte Festschrift zum 60. Geburtstag.* 2 vols. [Hildesheim, 1968–1984], 316–325); F. Jamil Ragep, "Tusi and Copernicus: The Earth's Motion in Context," *Science in Context* 14, no. 1-2 (2001): 145–153; and "Copernicus and His Islamic Predecessors: Some Historical Remarks," *History of Science* 45, no. 1 (2007): 65–81. On observatories in the Muslim world and their connections with European astronomy and astrology, see Aydın Sayılı (1960), *The Observatory in Islam* (Turkish Historical Society, 1960); Ann Geneva, *Astrology and the Seventeenth Century Mind: William Lilly and the Language of the Stars* (Manchester UP, 1995); and Håkan Håkansson, "Tycho the Apocalyptic: History, Prophecy, and the Meaning of Natural Phenomena," *Acta Historicae Rerum Naturalium Necnon Technicarum* 8 (2004): 211–236.

Chapter Eight

Return of the Turks

While the Toluid regimes were attempting to find a ruling method combining enough nomadic elements to retain the loyalty and confidence of the conquest elite while learning enough of local traditions to manage large populations and complex economies based on agriculture, their Turkic contemporaries were creating conquest empires with more diverse orientations toward both conquest and agriculture. Though these regimes were less populous and often less stable than the Toluid lands, they had great long-term significance. In the late fourteenth century, these Turkic empires enjoyed long-term control of Egypt and North Africa, succeeded the Ilkhans in Iran, the Levant, Iraq, Azerbaijan, and added Transoxiana. The number of Turkic sultanates of the fifteenth and sixteenth centuries was considerable, but this chapter will concentrate on the largest and most influential: the Mamluks of Egypt, the Jochids of the Russian steppe (today often called the Kipchak or the Golden Horde), the Chaghatay khans of Central Asia, and the Ottomans.

THE MAMLUKS AND THE MUSLIM MEDITERRANEAN

The word *Saracen* came into English via the French language sometime during the Crusades. The classical citations connect it to Arabic root words for "the east": *al-mashriq*—commonly contracted to *sharq*—in the sense of where the sun rises, or the Levant. It is a likely source of the Norse name for the Levant and the Abbasid lands: Sarkland or Serkland. In medieval European languages, forms of the word often meant Muslims generally or Arab Muslims more particularly, but in context, it often indicated Mamluks—perhaps an unintended irony (or given the learning of Frederick II and his contemporaries, perhaps not so unintended) since the early Mamluks were indeed from the east, usually of nomadic origin.

The history of Turkic migration into Abbasid territories and recruitment as *mamluk* had long produced a steady stream of Turkic (prominently Kipchak and Seljuk-related Oguz) migration into Egypt, where they served in similar mercenary positions for the Muslim dynasties based at Cairo during the ninth through the thirteenth centuries. A dynasty that arose directly from these Turkic migrations, the Tulunids, united Egypt and Syria in a ninth-century military regime that provided a template for Cairo-based sultanates that followed. Turkic commanders in the Levant became an essential element in the power of successive sultans of the Fatimids and Ayyubids in Cairo. During the wars against European Crusaders in the thirteenth century, *mamluk* military officers of the Cairo sultanates became a political force in their own right. The famed Ayyubid sultan Saladin (1138–1193) enlarged and gave first place to *mamluk* battalions; indeed, during the last decades of the Ayyubids, it is difficult to distinguish between the sultan's initiatives and those of his high-ranking *mamluk*. By the early thirteenth century, an Ayyubid sultan seeking increased leverage manumitted his *mamluk* on condition that they remain in the military and in his personal service. Nevertheless, over time, some *mamluk* developed grievances against the Ayyubid court. When a *mamluk* faction took advantage of the capture of Louis in 1250 to try to restore their political position, they were resisted by the court. They assassinated the sultan and installed a former sultan's widow in the position.

The *mamluk* continued to consolidate their power. Struggles between factions led to relative independence and rising influence in Cairo for *mamluk* based in the Levant. After a succession of struggles and assassinations, Kutuz (d. 1260) seized power at Cairo in 1259. *Mamluk* contingents opposed to Kutuz maintained their own bases in some parts of Syria. It was during the process of attempting to eradicate these holdouts that Kutuz was visited at Cairo by ambassadors from Hulagu, who suggested that Kutuz submit to the Mongols and provide a hostage bride. Instead, Kutuz had the ambassadors executed. With his newly centralized military forces in Syria, he was able to stop the inevitable Mongol revenge mission at 'Ayn Jalut in Syria in 1260, where he personally led the troops, executed the Mongol commander, and then proceeded to take back Damascus. On his return journey to Cairo he was murdered, and a new faction came to power under the long-lived sultan, Baybars (1223–1277). This court, which we commonly refer to as the Mamluks, referred to itself as the "regime of the Turks" (which appears in various forms in their Arabic and Turkish documents), and when Turkic *mamluk* lost control of the sultanate, subsequent rulers often referred to the state as the "regime of the Circassians" or, when *mamluk* of Mongol origin were in control, "regime of the Mongols" (a similar pattern can be observed in the Delhi sultanates, which also had sequential dynastic regimes).

The Mamluks maintained their Levant province, despite intermittent challenges from the Ilkhans. Like other Turkic states in agricultural zones before them—and their Toluid contemporaries—they made the ruler's household, bodyguards, personal treasury, and military an island of their own surrounded by the sea of farmers and merchants. They linked the Levant and North Africa by the Central Asian–style courier system. Revenues collected directly by the sultanate were used to support the sultan's armies, while the revenue portions that land grantees were permitted to retain was often used to support their own personal armies. Partly to alleviate the history of factionalism among the *mamluk* of the previous Ayyubid period and partly to support the growth of private and sultanal armies, the Mamluk rulers sought new recruits from a variety of peoples of the Black Sea and Central Asia. The sultanate's military became a bastion of professionalism and cultural diversity. Its most striking effect was the militarized professional ethos of horse culture. *Fûrûsiyya* was a combination of skills, values, and literature that not only distinguished one of the most vivid secular cultural traditions of medieval Eurasia but also clearly inspired European notions of chivalry that came after, as the Crusader armies became conduits of Muslim military vocabulary and concepts. The emphatic militarism in imperial culture afflicted the state with tension between centralized control over the sultan's income and military affairs on the one hand, and decentralized administration on the other— that is, a devolution of control to local officials and landholders of civil courts, commerce, and private daily life. *Mamluk* tradition defined military servitude as a prestigious status, and distinctions between soldier and civilian, Turkic and local, and palace and society were profound. Like the Toluids, the Mamluks often mitigated this tension by crossing the line between military and merchant realms themselves. The Toluids were active investors in merchant activities and occasionally produced serious scholars, and the Mamluks encouraged members of the sultanal families to take up careers as merchants, scholars, or civil officials. Nevertheless, the ironclad Mamluk relationship between revenue and military capacity helps to account for the instability of some periods of Mamluk history, since the wealthy province of Syria not only generated substantial revenue for local landholders but also considerable independence, including personal military resources.

In the later Mamluk period, the primacy of military spending also produced a revenue trap that resembled the one faced by the Toluids in their later periods: the tendency to bring profitable land under direct administration of the rulership in order to gain access to staple grains in particular gradually diminished the scope of privately held, taxable land. Unlike the Toluid regimes, the Mamluks were not strangers to Egypt and Syria, and they had learned well the Ayyubid policies for economic management. They continued the currency system of the Ayyubids, and the basic Ayyubid policies of *mamluk* landowners controlling their own revenue, though they modified the latter to make the terms of landholding conditional on continued military service. They knew well and had specific policies encouraging the production not only of staple grains but also of cotton and sugarcane, their major exports. They tightly monitored management of the Nile River, which was essential to irrigation and transportation in Egypt. They encouraged landholders to maintain irrigation systems, keep land under cultivation, and minimize or completely prevent land degradation by nomads. Activity outside the state monopolies (which were surveilled by special bureaucratic offices) was private and discretionary. Mamluk tax policies privileged merchants, even over the interests of religious charities. Income reserved for the sultanal household and its military dependents was clearly designated and assiduously monitored. The overall taxation scheme followed a pattern familiar from the Abbasid regions generally, with the qualification that the proportion of taxes sent directly to the state may have been unusually high.

They were also careful to exploit the capacity of their transport systems to convey—and tax—goods moving between Europe and the overland trade network, such as spices, dyes, medicinal herbs, cotton, wool, linen, honey, and cheese. This sometimes involved exclusive agreements—despite periodic interdiction by the popes—with Spain, Byzantium, and the Italian city-states of Venice and Genoa, relating not only to transport but also to exclusive supply of manufactured goods, such as cotton, silk, paper, soap, and glass. In the late Mamluk period, the sultanate responded to diminishing and irregular income from its provinces by declaring a state monopoly on the most lucrative trade goods. It is likely that the profitable trade prolonged the Black Death outbreak, as Kaffa on the Black Sea (an embarkation point for Kipchak *mamluk* on their way to Egypt), Cairo, and Venice were repeatedly reinfecting each other. Like Europe, Egypt is believed to have lost one-third of its population at the peak of the plague in the fourteenth century.

The Mamluks were, like their Central Asian contemporaries, Sunni Muslims and *gazi* warriors on behalf of Islam. Baybars in particular was keen to call upon traditional Islamic veneration of the caliph, whom he was hosting after 1258, by describing himself as an "associate" of the caliph—not a Heaven-endorsed ruler in the style of an Ilkhan padishah. It not only reinforced his legitimacy in his own regime, but became part of his rhetorical campaign against the Ilkhans. Baybars and many sultans following him found this gave some license to pursue a relatively liberal social and cultural agenda. They were patrons of mosques and religious schools but regularly extended their sponsorship to secular projects like hospitals and parks. This was not only consonant with their Turkic traditions of synthesizing formal religion with folk tradition but was also a continuation of liberalism in Egypt reaching back to the Fatimids, who had been Shi'i by heritage but had opened their bureaucracy to Sunni, Christians, and Jews. The comparative doctrinal flexibility of the Mamluks paralleled their pragmatism in strategic thinking. The sultan Baybars was wary of the possibility of an alliance between the Ilkhans and European popes and explored an alliance of his own with the Ilkhan enemies, the Jochids. By the middle 1260s, he felt confident enough of his position in Syria that he began a series of attacks on Makuria (a 700-year-old Christian kingdom to the south of Egypt), on European outposts in the Levant, and on Armenian nobles who had submitted to the Ilkhans. In 1268, he destroyed the European Crusader principality at Antioch, and a grand plan by Louis IX to invade Egypt from what is now Tunisia ended when Louis died in 1270. The next year, Baybars attacked the Christian kingdom at Tripoli, and in 1277, weeks before his death, he made a brief assault against the Ilkhans in their recently acquired territories in Anatolia.

Baybars' interest in Muslims in Sicily and the Italian mainland may have had two aspects: first, a view of Sicily as part of the Muslim world, and second, he looked to Sicily and Italy as keys to weakening European campaigns in the Levant. Sicily, like the southern Iberian peninsula, had been within a penumbra of occasional North African rule and continuous North African influence since at least the time of the Carthaginians in the early first millennium BCE. Muslim forces had wrested control of it from Byzantium at the beginning of the tenth century. From that time, its Muslim governors and largely Christian population had developed a cultural style in which contact with the scientific and artistic worlds of Muslim Spain, North Africa, and Cairo combined with Italian and Greek languages, folk cultures, and Christianity. In the late eleventh century, internal disputes among Muslim rulers in Sicily created an opportunity for invasion by the Normans, who had over a century and half had been establishing their regimes in southern Italy. Well into the twelfth century, the Normans continued to consolidate their position (actually, multiple positions) in Sicily.

But Sicily was not cured of its Mamluk-linked cosmopolitanism. In the late twelfth century, it was home to the young Hohenstaufen heir Frederick II, who grew up conversant with Latin and Arabic, and Christianity and Islam, and established one of Europe's first universities at Naples in 1224. He had become king of Sicily while still a boy, was appointed Holy Roman Emperor in 1220, and in 1229 became king of the Crusader kingdom at Jerusalem. While Frederick was in the Levant, his communications with both local Muslim rulers and the Ayyubid court were cordial, aided by the Muslim secretaries he had at the head of his entourage. Like his Norman predecessors in Sicily, he was accused in some European courts of being more Muslim than Christian, particularly for his interest in Muslim science. To deflect the charges, Frederick periodically enacted harsh restrictions on the Muslims in Sicily, including forced removals to the Italian mainland (where Baybars's ambassadors visited them). But whether in Italy, Sicily, or Jerusalem, Frederick was accustomed to Muslim ritual and scolded locals who suppressed it because of respect for his Christian affiliation.

When he died in 1250, his illegitimate son, Manfred, dominated the government and in 1254 declared himself king. The pope refused to acknowledge him, and in response Manfred rounded up the Muslims whom Frederick had exiled to Italy and commenced a war; hostilities concluded with Manfred excommunicated but in control of Sicily and substantial parts of southern Italy. In 1265, Manfred battled opposing Angevin monarchs for the Sicilian kingship. He died in battle, and a new pope confirmed the Angevins as kings of Sicily. Baybars had in fact actively aided Manfred when possible, and was relieved that trouble in Sicily and Italy after the fall of Manfred continued to hinder the Crusades. Continuous contact among the Mamluk sultanate, Sicily, and the Holy Roman Empire permitted a flow of influence through the Levant and across the Mediterranean, affecting European regional architectures, literatures, music and musical instruments (including the lute), dress styles, and pastimes. Details of both Sicilian and Italian conditions as late as the thirteenth century are provided today in part because of the friendship of its ruling family with the Syrian diarist who was Mamluk ambassador to the Hohenstaufen court in Sicily.

In the late fourteenth century, instability originating in Syria led to a series of coups and countercoups that ended with the securing of the throne by a Circassian, and for a long period it was Circassians rather than Turks who ruled the sultanate. By that time, two other great Turkic powers were a serious threat: the Timurids and the Ottomans (see Map 8.1). The Mamluks successfully negotiated an alliance with both the Ottomans and the Jochid regime on the Russian steppe to contain the Timurids and shortly afterward extended their own dominion to Cyprus. They also supported the Ottomans in their wars against Byzantium. But the configurations of large states in the Middle East changed again. The Safavids of Iran attempted to ally with Venice and with the Mamluks to challenge Ottoman control of Anatolia, after which the Mamluks were Ottoman enemies. In 1517, the Mamluk sultanate ended when its territories, including Syria, Cyprus, and the Arabian coast of the Red Sea, came under Ottoman control. Even after the demise of the sultanate, "Mamluks" remained a prestigious local military elite of the Ottoman empire.

THE FRANCHISE OF THE RUSSIAN STEPPE

The origins of Jochi's independent regime lay in the campaigns of Chinggis against the Kipchak Turks (see Chapter 6) and eventually against the Rus. Jochi's armies were overwhelmingly Turkic—recruited from the old Kara Kitai and Karakhan lands, northern Transoxiana, and especially the Kipchaks themselves. After Jochi died in 1227, his son Batu (1208–1255) continued the campaigns together with several of Chinggis's leading generals. Unlike

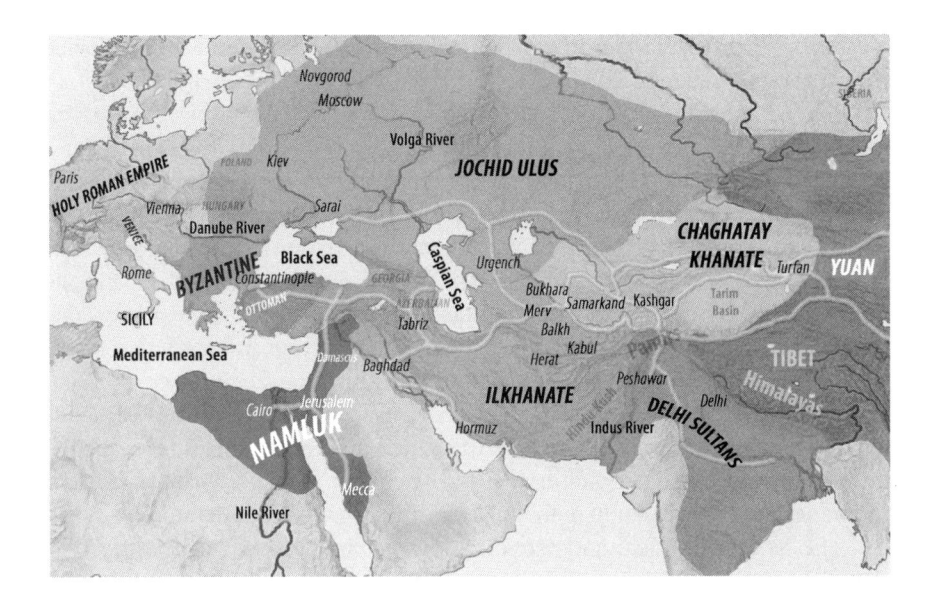

Map 8.1. Turkic regimes and the Byzantine empire, c. 1300.

Jochi—who had withdrawn from Karakorum and kept to himself on the steppe after Chaghatay had questioned his paternity—Batu was close to Ogedei and cooperative with his Toluid cousins. For the rest of his life, he concentrated on creating his own capital at Sarai (from a Turkic word for "palace") on the Volga River. Contemporary records in Mongolian simply called Batu's organization the *"ulus* of Jochi." Sixteenth-century Muscovite historians retrospectively referred to the khanate as the Golden Horde, possibly derived from the imperial genealogies in which the Jochids were referred to as the "golden" (*altan*) lineage, as were all the Chinggisids. The idea that the "Golden Horde" were called so because of the color of their tents is apparently in the spirit of a folk etymology introduced by later historians.

Just as the Mongols arriving in West Asia found the way to conquest eased by the disintegration of the Abbasid order, so the Mongols under Batu found the lack of centralized rule of what is now Ukraine and Russia advantageous. The largest city, Kiev, had since the tenth century been the center of a political federation built on legitimation by the Orthodox Church in Constantinople and domination by the aristocracy of the Rus, a people whose origins are now agreed to be in Scandinavia. The general population was Slavic and had been affected by a thousand years of invasions by Central Asian peoples, including the Skythians, Cimmerians, Huns, Alans, and Khazars. The Rus had been the last to arrive and had invaded the area from the north and west in the ninth century. They gradually established a political system shaped by the fact that the Rus dynastic founder had not established primogeniture, instead dividing his lands among his sons. Their collection of city-states constituted a vigorous trade network, but the princes were frequently at odds. There was additional constant pressure from steppe federations—greatest among them the Kipchaks—raiding the Rus territories and looking for grazing land. By the end of the tenth century, the Rus had subjugated and loosely Christianized the diverse population of the region. Close aristocratic ties with the church in Constantinople were cemented, and the influence of Byzantine civilization was firmly established in a pattern that resembled the rise of the Bulgar khanate. Trade between the Kievan towns and Byzantium was healthy, at least until the ruin and occupation of Constantinople in 1204 by French and Italian Crusaders. The Russians supplied Byzantium with furs, honey, leather, flax, burlap, and slaves. In return, they purchased wine, gems, religious art, and silk. There was an outstanding period of development in Kiev in the twelfth century in art and literature.

The precise political and economic conditions in Kiev of the early thirteenth century are matters of dispute among historians, which means that the impact of the Mongol invasion is in some ways unclear. Until fairly recent decades, the assumptions had been that the nobles of Kiev had rights of tribute extraction from the populations working their land, but in daily affairs farmers governed themselves through their village councils. The regime was understood to have never had much centralization and to be losing any it had by the late twelfth century. Going along with this was a thesis of declining economic output and commerce, perhaps as a direct consequence of conflict among the nobles over land and trade rights. More recent research suggests, instead, a thriving economy and external trade with Hungary, Poland, Byzantium, Scandinavia, the Middle East, and Central Asia. Standards of metalwork were particularly high, and together with textiles, leatherwork, furs, and some agricultural products made Kievan goods prized. Kiev itself was a city with a twelfth-century population around 40,000—a little more than London, a little fewer than Paris. Together with the other cities of the Kievan federation, the total urban and rural population must have amounted to something over five million. The lack of coherence of the political system was probably also exaggerated by earlier scholarship. There was certainly some degree of local autonomy in the villages, and each city had an assembly that could curb the demands of its prince; there may have been few institutions truly comparable to western Europe, where laborers were tied to both the land and the lord owning it. But the nobles were nevertheless bound together by extra-local income sources. They controlled the critical trade between the Baltic and the Black Seas and between the steppe and Byzantium.

Protecting the rights and distributing the proceeds kept the noble class together as did their consent to the basic Rus principles of succession within the lineage. There were a variety of models—most proximate the Bulgar and Khazar khaghanates (see Chapter 3)—to draw upon, and it is apparent that the Rus did that, creating a collegial state with a ceremonial and, in some ways, fiscal center at Kiev itself. They even had a "prince of princes" (or more literally, "high king," *velikii knyaz*) to parallel the "khan of khans" and probably inspired by it—for at least a short period Rus was a tributary of the Khazar khaghanate, and the Rus used the term *khaghan* among themselves from the ninth century onward. The collegial form of Rus government had the typical advantages and disadvantages but—as with other collegial governments in the Turkic style—cannot be dismissed as fragile or weak merely because of its collegial nature. There is every reason to think that, by the time of the first arrival of the Mongols, the federation was wealthy and relatively cosmopolitan, with Slavs, Khazars, and Turks of various backgrounds in high civil and military positions. The city-state of Novgorod was a northerly neighbor whose economy and political system mirrored that of the Kievan federation, though with a closer connection to Baltic trade. The first conflict between the Rus and the Mongols occurred in 1223, when a combined Russian and Kipchak army was defeated at the Kalka River and the Kievan grand prince captured and executed. The great onslaught did not come until the late 1230s, when a series of defeats for the Rus climaxed in the capture and spectacular pillage of the town of Riazan. The princes, like the Turkic sultans of West Asia, did not unite to oppose the invaders. In 1240, the central town of Kiev fell to the Mongols. Various tactical problems impeded Batu's progress, but Hungary, Poland, and parts of the Balkans remained under threat from Mongol forces for half a century.

Unlike the Toluids, Batu never considered it irresistibly lucrative to occupy the agricultural areas that came under his control. The Jochids were tightly focused on trade income and located their capital of Sarai on the Volga, where it could be connected to the steppe networks and to the trade across the Black Sea. Ibn Battuta (1304–1368?) visited in the early 1330s (probably) and found it to be a typical West Asian overland trade entrepôt—more populous than most—with the cultural, economic, and architectural character to be found in any Black Sea, Iranian, or Transoxianan city of its time. Europeans on the way to Karakorum (or, later, to Dadu) sojourned at Sarai and awaited permission to proceed. Batu's brother and successor Berke (1209?–1266) built a new Sarai for himself nearer to the Russian territories, about a day's ride from Volgograd and possibly on the site of the old Khazar capital. Berke's Sarai was destroyed in 1395 during an incursion by Timur (see below), and Berke's capital was sacked several times in wars against the Mongols or between rival Jochid khanates. Today, the sites of both cities are subjects of archaeological speculation. Travel between either of the two Sarais and the Rus cities was required—Mongol overseers had to visit the courts in each city, and Rus princes had to report to Sarai periodically to pay tribute and reaffirm their fealty (during the Karakorum period, they proceeded eastward to meet the khaghan). Batu and his successors built new extensions of the Mongol courier system through the Kievan territories, allowing the cities to be in closer communication with each other and with the steppe than previously. The road system was managed by a variety of officials of Mongol, Turkic, and Rus origin and in their respective languages, which allowed its reputation to spread quickly. European visitors, many of them influential noblemen representing the Holy Roman Empire and the Hapsburgs in particular, were amazed at being able to travel over 300 miles (500 kilometers) in 72 hours.

Batu was content to engage in a relationship with the princely families of Rus and Hungary in which he recognized their authority to rule their cities and they pledged him tribute and obedience. Russian princes acted as the Jochid khan's agents (primarily his tax collectors and census takers). They were often his ambassadors to the courts at Karakorum and, afterward, at Shangdu and Dadu. The peculiar form of domination imposed upon Russia by the Jochids was once commonly represented in Russian scholarship by the phrase "the Mongol yoke" (*Mongolo* or *Tatarskoye igo*). It suggests the exploitation of the strength of the Russian population, but what is remarkable about it is that it shows the Jochids controlling Russia from a distance—driving it at the end of a yoke, not riding it. The Jochids assigned their governors and military supervisors to the princely city states to make sure that wealth was being transferred as ordered and to watch for any sign of rebellion among the elites or the commoners. But the overall practice was to rely upon the princes—and occasionally the church—to complete the centrally important tasks. Like all other Chinggisid regimes, the Jochids saw essential government functions as census taking and tax collection. They completed the first census ever executed in Russia in 1257 with the aid of church clerics. Russia provided European visitors their first exposure to a state practice that would not be introduced in Europe itself until more than a century later and would not become widespread until the modern period. The princes were in effect given the Jochid franchise to govern and tax their cities as they saw fit once they had fulfilled their tribute and ritual obligations.

The relationship between the Rus princely families and the Jochid court grew close in political if not in spatial terms. The responsibility given the Rus aristocrats permitted their leaders—particularly Alexander Nevskii (1221–1263), then based in Novgorod—enough discretion that they designed and pursued their own military campaigns against the Swedes and the Teutonic Knights while the Jochids protected Rus's eastern and southern fronts. By the late fourteenth century, many leading lineages had married into the Jochid nobility or taken Turkic or Mongolian surnames, and long after the Jochids were gone from Russia, the Jochid Turkic dialect ("Tartar") was still used by rulers in Moscow. Certainly, the Jochid period left its own marks on the Russian language in the form of terms and phrases that remain part of colloquial Russian today. The physical distance kept by the Jochids from the Russian farmlands may be related to the lack of human and environmental damage from the conquests in comparison to China or Iran. Though there were no cities in Kiev or Novgorod on the scale of Baghdad, Damascus, Beijing, or Samarkand, the destruction at Riazan, Suzdal, Moscow, Rostov, Tver, and a dozen other cities may have resulted directly and indirectly in the deaths of one-tenth of the population. Rural Ukraine, which had been a fertile and well-populated region in the late Kievan period, underwent a severe depopulation, as the Mongols not only crossed it repeatedly in their campaigns against eastern Europe but also raided it continually to discipline villages that were uncooperative in the surrendering of their tax payments. Despite the physical destruction, evidence of archaeology and documents suggests that economic recovery after the cessation of warfare was brisk. Though the extractive demands of the Mongols were high and their monetary measures sometimes impractical (including importing Toluid paper money), the Russian territories regularly managed to pay their taxes in silver, which suggests not only regular surpluses in their income but also an economy functioning well enough to make the conversion of goods to cash convenient. It is also clear that tax burdens were increased not by the Mongols directly but by their tax collectors, the Russian princes, who routinely exempted their own lands from the tax and shifted the additional burden to the farmers.

In Batu's time, the Jochids were shamanists with an interest in Buddhism, but as in their language practices, so, too, in their religion they may have been influenced by Muslims among the Turkic nomadic population on which their armies were based. At the khan's capital of Sarai, mosques were plentiful, though there were also facilities for Christians (including those visiting from Europe) and Buddhists. Overall, the Jochids were more inclined to fight fellow Muslims and Mongols than to fight the Russian Orthodox Church. Berke converted to Islam in 1257, though Jochid Mongols were not ordered to convert until the early fourteenth century. He criticized Hulagu for murdering the last caliph in 1258 and declared his intention to fight the Ilkhans for control of the Caucasus. The initial Jochid–Ilkhan conflict in 1262 was inconclusive, and the two superficially Mongol domains remained at war on and off until the 1290s. During that time, the Jochids acknowledged the Orthodox Christian Church as the primary cultural authority in Rus and did not interfere with it. Both Turks and Mongols had a long history of acquaintance with Christianity in Central Asia, and the records of the Jochid period note several instances of Turks and Mongols becoming Orthodox converts and rising to high rank in the church in Russia. The Jochids had cordial personal contact with the church patriarchs and, in the 1250s and 1260s, issued declarations giving the church immunity from taxation and military conscription. Within a relatively short time, the church changed from an exclusive orientation toward Constantinople to a more Russian and Eurasian posture. Churchmen began using Russian to compose detailed histories of the Russian princedoms and introduced their own narratives of the Mongol conquests. Nevertheless, the Jochids did not engage closely with local or distant Orthodox Christian bureaucracy or feel—as the Toluids had—that the conquered culture had to be represented at the khan's court.

Despite the indirectness of Jochid control over the Rus territories, patterns of urban development and population movement were strongly affected. This was partly because of the role played by Alexander Nevskii—who had displaced his brother Andrei to become Grand Prince—in aiding the Mongol conquest. Alexander persuaded many of the Rus princes that it would be better to submit to the Mongols than to resist them. He was also the primary strategist in precarious Russian victory of the Teutonic Knights at Lake Chud (Peipus, bordering Estonia) in 1242, when the massively armored European knights exhausted themselves slipping around on the ice (and in the Eisenstein film went fictively crashing through it). In recognition of Alexander's service, the Jochids favored both Novgorod (under the rule of Alexander) and the emerging town of Moscow (under the rule of Alexander's son Daniel, 1261–1303). These towns eclipsed Kiev as political, cultural, and economic centers during the period of Jochid domination. This, in turn, encouraged a northward population displacement (i.e., away from the pasturelands and periodically plague-riddled trade cities in the southwest) and the opening of new agricultural land far north of the Caspian. Moscow was accessible to Sarai (old and new) thanks to the Volga waterway, which facilitated not only travel but also tribute conveyance from the city. The growth of Moscow was so remarkable in this period that the religious leader of the Orthodox Church, the Metropolitan, moved his headquarters there from Kiev.

Moscow's political preeminence was sealed in 1327 when the almost equally privileged city of Tver seethed with rebellion. Daniel's son Ivan, then the prince of Moscow, led an army of Turks and Mongols to quell it. Moscow was afterward made *darkhan*, exempt from taxation, and was given authority over tax collection for other Russian cities. Subsequently, the princes of Moscow were primary among all the princes, made permanent by adoption of a new pattern of primogeniture that stabilized the succession of princes descended from Daniel and Ivan. In the late fourteenth and early fifteenth centuries, the princes of Moscow tried several times to throw off Jochid rule. In a confrontation at Kulikovo in 1380, the Moscow forces defeated a large Jochid army, though at great cost—the Jochids sacked Moscow as a punishment and rescinded its tax exemption. By the end of the fourteenth century, the Jochids were responding by dismantling their government, allowing their own nobles to break away with their armies and herds to establish their own small khanates fighting for Jochid survival. In 1395, they were under assault from the forces of Timur. They gradually lost ground to him and his successors in the east and to Moscow in the west, surviving only as remnants. A branch, the White Horde, ruled much of southeastern Russia until the 1480s, and the khan of Crimea—the last ruling direct descendant of Chinggis—was not overthrown until 1783.

CHAGHATAY ROOTS, TIMURID TRUNK, MUGHAL FLOWERS

By the late thirteenth century, the Jochid and Chaghatay khanates had much in common and were often allies against their Toluid cousins. Both had unfulfilled ambitions in Transoxiana, were openly dependent upon Turkic military populations, and were Sunni Muslims. The least populous and most politically amorphous of the Mongol empires derived from the holdings and the descendants of Chinggis's son Chaghatay. But the Central Asian khanate was also the root of what became two of the most influential empires of the medieval and early modern worlds—the Timurids and the Mughals.

Chaghataids were often on the short end of *ulus* distributions during and after the conquest of Khwarazm. In the time of Ogedei, tribute from some of the richest cities in ostensibly Chaghatay territory was directed to the imperial coffers in Karakorum, and Chaghataids were frequently summoned the short distance to Karakorum for various tasks. In 1260, as the civil war began to split Mongolia, Berke on the Russian steppe was preparing for war against the Ilkhans, and Chaghatay's grandson Alghu (d. 1266) seized Jochid holdings in Transoxiana (see Map 8.1). Alghu and his successor continued to

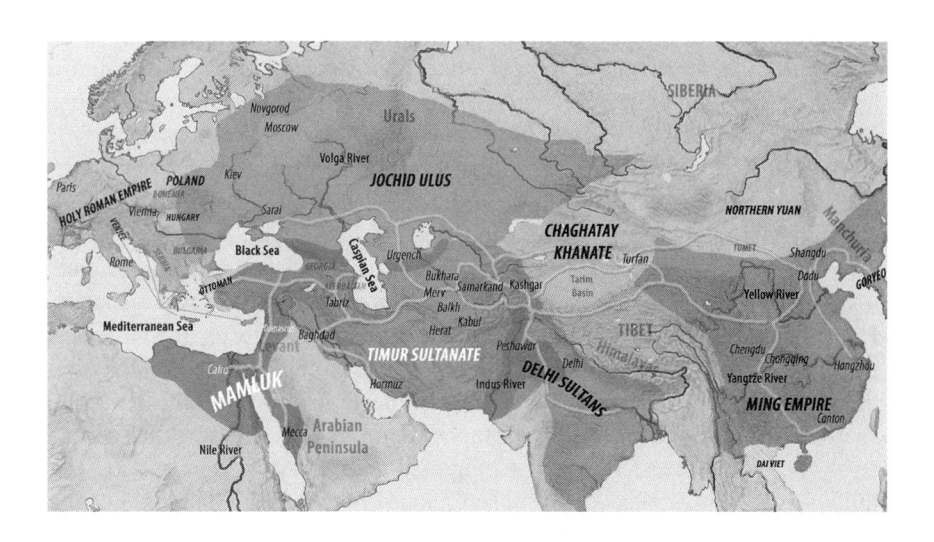

Map 8.2. Timurid-Ming Eurasia, c. 1400.

seek ways of exploiting both Jochid and Ilkhan weaknesses in hopes of absorbing more territories or treasure. The lack of success inspired the ambitions of Ogedei's grandson Kaidu (1235?–1301). He began his own campaigns to seize Chaghatay territory, and it was Berke who aided him by promising peace on Kaidu's western border and occasional troops. By the end of the civil war between Kublai and Ariboka, both Berke and Kaidu were confirmed enemies of the Toluid regimes. When Kublai attempted to install one of Chaghatay's grandsons as the new Chaghatay khan in 1266, it sparked a Transoxiana civil war in which the Jochids took the side of Kaidu. Sometime before 1270, the war concluded with Transoxiana being split between Kaidu and the Chaghatay khans, but each agreed to a formal pact to stay out of the cities and base themselves among the nomads.

Almost immediately, Kaidu persuaded Chaghatay to make a new war against the Ilkhans. When the Chaghataids lost the short war, a portion of the aristocracy defected to the Ilkhans, and many others pledged themselves to Kaidu, who appointed his own Chaghatay clients as khans. After Kaidu's death in 1301, Chaghatay khans eradicated what they considered Ogedeid influence and made themselves a virtual feudatory state of the Yuan empire. The disintegration of both Yuan and Ilkhan began in the 1330s, leaving Central Asia to fend for itself. Descendants of Chinggis Khan were still regarded as legitimate, and soldiers rising to power in the region tended to find credible Chinggisids to install as khans. The surviving religious affiliations surfaced, creating a discernible divide between the Buddhist and shamanic lands of eastern Chaghatay and the Islamic Sart territories that composed the western half of the Chaghatay domain.

In the later fourteenth century, a war leader named Timur (whose appearance we know well thanks to forensic reconstruction from his skull in 1941) began to unite Transoxiana. He served as a soldier and possibly a bandit in his early life—when he received a wound that caused him to limp for life, gaining him the sobriquet of Timur-i-lenk (later standardized by writers from Gibbon to Poe as "Tamerlane"—see the epilogue to this book for Christopher Marlowe's *Tamburlaine the Great*). His ancestors had been Mongol aristocrats from a lineage related to the Borjigins. Like Kaidu before him, Timur sought out acknowledged Chinggisids as his puppet rulers and framed his early career uniting Transoxiana as a champion of the Chaghatay khanate. He married into the khanal lineage and in 1370 and took effective control of the khanate. Though the Chaghataids became prominent Muslim converts in the earlier fourteenth century, they also protected some shamanic practices (particularly those associated with the worship of Chinggis's spirit) and actively promoted the ideology of Chinggisid legitimacy. After marrying into the lineage, Timur considered himself a son-in-law of the Chinggis lineage. With his credentials established and most of the Chaghatay territories under his control, Timur proceeded to create a recognizable state. As in the case of the Seljuks and Ilkhans, the Timurid rulers most often called themselves "sultan."

Timur was aggressive in championing Sunni Islam—he insisted that all Borjigins convert and sometimes referred to himself as the "Sword of Islam." On the other hand, he institutionalized the veneration of Chinggis's spirit and referred continually (if not accurately) to his conquests and empire as reconstitution of the empire of Chinggis. And both traditions incorporated the Persian political practices generalized to Central Asia and the Middle East by the Abbasid caliphate. The synthesis was a marked imperial posture. It may be most simply described as a court of nomad Mongol *gazi* instead of nomad Turkic *gazi*, and it would be inherited by the Mughals after the Timurids, despite the overwhelmingly Turkic cultural orientation of both dynasties. To Timur's Timurid and Mughal successors, he was a "Lord of Auspicious Conjunction" (*sahib-kiran*), in all its meanings of astrological destiny, messianic mission and supernatural protection. The title was assumed to go back to Alexander. Its specific reference was to the astrological conjunction of planets, particularly the conjunction of Jupiter and Venus that was believed to mark a temporal transition. Being born under it was a mark of a savior, a prophet, or a predestined conqueror. By the time of the Mongol conquest of Iran in the thirteenth century, it was an honored sobriquet of various rulers of the Islamic world, invoking the marriage of charismatic military prowess to the legal, ethical, and administrative capacities of civilization. Its astrological reference had been metaphorized as the convergence of conquest and justice—or, in the Timurid and Mughal context, the conjunctions of Mongol power and Islamic civilization. Those coming after him—most famously Shah Jahan (1592–1666)—invoked it to describe themselves as incarnating his combination of terror and justice, which is to say, the conjunction of nomadic warrior traditions with the long histories of settled civilizations. For a time under the Ottomans, the "Lord of Auspicious Conjunction" would become the last universal ruler, ushering in new age of God.

Timur gradually expanded his domain until his death in 1405. His realm came to include extensive agricultural and urban areas, particularly through Transoxiana and the Ferghana Valley, but his administration tended to the economic frontier between them and the pastoral reaches of the Kipchak and Mongolian steppes. He helped inflict the blows that fractured the Jochid regime on the Russian steppe and for a time controlled the Jochid court at Sarai. He drove the Ottomans to take refuge in the Balkans and persuaded the Delhi sultan to become his vassal. All the while, he constantly pressed his eastern front. He threatened the Ming rulers of China, who had overthrown the Yuan in 1368. But he never succeeded in eradicating all remaining Chaghatay khans. A small regime held out in what is now Xinjiang Province of China; technically, the Timurids and remnant Chaghataids were contemporaries in the fourteenth and fifteenth centuries (see Map 8.2).

In 1401, Timur repeated Hulagu's devastation of Baghdad. There and elsewhere, he may have consciously attempted to recreate the terror that he believed accompanied all the Mongol conquests. Historians often cite a total of "17 million" deaths for his conquests across Central Asia and the Middle East, but as in the case of Chinggis, it is impossible to arrive at a definitive total. Timur's own historians often claimed massacres twice the size of those estimated by historians sponsored by his enemies. What is certainly true is that Timur saw great strategic and ideological value in vivid displays of bloodthirstiness, a lot of them featuring severed heads—gathered into huge piles, hung from the belts of his troops, or made into trinkets or drinking vessels. The effect was as Chinggis and his sons had hoped in their own day: an incentive to surrender and pay tribute resulting in less pressure on the sultan to expend troops, horses, and cash on prolonged campaigns.

Like the Kara Kitai, Karakhanids, Seljuks, Ilkhans, and Chaghataids, the Timurids used Turkic for military affairs and the life of the imperial lineage and Persian for management of the civil state. Arabic was widely used for religious worship and some administrative tasks. The government structure was also on the template of these predecessors. The military was decimally structured and under direct control of the ruler, though he could grant both lands and troops to his subordinates. The ruler himself worked through a close group of trusted military and civilian advisers, and a large organization oversaw his household affairs and personal safety. And like the Seljuks and Ilkhans in particular, the Timurids were sponsors of Arabic-language work in mathematics, astronomy, philosophy, and theology. Timur established his capital at Samarkand (very close to his birthplace), and together with Herat and Bukhara it became the design center for western Eurasia. He liked his monuments and architectural ornamentation to be gigantic, and his appetite for sponsoring artists, technicians, and scientists was vast. The basic artistic themes associated with the Timurids were derivative, reaching back to Seljuk and Abbasid models: geometrically patterned tiles in blue and white, solid turquoise tiles, domed buildings, minarets, and colorful archways. In architecture and the plastic arts, Timur earned a reputation for grandiosity. The epitome of his taste was probably his immense Persian-style tomb in Samarkand.

After Timur's death, the political life of the Timurid elite was contentious and often violent, and they lost most of Iran to their former vassals, the Turkic Akkoyunlu. The Timurids remained dominant in Transoxiana and parts of present-day Xinjiang Province of China, and Ulugh Beg (1394–1449) used his considerable revenues from trade to continue his grandfather's legacy of ambitious architecture at his capitals of Samarkand and Bukhara. He founded hospitals and religious schools as well as major academies in both cities notable for advanced studies in astronomy and mathematics. To the tradition of the sultan as sponsor of civilized arts, he added the role of participant, becoming a competent mathematician and astronomer in his own right. He helped design the huge observatory in Samarkand (whose ruins survive today). His staff established the exact angle of the earth's equator in relation to the plane on which it revolves around the sun and completed the first catalog of visible stars since the time of ancient Greece. Babur (1483–1530) was born in modern-day Uzbekistan and in his teens began to compete among his Timurid cousins for control of his own territories. He made some progress and even held Samarkand for a time, but after being driven out he repaired to Kabul (in today's Afghanistan). For a time, his status in Kabul rose, as Timurid nobles neutralized each other and eventually acknowledged Babur as supreme among them (the padishah). He made peace with the new Turkic masters of part of Iran, the Safavids, and was able to recapture some of Timur's former domains. But continuing instability in both his agreements with other rulers and his relations with Timurid relatives caused Babur to conclude that the safest route was to India. The dynasties of Turkic rulers founded in northern India 300 years before, and having successfully deflected the forces of Chinggis 250 years before, were now destroying each other. A rival of the great Delhi sultanate requested Babur's aid in the 1520s, and Babur complied—then seized the Delhi rulership for himself. He established his own dynasty of Timurid rulers of India—later called the Mughals (that is, the Mongols). Babur himself is famous as a poet and memoirist, as well as patron of the arts of painting, architecture, and literature—especially in the contemporary version of Chaghatay Turkish (see Chapter 10), which became the early court language of the Mughals. They continued to see themselves in the roles of both conquerors and civilizers, in what they understood was the special legacy of Timur.

THE NEW EMPERORS OF THE CITY

From Roman times, Constantinople was the single essential metropolis between Europe and the Middle East. It was also one of the world's largest cities before its multiple sackings and brief occupation by Crusaders in the early thirteenth century. Anatolia had once been under the authority of Constantinople, but the Seljuks had seized a major portion of it for the Abbasid caliphate in the eleventh century. Over time, the Seljuks based in Anatolia weakened their ties to Baghdad and strengthened their ties, including marriage ties, to Constantinople (see Chapter 5). But the future cultural character of Anatolia was determined when a new power arose there at the end of the thirteenth century. Within a century and a half, Constantinople would regain its international character as an anchor of civilization—but with a difference. Its past names of "New Rome" or "East Rome" were superseded east of the

Bosphorus (a passage from the Black Sea to the Mediterranean that modern Istanbul straddles) by Konstantiniyye. Over a huge region to its east and west, it was simply called "the city" (the source of the modern name Istanbul)—the seat of true emperors. The early Ottoman leaders were called by the traditional title of *bey* (the same as Turkic *beg*). During roughly the same period, they also emblemized their pre-Islamic, Turkic origins by incorporating the title khaghan (*khakan*). After the final demise of the Seljuks they began to add sultan and padishah to their titles (see Chapter 11). At some point, they also assumed the title of caliph (though as an overt title it could have been quite late), giving the Ottoman sultan independence from the judgments of Muslim clergy. They were the first Eurasian rulers to transcend the division between secular government and its spiritual legitimation—that is, they created the first self-legitimating early modern rulership. With the capture of Constantinople, Mehmet II (1432–1481) became an emperor (*imparator*), also styled *kaysar-i Rum* (Caesar of Rome).

The Seljuks who had driven the Byzantines out of Anatolia had originated among the Oguz Turks of the western steppe (see Chapters 5 and 6). In the Seljuk period, Oguz Turks continued to migrate toward Anatolia, Syria, and Egypt. In the last years of the thirteenth century an Oguz leader, Osman (in Arabic, 'Uthman), a local military commander in a coastal region of northwestern Anatolia, collected an army of Oguz followers and Byzantine defectors and began to capture towns of the valley of Anatolia's longest river, the Sakarya (see Map 8.3). After Osman's death, a son continued the campaigns, and over the course of the fourteenth century, the group—the elites calling themselves Osmanli and called by historians the Ottomans—gained control of most of Anatolia and crossed their corner of the Mediterranean to seize Venetian possessions in Greece in the fourteenth century (see Map 8.4). From there they proceeded toward the Balkans where they ended the Serbian empire by decimating Kosovo in 1389. In an extraordinary encounter of 1396 at Nikol in modern Bulgaria, the Ottoman armies decisively defeated an allied Christian force—a papally endorsed crusade specially formed to prevent Muslims from conquering any more of Europe—composed of a few tens of thousands of volunteers from England, France, the Balkans, Venice, Hungary, the Second Bulgarian Empire, and several regions of what is now Germany. This Battle of Nicopolis was a turning point in many ways. Bulgaria collapsed and became an Ottoman dependency. In 1417, Wallachia (an ancestor state of modern Romania) signed a peace treaty with Ottoman. Hungary, whose kings were gaining control of the Holy Roman Empire, was forced to revise its ambitions for ruling the Balkans, and soldiers returning to their homelands from Nicopolis carried stories of the ruthless Ottoman execution of their prisoners (according to Ottoman historians, to avenge Christian execution of Ottoman prisoners in earlier encounters).

Despite such successes on their western front, on the east the Ottomans were experiencing a profound challenge from Timur, who after conquering former Ilkhan lands in Iran, Iraq, Azerbaijan, and Armenia, was pushing into Anatolia. The Ottomans attempted to block him at Ankara, but they were outnumbered and probably disorganized since a large part of their force was still in Greece and the Balkans. Timur occupied almost all of Anatolia, and the Ottoman sultans decamped to Edirne, at the neck of land that connects modern-day Turkey to both Greece and Bulgaria. In the ensuing decade, the Ottomans were dependent upon their Balkan and Greek holdings for revenue and upon an alliance with Byzantium for protection against the Timurids. Constantinople became a familiar neighborhood. Struggles for succession among Ottoman sultans were sometimes tipped by Christian nobles of the Balkans, who had a hand in the rise of Sultan Mehmet I in 1413. In the subsequent four decades, Ottoman sultans were able to reclaim much of Anatolia (thanks to the decentralization and internal conflict among the Timurids) and consolidate their holdings in the Balkans by battling Hungary and Venice. The Byzantine empire was reduced to a sliver along the coast of the Black Sea. In 1453, Sultan Mehmet II—at the age of 21, near the beginning of his second reign as sultan—was able to exploit resentment against the Byzantine role in a recent struggle for the Ottoman throne to end all treaties with Constantinople. In a fairly expeditious artillery and infantry siege, the city fell to him. Konstantiniyye was no longer a hole in the Ottoman empire but now the jewel at its center. In the following century, the Ottomans concentrated on expanding into the remaining Venetian outposts in the western Mediterranean; into Mamluk territory in Egypt, Tunisia, and Libya; into Safavid territory in the Caucasus, Iraq, Palestine, Syria, and the western edge of the Arabian Peninsula; into former Jochid territory in Crimea; and ultimately, into Ukraine (see Map 8.5). A century later, they controlled much of what today is Somalia. By the end of the sixteenth century, they were a formidable sea power challenging Portugal, Spain, and England for control of trade lanes through the Mediterranean and the Persian Gulf. They attacked Vienna twice and eventually smothered the fairly strong emergent state in Hungary. By 1600, the empire occupied about 900,000 square miles (about 2.25 million square kilometers, see Map 8.6).

The Ottoman conquerors did not come to Constantinople as the same followers of Osman who had started attacking villages in Anatolia a century and a half before. Osman had considered himself a *gazi*. The Ottomans of Mehmet II's day did not rely only on Turkic horsemen and *gazi* zeal. They had developed from masters of the horse and sword to masters of cannons and firearms. Especially after their artillery siege of Constantinople in 1453, they were feared by the European powers for their advanced production and deployment of gunpowder weapons of all sizes. And they had also perfected a high art of diplomacy with the Mamluks, the Jochid Mongols, and the

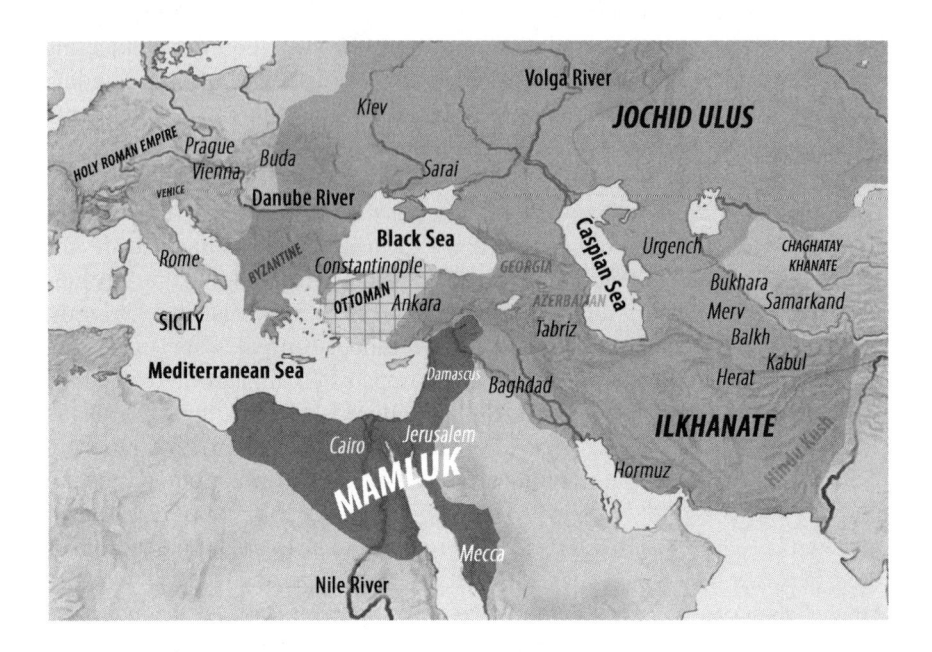

Map 8.3. Growth of the Ottomans, c. 1300. *Note*: Ottoman territories are cross-hatched and contested areas are shaded.

states of the Balkans and Europe. Mehmet II's troops, regardless of their background, were Muslim (a large number of them converts from Orthodox Christianity), and their goal was to advance the faith in the Balkans. Mehmet II was a Sunni Muslim, but he, like his predecessors, had lived for decades in the ambit of the Greek- and Slavic-speaking worlds of Orthodox Christianity, and his courtiers included Balkan princes and nobles. He permitted the Orthodox Christian hierarchy in former Byzantine lands to retain all their practices and privileges. Rewards aside, the distrust by Orthodox Christians of the Latinate Christians of Rome—and particularly the empire of Venice—may have hastened their reconciliation to Ottoman rule. The ways in which the Ottomans organized their military grew directly from their position at the interface of the Christian and Muslim worlds. The Turkic states had been largely collegial in origin, and even after establishment of a khanship or sultanship, many experienced instability because of residual privileges of the Turkic elites.

A strategy often used was to keep the ruler's segment of the military larger than those of his challengers. In the Ottoman case, it was also useful in curbing the independence of the minority of still-nomadic Oguz Turks entering the Ottoman forces. A rich source of new troops was outright capture or forced surrender of young men and boys from conquered communities. Once

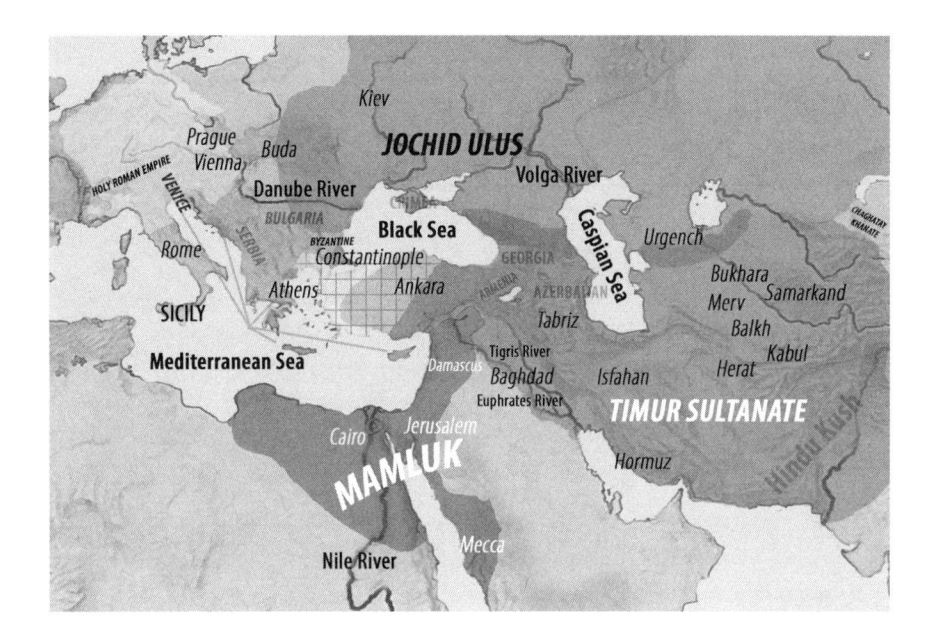

Map 8.4. Growth of the Ottomans, c. 1400. *Note*: Ottoman territories are cross-hatched and contested areas are shaded.

the Turks entered the Muslim world and began to develop their own sultanates, this practice conflicted with the principles of Islam, which forbade enslaving Muslims. The Ottomans found themselves surrounded by populous Christian regions, many of which they proceeded to conquer. Afterward, they required the surrender of boys for military service. The new military slaves were converted to Islam and made property of the sultan. Care was taken that the general labor force not be pinched by these practices. Urban populations and the families of technicians were exempt, as were families in which a son was the sole breadwinner. Many of the taken were trained in traditional Turkic horseback archery, and the infantry—called the "New Army" (*yeni ceri*), or Janissaries—were trained in firearms and *mélée* weapons. The sultan's house guard was selected from the boy converts, and many were trained for scribal duties. Others were chosen to pursue religious studies and become the leaders of Muslim communities within the empire.

The sultans were able to use this substantial stream of newly converted boys to build both their personal armies and a tight personal bureaucracy. This class of converts from Greece, the Balkans, or Christian communities in Anatolia soon became prestigious (as some forms of slavery in the Turkic world had always entailed prestige). They had high salaries, intimacy with the sultan and his household, and exceptional medical care. After the late

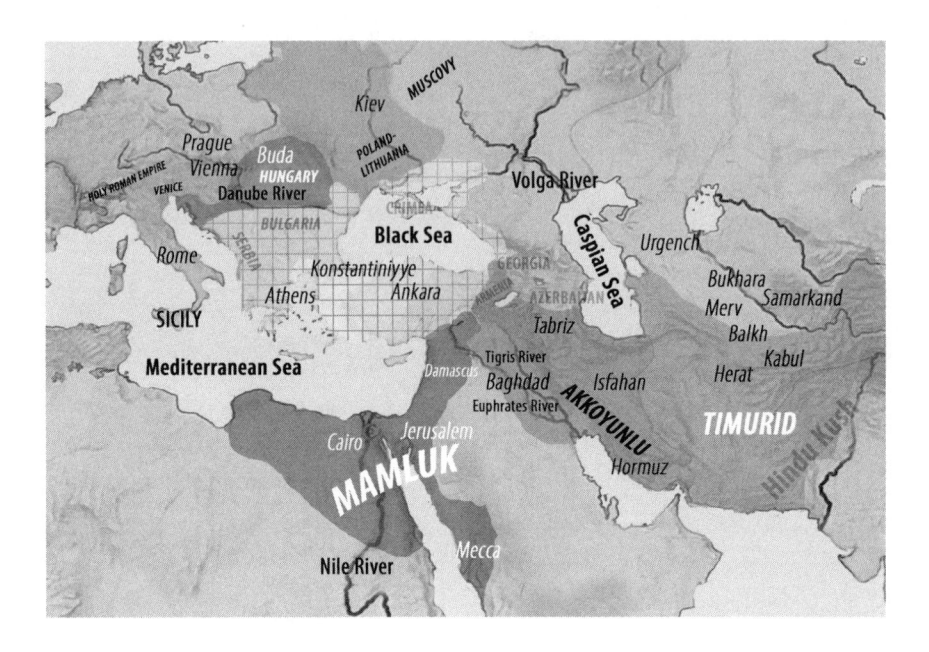

Map 8.5. Growth of the Ottomans, c. 1500. *Note*: Ottoman territories are cross-hatched and contested areas are shaded.

1500s, Janissary sons could be admitted to Janissary status, which created a large, influential, hereditary class. The state had a bit more trouble keeping imposters out than coercing new boys in, and the forced collection was discontinued in the seventeenth century. But the Janissaries continued to grow as a dominant political class, the sort of political deformation that Turkic leaders had always mistrusted. Because the Janissaries (who at their height may have numbered 200,000–300,000 out of an empire-wide population of less than 30 million) supplied both the advanced military units and the bureaucracy, the Ottoman government was always fixed on military affairs. This was inspired partly by the steppe tradition of putting financing of the military above all else in government. It also drew heavily upon the Turkic institution of the *keshig*, the small group of multifunctional officials around the khan who ran his military, communications systems, and bureaucracy. The founder, Osman, had had a *keshig* of trusted organizers around him, and in later decades, this became more elaborate.

The priorities of the government closely resembled those of earlier and contemporary Turkic khanates and sultanates: census taking of the potential military-conscript and tax-paying population, land registration, and tax collection. The financial administration of the central government was well staffed by a specialized bureaucratic cohort, "men of the pen," not only

Map 8.6. Growth of the Ottomans, c. 1600. *Note:* Ottoman territories are cross-hatched and contested areas are shaded.

trained in literate tasks but also in the specifics of fiscal accounting. With this restricted view of state responsibilities, the Ottomans kept the government small by delegating as many tasks—even critical tasks—as possible to local elites. Often, whether in the Muslim or the Christian territories, these elites were clergymen, who in function became extensions of the state (in fact some had been prepared for the clergy while technically slaves of the sultan). To the extent practical, they were given the discretion to resolve conflicts on the basis of the religious law that predominated locally. Like the Mongols in the Ogedeid period, the Ottomans divided their territories into larger units overseen by enfeoffed governors, and each of these units was in turn divided into smaller units, overseen by enfeoffed magistrates. The divisions of Anatolia were clearly the blueprint for the modern provinces of Turkey. The Turkish name for province, *il*—a subordinate replica—reflected the Turkic and Mongol political tradition of making subordinate divisions smaller-scale iterations of the higher division or central government, the manner in which Kublai had reordered the administration of China. Often, institutions of partly or primarily steppe origin had the names of Islamic institutions reaching back to the Abbasids. The *keshig*, for instance, translated to the *divan* (from Arabic *diwan*), the small office headed by the *vizier* (from Arabic *wazir*). In the Ottoman case, from the early fourteenth century on, the vizier took responsibility for appointing and supervising officials and became a supremely powerful office.

The Ottomans subscribed, with increasing explicitness, to the *dar al-Islam* concept and the liberal Hanafite jurisprudence they had inherited from the Seljuks (see Chapter 5). They were protectors of Sunni Islam, not only in their roles as sultans but later also as caliphs, and considered themselves entitled to rule any areas where Muslims were in substantial number. They put this into practice in later centuries by claiming patronage of Muslims in the Russian territory of Crimea. On the other hand, the *dar al-Islam* was in principle a space in which Christians and Jews were also protected. The sultans sponsored Christian charitable schools and hostels for the poor; they were also on cordial terms both with the patriarchate that governed Greece on behalf of the empire and with the head rabbi of the Jewish community. Also like the Seljuks, the Ottomans recognized nonorthodox Muslim sects, including Shi'i, Ismaili, Druze, and Alawite. Sufism in all forms was commonly practiced throughout the Janissary class, and members of the Ottoman ruling lineage sponsored Sufi teachers and schools. There were episodes, sometimes during war with the Mamluks in Egypt or Safavids in Iran, when sultans became suspicious of certain groups, and Jews were always vulnerable to falling out of favor with the court. In such times, there were commonly forced removals or revocation of tax exemptions, and in uncommon instances, there could be massacres of targeted populations. These were exceptions to the general Ottoman posture of protector of religious faiths, a posture resembling that of the Ilkhans and the Yuan. Like the Ilkhans and the Yuan, they institutionalized a multiplicity of legal codes. The sultans were lawgivers in their own right and administered a set of secular regulations, the *kanun* (canon), largely based on traditional Turkic law and often referred to as *yasa*, the term also used in reference to the legal code attributed to Chinggis Khan. Matters relating to trade, or not covered by religious law, or on which there was an irreconcilable conflict between the legal precepts of disparate religions were referred to the *kanun* and imperially commissioned judges. Otherwise, disputes and punishments were managed within recognized religious communities (see Chapter 10) and infrequently impinged upon state resources.

Accession to the sultanship was not by primogeniture, but eligibility was normally limited to the sons of the sitting sultan, who were educated in schools within the palace (which also educated high-ranking Janissaries). The Ottomans were notorious for adhering to the ancient Turkic pattern of a new ruler eliminating likely competitors (usually his brothers) and making politically stabilizing fratricide legal. The practice was never unique to Turkic regimes, and there is evidence for it in the histories of the Sasanians and the Byzantines (who claimed they got it from ancient Rome), both well within the range of sources of Ottoman institutions. The Ottomans were not shy about defending the practice, and in a letter to Timur, they answered his criticism by claiming that history showed that "two sultans cannot live in one country." In effect the practice seems to correspond to centralization of the state. It was not much in evidence before 1400, when the young Ottoman regime was struggling against fragmentation from within and dismemberment from without. Nevertheless, it is recognizable as part of the transition from a traditional collegial political pattern to a firm adherence to Islamic principles of monarchy. Mehmet II himself established rules for distinguishing between legal execution of contenders for the sultanate and illegal murder. Still, practice of legal sultanal fratricide was clearly constrained; at least 11 sitting sultans were displaced by competitors who had evidently not been eliminated. It is an interesting feature of Ottoman history (from 1299 to 1922) that for long periods when the ruling lineage seemed unable to find sufficient talent to control the state, men and women (see Chapter 11) of ability nevertheless came forward to perpetuate dynastic as well as imperial rule. In the seventeenth century, the Ottoman sultans were primarily a ceremonial presence. For the first half of the seventeenth century, the empire was run by a succession of women leaders; during the latter half of the seventeenth century, viziers ran the state.

The long history of Turkic comfort with Sartic culture and economic ideas could be observed in the differences between their ideas of how cities should be treated and how the countryside should be treated. The population of the Ottoman empire at its greatest extent was concentrated in the Balkans, Greece, and Anatolia—not surprisingly, the regions where agriculture was oldest and best developed. These regions accounted not only for most of the income of the Ottoman elites but also the majority of military conscripts. Like the Mongols, the Ottomans used what is best described as a "cadastral survey," a combined study of landholding and habitation in any designated territory. The Ottoman court held extensive lands throughout the empire and especially in newly conquered areas sought precise designation of their property, as well as the lands they had gifted to military and civil officials (who lived on the income instead of salaries). These surveys were conducted freshly, as in the Balkans, or on the basis of existing cadastral surveys (as in lands taken from the Mamluks, who also employed a version of the cadastre themselves). Until well into the early modern period, the vast majority of land was controlled directly or indirectly by the Ottoman imperial court. But a comparatively small amount of the revenue from indirectly controlled land went to the treasury since it was divided on a stipulated ratio between the local landholder and the ruler. A substantial amount of non-imperial land was also owned by religious foundations that managed it for the support of schools, mosques, public baths, and hospitals. The right of the sultans to revoke grants of land to local officials (though not to religious foundations) was always reserved and may have contributed over time to a lack of investment and innovation in local agriculture. Sporadically, the state created incentives to landowners to make farming more efficient and commercial, but the rate of growth in the countryside seems never to have matched that of the cities.

As a consequence, the Ottomans were always keener to invest in and develop the cities, from which they derived taxes directly. The principle was underscored with development of sea trade and Ottoman ports. The great cities of the empire, and above all Konstantiniyye, provided tax advantages to merchants of all religious backgrounds and sent out invitations to Jews in Christian Europe to migrate to the trade cities (this is the background of the Ladino, the Jews who fled the Spanish Inquisition to settle in the Ottoman cities from 1492 on). The sultans spent from their own treasury to keep the streets of the great cities passable and the religious facilities attractive. They instituted an effective system of direct taxation that permitted a steady flow of cash toward the palace as the critical trade networks connecting Ottoman cities to Europe, North Africa, Russia, Central Asia, and India matured. Ottoman imperial income increased steadily into the sixteenth century and then, in the early modern period, doubled. Konstantiniyye, with a population of perhaps 400,000 by 1500, regained its status as one of the three or four largest cities in the world.

As cultural patrons, the Ottomans were the most cosmopolitan rulers of the fifteenth and sixteenth centuries. Like the Timurids and the Mughals, the Ottomans became renowned throughout Eurasia for their architecture, which was in many ways seen as a revival of the glories of Abbasid Baghdad. But in the age of the great architect Sinan (1490–1588) (with a possible minor influence from the 1502 and 1505 visits of Leonardo da Vinci [1452–1519] to Konstantiniyye), Ottoman architecture incorporated structural influences from Byzantine and Roman church design, which later influenced some Mughal styles. Persian themes in turrets, minarets, arches, and tiled courtyards prevailed. The intertwining developments of Ottoman literature (see Chapter 10), painting, and illuminated books continued the development of this complex that had begun in the Seljuk and Ilkhan periods. Chinese artistic themes (particularly in the representation of landscapes) combined with Byzantine traditions of portraiture. In the fourteenth century, the sultans built within the palace one academy for Greek-speaking painters and another for Persian speakers. Small paintings—sometimes impossible to distinguish from book illustrations—in the Ilkhan style were highly valued. Abstract designs became popular, many of them inspired by Persian and Arabic calligraphy (also represented in the stylized signatures—the *tughra*—of the sultans). Workshops for book production—from papermaking to copying and bookbinding—were in or near the palace complex. The Ottomans were also well-known patrons of musical composition and performance. They shared this with many early medieval empires entering China from north or northeastern Asia—among them the Northern Wei, Sui, and Tang of China, all of whom had promoted the earliest traditions of musical theater in China (see also Chapter 10). Select Janissaries were trained as musicians, especially for military marches; their style of music became so well-known internationally that it influenced Mozart and Beethoven. Like everything Ottoman, their music was eclectic, based on the folk melodies of Central Asia, the Caucasus, Iran, and Byzantium, and played on a variety of wind instruments and drums. Percussion also accompanied the shadow-puppet shows (a form well-known across Eurasia), of which the sultans were fond. Several sultans were accomplished musicians and composers.

In the sultanal tradition also represented by the Ilkhans, Yuan, and Timurids, the Ottomans were generous and sometimes demanding patrons of learning. In the late 1500s, they ordered a large observatory and academy be built at Galata, outside Konstantiniyye, under the direction of Taqi al-Din Muhammad ibn Ma'ruf (1526–1585), deliberately emulating the examples of Hulagu, Kublai, and Ulugh Beg—as well as the project going on at the same time in Denmark, where the king was sponsoring a new observatory, academy, and printing operation designed by Tycho Brahe (1546–1601). During 1577–1578, both Tycho and Taqi al-Din were observing the passage of the Great Comet (C/1577 V1) through the sky. Each came under pressure from his royal patron to make prognostications on the basis of the comet. Tycho erroneously predicted imminent "violence and warfare" as well as political crises that seemed to be associated with the house of Hapsburg (a frequent object of prophecies across eastern Europe and the Muslim world at the time). Taqi al-Din erroneously predicted a glorious Ottoman victory over the Safavids in Iran. Predictions of disaster are probably better than predictions of triumph since few will complain if they do not come true. Tycho is remembered for his scientific, not his superstitious, involvement with comets. He ultimately had to abandon his observatory, primarily for political reasons, but moved to a newer observatory in Prague. Taqi al-Din, in contrast, found that his observatory was quickly engulfed in the ongoing debates among Islamic scholars regarding the impiety of using the skies for opportunistic and possibly ungodly prognostication. The observatory was ostentatiously destroyed, but Taqi al-Din continued his work in astronomy, mathematics, and optics under the protection of powerful Ottoman officials. After his death, Tycho's work in Prague continued with possible specific advantage from Taqi al-Din's precise triangulating calculations for determining the variations in the sun's trajectory. The destruction of the Galata observatory is sometimes seen as a critical moment in the drift away from science in the Ottoman world, and in the Islamic world as a whole, while the contrasting experiences of Tycho and Taqi al-Din are often read as the point at which the flow of science from the Muslim world to Europe was reversed.

This could be over-reading. In the history of Muslim observatories, the Ilkhan academy at Maragha stood out for its longevity. Other observatories of the Seljuks and Timurids—not to mention the incomplete projects of the Mamluks—were in operation only a bit longer than Galata, often declining after the death of their guiding scientists or the cessation of imperial protection resulting from continual criticism from conservative clerics. But the accumulation of knowledge across the Muslim world from the sporadic operation of observatory academies was immense in comparison to knowledge accumulated in Europe or China before 1600, and the Ottomans were great curators of accumulated knowledge in all fields. The palace in Konstantiniyye included a large library, today part of the Topkapi Palace Museum. The greatest builder of the library, and perhaps the greatest science and arts patron of the fifteenth century, was Mehmet II. He commissioned the systematic recovery and translation of the works of Ptolemy and imported scholars from Samarkand to collect books on and teach astronomy and mathematics. He gathered his Greek and Central Asian scholars into imperial academies and published their works. And despite the destruction of the Galata observatory, Taqi al-Din's contributions to timekeeping, mathematics, physics, and optics continued and were gaining influence throughout the Ottoman world and Eastern Europe when Giordano Bruno was burning in Rome. If there is a moment in which Europe became scientific and secular while the Islamic world became obscurantist and pious, it is not likely to have occurred before the seventeenth century. In both Islam and Christendom, science and faith were locked in a struggle—both within individual scientists and intellectual communities—through the early modern period.

The Ottomans were more competitive with Europe in diplomacy, which they had to learn the hard way. They survived the demise of the Seljuks by clever bargaining with the Mamluks, the Jochids, and the Timurids and barely survived the Timurids by allying with Byzantium. After the late sixteenth century, the rise of imposing challengers—Portugal, the Hapsburgs, and Safavids foremost among them—required close study of foreign communications and the intricacies of treaty-making. They worked out an alliance with France in the sixteenth century that allowed each empire to gain coveted territory (France along the Mediterranean coast and the Ottomans in Hungary). When Philip II of Spain formed a coalition that defeated the Ottoman fleet at Lepanto in 1571, the Ottomans found time to rebuild their fleet by seeking out Venice as an ally. European resentment of the high Ottoman fees for access to the land routes of Eurasia helped inspire Spain and Portugal to send mariners along the west coast of Africa in search of their own routes to Asia, but the rising esteem of Ottoman products—primarily coffee and carpets—in Europe made the loss of revenue negligible. In Crimea, the Ottomans were challenged in the late sixteenth century by the post–Jochid Muscovy state (see Chapter 11). They enlisted a lineage of Chinggisid aristocrats (lately resident in Konstantiniyye) and installed them as khans of Crimea. Crimea remained an Ottoman ally through the sacking of Moscow in 1571, but afterward became a problematic pirate state for a century, bringing trouble to both eastern Europe and the Ottomans themselves.

The influence of the Ottomans was perhaps the greatest of the Turkic and Mongol states surveyed in these chapters. They ruled most of North Africa until the eighteenth century and indirectly most of the Arab lands until the opening of the twentieth century. The fourteenth- and fifteenth-century empire tended to make its impressions on Europe and Iran through military performance, particularly the advanced use of large guns. But in the sixteenth and seventeenth centuries, the Ottomans emerged as masters of strategy by carefully positioning themselves as enemies of the Hapsburgs and the papacy, making them appealing to England and France as possible allies. The flow of communications, ambassadors, military advisers, and merchants between Europe and Konstantiniyye provided a channel for Ottoman influence to persistently reach Italy and France and, later, England, raising the hope that the Ottomans might be the critical accelerating force in the cracking of the traditional strategic hierarchy in Europe.

READING NOTES: RETURN OF THE TURKS

On astronomy and observatories in the Muslim world, see Chapter 7 reading notes.

For general background on the period of this chapter, a classic source is Rashid al-Din's, *The Successors of Genghis Khan*, trans. John Andrew Boyle (Columbia UP, 1971). It is useful to consult David O. Morgan, *The Mongols*, (Introduction reading notes); Stephen F. Dale, "The Rise of Muslim Empires," in *The Muslim Empires of the Ottomans, Safavids, and Mughals* (Introduction reading notes), 48–76, and "The Islamic World in the Age of European Expansion, 1500-1800," in *The Cambridge Illustrated History of the Islamic World*, ed. Francis Robinson (Cambridge UP, 1996), 62–89; André Wink, "Post-Nomadic Empires: From the Mongols to the Mughals," in *Tributary Empires in Global History*, ed. Peter Fibiger Bang and Christopher A. Bayly (Cambridge UP, 2011), 120–131; and Robert D. McChesney, *Central Asia: Foundations of Change* (Princeton UP, 1996); Devin Deweese, *Islamization and Native Religion* (Pennsylvania State UP, 1994). And for a different perspective, see Eve M. T. Powell, *Tell This in My Memory: Stories of Enslavement from Egypt, Sudan, and the Ottoman Empire* (Stanford UP, 2012).

For general background on the Mamluks, see Carl F. Petry, *The Cambridge History of Egypt, Volume 1: Islamic Egypt, 640-1517* (Cambridge UP, 1999); Peter Malcolm Holt, *The Age of the Crusades: The Near East from the Eleventh Century to 1517* (Addison Wesley Longman, 1986); and Jonathan Harris, Catherine Holmes, and Eugenia Russell, eds., *Byzantines, Latins, and*

Turks in the Eastern Mediterranean World after 1150 (Oxford UP, 2012). On connections with Sicily and Italy, see Julie Anne Taylor, *Muslims in Medieval Italy: The Colony at Lucera* (Lexington Books, 2005). Charles J. Halperin reviewed and contextualized the debate on whether the Mamluks were influenced by, or inclined to make diplomatic approaches, to the Ilkhans in "The Kipchak Connection: The Ilkhans, the Mamluks and Ayn Jalut," *Bulletin of the School of Oriental and African Studies* 63, no. 2 (2000): 229–245.

On Mamluk state and society, see Winslow Williams Clifford and Stephan Conermann, eds., *State Formation and the Structure of Politics in Mamluk Syro-Egypt, 648-741 A. H./1250-1340 C. E.* (Vandenhoeck & Ruprecht P, 2013); Yuval Ben-Bassat, ed., *Developing Perspectives in Mamluk History* (Brill, 2017); Nasser Rabbat, "Representing the Mamluks in Mamluk Historical Writing," in *The Historiography of Islamic Egypt, c. 950-1800*, ed. Hugh N. Kennedy (Brill, 2001), 59–75; Peter Malcolm Holt, "The Position and Power of the Mamluk Sultan," in *Muslims, Mongols and Crusaders: An Anthology of Articles Published in the Bulletin of the School of Oriental and African Studies*, ed. G. R. Hawtings (Routledge, 2005); Thomas Asbridge, *The Crusades: The Authoritative History of the War for the Holy Land* (Simon & Schuster, 2010); Michael Winter and Amala Levanoni, eds., *The Mamluks in Egyptian and Syrian Politics and Society* (Brill, 2004); Amina Elbendery, *Crowds and Sultans: Urban Protest in Late Medieval Egypt and Syria* (The American University in Cairo P, 2016); Kristen Stilt, *Islamic Law in Action: Authority, Discretion, and Everyday Experiences in Mamluk Egypt* (Oxford UP, 2011); Ruth Kark, "Mamlūk and Ottoman Cadastral Surveys and Early Mapping of Landed Properties in Palestine," *Agricultural History*, 71, no. 1 (Winter, 1997): 46–70; Winter, "The Re-Emergence of the Mamluks Following the Ottoman Conquest," in *The Mamluks in Egyptian Politics and Society*, ed. Thomas Phillipp and U. Haarmann (Cambridge UP, 2007).

On Mamluk trade, see Adel Allouche, *Mamluk Economics: A Study and Translation of al-Maqrizi's Ighathah* (U Utah P, 1994); Georg Christ, *Trading Conflicts: Venetian Merchants and Mamluk Officials in Late Medieval Alexandria* (Brill, 2012); and R. Stephen Humphreys, "Ayyubids, Mamluks, and the Latin East in the Thirteenth Century," *Mamluk Studies Review* II (1998): 1–17.

For the training and varied status of Mamluk riders, see David Ayalon, *The Mamluk Military Society* (Variorum, 1979) and "Notes on the Furusiyya Exercises and Games in the Mamluk Sultanate," *Scripta Hierosolymitana* 9 (1961): 31-62; Ulrich Haarmann, "The Late Triumph of the Iranian Bow: Critical Voices on the Mamluk Monopoly on Weaponry," in *The Mamluks in Egyptian Politics and Society*, ed. Thomas Phillipp and U. Haarmann (Cambridge UP, 2007), 174–187; and Reuven Amitai, "The Logistics of the Mongol-Mamluk War, with Special Reference to the Battle of Wādī'l-Khaznadār,

1299 C. E.," in *Logistics of Warfare in the Age of Crusades*, ed. John Prior (Surrey, 2006): 25–42. The best-known Mamluk illustrated manual on horsemanship, *Nihāyat al-su'l wa-al-umnīyah fī ta'allum a'māl al-furūsīyah* (not later than 1348), has been put online by the Qatar Digital Library: https://www.qdl.qa/archive/81055/vdc_100000000044.0x0003ca. See also John Masson Smith Jr., "Ayn Jālūt: Mamlūk Success or Mongol Failure?" *Harvard Journal of Asiatic Studies*, 44, no. 2. (Dec 1984), 307–345 and Charles J. Halperin, "The Kipchak Connection: The Ilkhans, the Mamluks and Ayn Jalût," *Bulletin of the School of Oriental and African Studies*, 63, no. 2 (2000): 229–245.

For background on the Jochids—the Golden Horde, or Kipchak Horde—see Nicholas V. Riasanovsky, *A History of Russia*, 6th ed. (Oxford UP, 2000); Paul Bushkovitch, *A Concise History of Russia* (Cambridge UP, 2011); Geoffrey Hosking, *Russia and the Russians: A History* (Belknap Harvard, 2001); John Fennell, *The Crisis of Medieval Russia: 1200-1304* (Longman, 1983); Charles J. Halperin, *Russia and the Golden Horde: The Mongol Impact on Medieval Russian History* (Indiana UP, 1987); Leo De Hartog, *Russia and the Mongol Yoke: The History of the Russian Principalities and the Golden Horde, 1221-1502* (I. B. Tauris, 1996); Janet Martin, *Medieval Russia, 980-1584* (Cambridge UP, 2003); Charles J. Halperin, "The Missing Golden Horde Chronicles and Historiography in the Mongol Empire," *Mongolian Studies* 23 (2000): 1–15; and Nevill Forbes and Robert Mitchell, trans., *The Chronicle of Novgorod 1016-1471* (Academic International/Orbis Academicus, 1970).

The following have also been influential in this chapter: Donald Ostrowski, "The 'tamma' and the Dual-Administrative Structure of the Mongol Empire," *Bulletin of the School of Oriental and African Studies* 61, no. 2 (1998): 262–277 and *Muscovy and the Mongols: Cross-Cultural Influences on the Steppe from 1304-1589* (Cambridge UP, 1998); Charles J. Halperin, "Russia in the Mongol Empire in Comparative Perspective," *Harvard Journal of Asiatic Studie*s 43, no. 1 (Jun 1983): 239–261; Nicola di Cosmo, "Mongols and Merchants on the Black Sea Frontier in the Thirteenth and Fourteenth Centuries," in *Mongols, Turks and Others: Eurasian Nomads and the Sedentary World*, ed. Reuven Amitai and Michal Biran (Brill, 2005), 391–424; A. P. Martinez, "The Eurasian Overland and Pontic Trades in the Thirteenth and the Fourteenth Centuries with Special Reference to Their Impact on the Golden Horde, the West, and Russia and to the Evidence in Archival Material and Mint Outputs," *Archivum Eurasiae Medii Aevi* VII (1987–1991): 127–222; Peter B. Golden, "The Qıpčaqs in Georgia," *Archivum Eurasiae Medii Aevi* VII (1987–1991): 45–64; and Thomas Allsen, "Mongols and North Caucasia," *Archivum Eurasiae Medii Aevi* VII (1987–1991): 5–40.

On problems of a "Eurasian" school in Russian historiography, see Chapter 11 reading notes.

On the Chaghatay khanate, see Michal Biran, not least for her study *Qaidu and the Rise of the Independent Mongol State in Central Asia* (Curzon P, 1997); "Rulers and City Life in Mongol Central Asia (1220-1370)," in *Turko-Mongol Rulers, Cities and City-Life in Iran and the Neighboring Countries*, ed. David Durand-Guedy (Brill, 2013), 257–283; "Central Asia from the Conquest of Chinggis Khan to the Rise of Tamerlane: The Ögodeied and Chaghadaid Realms," in *The Cambridge History of Inner Asia, Volume 2*, ed. Golden, di Cosmo, Frank (Chapter 6 reading notes), 46–66; and "Diplomacy and Chancellory Practices in the Chagataid Khanate: Some Preliminary Remarks," *Oriente Moderno* 88, no. 2 (2008): 369–393. See also Jeff Eden, *The Life of Muhammad Sharif: A Central Asian Sufi Hagiography in Chaghatay*, with a contextualizing appendix of special interest by Rian Thum and David Brophy (Austrian Academy of Sciences P, 2015).

For the Timurids, see Beatrice Forbes Manz, *The Rise and Rule of Tamerlane* (Cambridge UP, 1989); *Power Politics and Religion in Timurid Iran* (Cambridge UP, 2007); and "Mongol History Rewritten and Relived," *Revue des mondes musulmans et de la méditerranée* 89–90 (2000): 129–149 (see also Chapter 11 and its reading notes). My comments on Timur's reification of a nomadic economic frontier are inspired by Manz, "Temür and the Problem of a Conqueror's Legacy," *Journal of the Royal Asiatic Society* 8, no. 1 (1998): 21–41, esp. 31–32. See also Daniel T. Potts, "The Mongols and the Timurids," in *Nomadism in Iran : From Antiquity to the Modern Era* (Oxford UP, 2014), 188–213; Ralf Kauz, *Politik und Handel zwischen Ming und Timuriden: China, Iran und Zentralasien im Spätmittelalter* (Reichert, 2005), which has been summarized in English and amplified by Rajkai Zsombor Tibor, *The Timurid Empire and Ming China: Theories and Approaches Concerning the Relations between the Two Empires* (Eötvös Loránd U, 2015).

For the transition to the Mughals, see Stephen F. Dale, *The Muslim Empires of the Ottomans, Safavids, and Mughals* (Introduction reading notes); John F. Richards, *The Mughal Empire* (Introduction reading notes); Richard M. Eaton, *The Rise of Islam and the Bengal Frontier, 1204-1760* (U California P, 1996); and *A Social History of the Deccan, 1300-1761: Eight Indian Lives* (Cambridge UP, 2008).

On its origins of "lord of auspicious conjunction," see Naindeep S. Chann, "The Lord of Auspicious Conjunction: Origins of the Ṣāḥib-Qirān," *Iran & the Caucasus* 13 (2009):1:930110; see also Dale, "The Legacy of the Timurids" (*op. cit.*), Geoffrey Parker, "Messianic Visions in the Spanish Monarchy, 1516-1598," *Caliope: Journal of the Society for Renaissance and Baroque Hispanic Poetry* 8, no. 2 (2002): 5–24; Lisa Balabanlilar, "Lords of the Auspicious Conjunction: Turco-Mongol Imperial Identity on the Subcontinent," *Journal of World History* 18, no. 1 (Mar 2007): 1–39; Kaya Şahin,

Empire and Power in the Reign of Süleyman: Narrating the Sixteenth-Century Ottoman World (Cambridge UP, 2015); Azfar Moin, *The Millennial Sovereign: Sacred Kingship and Sainthood in Islam* (Columbia UP, 2014); Stephen P. Blake, *Time in Early Modern Islam: Calendar, Ceremony and Chronology in the Safavids, Mughal and Ottoman Empires* (Cambridge UP, 2013). As Muhammad Abdul Ghani noted in *A History of Persian Language & Literature at the Mughal Court* Part I (The Indian Press Ltd., 1929), *sahibqiran* was the literary equivalent of Arabic (from Greek) *Zulqarnain*—generally but not universally accepted as a reference to Alexander the Great as the lord of two "horns," or ages. On the meaning and fate of Suleiman's four-realms tiara representing him as *sahib-kiran*, see Gülru Necipoğlu, "Süleyman the Magnificent and the Representation of Power in the Context of Ottoman-Hapsburg-Papal Rivalry," *The Art Bulletin* 71, no. 3 (Sep 1989): 401–427.

This chapter has been influenced by a debate in English-language historiography and anthropology. Paul Wittek (1894–1978) had emphasized that the Ottoman founder and his supporters had weak ties to their nomadic roots and relied heavily on their *gazi* ideology to attain unification. Rudi Paul Lindner challenged this in 1983, with his *Nomads and Ottomans in Medieval Anatolia* (Indiana UP, 1983), which described the earliest Ottomans as much more traditionally Turkic and nomadic, with the result that after the empire of the state, they harbored a special wariness of the destabilizing effects of nomads and were careful to control them with regulation and taxation. Lindner's work on this topic remains somewhat controversial. For further background on Ottoman history, see Halil İnalcık, *The Ottoman Empire: The Classical Age 1300-1600* (Phoenix, 1973); Caroline Finkel, *Osman's Dream: The History of the Ottoman Empire* (Perseus, 2007); and Rudi Paul Lindner, "Anatolia, 1300–1451," in *The Cambridge History of Turkey, Volume 1: Byzantium to Turkey, 1071-1453*, ed. Kate Fleet (Cambridge UP, 2009), 102–137. On ideology and historiography, see Cemal Kafadar, *Between Two Worlds: The Construction of the Ottoman State* (U California P, 1995) and Rudi Paul Lindner, *Explorations in Ottoman Pre-History* (U Michigan P, 2005). Also see Chapter 11 of this book. For the question of when the Ottoman rulers might have assumed the title of caliph—whether rhetorically or with political intent—see Finkel, *op. cit.*, 110–111.

The following works have also been influential in this chapter: Herman G. B. Teule, "Introduction: Constantinople and Granada, Christian-Muslim Interaction 1350-1516," in *Christian-Muslim Relations: A Bibliographical History, Volume 5 (1350-1500)*, ed. David Thomas and Alex Mallett (Brill, 2013); İlker Evrim Binbaş, "A Damascene Eyewitness to the Battle of Nicopolis," in *Contact and Conflict in Frankish Greece and the Aegean, 1204-1453: Crusade, Religion and Trade between Latins, Greeks and Turks*, ed. Nikolaos G. Chrissis and Michael Carr (Ashgate Publishing, 2014); Varlik

Nükhet, *Plague and Empire in the Early Modern Mediterranean World: The Ottoman Experience, 1347–1600* (Cambridge UP, 2015); and J. M. Rogers, *Sinan: Makers of Islamic Civilization* (I. B. Tauris, 2006).

Part IV

The Forge

Chapter Nine

Dissidence and Doubt

The figure of Thomas putting his finger into Christ's wound exemplified the ancient Eurasian dichotomy of light and dark, at base a matrix of questioning: doubt about the reality of the world perceived by the senses, doubt about deceptions by a Satanic figure, doubt about the authority of teachers and priests deployed by the hierarchical religions to shepherd the masses. That dualism percolated into the realms of hierarchical religions across Eurasia. It provoked sectarianism, expanded popular access through simplification of some religious and liturgical practices, and in some ways linked medieval theology to ancient cosmology. The reactions of religious and secular authorities of the later middle ages differed. In some regions, dualistically inspired methods were welcomed even if the cosmology was not. Some religious domains accepted mystically oriented teachings as legitimate variations on orthodoxy. Others interrogated, tortured, and killed those targeted as dualists, charging them as deeply subversive heretics whose doubts about reality and ideologies of personally attained enlightenment were poison to the faithful. These differences could be simultaneous, one region suppressing religious dissent for its own reasons, another at the same time accommodating or even welcoming it as a companion of both religious education and scientific inquiry. The destiny of dissidents was dependent on many factors, among them the position of the rulership in relation to religious hierarchs—a position that changed in a fairly regular way in the post-nomadic regimes.

DOCTRINAL PLURALISM IN STEPPE REGIMES

Scholars of Mongol history counsel calm when considering the cliché that Chinggis Khan was an advocate of religious "tolerance." The conventional wisdom has its locus classicus in Gibbon, whose *Decline and Fall of the Roman Empire* was closer to a decline and fall of all empires before the seventeenth century, including the Chinese, the Abbasids, the Russians, and victims of Mongol predation. Looking back from the eighteenth century, Gibbon was conscious of a cleft that separated medieval Europe from his own time. In his view, the repressive religious policies of the medieval Europeans were primary signs of backwardness, and he pointed out that in the "medieval" period not everybody was actually "medieval":

> The Catholic inquisitors of Europe, who defended nonsense by cruelty, might have been confounded by the example of a barbarian, who anticipated the lessons of philosophy, and established by his laws a system of pure theism and perfect toleration. His first and only article of faith was the existence of one God, the Author of all good, who fills by his presence the heavens and the earth, which he has created by his power. The Tartars and Moguls were addicted to the idols of their peculiar tribes; and many of them had been converted by the foreign missionaries to the religions of Moses, of Muhammad, and of Christ. These various systems in freedom and concord were taught and practiced within the precincts of the same camp; and the Bonze, the Imam, the Rabbi, the Nestorian, and the Latin priest, enjoyed the same honorable exemption for service and tribute: in the mosque of (Bukhara) the insolent victor might trample the Koran under his horse's feet, but the calm legislator respected the prophets and pontiffs of the most hostile sects.

What we mean by "tolerance" does not correspond very well to the postures toward the religion of Chinggis, Ogedei, Mongge, or Kublai. The Mongols had their own religion, which they did not consider transferrable to others except in the required worship of Chinggis's votive figure (and the penalty for refusing could be death). A minimal interference in the practice of one religion or another, especially in densely populated regions, was good for business. Clerics could often be enlisted as administrators, and a series of religiously inspired revolts was not what the Mongols had in mind. Indeed, the time and place of Mongol domination of Eurasia was remarkably free of sectarian religious strife in comparison to contemporary Europe or the Muslim, South Asian, and East Asian worlds afterward. But neither a positive affirmation of the right to choose a religious affiliation nor a warm embrace of religious diversity was part of Mongol political ideology.

What is more interesting is Gibbon's assumption that Chinggis's "tolerance" was an isolated anticipation of modernity. To him, modernity welled up from a European spring; it did not flow in rivulets from another source. It was only a curiosity that it had spurted here or there from other ground. And it was a rebuke to those medieval inquisitors who, with their nonsense defended by cruelty, had delayed Europe's passage to science, liberty, and civility. But the connection of religions to travel over the Eurasian land network was intimate, and any community in contact with the network frequently encountered representatives of far countries and novel religious views. The closer any town or city was to the well-traveled center of the Eurasian knowledge core, the more religious ideas it encountered; those at the peripheries of the system, whether in Europe or China, encountered fewer and may have marveled at them more.

The thirteenth century was a particularly rich period of cultural exchange and highly refined debates, particularly about religion. The Mongols, like the Turks before and after them, were by tradition great collegialists and were comfortable contesting important issues—wealth, war, succession—in public. When Chinggis asked the representatives of Daoism and Confucianism to debate the virtues of their beliefs, he was following predecessors who often pitted religious spokesmen against each other in contests over augury or morality: Alexander, the Seleucids, Constantine, and the Sasanians; the Tang emperors, who demanded repeated divination competitions between Buddhists and Daoists; and the Byzantines, who had court debates on policies regarding Jews and the doctrinal debates with the Umayyad caliphs and with Latinate churchmen. The most proximate inspiration for Chinggis's debates may have been those held by the Naiman Kuchluk (see Chapter 6) after seizing the rulership of Kara Kitai. He held public debates among Christian, Buddhist, and Muslim clerics, which he hoped would loosen the hold of Islam on his majority population (this failed).

In 1254, William Rubruck—the Franciscan who was originally sent by Louis IX of France to help German slaves on the Russian steppe and then, by a series of misadventures, ended up in Karakorum—was ordered by Mongge to participate in a prepared debate with representatives of Daoism, Buddhism, and Islam. The debates were held ladder fashion (like Mongol competitions in wrestling, archery, and horse racing). Mongge had advised Rubruck that the individual religious systems were like the separate fingers of the hand—none truly separated from the others, none superior, but each with a distinct function. To the khaghan, the Abrahamic religions were all about the same, so much so that he ordered the Christians and Muslims to form a single team. Later, Mongge dictated a letter to Louis IX recommending that Christians stop squabbling since their doctrinal differences were negligible. The Abrahamic team was lucky enough to be eliminated in the early rounds. In the final match, the Buddhists defeated the Daoists and then demanded that the losers be criminally tried for theft, fraud, and various other abuses in China. Mongge ordered that some tracts of the leading Daoist be destroyed. Further competition as well as criminal prosecutions were delayed because the Karakorum court was embroiled in problems associated with their campaigns in Iran and Korea. Mongge considered the debates important enough (to the empire's search for supernatural efficacy, if not to spiritual enlightenment) that he instructed his youngest brother Ariboka to convene a subsequent contest between the Buddhists and the Daoists; the Abrahamics were no longer regarded as competitors. The contest concluded with Ariboka beating to death the same ostensibly immortal Daoist accused of crimes in 1254. Disappointed, Mongge told his brother Kublai to organize the next event at his capital, Shangdu, in 1258. Kublai added the bookish Confucians and Tibetan Buddhists—practitioners of ecstatic Tantrism, which the Yuan would prove most attracted to during their rule of China—to the debate rounds. The Buddhists of various sects quickly impressed Kublai with their grasp of Sanskrit and Tibetan texts as well as Chinese. Confucians were adept as historians and legal reasoners. Kublai liked both, but declared the Daoists unpersuasive. Their writings were ordered to be destroyed, and their temples lost tax exemption.

Kublai's allies the Ilkhans did not repeat Kuchluk's mistake of sponsoring public debates in which Islam was challenged by Christians or Buddhists. But they did take advantage of the relatively privileged position of Christians in their regime to explore strategic advantages in their wars against the Mamluks. Rabban Sauma (1220–1294) was a Christian cleric of rather unclear Turkic background born at Dadu, who had come west with a colleague to meet with the Christian hierarchs in Baghdad. In 1285, the Ilkhans recruited him to go to Constantinople, Rome, and then on to France to advertise the Ilkhan court, and he set out with a large entourage of interpreters (he could handle Chinese, Uighur, and Persian himself but needed help with Latin and Italian). Sauma was a debating adept, and at Rome in particular, he discoursed with a group of cardinals. They conducted searching forensics on the theological points that Latinate Christians were convinced branded the Greek Christians as deviant and the Central Asian Christians as heretics: the source and nature of the Holy Spirit and its relationship to God and Christ as father and son. Sauma asked the cardinals to solve for him the riddle of how, in a trinity of equal parts, one could be original and two derivative. Though their theological disputes were unresolved, Sauma charmed the pope into friendly gestures toward the Asian church and interested, at least temporarily, the monarchs of England and France in an alliance with the Ilkhans against the Mamluks. For a variety of reasons, the alliances were never realized, but a flurry (in thirteenth-century terms) of exchanges between Tabriz and Europe ensued.

The debates held by the Mongols are often seen not in the context of rhetoric and academic venue but rather in the context of religious plurality. In this respect, the debates at Karakorum, Shangdu, Rome, and Paris are emblematic of a long-standing characteristic of steppe polities: the reluctance, and in many cases inability, to practice any sort of religious exclusivity. This avoided the dangers of powerful religious factions capturing the loyalty of a ruler and expanded the range of supernatural tools that might be available to him. By the late thirteenth century, the Mongols were already expert at keeping the hierarchical religions at arm's length, extending an old tradition among Central Asian rulers (see Chapter 3). In the Toluid empires, Kublai had his closest relationship with Tibetan Buddhists but was more a patron than a believer, and the Ilkhans were sometimes educated as Christians before converting to one or another sect of Islam. The Chaghatay leaders were nominal Muslims but maintained the cult of shamanic Chinggis worship, the Jochid khan Berke was a Muslim but regarded it as a personal choice after long acquaintance with the religion and did not in his time impose conversion on his troops and slaves; the Jochid khans were not consistently Muslim until the early fourteenth century.

This was not a Mongol posture but was part of Central Asian political tradition. From their earliest arrivals in the Middle East, North Africa, and the Balkans, Turks had been minorities. In the days of the Sasanian and early Byzantine empires, nomads clearly tended to synthesize their shamanic traditions with the dominant hierarchical religions, primarily Christianity and Zoroastrianism. Early Turkic states isolated their surviving shamanism in court life, while their military populations became more syncretic and doctrinal communities were recognized in civil life. This resulted in a number of periods in which a post-nomadic court patronized a different religion from the majority of the population. The Bulgar khaghans were shamanists for a period when their majority Slavic population were Christian, and it is likely that the Khazar khans were Jews for a period while their military population were shamanists and their civil populations were Buddhists, Manichaeans, Christians, and Muslims. The Kara Kitai were Confucianists and Buddhists while their majority population was Muslim. In later times, the Delhi sultanates were Muslim while their majority population was Hindu, the Ilkhans were Buddhists while their majority population was Muslim, and the Jochids were Muslims while their majority population was Christian. Religious accommodation was, for most Turkic and Mongol states, a matter of survival.

Islam was a new and different medium in this regard. Unlike Central Asian Christianity, Manichaeanism, or Mahayana Buddhism, Islam in principle was totalistic—only the "peoples of the book" were permitted to live within the Muslim realm; all others had to convert or suffer punishment, usually in the form of higher taxes or lower status (including enslavement). At the same time, Islam introduced an element of religious accommodation toward designated confessional communities that went beyond the indifference that the Turkic and Mongol courts had evinced in eastern Eurasia and Transoxiana. In practice, the Turkic states and the Mongols after them rarely pursued totalizing policies. Those that came closest to eradicating all religions outside those protected by Islamic teaching could not do much to stem sectarianism within Islam. This was a fundamental factor in the Seljuk championing of the *dar al-Islam* concept (see Chapter 5)—a domain in which Sunni Islam was sovereign but variant beliefs accepted. Even the Timurids—

whose pronouncements were staunchly orthodox, repeatedly invoked the caliphate, and justified the conquest of Iran and Iraq as reclamations from the infidel imposters the Ilkhans—were accommodating of other Muslim sects, and the posture was continued by the Mughals.

We often use the word "dissidence" today to mean vocal or even physical opposition to an established order, but its literal meaning is simply to sit apart from the dominant social or ideological groups. This is a universal phenomenon in human societies, but the reactions to it by state formations and religious hierarchies is significant. Not only did Turkic regimes tend to accommodate such sectarian differentiation, they actively relied upon its dynamics in their state development (see Chapter 10). As the early post-nomadic states had been wary of centralization and accumulation of power—whether by an individual or a clique—so the later post-nomadic states attempted to keep power dispersed by broadcasting favor among competing groups, sponsoring the disadvantaged against the privileged, and immunizing themselves against the authority of any local religious or philosophical system. The Mamluks of Egypt were characteristic of this practice of Islamic pluralism. Although they perpetuated many Ayyubid practices and attitudes, they never returned to the severity of Ayyubid domestic policies against Coptic Christians or Muslim sects, particularly the Shi'ites and Ismailis. Like the Seljuks, the Ilkhans, and the Timurids, the Mamluks also welcomed the liberal and accommodationist legal interpretations of the Hanafite jurists—though they gave priority to a more conservative school. The Mamluk sultans were also patrons of Sufist (see below) teachers and congregations and repeatedly penalized the most prominent critic of Sufism, ibn Taymiyya (1263–1328, born to an Arabic-speaking family residing just inside the borders of modern Turkey and probably of Kurdish descent). It may have increased Mamluk impatience with him that he was a consistent critic of a variety of influences arising from Turkic and Mongol conquest of the Muslim world—Sufism (particularly of the Bukharan style), the Hanafite legal school, religious pluralism, Christianity, and the Ilkhans themselves. The Ottomans drew upon the history of Turkic pluralism, even before their conquest of Constantinople, by issuing special invitations to Jewish merchants and scholars to settle in Anatolia. Mehmet II learned both Latin and Greek to read philosophical texts and invited the most famous Greek scholars—some of them converts to Islam and some of them still Orthodox Christians—to lecture both at court and in the schools sponsored by the court across the empire. The sultan also sponsored schools of Christian theology. By the fifteenth century, the empire had the greatest concentration in the world of knowledge of mathematics, engineering and architecture, weaponry, and cartography.

THE SCIENCE OF REALITY IN MEDIEVAL EURASIA

The historian Christopher Beckwith wrote in detail (see reading notes) of the development and dissemination of a particular style of debate across medieval Eurasia. In essence, he was looking at the evolution of rules for constructing oppositional arguments on various subjects (primarily cosmology and theology). The origin of these practices, he hypothesizes, was in Central Asian educational traditions, probably in the vicinity of ancient Gandhara (see Chapter 1 and Map 1.1), where Indian and later Greek philosophies were known and compared. Early monastic traditions and early academic traditions are impossible to distill from each other. South Asian monasticism appeared to have an influence on religious life of the Levant in the first millennium BCE, and in the first millennium CE expanded through Christian communities of Anatolia, the Balkans, and Central Europe. Certainly, by the last centuries BCE, academic centers adapting some monastic institutions to philosophical study and teaching were evident in South Asia, Central Asia, and Greece. In the confessional age, academies thrived under religious patronage throughout the Islamic world. Those at Fez and Cairo were operating hundreds of years before European theologians founded their earliest universities at Bologna, Paris, and Sicily. Constantinople was an open conduit of knowledge, from the Abbasid domains to the Byzantine empire and from there to all of Christian Europe, while scholars—philosophers, mathematicians, physicians, historians—of Islamic Spain were read in scattered parts of southern France.

Europe in the time of Charlemagne appears to have been an intellectual and technological dependency of the Byzantine–Muslim world. What Europeans north of the Pyrenees and west of the Balkans lacked was knowledge of Greek and good transportation to get them as far as the Iberian emirates, Constantinople, or the Levant. It would not be quite right to say that in these centuries, Europe—particularly Europe west of the Balkans—had lost all contact with the Greek legacy. They read Augustine of Hippo (35–430), who made references to his study of Plato and whose *City of God* was a discernibly Platonist (or as Christians attributed Platonic influences to Paul, "Pauline") text. Boethius (480–524), was a church official in Rome had standing for medieval European scholars; his two sons, in the sixth century, made some of the last direct comments on Aristotle and Plato surviving in early medieval writing. But Europeans were not known to write about Greek philosophical texts after that time, and as mentioned earlier, they lost common knowledge of the Greek language after the eighth century (see Chapter 4).

By that time, contrapuntal dialectics were widespread through the Greek, Arabic, and Chinese academic worlds. The source venue for application of early argumentation was a collection—a college—of teachers and students, an institution attested in early Indian texts and possibly an influence on ancient Greek academies. Public discourse, conducted before qualified audiences and judged by the criteria of these rhetorical forms, spread to the Islamic world soon after the creation of the Umayyad caliphate, which established colleges across the Levant, Iran/Iraq, North Africa, and Spain. Though the written form is what we know today, these techniques were most frequently employed in oral, public debate. It would have been logical for William Rubruck to have used these methods when ordered to argue the value of Christianity at Mongge's court at Karakorum—indeed, in preparation for the debate, William argued the opposite proposition, for Buddhism, a distinct technique of the dialectical tradition. And it is equally likely that Rabban Sauma used these techniques when debating the cardinals in Rome.

Beckwith notes that, although the Muslim scholastic world often claimed credit for preservation and development of the Greek philosophical heritage, the better attribution might include northwest Indian scholars at Gandhara and connected communities of the pre-Islamic era. From there, it was transmitted (along with texts and ideas) to both the Mahayana Buddhist and the Islamic worlds. The Gandharan nexus can be assumed to have had many continuities with early Indian philosophical speculation, mathematical work, and astronomy. In pre-Buddhist times, Indian texts already showed evidence of advanced mathematical features (including sine functions and the first representation of zero) and formal logic. Logicians—like mathematicians and natural philosophers—were usually members of the Brahmin priestly class, and the development appears to have been dialectical, probably dependent upon the kind of courtyard debates that are referred to in early Indian texts. There was speculation—perhaps with direct stimulation from Plato and Aristotle, after the establishment of regular connections by the Seleucids (see Chapter 1)—on issues of universal forms and on whether reality was immanent in the phenomenal world. In an attempt to distill reality from illusion, there was a formal approach to exclusive categories with proofs of truth or falsehood. The centrality of Plato in these early traditions was powered in significant degree by his proposition that the inconstancy of material entities—their inevitable processes of growing, aging, and weathering—suggests that their apparent form at any point in time cannot be their true form. Instead, they partake of a defining essence that transcends the hazards of time and chance. Their essence was in fact their function in the real universe that was only dimly perceptible to the intuition of philosophers and invisible to the general run of mankind. This duality of one original and superior world of truth and one reflected and degraded world of material illusion would haunt the philosophical and religious systems of Eurasia to the present day.

From an early point, Buddhist logicians—almost always attached to monastic colleges—realized the need to grapple with formal proofs of reality. Ultimately, the problem of Buddhism's insistence that the phenomenal world is an illusion challenged philosophers to explain how Buddha himself came to this realization and how any living human might be enlightened. Many concluded that for enlightenment to occur, there must be consciousness, and as a result consciousness is real. But logically, nothing beyond consciousness could be proved to exist because the possibility that anything that appears to be outside consciousness is only a production of consciousness itself could not be excluded. The opposing argument tended to follow the outlines of early Indian philosophy, proposing that phenomena are composed of real but infinitely transient particles. Buddha, truth, and consciousness were one unified and permanent reality, and empirical observation of the phenomenal world was nevertheless an exercise in reality. By the early centuries CE, the main school of Buddhist logicians (Yogachara) had established two pillars of the method of determining truth, particularly the reality of phenomena, of perception and of logical inference. But Buddhist logicians were constantly debating among themselves and with Hindu logicians. The result was perpetual synthesis and the diverging of new discourses of logical theory, eventually producing an influential school of the northeast Indian philosopher Dharmakirti (sixth to seventh centuries).

These influences along with the institutions of monasteries (including scribal facilities) and colleges were evident in the Gandharan triangle and spread not only westward toward Jewish, Christian, and later Islamic zones but also eastward toward China, Korea, and Japan. Ancient Chinese philosophy had several schools of logic and linguistics, but they had been suppressed after the establishment of state Confucianism during the Han period. Several schools of ostensibly Confucian philosophy continued the logical and linguistic studies of the pre-imperial period, refusing to endorse the older schools by name but striving to subsume their basic principles. This classical "Confucianism" was firmly rooted in accepting the reality of the natural world and human history. To some degree, it could be challenged on these points by Daoism, but—except for the centuries of disunion between about 200 and 600 CE—the political and social influence of Confucianism kept Daoist influence modest among the literate elite. The earliest significant influences of Buddhism on Chinese society were evident in the elite cultures of the Xiongnu, Sarbi, and Turkic states of the third to seventh centuries as well as the Sui and Tang empires in China, the early period of the Tibetan empire, the Shilla state in Korea, and the Nara and early Heian periods of Japan. The sectarian differentiation of Mahayana before coming to East Asia facilitated its adoption. Practices could vary from highly disciplined, textually based study to extremely simple faith based approaches that required minimal textual knowledge and few esoteric practices. The latter contributed to the spread of Buddhism among commoners, as temples often combined Daoist imagery of hell and judgment with Buddhist representations of salvation. The belief that instant enlightenment could result from selfless repetition of the Buddha's honorific was widespread. Among the better educated, this was accompanied by training in meditation, usually focused on one or another short passage (*sutra*) from the translated Buddhist texts. The best-known technique, Zen (the Japanese term, from Chinese Chan, itself from Sanskrit *dhyana*), became a fixture of both elite and popular culture across China, Vietnam, Korea, and Japan by the ninth century.

It was the impact of Buddhism in China that slowly changed the world of Chinese philosophy, and it happened mostly in the late Tang and Song periods. Several prominent founders of so-called neo-Confucianisn—among them Cheng Hao (1032–1085) and Lu Xiangshan (1139–1192)—had spent years in study of Buddhism (and often Daoism) before dedicating themselves to Confucian teachings. For them, the reality of the world was not self-evident, and proving that it was real required theorizing about cosmology, perception, and above all, the mind. Speculative Confucians (who called themselves specialists in the study of "principal," or immanent cosmological patterning) divided along the lines of a rationally based mind/matter dichotomy on the one hand and an intuitively based identity of mind and matter on the other. In general, the Chinese world of speculative philosophy after the impact of Buddhism showed a trait that was widespread across Eurasia, including those traditions that had constructed the ideal/real dichotomy as a debate between Plato and his student Aristotle: idealist claims that knowledge of reality was accessible only by disciplined intuition were in general the objects of criticism from rationalist assertions that the phenomenal world has a reality independent of human consciousness, perception, and linguistic expression—and is accessible through teaching and reason. The importance of the confessional-age context (see Chapter 4) is critical here because the pervasive dichotomy of spiritual and military authority was conceptually hospitable to the rationalist mind–matter dichotomies and their metaphors. The idealists were never eradicated, but they were always under suspicion. Idealist neo-Confucians could be accused of being crypto-Buddhists, and Islamic and Christian idealist philosophers could be accused of gnosticism, mysticism, or outright paganism. In certain periods, religious and political authorities claimed a ubiquity of subversive idealisms as justifications for persecutions of individuals and groups. In the Chinese case, the establishment of Confucian orthodoxy (first by decree during the Yuan period and then by institutionalization in the examination system of the Ming) provides a particularly clear illustration of the investment of the late medieval state in both rationalism and popularization.

The advantages of a rationalist orthodoxy to the state are clear enough: The mind–body (often represented as the struggle between moral reason and natural instinct) dichotomy allows efficient legitimation of the authority of officials, the law, and teachers as necessary intercessors in the perfection of reasoning. In contrast, idealist propositions of personal revelation and intuitive knowledge was always a potential justification for solipsism, dissidence, resistance, and rebellion. Idealists such as Wang Yangming (1472–1529) claimed to be unqualified Confucians by affirming the reality of the material universe and asserting the universality of an organizing causative force. For this reason they argued that rationalists and idealists—if they used the correct methods—must ultimately arrive at the same moral truths. But critics of Wang protested that his philosophy licensed every individual to seek truth without the discipline of teachers or the law. Moreover, Wang's claim that knowledge was never valid without the action it entailed was an invitation to rebellion and assassination. This aspect of Wang's philosophy had a deep impact in Japan of the seventeenth, eighteenth, and nineteenth centuries. Nevertheless, from the time of Wang Yangming's writings in the early 1520s to today, even authorities who recognized the dangers of the individual discretion that Wang's idealism prescribed did not advocate jailing or executing those who espoused it (at least, not merely for the act of espousing it).

On another level, declaring an orthodoxy within Confucianism—advocated by Xu Heng (1209–1281) and other unlikely scholars who had shot to the top of the Yuan bureaucracy—allowed the Yuan state to blunt the effects of literati factionalism on the court in parallel to the Ilkhanate's insulation of itself from religious factionalism. The Yuan declaration of orthodoxy settled the issue of philosophical competition of the Song period, when academies and social networks attempted to gain influence over the examinations and political appointments. It also changed the accessibility of high-level literacy and political aspiration on the ground. The works of the Song arch-rationalist Zhu Xi (1130–1200) were easily selected as the advantageous works to read. The retention of the orthodoxy through most of the Ming period and all of the Qing amplified the effects of newly popularized and vernacularized philosophical and academic discourse as the examinations became again the primary avenue to bureaucratic appointment.

While Buddhism was having its multifaceted impact on philosophy in East Asia, the effects of early Indian philosophy and mathematics, with or without the overlay of Buddhist logic, were having their own effects on the nearby Islamic world. Royal patronage had played a certain role in the emergence of Hindu and Buddhist discursive communities; imperial patronage had its share in the rise and establishment of neo-Confucian philosophers; and caliphs of the early Islamic empires always sponsored institutions for theological, mathematical, and astronomical study. Nevertheless, the patronage role of the Turkic sultans of the Islamic world was unusual. Their tendency to sponsor multiple competing sects produced a concomitant increase in the number of schools. Under the Mongol regimes as well as the Timurids and Mughals, chartering of research institutes (often on palace grounds) produced new opportunities for diversity of influence and the refinements of long-term debate—in person or via written treatises. In the ninth century,

Arab scholiasts were still building the foundations of Muslim philosophy at the academy in Baghdad founded for the purposes of translating Greek philosophical texts and Sanskrit mathematical treatises into Arabic. They also did some early writing on the problems that would occupy virtually all philosophers of the Muslim and Christian worlds: reconciling religion and natural philosophy (i.e., what we now mean by "science"). These early scholars offered no very great synthesis beyond the suggestion that there was a categorical distinction between spiritual knowledge—and especially prophetic revelation—on the one hand and rational observation of the natural world on the other.

Later in the century, scholars developed a field of speculation (which they customarily credited to Aristotle's influence) that would become critically important to most of the philosophers of medieval Eurasia: the use of formal logic to develop a science of method. In the Seljuk period, Muslim scholars writing in Arabic extended the problems of perception and philosophy of knowledge to investigations of optics and light, which would remain a preoccupation of philosophers into the early modern period. Ibn Rushd (Averroes; 1126–1128), by far the most influential in Europe among these Islamic philosophers, defended the scientific inquiries of mathematics, motion, astronomy, and optics from charges of blasphemy. In the Seljuk period, he explored the different kinds of being among entities, distinguishing that which is uncreated and creating, moving others but never itself moved—uniquely, God—from that which is created and animated, limited in time and attributes—the natural world. He also speculated on the agency by which spiritual but not ultimate beings (of the category of *djinn*, which in this context can be compared to angels, *bodhisattva*, or the ancient *asura* and *deva*) caused movement and change in the world because of their pursuit of the love of God (an idea parallel to Plato's concept of motion and action generated by a pursuit of the good).

Europeans regained some access to the texts of Aristotle or Plato by way of the great philosophers of the Abbasid and early Seljuk periods. These were translations into Latin from Arabic from Greek, and some commentaries on cosmology and logic may have gone from Sanskrit to Arabic to Latin. European philosophers who became enthusiastic about Ibn Rushd (the "Averroists") tended to claim that reality was bifurcated—one aspect controlled by rules applying to God and one aspect controlled by rules applying to the natural world. Only in regard to the natural world should strictly rational methods apply. This dualism—which was frequently associated with idealist neo-Platonism—got them branded as heretics (famously by Thomas Aquinas, who wrote a tract about it) and their writings banned at the end of the thirteenth century.

A victim of the vagaries of public debate in medieval Europe was Peter Abelard (1079–1142), a lecturer with a blazing early reputation in Paris. He was a hero of the contrapuntal dialecticians and famous for his early work, "Yes and No" (*Sic et non*). As a philosopher, he tended to favor Aristotle over Plato (or, the ostensible Aristotle over the ostensible Plato) and was an advocate for "nominalism" against "realism." In this he was in line with other nominalists like Thomas Aquinas and Albertus Magnus, all combatting widespread but often vague Platonist ideas. Abelard was later pushed into silence as a result of personal conflict (which included his castration by thugs working for the uncle of his beloved, Héloise) and doctrinal disputes with the Roman Church. His early subject was dialectical method, logic, and philosophy, but he later moved on to theology. After being charged with heresy in 1121 and convicted, he was forced to burn his own theological treatise. For a short time, he lived as a hermit and then took up leadership of a new monastery (where Héloise was in residence). He rewrote his lost work and, in the last years of his life, taught at a small monastery outside Paris. This got him into trouble again, and he was excommunicated. But the intervention of high-ranking church authorities persuaded the pope to lift his excommunication just before Abelard died.

With consistency, Abelard argued what he considered the Aristotelian position of the reality of the phenomenal world in its own right and that ideal forms were immanent in the material world, not derived from another realm (very similar to the earlier proposition of Hindu cosmologists). Nevertheless, when he moved on to theology, Abelard's speculations on the rational origins of knowledge and the arbitrariness of language brought him into conflict with a number of church doctrines, especially the nature and comprehensibility of the Holy Trinity—fortunately, when Rabban Sauma arrived in Paris nearly a century and a half later to debate some of the same issues using many of the same techniques, everybody was in a better mood about it. In his autobiography, Abelard commented that at the depth of his troubles, he considered leaving Christendom altogether and living among the "heathen." He did not specify which corner of heathendom attracted him, but it is not difficult to guess since he makes a clear reference to the special tax that Muslim states levied on Christians. Evidently, he was considering moving to Andalusia or to Seljuk Anatolia. Since he chose for his surname "Abelard," the name of one of the original leaders of the Crusades against the Seljuks, it could well have been in that direction he was looking. Either would have been appropriate because virtually the entire framework of university debate and philosophical inquiry in Abelard's lifetime was a product of the influence of Central Asia and the Islamic world.

The odd thing about the ferocity with which Abelard, Aquinas, and others pursued their intellectual battle against "realism" (i.e., what I am calling idealist cosmology) was that their opposition to Plato and Platonist Christian commentators—among them Augustine, John Scotus (810–877), Anselm of Canterbury (1033–1109), Bernard of Chartres (d. c. 1125), and John of Salisbury (1120–1180)—was constructed without much direct reference to the works of either Aristotle or Plato. The problems most frequently debated were whether the existence of God could be logically proved, the nature of the soul, the identity of the Holy Spirit, and how Christ could have been both divine and human. Of the four, the last was most dangerous and, of course, had never been of interest to either Aristotle or Plato. The terms in which medieval European philosophers framed their arguments were much more like the concepts of Zoroastrianism, Manichaeanism, and venerable Eurasian folk religions than anything to do with Aristotle or Plato. This was particularly visible in the debates over the nature of Christ since it was actually a traditional Eurasian dualist—and not necessarily Platonist—position to refuse to accept that spiritual light and Satanic matter could be irreducibly combined in a single entity. The "nominalists"—deniers of an ideal realm—complained widely of Platonism and Nestorian-style heresies, suggesting they felt themselves surrounded by them. The self-described Aristotelians were basic rationalists of the mind–matter dichotomy sort on other matters and, in most but not all cases, were eager to affirm church authority in teaching and the law, just as their contemporaries in China were eager to affirm the authority of the state in teaching and the law. But in general, even the most strident nominalists were still reliant upon idealist concepts for understanding the soul and the agency of the Holy Spirit, and in many cases, for their reasoning about the existence of God.

The treatment of Abelard (and other European "heretics" between about 1000 and 1600) was a contrast to the treatment of divergent philosophy in the Islamic world of the same period. This is not to say that the Islamic world nurtured religious free-thinking. Extreme religious heretics attempting coups d'état, or Christians attempting to convert Muslims, or apostate Muslims, were in a few instances executed, sometimes by fire. But philosophers were not considered threats in themselves. An illustrative example is Ibn Sina (Avicenna; 980–1037). Criticism of him by Ibn Rushd produced the impression that Ibn Sina was a Platonist, a gnostic, or a "mystic." This was not quite true. He was a great admirer of Aristotle and, if anything, attempted a synthesis of Aristotelian and Platonic problem solving: that is, he sought the great Eurasian philosophical goal of finding the surest means to affirm whether reality was at root phenomenal or noumenal, and exactly how it attached to God. Despite the rejection of Ibn Sina's work by strict rationalists and orthodox religious authorities, it was never banned. Philosophical dissidence, perhaps primarily because of its associations with the sultanal academies, was as essential to the state as was religious dissidence.

Much about Ibn Sina was uncommon. He was a product of the Sartic world, not of Baghdad: raised outside Bukhara (which in his lifetime, was passing from the Samanids to the Seljuks); familiar with the great libraries of Balkh (his father's native town), Gorgan, Isfahan, and Hamadan; educated as a jurist of the Hanafite school; and writing not exclusively in Arabic but occasionally in Persian. In early life, he supported himself by tutoring students in Euclid and Ptolemy. Much of his theory of knowledge came from his understanding of Aristotle's rationalism, and he borrowed a great deal of Aristotle's cosmology as well. He also shared some reasoning with Ibn Rushd on the proof of God as that which must be first, prior, uncreated. And generations—really, centuries—of readers were charmed by his imaginal concept of a man created in an instant, floating in the air but having no sensations and in fact no physical attributes; his consciousness of being would in itself prove the existence of the soul and that it precedes and transcends the material existence of the body. Ibn Sina's theory of reality relied upon an idea of universal forms (the hated target of Ibn Rushd and Abelard), meaning a perfect reality imperfectly and unreliably reflected in the phenomenal world. In his later career, he offered a detailed explanation of causation as the agency by which the real world emanated to the phenomenal world and speculated on the possibilities for human apprehension of the reality behind illusion. This took him back through early Abbasid philosophy to the basic questions of classical Indian and Greek thought (with cognates in medieval Europe and China): the primacy of being and whether the powers of action that cause phenomena and perception are part of the primal unity (for Ibn Sina, God) or in some way derivative and amenable to rational analysis.

Like many idealist thinkers from earliest times, Ibn Sina attributed the properties of noumenal conveyance, truth, constancy, and spiritual illumination to light. The sciences of light, reflection, refraction, and perception were deeply explored by mathematicians from an early period. Ibn Sina's interest in Euclid was an important influence on him in this regard, as were the ninth- and tenth-century works by Baghdad scholars who discovered that visual perception of movement and color is the result of light entering the eye under the principles of refraction. Ibn Sina and his contemporaries also became certain that light moves—meaning that it is not instantaneous or uncreated but has an attribute, speed—and that it moves much faster than sound. For Ibn Sina, light was the possible point of reconciliation for idealists and rationalists. It was created and moved as a transitional or causative agent but had within it the immanent reality of the truer world from which it emanated.

Successive waves of Arabic and then Persian scholarship were transmitted to Europe via both Cordoba and Constantinople, leading to the spectacular career of Roger Bacon (1220–1292). He was not only a reader of the Latin translations of a wide range of Arabic scholarship but was also a friend of William Rubruck and conceivably encountered Rabban Sauma at Paris. He is reasonably considered a philosopher, but his major completed work was essentially a catalog of knowledge at the time. It was not unprecedented in concept, following the basic outlines and methods of Vincent of Beauvais's

Great Mirror of 1244 (see Chapter 10). But Bacon's work gave greater emphasis and development to scientific knowledge as contrasted to history and myth. It was almost entirely a synthesis of knowledge transmitted to Europe by Muslim philosophers—the works of Aristotle, Plato, and Euclid; Central Asian pharmacology as synthesized in Gandhara, China, and Baghdad; mathematics from Greece, India, Gandhara, and Baghdad; astronomy drawing upon constructs and observations from Gandhara, Baghdad, Samarkand, and China; alchemy from across Eurasia, including a description of firecrackers powered by charcoal, saltpeter, and sulfur; optics inherited from classical sources and advanced by experiment and speculation in Baghdad and Cordoba; and linguistics from Gandhara and Baghdad.

Bacon has sometimes been described as a visionary anticipating the empiricism and skepticism of modern thought. But he is most remarkable for his ability to catalog the information available through the monasteries and libraries of his time. His work helped make possible Europe's intellectual transition from a dependency of the Muslim world to an independent producer of objective knowledge. The key to Bacon's relative lack of trouble from secular and religious authorities seemed to lie in his distance from genuine philosophical—in the European environment, inevitably religious—speculation. He represented a kind of border beyond which European philosophers who retained a Platonic, Pythagorean, or gnostic flavor (or combined it with newly imported Egyptian mysticism to evince "hermeticism") were increasingly at risk—culminating with the burning of Giordano Bruno in Rome in 1600. In contrast, those like Kepler and Copernicus, who carefully reconciled their hypotheses to church teachings or, like Newton, kept their mystical interests private in their own time (and helpfully obscured by some biographers), could carry on to produce the intellectual foundations of Europe's so-called scientific revolution and the myth that it was essentially Aristotelian in inspiration.

Historians sometimes (less now than in the past) invoke an "idea of science" when explaining why Central Asia, or Tibet, or India, or the Muslim world was not the source of modern scientific thinking, and why such thinking should be so strongly evident in eighteenth-century Europe. The notion attributes to Aristotle a precocious scientific ethos and then suggests that anybody fighting the ostensibly "Aristotelian" fight of the medieval and early modern periods was pursuing the "idea of science." But the weakness begins with the Aristotelian paradigm and its supposed opposition to Platonic idealisms from classical to modern times; from India to Gandhara to Baghdad to Paris, ancient and medieval philosophers were repeatedly finding overlaps and syntheses between the two. It is hard to argue that the Aristotle/Plato dichotomy was much more than a heuristic and rhetorical device for discussing issues of reality and perception—and to usefully marginalize and if possible eliminate troublesome dissidents who had (or could be accused of having) dualist or idealist tendencies. To the extent that the distinction is meaningful, most of what we today regard as scientific inquiry in the ancient and medieval world was connected to doubts about the reality of phenomena and skepticism of matter—the opposite end of the spectrum from Aristotle and the Peripatetics.

But those who invoke the "idea of science" imply that only Europe could genuinely inherit it. Beckwith, for instance, finds that translating and studying Aristotle could impart a weak scientism to other cultures and suggests this happened in the Islamic world, but was suppressed by harsh orthodox critics such as al-Ghazali (1058–1111)—and he could have mentioned ibn Taymiyya as well. Beckwith implies that Ibn Sina was imprisoned for his philosophical views, which is not regarded today as probable (he was certainly imprisoned, but it appeared to be as a result of a dispute involving his patron). Though al-Ghazali could be a harsh critic, he mainly insisted that philosophers stick to science and leave religion alone. Even with respect to religion, al-Ghazali made clear that only one part (the idealist part) of Ibn Sina's thought was problematic, and he credited Ibn Sina with inspiring part of his own theological commentaries. In Syria, the Mamluks imprisoned and fined Ibn Tamiyyah, probably repeatedly, for his criticisms of unorthodox philosophers (Ibn Sina in particular). In the worlds of the post-nomadic rulers of the Middle East, India, and China, ideas—including what might be called "ideas of science"—were common currency and resulted in bodily penalty.

The reasons Europeans of the seventeenth and eighteenth centuries started getting self-consciously scientific surely involved many factors that are not part of this discussion, but it is worth pointing out that the war against the "idea of science" was waged more fiercely in medieval Europe than anywhere else in Eurasia. Objective sciences of the natural world—astronomy, pharmacology, physics, optics, mathematics, and linguistics—were disseminated all over the continent, particularly when waves of post-nomadic rule over Iran/Iraq, Central Asia, and China created the transportation infrastructure, institutional nodes, and discursive fluidity to make them almost universally available to literates after about 900 CE. Rationalism, often with explicit reference to Aristotle, was welcomed and, more often than not, given the more authoritative position. From the perspective of the transmission of ideas and local responses to them, Europe is distinct in two obvious ways: its interval without direct access to the natural philosophy of the ancient Greeks and the hostility of its religious authorities to certain kinds of philosophical speculation. The worlds of the sultans produced classic and novel science without much ado. Speculation was accommodated—even if not always welcomed—and knowledge proceeded without the steady production of inquisitions, martyrdoms, or underground networks of occult, hermetic, or mystical teachings. Once new, strong post-nomadic rulerships (see Chapter 11) undermined religious authority and eradicated some of the regional discretion to punish or reward natural philosophers, it was the novelty of "science" that made it easy for Europeans of the seventeenth century to define, and which gave it much of its power. History suggests that Europe's centuries of dependency and repression are more likely to be factors in its later intellectual transformation than any "idea of science" that was absent in the vaster Eurasian world. And this appears to be paralleled by the interactions of repression and subsequent liberation in the spiritual and political realms.

LIGHT, DISSIDENCE, AND INDEPENDENT LEARNING

From the earliest beginnings of discursive studies, public debates, collegiate education, and academic writings, the question was why speculation and rationalism were needed at all in environments in which the hierarchical religions of Buddhism, then Christianity, and then Islam claimed to provide all the answers—whether on origins of the universe, destiny of the soul, or the meaning of good works on Earth. In all these environments, orthodox religious authorities posed the question to the philosophers repeatedly: Why was doctrine not enough? None of these doctrinal systems was immune to subversion by the widespread assumptions of the ideology of light and dark that had pervaded Eurasia before the doctrines had emerged. What philosophers in Islamdom and in Christendom saw as the classic question between Aristotle and Plato was never fully resolved. It was impossible for the reality of the material world to be taken for granted forever; there was too much suppressed writing and secret teaching from idealists of all varieties challenging the proposition over many centuries. Even for those convinced that the natural world was real in every sense, the hypothesis of a single, unifying God was constantly being pursued as an independent problem, one that would be best reconciled, whether by contrivance or convergence, with religious doctrine. Across medieval Eurasia, the propositions of God, soul, and destiny were never regarded as unquestionable, and scholars worked in cognate ways to develop the intellectual technologies to question, hypothesize, and debate.

It is significant that the Muslim Turkic regimes of the thirteenth and fourteenth centuries not only observed the religious obligations from the Quran to protect all the Abrahamic religions but also added a liberality that set them off from much of the rest of Eurasia and North Africa. Their tendency to preserve at least some shamanic lineage rituals at court and their long historical association with various kinds of Christianity might have been influential in this. But it is equally likely that their attractions to folk literature and pastimes (see Chapter 11) were not separate from an interest in folk religions, particularly the basic ideas of light and dark, soul and body, appearance and reality, and spiritual intercessors that over time frayed the edges of all the hierarchical religions. When Hulagu destroyed the Ismaili headquarters and library at Mount Alamut in 1256, he came away with a remarkable adviser, Nasir al-Din Tusi (see Chapter 7). At the beginning of the campaign, Tusi had been inside the fortified city where he had been living under the protection of the small Ismaili state at least since the late 1230s. In the course of Hulagu's siege of Alamut, he encountered Tusi as an interlocutor, and after the destruction of the Ismaili state, Hulagu took Tusi on as a general guide to things Persian and Muslim. Under the sponsorship of the Ilkhan court, Tusi wrote comprehensively on all sects of Islam and all varieties of Muslim philosophy. He had been born into a family of Shi'ites and later allied himself with the Ismailis, but his strongest sympathies seem to have fixed to a school of mystical philosophy called in English "illuminism" or "illuminationism"—based on an Arabic term (*eshraq*) that shared roots with the European word *Saracen* and the Arabic inspiration for the term Levant (see Chapter 8). The school was strongly associated with the legacy of Ibn Sina's idealist cosmology and theory of knowledge in which he had made intuitive apprehension of and imaginative anticipation of God equal to or better than reason. He wrote a specialized essay on gnostics in which he credited them with wisdom in overcoming the deceptions of material existence and achieving knowledge that is closest to perfect—engaging soul, mind, and body in a unity of knowledge and bliss. This provided critics such as Ibn Rushd enough evidence to condemn him as a neo-Platonist mystic, the guise in which he is known to much of Islamic and European history of thought. But it provided the illuminationists a link to ancient Eurasian gnostic ideologies.

The most prominent—if a bit late in the development overall of illuminist theology—philosopher was Suhrawardi (1154–1191) who, writing in Persian, synthesized the ancient light–dark cosmological ideas of Eurasia, particularly Zoroastrianism, with the teachings of Plato and Ibn Sina. His theology was based explicitly on light as both a spiritual and physical force and the source of all energy in the universe, including the agencies by which God and lesser spiritual presences effected causation in the phenomenal world. Suhrawardi posited that many of Aristotle's attitudes toward evidence and reason were valid, but as he matured he came to believe that true knowledge is spiritual and arrives through mystical transcendence of the limitations of the body. Late in his life, he got into trouble in Syria by advocating subjective reading of the Quran—interpretations arrived at by individual reasoning and intuition, a religious cognate to his Chinese contemporary Lu Xiangshan's theories of investigation of nature and history by reliance on consciousness. The circumstances of Suhrawardi's death are unclear, but it is possible that he is an example in medieval Islam of a philosopher being executed for heretical ideas—in this case, ideas relating in the most intimate way to the religious instruction and Quranic interpretation. He had, in other words, violated al-Ghazali's precept that the philosophers should stick to philosophy.

Suhrawardi's cosmological ideas had the strongest possible kinship to the Sufist movement. Sufism is often characterized as "mystical" because it encourages practitioners to seek a merging of their identity with that of God outside the rational and ethical teachings of religion. It posits an original reality that is precisely positioned between light and matter, an undifferentiated state in which God exists uniquely. The believer is impeded in his or her progress toward unity with God by actions of a Satan or demiurge, who has created the material world. The struggle against the false world, to arrive at communion with God, is the Sufist's struggle, or *jihad*. Because Sufism has in most periods been accepted as a fully Islamic teaching, some historians of Islam dislike looking to non-Islamic inspirations for Sufi concepts and methods. Others see Sufism to be an inheritance from all prophets of the Abrahamic religions, including Daniel, Abraham, Moses, Jesus, and Muhammad—all of whom can be seen as Sufis first and prophets of particular religions second, an idea close to Mani's notions of prophetic legacy. Most non-Muslim scholars consider the roots of Sufism to lie not only in Islam but also Zoroastrianism, Platonism, Christian Gnosticism, and Manichaeanism. Certainly, Sufism suggests a strong continuity with the Eurasian belief systems of light and dark that persistently seeped into all the hierarchical religions. These would include tantric Buddhism—the teachings of independent access to enlightenment—which shared some practices with Sufism and also had a reception at the Yuan court that paralleled Sufism's status in the Seljuk and Ilkhan regimes.

To overcome the phenomenal obstacles and unite with God, the Sufist believer must enter into a transcendent state, often achieved through music, drumming, dancing, meditation, or drugs. The state of receptivity to truth is believed to be increased by practice of asceticism in dress, diet, and living conditions. It is through immersion in the noumenal world of truth that the believer becomes one with God. Like the gnostic formulations of Zoroastrianism, Buddhism, Judaism (whose Karaites were thriving alongside the Sufis in the Islamic world), Christianity, Manichaeanism, and East Asian idealist intuitionism (of the Lu Xiangshan/Wang Yangming variety), Sufism is a path of personal salvation that obviates conventional priests, congregations, temples, and hierarchical authority. Not only its cosmology but also its geography link Sufism with Central Asia. The proposition that innate knowledge and intuition are essential to religious completion was taught by several reputed "mystics" from an early point after the establishment of Islam, particularly in Baghdad and nearby parts of Iraq, and later became influential in Andalusia and Egypt in Islam's early centuries. But after the Abbasid founding in 750, Persian poetry became the primary vehicle for the expression of

Sufist ideas and sentiments, and the foci of Sufist/illuminist influences moved to eastern Iran and Transoxiana; Omar Khayyam—whose mathematical ideas as well as poetry incorporated intuitionist propositions—was born in Nishapur in 1048 and educated nearby, and the most noted Sufi poet of the period, Jalal al-Din Rumi (1207–1273) was born and educated in Balkh before he moved to the sultanate in Anatolia, which inspired his later epithet of "Rumi"). The most influential Sufi sect of the later medieval period, the Naqshbandiyyah, was founded at Bukhara in the fourteenth century.

Sufist themes were pervasive in the court practices, personal beliefs, patronage preferences, and artistic efforts of Turkic sultans of the Ilkhan, Mamluk, Ottoman, Timurid, and Mughal courts. It has been of some interest to historians that the Sufist emphasis on transcendence and ecstasy—on an intuitive encounter with truth that bypasses rational and moral teachings—recalled the most ancient and widespread elements of popular religion across Eurasia and especially across Central Asia (see Chapter 5 reading notes). This need not mean that Turkic courts regarded Sufis as shamans. It might only mean that they regarded Sufis as using means of spiritual access that paralleled those of traditional shamans; in this sense, Timur may have been completing a circle by looking to Sufis to confirm his own shamanically derived spiritual powers. What is probably most significant is that the mainstream Sufist school's outlook was accommodationist, blunting what would otherwise be sharp edges of sectarian disputes that could threaten the Turkic regimes. When there were exceptions—as an episode of political interference by the extreme sect, the Hurufiyya at the Ottoman court of Mehmet II—there could be violent purges or exiles. The tendency of Turkic courts was to patronize Sufi sects (a different issue from any appeal it had for Turkic populations), and particularly moderate ones. Such patronage preserved a state diffidence respecting all sorts of religious partisanship, while complementing the interest of these regimes in vernacularization of language and the performing arts (see Chapter 10).

The importance of the political and cultural agendas of the post-nomadic states in fostering religious ideas adumbrating modernity is evident by a comparison of the Sufis with a contemporary group, the medieval European Cathars (Albigensians). Historians sometimes link the Sufis and the Cathars through their apparent shared gnostic or dualist inspirations, but there is a more important reason to discuss them together at this point. As in the case of scientific knowledge in medieval Europe, it appears that political context was decisive. There were important reasons the Cathars were hunted to extinction while the Sufis enjoyed rising influence and prestige. During and after the demise of the Cathars, authorities of the Catholic Church proposed a history linking them to widespread Eurasian ideas that, as early as the fifth century, the Christian Church had attempted to expunge. In this narrative, gnostic troublemakers whom the Byzantines had settled in the Balkans were continuously migrating toward central and western Europe, and Bogomil communities caught on the Roman side of the religious split in 1054 (see Chapter 4) contributed to a popular, rural interest across Central Europe in gnostic Christian beliefs. These included a cosmic struggle between God and Satan—the latter being the world-making god of the Old Testament, the identity of Christ as a being of truth and light, the intuitive access to truth without priestly intervention, and the importance of living apart from secular society. In the late twelfth century, a specific sect consolidated itself in southern France, calling themselves the pure ones (*cathari*—a name used earlier by some heterodox sects) and recognizing both men and women as perfected teachers. They added an interesting doctrine on reincarnation: the soul would continue to reincarnate until it achieved complete alienation from its earthly forms. They began to organize their communities in hierarchies that superficially paralleled the Catholic Church.

In the mid-eleventh century, regional church councils responded to the challenge to their authority by declaring the Cathars heretics and plastering them with charges of neo-Platonist radicalism. This began a century of inquisition, torture, and execution. The usefulness of the gnosticism-to-Catharism narrative to church authorities attempting to hereticize reformers and dissidents is clear enough, and the evidence confirming precise parallels between Cathar beliefs and any Central Asian belief system is murky. Major revisions by historians now portray the Cathars not as proto-Protestants but rather as fairly orthodox Catholics attempting to reform their local congregations while promoting religious teaching and liturgy in their own languages. Nevertheless, for heretical narrative to be completely untrue, the Cathars would have to be one of the few religious sects of medieval Eurasia not influenced by folk ideologies of light and dark, a forged world, and idealist awakening, which was frequently associated with demands for self-education through vernacular rendering of sacred texts. The predicament of the Cathars became even more political when many found refuge under the protection of Raymond VI in Toulouse (which had briefly been under Muslim control in the eighth century and subsequently was in economic and cultural contact with Andalusia). In 1206, Raymond was excommunicated (and again in 1209). Shortly afterward, Philip II of France undertook a Crusade, endorsed by Pope Innocent III, to exterminate the Cathars. The wars persisted until 1255 (about the time that Mongge was advising Christians to stop killing each other over trivial differences), at which point Toulouse and other regional governments that had supported the Cathars were absorbed into the kingdom of France. The last of the Cathars disappeared into the torture chambers or died on the battlefields or in their villages. It was the extermination of the Cathars that gave English speakers their deathless motto, "Kill them all, and let God sort them out." It was the response of the abbot, Arnaud Amalric, to the question of how to distinguish heretics from Catholic villagers who had refused to separate themselves from the Cathars when the Crusaders surrounded the town of Béziers in 1209.

Both Sufism and Catharism (even if it was a reform movement) questioned the orthodox religious authorities. But in Seljuk Anatolia, the Sufis were able to develop their culture and they became politically influential while, in Capetian France, the Cathars were hunted down and killed. The traditionally Turkic segmentation of the Seljuk federation, together with the traditional insularity of the sultanal court from sectarian strife, permitted the Anatolian courts to patronize the Sufis without being threatened by inquiries from the caliphate. If Phillip II had not been in the process of consolidating France and determined to wipe out the counts of Toulouse, it is possible that the Cathars would have survived and become influential too.

When the Cathars were forming their network in southern France, in western France the Waldensians also began to claim the right to preach for themselves, without instruction from or permission of the church or local clergy. Their reasoning for such authority was classically idealist: the Holy Spirit could supply them with intuitive understanding of God and his purposes, without the intervention of teaching by the church. To support their self-preaching enterprise, the Waldensians had the Latin Bible translated into their local dialect, and they began to reject implements of worship that they deemed not consistent with scripture. Eventually, they denied the efficacy of the saints and the sacraments—including infant baptism and marriage. They refused to be recruited or impressed for warfare, which they regarded as a secular perversion of God's will. Like the Cathars, they allowed women to preach and lead their communities. And like the Cathars, the Waldensians were condemned as heretics and persecuted in France. They found protection in a few localities of Italy where sympathetic aristocrats were strong and in the Alps where political control of any kind was weaker. But the combination of a new papal Crusade against them and the opportunity to seek fellowship with other dissident sects drastically diminished their numbers in the early sixteenth century. Surviving communities were massacred in Italy in 1545 and in the Alps in 1655.

It is of interest here that the reservoir of idealist-themed heretical teachings in Europe of the fourteenth and fifteenth centuries was in and around what today is the Czech Republic—"Bohemia," sometimes a state, and with shifting borders, but always a pump of cultural influence into central Europe. It was on the medieval interface between the Avar–Bulgar–Magyar zone of continual steppe contact (see Chapter 3) and the eastern front of the Latinate Frankish empires. It was also bordering on the Balkans, to which gnostics (and, later, Hurufi's and Jewish kabbalists) continually migrated from the Ottoman territories. In the fourteenth century, the city of Prague became one of the most important intellectual centers in Eurasia. It was the personal capital of Holy Roman Emperor Charles IV (1316–1378), whose mother was a Bohemian aristocrat, and he resisted pressure to move his capital farther west after his investiture in 1347. In 1348, he created Charles University, which would become central to what historians sometimes refer to as the "Bohemian Reformation," or what Czech historians today call the "first" reformation. The university cemented the intellectual ties between Prague and Paris, Rome and the cities of Poland, and Germany (especially Nuremberg) and Hungary.

Jan Hus (1370–1415) was born in southern Bohemia and read the writings of the English theologian John Wycliffe (1330–1384), whose life had been punctuated by various troubles because of his criticisms of the Roman Church. Wycliffe died a natural death but later was condemned as a heretic, and religious authorities burned his corpse the year that Hus himself was burned at the stake. Wycliffe was a critic of ostensibly Aristotelian nominalism and considered the church the primary source of ignorance and illusion in the world—a recognizable if not explicit idealist thesis that the church was playing the role of Satan. The rationalists had epistemological as well as theological arguments for church authority, which Wycliffe strenuously refuted. He oversaw a huge project to translate the entire Bible into English so that worshippers could read it and interpret it for themselves. Wycliffe also decried the doctrine of transubstantiation of the host since, like a good idealist, he did not believe that material and spiritual elements could be transformed into each other. Wycliffe also had been a strong advocate of the idea of predestination—that is, the proposition that, in an invisible realm, there exists a true church consisting entirely of those selected by God for salvation. Predestination was not new with Wycliffe. In various forms it had been at least a fleeting part of the doctrines of Hinduism and early Buddhism, Judaism, early Christianity, and Islam; their persecutors claimed that the Cathars believed it and the Waldensians in their late period certainly believed it, though likely as a result of the influence of Wycliffe, Hus, and John Calvin. Predestination's logical connection to idealist assumptions is clear enough. It proposes that the world as we perceive it—in which humans appear to have free will and the ability to make themselves worthy of salvation—is an illusion. In the true realm, the salvation of those who will be saved (or spiritually completed) is already a fact (since time is only another illusion of the phenomenal world). God knows who will be saved, and therefore it has already happened. Humans have no agency to change God's knowledge. Nevertheless, the fate of those not on the list of the saved was the object of a good deal of speculation from diversifying religious sects in Christian Europe (and to some degree throughout the Islamic world).

Hus found predestination incontrovertible and was attracted to Wycliffe's rejection of priestly authority and transubstantiation of the host. He lived in a period when popular Christian movements were thriving in Prague and nearby districts, combined with demands for local independence from the church.

Like Wycliff, Hus's stated goal was to reform the church, not divide or destroy it, but his teachings nevertheless inspired independent Christian communities of worship. From his base at Charles University, Hus became one of the most influential academic authorities for the popular reform movement. But papal politics, in which Bohemian institutions were critically important, led to his undoing. In his lifetime, the church was split into two papacies and was teetering on a third. Hus threw in his lot with the losing pope and eventually got into a dispute about the sale of indulgences. The result was excommunication and a series of trials culminating in a demand that he recant his beliefs or burn, the former of which he refused. Following Hus's martyrdom, his movement continued in a new sect based on his teachings as well as related idealist (Augustinian, mostly) movements that resisted papal authorities and led to sporadic social disorder. Hus is widely important because of the impact of his and Wycliffe's ideas of individual and communal autonomy of scriptural interpretation and the rejection of what were regarded as superstitious, nonbiblical institutional impositions by the church. These ideas strongly influenced other reformers, including Martin Luther. Hus's theories of predestination also touched a wider movement culminating in the work of John Calvin (1509–1564), who like the Waldensians, fled to the Alps to escape religious authorities. Calvin independently found justifications for predestination in the idealist writings of Augustine, elaborating the revival of European idealist religious thought.

But Hus was part of a larger legacy of dissidence from the European–Central Asian frontier. Peter Chelchiky (1390–1460) was not educated as a churchman and worked for at least part of his life as a farmer. Most biographers believe that he was either a Waldensian in his youth or knew a great deal about their beliefs. He extended Wycliffe's and Hus's critiques of the church to the state. In the same way that he found the church sacraments to be profane inventions, he found the demands of the state for obedience to be without justification. Chelchiky particularly condemned the willingness of Christians to participate in capital punishment or war. The excuse used for these by the state, he argued, is to fight evil. But the source of evil was Satan, the creator of this world, and there was no hope that Christians could defeat it in this world. He thought the only responses to evil were those practiced by Christ—peaceful resistance and self-sacrifice if necessary. He added to it a social code of equality and plain living, an echo of not only the Cathars and Waldensians but also idealist sects, back to the earliest roots in the Levant and South Asia. Chelchiky's ideas are recognizable ancestors of those of modern dissident sects, including the Moravians, Quakers, and all orders of Mennonites.

The idealist traditions in Czech religion continued with Jan Komensky (Comenius; 1592–1670), who joined and rose to high rank in the religious sect that Chelchiky founded. By his time, the movement for Bohemians' cultural and religious independence had reached the point of war with the Holy Roman Empire (the Thirty Years' War, 1618–1648), which caused Komensky and his congregation to relocate to Poland. He formed theories of secular education and Latin-based scientific discourse that later created a demand for him across Europe—and western Europe in particular—as an adviser in the development of popular, state-sponsored educational programs, making him a critical figure in Europe's modernization. But in the vein of this book's discussion, Komensky is a personification of the overall paradigm of the idealist, dualist ideology that remained ubiquitous across Eurasia. For Platonists, it had been the challenge to prove the reality of the phenomenal world and how it works. For medieval religious dissidents—and some approved visionaries, like Hildegard von Bingen (1098–1179) and Eckhardt von Hochheim (1260–1328)—it inspired the constant imagery of light as the messenger from the noumenal to the phenomenal realms, and "enlightenment" as the act of transcending the limitations and confusions of the material world. Komensky believed in ecstatic revelation and prophecy, and in his book *Light and Darkness* (*Lux et tenebris*), he compiled a history of Bohemian prophecy. He was also—showing his kinship with ancient gnostics as well as contemporary Islamic visionaries—a millennarian (he thought the end would arrive in 1692, and he mentioned particularly obliteration of the papacy and the Hapsburgs). But perhaps his most unreconstructed idealist statement was his remarkable didactic text, *Labyrinth of the World*. In it, he uses an extended metaphor that could have come from *The Republic* or *The City of God*: It is a parable of a searcher entering a strange town of twisting streets. He acquires two guides, one of whom is a personification of the thirst for worldly knowledge and the other is a personification of conventional wisdom. Their intention is actually to confuse him, and they even resort to making him wear a pair of eyeglasses that interferes with his vision. As a consequence, he sees only ugliness and sin. But eventually, he encounters Christ, who informs him that all along, the truth was inside him. Komensky removes the crippling spectacles and finds the invisible church in the real world, leaving the illusions of the material world behind. Komensky was not an exception among early European intellectuals who devoted their sponsored and public work to ostentatiously "rational" and "scientific" projects while laboring privately to pursue idealist projects in decoding textual and astronomical phenomena to find noumenal truths. Like Newton after him, Komensky was driven by an idealist's doubts to a rationalist's responses.

Since I am arguing that such gnostic, dualist, or "Platonic" influences were virtually ubiquitous, there would appear to be no necessity to demonstrate direct links from Central Asian culture to early modern European changes in the direction of secularism, scientific inquiry, and discourses of individual liberty. But with respect to Europe, a consideration of the critical role of the Balkans (and by extension the Alps) and Eastern Europe in the early modern transformation suggests that influences were both local and distant—and above all, that it is not influence alone but the reaction to influence that determines large changes. Medieval and early modern Bohemia was peculiarly placed to evince with some precision the cumulative cultural influences from both Central Asia and the Muslim Turkic world. The course of the Thirty Years' War eventually shifted political and military attention to Germany and western Europe, obscuring part of the role of eastern Europe in the transformation of European intellectual life on the broad medieval/early modern cusp. But the Bohemian theater demonstrates that religious authorities in premodern times could not eradicate the philosophical and religious engine of idealism in Eurasian cosmology. Instead, the hierarchical religions all integrated threads of idealism into their sectarian fabrics. In both the Islamic world and Christian Europe, the role of idealist convictions in generating systemic study of the material world is clear, and in both cases it is equally clear that critical perspectives on political orders followed.

READING NOTES: DISSIDENCE AND DOUBT

It is common to use Gibbon's comments as a starting point for discussions of religion among the Mongols. For two other recent examples, see Christopher P. Atwood, "Validation by Holiness or Sovereignty: Religious Toleration as Political Theology in the Mongol World Empire of the Thirteenth Century," *The International History Review* 26 (Jun 2004): 237–256 and Jack Weatherford, *Genghis Khan and the Search for God* (Viking, 2016). See also Peter Jackson, *The Mongols and the Islamic World: From Conquest to Conversion* (Yale UP, 2017), 303–304. The long-standing historical axiom that traditional shamanism predisposed the receptivity of Turks and Mongols to Sufism and Islam is reviewed and qualified by Reuven Amitai-Preiss, "Sufis and Shamans: Some Remarks on the Islamization of the Mongols in the Ilkhanate," *Journal of the Economic and Social History of the Orient* 42, no. 1 (1999): 27–46.

The idea of ubiquitous presence of folk beliefs is partly inspired by my reading many years ago of Carlo Ginsberg's *Ecstasies: Deciphering the Witches' Sabbath*, trans. Raymond Rosenthal (U Chicago P, 2004), in its view of European "witchcraft" and "heresy" as inheriting a pre-Christian worldview; this book is a further exploration of such ideas in wider parts of Eurasia. On the dynamics of dissidence, heresy, and persecution, see Steven Runciman's classic study of alienizing influences from the Middle East and nomadic Asia: *The Medieval Manichee: A Study of the Christian Dualist Heresy* (Cambridge UP, 1947); see also Milan Loos, *Dualist Heresy in the Middle Ages* (Prague Academia, 1974) and Yuri Stoyanov, *The Other God:*

Dualist Religions from Antiquity to the Cathar Heresy (Yale UP, 2000). On the connection of heresy in European thought with Satanic or chthonic beliefs, see David Frankfurter, *Evil Incarnate: Rumors of Demonic Conspiracy and Satanic Abuse in History* (Princeton UP, 2006).

On the general dynamics of heresy and persecution, see three seminal works by Robert I. Moore: *The Origins of European Dissent* (Blackwell, 1977, 1985); *The Formation of a Persecuting Society: Authority and Deviance in Western Europe, 950-1250* (Blackwell 1987, 2007); and *The War on Heresy: Faith and Power in Medieval Europe* (Harvard UP, 2014). The last is Moore's magisterial revision of the traditional historicization of the Cathars. See also Caterina Bruschi and Peter Biller, eds., *Texts and the Repression of Medieval Heresy* (York Medieval P, 2003); Christine Ames Caldwell, *Righteous Persecution: Inquisition, Dominicans, and Christianity in the Middle Ages* (U Pennsylvania P, 2000); David Nirenberg, *Communities of Violence: Persecution of Minorities in the Middle Ages* (Princeton UP, 1996); John Christian Laursen and Cary J. Nederman, eds., *Beyond the Persecuting Society: Religious Toleration before the Enlightenment* (U Pennsylvania P, 1998); Talal Asad, "Medieval Heresy: An Anthropological View," *Social History* 11, no. 3 (1986): 345–362; Cary J. Nederman and John Christian Laursen, eds., *Difference and Dissent: Theories of Toleration in Medieval and Early Modern Europe* (Rowman & Littlefield, 1996); Samuel Hosain Lamarti, "The Development of Apostasy and Punishment Law in Islam, 11AH/632AD-157AH/774AD" (PhD diss., Glasgow University, 2002); Julian Baldick, *Imaginary Muslims: The Uwaysi Sufis of Central Asia* (NYU P, 1993); and Charles Halperin, "The Ideology of Silence: Prejudice and Pragmatism on the Medieval Religious Frontier," *Comparative Studies in Society and History* 26, no. 3 (Jul 1984): 442–466. The metaphysical and occult preoccupations of modern scientific thinkers have been noted by many biographers, but for a recent survey from Newton to William James see Jason A. Josephson-Storm, *The Myth of Disenchantment: Magic, Modernity and the Birth of the Human Sciences* (U Chicago P, 2017).

On the history of specific heresies, see Dmitri Obolensky, *The Bogomils: A Study in Balkan Neo-Manichaeism* (Cambridge UP, 2004; re-issue of 1948 original); Peter Biller, *The Waldenses, 1170-1530: Between a Religious Order and a Church* (Ashgate, 2001); Euan Cameron, *Waldenses: Rejections of Holy Church in Medieval Europe* (Blackwell's, 2001); Martin Aurell, ed., *Les cathares devant l'Histoire: Mélanges offerts à Jean Duvernoy* (L'Hydre, 2005); Uwe Brunn, "*Cathari, catharistae et cataphrygae*, ancêtres des cathares du XIIe siècle?" *Heresis*, 36–37 (2002): 183–200.

A critical contribution to understanding the institutionalization of Greek importations into Arabic academics of the Abbasid period is Dmitri Gutas, *Greek Thought, Arabic Culture: The Graeco-Arabic Translation Movement in Baghdad and Early 'Abbasid Culture* (Routledge, 1998). On the background to the connections and interactions of Islam, Judaism, and Christianity across the Balkans and the Levant as well as via Andalusia and North Africa, see Peter F. Sugar, *Southeastern Europe under Ottoman Rule, 1354–1804* (U Washington P, 2012); David Nirenberg, *Neighboring Faiths: Christianity, Islam and Judaism in the Middle Ages and Today* (U Chicago P, 2014). On the reflected influence from Hinduism and Buddhism via the Islamic world, also see Chapter 2 reading notes. Especially important to this chapter (and to Chapter 9) is Siglinde Dietz, "Buddhism in Gandhara," in *The Spread of Buddhism*, eds. Ann Hierman and Stephan Peter Bumbacher (Brill 2007), 47–74. See also John Walbridge, *The Leaven of the Ancients: Suhrawardi and the Heritage of the Greeks* (SUNY P, 1999); Georges Dreyfus, *Recognizing Reality: Dharmakirti's Philosophy and Its Tibetan Interpretations* (SUNY P, 1997); and Michal Biran, "The Islamization of Hülegü: Imaginary Conversion in the Ilkhanate," *Journal of the Royal Asiatic Society* 6, nos. 1-2 (2016): 79–88; Mehdi Aminrazavi, *Suhrawardi and the School of Illumination* (Routledge, 2014); Roy Mottahedeh (referring to the subject as Sohravardi), *The Mantle of the Prophet* (Oneworld, 2002, 2008, 2014).

For Beckwith's tracing of rhetorical traditions, *Warriors of the Cloisters: The Central Asian Origins of Science in the Medieval World* (Princeton UP, 2012) follows the direct effects of Central Asian political and scholastic culture upon wider reaches of the continent; see especially "From College and *Universitas* to University" and "Transmission to Medieval Western Europe," 37–49. See also John M. Hobson, "Countering the Eurocentric Myth of the Pristine West: Discovering the Oriental West," in *The Eastern Origins of Western Civilisation* (Cambridge UP, 2004), 1–31 and on Rabban Sauma, see Morris Rossabi, *Voyager from Xanadu: Rabban Sauma and the First Journey from China to the West* (re-issued U California Press, 2017). On philosophical discourse in medieval Europe, see Bruce R. Berglund and Brian Porter-Szűcs, eds., *Christianity and Modernity in Eastern Europe* (Central European University P, 2010); Edward Grant, *The Foundations of Modern Science in the Middle Ages: Their Religious, Institutional and Intellectual Contexts* (Cambridge UP, 1996); Brian Davies, "Aquinas, Plato and Neoplatonism," *The Oxford Handbook of Aquinas* (Oxford UP, 2012); this chapter has also been influenced by Frances A. Yates, *Giordano Bruno and the Hermetic Tradition* (Routledge, 2002; re-issue of 1964 original). On Abelard's contemplation of moving to the Muslim world, see Peter Abelard, *Historia Calamitatum: The Story of My Misfortunes*, trans. Henry Adams Bellows (CreateSpace, 2013), 34–36.

On Ibn Sina (Avicenna) and scientific discourse, see Roy Mottahedeh, *The Mantle of the Prophet: Religion and Politics in Iran* (Oneworld Publications, 2000); Idris Zakaria, "Ibn Sina on 'Pleasure and Happiness,'" *Advances in Natural and Applied Sciences* 6, no. 8 (2012): 1283–1286; Shams Constantine Inati, *Ibn Sina and Mysticism: Remarks and Admonitions* (Kegan Paul International, 1996); E. S. Kennedy, "The Exact Sciences in Iran under the Saljuqs and Mongols," in *The Cambridge History of Iran, Volume 4: The Period from the Arab Invasion to the Saljuqs* (Cambridge UP, 2008), 659–680; Daniel Sheffield, *In the Path of the Prophet: Medieval and Early Modern Narratives of the Life of Zarathustra in Islamic Iran and Western India* (NELC, 2012); and Farhad Daftary, "Nasir al-Din al-Tusi and the Ismailis," in *Ismailis in Medieval Muslim Societies* (I. B. Tauris, 2005), 171–182. Ehud Benor compares Maimonides and Ibn Sina on questions of self-sufficient consciousness, God and creation in *Ethical Monotheism* (Chapter 2 reading notes), 108.

On the background of Islamic, and particularly Sufist, mysticism from the Seljuk to Timurid periods, see Beatrice Forbes Manz, *Power, Politics and Religion in Timurid Iran* (Cambridge UP, 2007); Nathan Hofer, *The Popularisation of Sufism in Ayyubid and Mamluk Egypt, 1173-1325* (Edinburgh UP, 2015); Julian Baldick, *Mystical Islam: An Introduction to Sufism* (NYU P, 1989); Fritz Meier, *Essays on Islamic Piety and Mysticism* (Brill, 1999); Nikki Keddie, *Scholars, Saints, and Sufis: Muslim Religious Institutions in the Middle East since 1500* (U California P, 1972); Leonard Lewisohn, *The Legacy of Medieval Iranian Sufism* (Khanigahi-Nimatullahi Publications, 1992); Tor Andræ, *In the Garden of Myrtles: Studies in Early Islamic Mysticism* (SUNY P, 1987); Dick Davis and Afkham Darbandi, *The Conference of the Birds* (Penguin Classics, 1984); and William C. Chittick, *Faith and Practice of Islam: Three Thirteenth Century Sufi Texts* (SUNY P, 1992). Among the critics of some Sufis, Ibn Taymiyya is often considered an intellectual predecessor of Wahhabism because of his strenuous opposition to religious accommodation, which he thought in many cases was acceptance of idolatry and paganism. See Emmanuel Sivan, *Radical Islam: Medieval Theology and Modern Politics* (Yale UP, 1990); Yahya Michot, *Ibn Taymiyya: Muslims under Non-Muslim Rule* (Oxford UP, 2006); and Wael B. Halloq, *Ibn Taymiyya against the Greek Logicians* (Clarendon Press, 1993). For the illuminist and Sufi themes in the literary work of Omar Khayyam, see Ali Dashti, *In Search of Omar Khayyam* (Routledge, 2012), esp. 119–122.

Chapter Ten

Intimations of Nationality

The tolerance for folk and local belief systems under the post-nomadic rulers was fostered not only by their tastes but also by their strategic preferences for taming or displacing established authorities in religion and governance. They not only rearranged government and religious administration at the top to constrict the discretion—and in some instances, participation in any meaningful form—by old elites but also used patronage at the bottom to encourage new forms of literature and the arts that were popular among the majority of the population. In addition, through their development of urban commercial networks in North Africa, Anatolia, and the Levant as well as promotion of trade across the Mediterranean, they provided much of the market for nascent printing enterprises. The results included the rise of standardizing vernacular languages in performance and writing, providing new venues for the construction of identities along the lines of what in the modern period we recognize as nationality.

THE STATE AND OBJECTIFIED IDENTITY IN CHINA

Division and status were essential considerations in the administration of any civilian population. Some lines of division—most of which carried inherent status—were provided by histories and institutions of the agrarian societies. Eurasian societies after about the third century BCE were generally organized into communities—whether urban precincts or rural villages—that were marked not only by economic cooperation and lineage affiliations but also confessional solidarity. Increasingly, the confessional orientations were hierarchical—congregational leaders reported to regional authorities, who often communicated with some spiritual or doctrinal center. In many cases, separations of the civil population were not doctrinal, but based on histories of migration, frequently coerced. In China's traditional methods of identification, individuals outside the imperial lineage and not held in slavery were labeled in their biographies by their native places, which often corresponded to the county-level districts in which they were born. The Xixia and Kitan had a special problem because each was ruling a territory that was largely pastoral in economy; in their early periods agricultural areas formerly part of a state running on Chinese administrative principles were augmentations of their domains. They responded with pluralistic systems of administration and law, in which the Chinese-speaking farmers (and in a small number of cases soldiers or officials) were objectified minorities. They used the term *han*—from the name of the Han empire—together with native place to identify these subject populations. The Kitans added a refinement to this by using the traditional concept of the aristocratic estate (the *ordo*; see Chapter 3) to organize such subject populations under their aegis. These populations—primarily the Han and Bohai—were in this way tagged as captured and, when the emperor was so inclined, distributed for work on farms, necropolii, and military support facilities. When still living in their native districts, they were governed by what was understood to be Chinese law, often administered by Chinese officials, and their tax obligations were rendered in familiar Chinese weights and measures.

The Jin continued these practices but with a difference. They controlled much more of China, and so their conquered, Chinese-speaking, and largely agricultural population was much larger than had been the case with Xixia or Kitan. The Jin instituted a more elaborate (or, in any case, better-documented) system of civil administration that acknowledged the *han* population and the traditions of Chinese law and taxation as majority. They instituted a "System of Han Officials," by which Chinese-speaking scholars who had been chosen through examinations shared government duties with Jurchen officials. It was the conquering Jurchen population and the third category of Tibetans and Tangguts that were set off from the majority by channels of education, examination, military assignment, and family administration. Indeed, over time, some of the Jin rulers became anxious that the Chinese majority would diminish the sense of distinctness that should be retained by the Jurchen conquerors and embarked upon programs to historically and administratively objectify Jurchen identity in an attempt to keep the Jurchens working, speaking, and acting like their Jurchen ancestors.

The Mongols, who in the Chinggis period had already started to consolidate political status and cultural identity in their taxonomy of sovereign and subject peoples (see Chapter 6), adapted the Jin identity system and much of Jin law as they developed what would be the Yuan empire in China. Mongols, regardless of lineage affiliation, were highest on the ladder. After them came the hugely varied population (in fact, called in Chinese, the "various categories," or *semu*) of Muslims, Jews, and Christians from the Sartic world, imported to oversee the critically important financial affairs of the empire. Third was the group called *han*. This primarily meant the entire civil population of the former Jin state, with Jurchens subsumed under the *han* designation. And at the bottom of this series were the *man*, drawn from a pejorative Chinese word for "barbarians" of the south but, in this case, applied to Chinese speakers as well as native cultural minorities of the area south of the Huai River. The system as a whole was intended to stabilize the Mongols as conquerors and the Sarts and *han* as their helpers, with the *man* represented unambiguously as the conquered. Mongols actively enrolled in the military were usually not taxed or were only incidentally prodded for tribute. Sarts were destined for employment in valued and potentially lucrative bureaucratic positions, though many were in commerce and finance in addition to or instead of government work. *Han* were preferred over *man* for the reduced number of civil appointments in law, history, and local administration. These categories were not racial in Yuan times, and the number of categories was never fixed at four. Koreans were another category, Tibetans were another category, and there were minor categories of various degrees of permanence. There was a special court where individuals or groups could petition to have their status (and perforce their identity) changed, usually because of mixed parentage, marriage, or work assignment. But these were also functional divisions. Mongols could enter the civil administration and even be scholars and researchers, but most were soldiers. *Han* could serve in the military, and some did for generations. But in general, they were regarded as men of civil and not military pursuits. These long-term ascriptions of the Mongols as warriors and the *han* as literati stuck and still affect our reading of Yuan and Ming history.

Korea was deeply impressed by the hereditary category scheme. The fall of the Yuan in 1368 was followed in fairly short order by the 1392 overthrow of the Goryeo vassal dynasty. The new Joseon state proceeded to establish and maintain close relations with the new Ming government in China but retained a good number of Mongol institutions, including the use of Mongolian itself as a lingua franca in Korea and Manchuria. They also retained the Mongol status system, with a twist: Koreans were to be the favored group, with Mongols, Jurchens, and Chinese to be registered as hereditary aliens. By the sixteenth century, these statuses had become racial, in the sense that they were perceived as permanent and heritable limits of assimilability.

In many ways, the transition in China from Yuan to Ming in 1368 was more ideological than structural. The Ming were strong in their pronouncements of protecting the *han* and defeating the Mongols (i.e., the "northern slaves," the "northern barbarians," and so on) and revived the examination system for purposes of staffing a new civil bureaucracy. Partly to symbolize their rejection of the Mongols, they established their imperial capital at Nanjing (the "southern capital"), rather than at Dadu—which they now referred to as the "northern capital" (Beijing). But in basic outlines, their government resembled that of the Yuan. In their new capital, they built a replica of the observatory at Beijing and attached to it their own Muslim academy of astronomy, mathematics, and cartography. They retained the provincial scheme of administration, including the military garrison system introduced under the Yuan. They retained the Yuan arrangement of a unique reporting relationship with Tibet, which continued under the administration of its religious hierarchs. Though the examinations were revived and staff sought for a civil government on the model of Han and Song, even at its highest staffing the government remained smaller than the Song government had been, despite that fact that Ming was a much larger empire. Most important to this discussion, Ming continued the Yuan precedent of hereditary social categories. Cultural minorities were carefully identified and documented, but the Ming added hereditary professional categories, meaning that future government officials could report themselves as the candlemakers, bricklayers, and pig breeders that their ancestors had been.

Large communities of descendants of the Sartic immigrants of the Yuan period remained in Ming China along with smaller and somewhat isolated Mongol populations in Yunnan and Gansu. A well-known Jewish community at Kaifeng survived in some form into the nineteenth century. Muslims were influential in the imperial academies, the army, and overland commerce. The first Ming emperor—if only in competition with the remaining Turkic states (most important the Chaghatay and Timurid) to secure the loyalty of the Muslims—built several impressive mosques in the cities with the largest numbers of Muslims, gave grants to Islamic schools, and in various ways publicly commemorated the service of Muslim soldiers. In ensuing decades, the Ming state was careful not only to recognize but constrain Muslims. Part of the reason that the Ming insisted upon an ascribed cultural identity for each individual was that their marriage laws forbade identified *han* from marrying a member of a recognized cultural minority. Muslims, on the other hand, were required to marry *han*; in general, Muslim communities were sustained by the marrying of Muslim men to *han* women, after which the women would be converted. A similar policy applied to Jews so that, within a few generations, members of the Muslim or Jewish communities could be distinguished from the majority Han population only by law and community affiliation.

In their early decades, the Ming had experimented with a severe constriction of foreign trade. The proposition was that vigorous overland trade was a characteristic of Mongol rule and that it had benefited only Mongol aristocrats and their Sartic clients. As a large agricultural economy, China might be self-sufficient, and currency would be easier to stabilize without foreign trade. But within a short time it became apparent that the economy was not self-sufficient and the Muslim communities were an essential tool in the reconstruction of trade patterns. Overland trade was revived, and to announce the Ming return to Indian Ocean commerce, the voyages of Zheng He (1371–1433) began in the early fifteenth century (see also Chapter 11). Zheng was descended from the prominent Yuan-period governor of Yunnan, Sayyid Ajall Shams al-Din Omar (1211–1279), a Khwarazmian who was in the Dali state at the time of the Mongol invasion (see Chapter 6) and, after surrendering, was appointed governor of the former Dali territories. Zheng was a boy when the Ming captured Yunnan, and he was castrated in order to facilitate his service as domestic help, but his talents allowed him to rise quickly in the ranks of the Ming army. His family had long practiced the pilgrimage to Mecca, and so his familiarity with the geography and contacts in the merchant networks were assets. Beginning in 1405, he was commissioned to lead a flotilla through the Indian Ocean to collect back taxes from communities of Chinese who had illegally migrated to Southeast Asia and to announce the renewal of Chinese trade in the ports of Southeast and South Asia, the Persian Gulf, and East Africa. On subsequent voyages, he reached Hormuz and sailed along the entire southern coast of the Arabian Peninsula and the northeast coast of Africa, reaching south of Mogadishu. At about the same time that the emperor was preparing for Zheng He's expeditions (and after the death of Timur in 1405), the court sent land expeditions led by Chen Cheng (1365–1457) as far west as Herat and back, crisscrossing Timurid territory with messages of commercial cheer and diplomatic pragmatism.

In time, the Ming imperial family came to rely upon the trade as the Yuan imperial family had before them. They were equally reliant upon Muslims who were key to financing and managing both the overland trade and, increasingly, the overseas trade throughout the Indian Ocean. These "Chinese" Muslims, known in the Ming period and after as the Hui (to distinguish them from the far less numerous Turkic-speaking Muslims of Eastern Turkestan), became a firmly institutionalized identity. Like other minority cultural identities of the Ming period, its legal definitions and restrictions provided a powerful matrix for the contrasting *han* identity of the period.

OBJECTIFIED IDENTITY UNDER THE SULTANS

Even before Islam, governments across the Arab and Persian worlds had to deal with negotiating the status of dependent populations, whether serfs, agricultural slaves, sexual slaves, military slaves, or technically free but still dependent populations. In the early Islamic period, conquest followed by decades or centuries of progressive conversion of conquered populations introduced new complexities. Processes of social transposition between dependency and freedom could intersect with conversion or resistance to it, and in the Abbasid period particularly, dependency moved from a private relationship to a publicly regulated one, allowing the state to take on powers of objectification and reification in fundamental elements of status. Various identities were administratively constructed and recognized, often (particularly in the case of the Turks) given strong literary archetypes, channeling both career assignment and cultural patronage. All the regimes arising from the Abbasid territories—whether Persian (as with the Samanids) or Turkic, (as with the Ghaznavids)—adopted and developed these political tools for the classification of populations and the bureaucratic appendages that made it possible. These were the broad state characteristics of later sultanates of the Karakhans (formed from Karluk and other remnants in tenth-century Transoxiana), the Seljuks, the shahs of Khwarazm, and the emperor sultans of the Ottomans and the Mughals as well as the Tulunid and later Mamluk states in Egypt and Syria, and dozens of small states across Arabia, Africa, and Southeast Asia from the tenth century to the present.

In the early centuries of Islam, the doctrine of the "peoples of the book" was virtually a mandate for the state (however small) in all its modern meanings. The doctrinal communities had to be recognized and their statuses made visible and credible; their differentiated legal rights and tax status mediated; and their safety assured. This was a formula for an expansive empire since early Muslim states began with a speck of believers and within decades had spread to millions. As a historical proposition, religious dissidence and legitimation of the state were coterminous in Muslim ideology. The Turkic regimes of the thirteenth century exercised their own approaches to state construction and objectification of community identities, but all alloyed the traditional Turkic systems of identification with Muslim principals of doctrinal plurality within the recognized religions. In the Mamluk, Seljuk, Ilkhan, and middle Ottoman states, this was done on the basis of religion and on the model of Islamic precedent for state modulation of religious plurality. The systemic application of a public, institutionalized cultural or religious and cultural identity was in most cases the essence of state activity, apart from military administration and financial management.

As Muslims, the Jochids recognized Christianity and had many reasons for wishing the Christian church in the old Kievan territories to remain largely intact. The churchmen were a help in documentation and administration of civil life in Russia—particularly taxation—and allowed the Jochid state to remain small. Indeed, the church for the first time was able to free itself of the need for patronage and protection of the Rus nobles, and its tax exemptions allowed it to acquire huge tracts of productive land on which large and ornate monasteries proliferated. The growing ability of the church to document Russian life, in the Russian language, allowed the establishment of taxonomies with long-enduring effects. Because the church was permitted to work as a shadow state, it could inculcate concepts of identity that isolated and targeted the Jochids themselves in order to, by contrast, define a Russian community. While the thirteenth and early fourteenth centuries in Russia were free of religious strife relative to western Europe, the church built up sufficient power that the weakening of the Jochid regime in the fourteenth century and emergence of a new power base at Moscow allowed the church to unleash an inquisition. The introduction of Russian as a liturgical language had not been accepted by all, and those favoring a return to Greek after the demise of the Jochids were targeted for torture and execution. "Christian" became a Russian term for any Russian-speaking commoner. By the early fifteenth century, the church had established Russian Orthodox practice as the indelible mark of a "Russian"—as contrasted to Jews, Muslim Tatars, and dissident Christians. In combination with the Jochid-era striations of social identity by rank, tax liability, and military obligation, the foundation of later "estate" (*soslovie*) identities in Russia was laid.

In the Turkic governments ruling Muslim countries, a different kind of taxonomy of identity was evident. In the first caliphates, the Umayyads and Abbasids, expansion of Islam was by definition into areas where Christians and Jews were majorities. Their adherents had to be identified to distinguish them from pagans (Zoroastrians, Manichaeans, and so on) and to levy the special tax on them that Muslims did not pay. The word used to objectify their religious affiliation was *millah*. It occurs in the Quran a number of times, often in connection with Judaism. It probably was derived from a Hebrew or Aramaic *millah* in the sense of something like Greek *logos*—the "word," or revelation, of a prophet. Moses and Jesus were both recognized as prophets, and so their communities of believers had the status of *millah*. But the greatest of prophets was Muhammad, and *millah* unspecified usually meant, in common writing, the community of Muslims (as in *ulum al-millah*, "Muslim science"). In the Umayyad and Abbasid state systems, *millah* were legally constructed, protected communities of believers with their own attributes regarding taxation, military obligation, and legal jurisdiction in the cases of blasphemy or personal disputes. *Millah* quickly also came to mean communities of people associated with distinct languages, dress, and customs. Ancestry was not part of the equation. The imperative to convert as many willing Christians and Jews as possible was paramount. To that end, they were pressured to convert by being required to pay the special tax levied on them and not being permitted to arm themselves, ride horses, or live in dwellings that allowed them to see into the courtyards of Muslim neighbors.

The Mamluks were able to combine Sunni zealotry (particularly in denunciation of the Ilkhans) with recognition of the Christian, Jewish, and sectarian Muslims as legitimate doctrinal communities. They followed the custom of the Ghaznavids and Seljuks by allowing communities of Christians and Jews to manage their own affairs through leaders recognized and legitimated by the sultan. Nevertheless, Christian communities under the Mamluks were vulnerable to suppression or eradication if they were in strategically sensitive territory—as in the Levant, where both Greek Orthodox and Maronite hierarchies might be suspected of being in collusion with either the Ilkhans or the Crusaders. Vandalization of Coptic churches or other property in Egypt was rarely punished with much energy, and on several occasions the sultans banned Christians from serving as government officials. Not surprisingly, there were massive conversions of Copts to Islam over the course of the fourteenth century. Whether identified as Muslim, as protected *millah*, as pagans (generally found among Bedouin nomads), or as converted orthodox Muslims, group identity was a matter of careful documentation and legal construction.

In Ilkhan Iran/Iraq, the basic requirement of religious identification was also important. For civil society as a whole, the Ilkhans adapted the legal designations that had been common among the Seljuks, separating the untaxed soldiers and clerics from the taxed farmers and laborers, but they added another division for the Mongols (and over generations this became complicated because of the tendency of occupying populations to assimilate with the Muslim, Persian-speaking majority). In city and village life, such formal identification was necessary because of the plural legal system used by the Ilkhans (a cognate to the plurality of law in Yuan China): as a general matter, Mongols were administered under Mongol law; Muslims, Jews, and Christians, under Islamic law; and special imperial courts recommended solutions in the event that litigants could not all be served by a single legal system. One of the most stubborn problems was the contradiction between the traditional shamanic method of animal slaughter among the Mongols, which required that no blood be spilled, and the Islamic code of cleanliness, which required the draining of blood from the carcass. Muslims were also repelled by the worship of idols that is fundamental to shamanism and complained of circumstances in which they were not properly concealed from view.

The most famous of the religious identity systems of the Muslim world was instituted by the Ottomans: the *millet*—derived from the plural of *millah*. Use of the term in the early Ottoman period is unclear, and before the sixteenth century, there was no uniform, free-standing legal description of a semiautonomous millet institution. In Mehmet II's time, degrees of self-governance were constructed ad hoc for Orthodox Christians and Armenian Christians and elaborated over time. The Ottomans had a relatively large population of Jews, who in the fifteenth century had been invited by the sultans to leave Spain and Byzantium and settle in Anatolia, with some concentration in the city of Bursa. The leaders of the community were helpful in facilitating commerce and financing. In occasional interactions with the sultans, the head rabbis were treated cordially. By the end of the fifteenth century, the "Jews" as an administered population were given the right to select their own leaders, a privilege eventually extended to most of the religious communities. As part of the same development, more obligations for management of civil life devolved to the communities as the sultans focused on military government. But it was not until the nineteenth century that the empire began to multiply the recognition of communities all called millet, on the basis of language and proximity as well as doctrinal affiliation, and ultimately to add ancestry to the criteria of identity. By the end of the Ottoman period, Roman Catholic, Syriac Orthodox Christians, Samaritans, Druze, and both Orthodox and Karaite Jews were recognized, but Muslim sects distinguished by doctrine alone and regarded as heterodox—Shi'i, Ismaili, Kharajite, and others—were not admitted to the millet registers. Today, *millet* means "nation" in modern Turkish, a product of the late Ottoman process of national and ethnic differentiation that the Ottoman institutions fostered over centuries.

In the earliest Ottoman policies of identity construction, recognition of the group entailed deformation of its existing structure. At first, the Ottomans put all Christians in the empire under the authority of the Orthodox patriarch. The evident reason was that, for the Ottoman court, the *millet-i-Rum* literally meant the Byzantine territories subsumed in the Balkans, Greece, and Anatolia; it was a super-province of the empire, with its own language and cultural institutions but not necessarily a delimited space. This meant that issues of regional discord, such as the language to be used for worship, were to be decided universally by the patriarchate. In the former Bulgar territories, there was a legacy of local vernacular from the time of the khaghanate that Byzantine religious authorities had permitted to become the basis of a Bulgarian autonomous orthodox church, later licensed to use Old Church Slavonic along with Greek in its liturgies. This legacy became an immediate source of tension with the Ottoman patriarchate in Konstantiniyye, which in the fifteenth century issued the order to abandon liturgical use of Bulgarian and other Balkan languages in favor of Greek, the single language to be used by all encompassed by the Christian super-province. Only in the nineteenth century, as the number of recognized millets rose and new Balkan millets were created, did the use of Slavic in Balkan communities become legally common again.

Slowly, the administrative structure molded itself around historical communities when circumstance could make them legible to the Ottoman state. The Armenian Orthodox Church had its own doctrinal orientation—one that bore some kinship with Central Asian Christianity—and a history of independence recognized by the Byzantine and then the Seljuk courts. This inspired the early Ottoman decision to recognize an Armenian Orthodox millet. But in reality, the Ottomans controlled only the western edge of the Armenian religious continuum, with the rest under control of the Safavids based in Iran after 1502. As a result, Ottoman construction of an Armenian millet edited out most of the existing religious hierarchy and imposed an arbitrary patriarchate. Even the small patch of historical Armenian territory held by the Ottomans encompassed a variety of linguistic and doctrinal communities who, like those of the Balkans, were forced to trade local differentiation for recognition and a significant degree of independence for the larger community. Serbia, on the other hand, was entirely under Ottoman jurisdiction and came with a history of legal and cultural distinction. The Serbian branch of the Orthodox Church sprang from the administrative independence of Serbia under the Byzantine Empire. In 1219, a civil law code covering both religious and secular matters was completed in Serbian Cyrillic and accepted across the Balkans as a standard. The Ottomans appeared to consider it a working plan for their own Balkan administration.

The millets—meaning the community-defining institutions that functioned as millets, whether or not they were called that in Ottoman regulations—were critical to coherence of the early and middle Ottoman empire, but they were also part of the overall plan of Ottoman government. Like most of the post-nomadic regimes, the Ottomans preferred a small state to a large one. They relied upon the ancient collegial practices of the Turkic regimes, with a tight group of trusted advisers and functionaries and a substantial stratum of skilled bookkeepers to oversee the imperial finances. They were careful to staff a judicial system that would take on enough work to keep decisive independence out of the hands of any defined community. The religious and legal structures of millet civil administration were intersected by the assignment of regional governors who separately oversaw taxation and public order in the Balkans, Greece, the Caucasus, the Levant, Arabia, and North Africa. Outside the capital, they delegated many responsibilities for civil management to governors and religious leaders. Millet administration not only took some pressure off civil bureaucrats but also judges. Disputes were to be resolved within the millet according to its own religiously based laws whenever possible. The imperial legal system was for trade disputes, capital crimes, and civil matters between individual members of different millets if their communities' legal precepts were irreconcilably opposed.

Institutionalization of communal identity changes the cultural phenomena of identity. The original prescriptions for recognition—that is, construction—of doctrinal communities inevitably introduced criteria of regional affiliation, language use, and heritability. These all happened with the Ottoman identities over time and bequeathed various kinds of meaning to millet (religion, language, and even race) and to continuations of the term to mean "nation" in the twentieth century to nations that had been part of the Ottoman empire. These methods of objectified identity across the post-nomadic world superficially resembled the "national" (i.e., regional) elector practices of central and eastern Europe but were different in a critical way: they radiated not from the aristocracy and nobility down but from the individual up, through a process of careful bureaucratic construction of identity based on language, religion, and ancestry.

COMMON PARLANCE

The structures of objectified cultural identity put in place by the Turkic and Mongol regimes were for the most part built upon recognition of genuine differences, even if the codification of those identities was independent of the ways the identities were lived. It would be misleading to say "preexisting" differences since such institutions generate continual cultural differentiation within and between legally constructed populations. But in the Ottoman case, the millet concept gradually responded to cultural particulars beyond religion, and in the Chinese and Korean cases, the categories extended beyond status and function—most obviously to language and language performance arts, including theater, story cycles, and popular fiction.

In concrete terms, just as horses permitted Eurasia to be one reticulated, technological community, tea and its social accompaniments contributed to the creation of a medieval wave of vernacular, secular literature. Perhaps more than other ubiquitous medieval products—including textiles, spices, medicines, and weaponry—tea was accompanied by social changes that influenced the means and scale of social communication. In fact, these changes gave tea opportunities to create more changes. The product had been used in China from probably the fourth century, but it was during the tenth century—during Song and Seljuk times—that town and city teahouses became thriving businesses. Urbanization had changed collective socializing from family and village gatherings to urban settings in which strangers gathered for tea and entertainment; in the twelfth through fifteenth centuries, the advantages of cities under post-nomadic rule buoyed the economy and cultural milieu of tea, social exchange, and performance.

In western Eurasia, tea combined with the technology of early samovars to create warm, fragrant atmospheres. Well before the Bronze Age, potters in Azerbaijan are known to have been making multilevel cooking chambers, with central heating tubes leading from an open fire below the chamber to a chimney above. In ancient Greece, bronze "auto-warmers" (*authepsa*) were made with the characteristic central tube through them, allowing a coal fire below to heat water in a bronze cauldron. This type of cooker spread through western Asia in Seleucid times and later. It was probably again in Azerbaijan that a novel, integrated fire chamber and water cauldron appeared, leaving the central tube sealed at the bottom and filled with burning coals. As tea spread across medieval Eurasia, such appliances became common across Central Asia, Iran, and the Caucasus. Possibly in Jochid times, it became the Russian means of heating a medicinal brew. When black tea was introduced to Russia from Mongolia in the early seventeenth century, the samovar—a Russian translation of the original Greek term—rapidly evolved to boil water and concentrate the tea. Teahouses and, in western Eurasia, the ancestors of samovars, were constituent components of the commercial establishments that were changing social communications. In virtually all teahouses, acrobats, storytellers, actors, musical entourages, and poets entertained the crowds. Vernacular speech became somewhat more standardized with the larger scale of public interaction, and a venue of exchange between performers with written texts was enriched. Some performance became based on texts, and some texts became crystallizations of what had been oral.

The history of particular themes and forms of oral literature among the Turks is difficult to reconstruct with precision. Turkic peoples had access to various writing systems for virtually their entire history on the steppe, but the nature of oral literature is that it is distinguished by the plasticity of performance and transmission as well as the constant adaptation to the language and tastes of the audiences. The origins of specific story cycles among the Turkic peoples are believed to trace back, at the latest, to oral performances of the Gokturk period. They frequently featured heroes in search of love or war glory and were punctuated by trickery and tragedy. Many of the stories were alloyed with others, particularly in times of political integration, and they occasionally shifted venues as political centers of gravity shifted. Both the Seljuks and the Ilkhans encouraged the commission to writing of some of the stories in Oguz Turkic, but few were completely written before the seventeenth century. These stories were told through song with stringed accompaniment; some melodies survive. Many stories incorporated a theme of searching for immortality or escaping death, paralleling the plots of the Alexander Romance (which itself changed over time with the infusion of Turkic story elements). In a few details, there may also have been some influence from Greek myth. The storytellers were called in Turkic languages and in Mongolian by the same term, *bakshi*, which comes from a Tang-period Chinese word for a scholar. They were living repositories of historical memory and also had license to edit the stories as they liked and pass them on to their students.

Popular oral literature across the Turkic spectrum had always celebrated heroes of various backgrounds and fates, but in the Seljuk period and later, these heroes were with increasing frequency associated with the definition of discrete groups in search of freedom from earlier empires or rival Turkic federations. Traditional narratives became founding myths of identity among Turkic groups. In the fourteenth or fifteenth century, a version of the tale of Dede (Grandfather) Korkut was produced in writing. It is agreed to be based upon a much earlier epic, probably from the tenth century or slightly before, of the struggle of the Oguz to free themselves from Kirgiz domination (which fits nicely with the known history of Oguz migration from the western steppe toward the Caucasus and Anatolia; see Chapter 8). The Oguz Turks were the source of the Seljuks, the Ottomans, and the Akkoyunlu who appeared in the Caucasus in the fourteenth century and eventually ruled part of Iran. The first redaction of the Korkut epic was possibly done under Akkoyunlu sponsorship, perhaps with an eye to flattering the Ottoman court. The story captures the transition of the Oguz from independent nomadic life to more organized and even settled life under heroic leaders. The name used in the epic for the redefined population of Oguz descendants is Turkmen, which became generalized as a way of distinguishing Oguz descendants from Kipchak or Karluk Turks. The genealogies inserted into the book in the earliest surviving written version specifically establish the Seljuks and then the Ottomans as descendants of the hero–ruler, Oguz Khan. The story appears to have been of incidental interest to the early Ottoman court but became important in the late Ottoman period as nationalists sought a defining narrative of descent that unequivocally distinguished them from Greeks, Armenians, and from other Turkic groups.

Seljuk court promotion of written Oguz Turkic epic literature and poetry was accompanied by sponsored academic promotion of scholarship on Turkic languages. Mahmud Kashgari (1005–1102)—a native of the Karluk-speaking Karakhanid territories—produced his comparative compendium of Turkic languages (*Dīwān Lughāt al-Turk*, written in Arabic) in the 1070s at Baghdad, ostensibly for the use of the caliph and his court in communicating with both the Seljuks and regional *mamluk* regimes. It was in essence an encyclopedia of linguistic, historical, and geographic knowledge of the Turks, including a collection of emerging poetry and religious commentary in Turkic; such literature continued to grow in importance in subsequent centuries, including the Turkic poetry of the Sufist poet Rumi (see Chapter 9). Though his work was used to support the language pluralism of the Abbasid–Seljuk period, Kashgari was an unusual advocate for recovery of cultural independence by Turks, whom he thought should purge their language of vocabulary and stylistic influences from standard Persian and Persian dialects used for commerce. For his rejection of cosmopolitan language and any non-Islamic religious influence, Kashgari was in later centuries regarded as a prophet of pan-Turkic identity.

To the Turkic courts and elites, language use was not intended in this period to be exclusive, and they continued to sponsor work in Persian. Throughout Iran, Azerbaijan, Transoxiana, Afghanistan, northern India, and parts of Iraq, traditions of Persian storytelling not only helped enliven the sultan's policies of Persian-language promotion but also provided some of the basis for early secular and popular writing in the language. Like the Turks, the Persians had a rich tradition of storytellers of various specializations who performed not only in villages but also in city streets, teahouses, and martial arts clubs. Stories could be acted out in front of a theatrical backdrop of canvas or silk. Plots often focused on legendary kings or war leaders of ancient Iran or the Seleucid empire (including Alexander). Sultans frequently subsidized such performances for both their own entertainment and popular appeal.

Such traditions were combined with biblical narrative and fairly straightforward Islamic history in the *Shahnameh* (*Shahnama*, *Shahname*, and so on), often considered the blueprint for modern national identity epics. The name meant, literally, a written account of the kings, or shahs, and its *nameh* component had been used previously with respect to didactic biographies or political commentary. The work in medieval Persian was a Ghaznavid–Seljuk period creation of Hakim Mansur (940–1020)—known by his literary name of Firdawsi (transliterated in many variants)—and completed in 1010, though the oldest surviving manuscript of the work dates to 1217. Translating archaic Iranian into contemporary Persian was a major literary enterprise of Samanid and Ghaznavid times, and translation from Sasanian chronicles in particular provided some of the content of the *Shahnameh*. It is the longest-known poetic saga, at about 100,000 lines, and is a broad narrative of the origins of the Iranian people from the times of the Avesta (see Chapter 2), through an age of heroes, to the documented history of the Islamic era. Firdawsi was a native of eastern Iran and was raised in the vicinity of Tus, on the Iran/Transoxiana border, later the ancestral town of Nasir al-Din Tusi (see Chapters 7 and 9), and close to the hometowns of Omar Khayyam and Rumi. For the first part of his life, the region and most of Iran was under the control of the powerful Samanid sultanic dynasty—Persians—of the Abbasid caliphate. Firdawsi saw Samanid power recede as the Turkic Ghaznavids and later the Seljuks became dominant. The Samanids had promoted Persian as the poetic language of Iran, and Firdawsi wrote his poem in the standard Persian of the time. The *Shahnameh* (see also Chapter 11) was a milestone in the popularization not only of written Persian but also of nonreligious writing that explicitly reminded listeners of the deep connections between pre-Islamic history and Iranian culture. Firdawsi concentrated on the adventures and virtues of heroes of ancient and Sasanian Iran, particularly praising a hero who recaptured and preserved the knowledge of the Zoroastrians. Islam condemned Zoroastrianism as paganism, and at least some of the Zoroastrian texts that Firdawsi used as indirect sources were disappearing in his lifetime. He was not the only Persian speaker of the Ghaznavid era attempting to preserve (with mixed success) ancient Iranian texts, and prominent scholars involved in the activity tended to come from eastern Iran and Transoxiana; the similarities of their concerns to controversial Ibn Sina (Firdawsi's near contemporary), also from this Sartic world and also struggling to integrate Zoroastrianism into a new school of thought ("illuminationism"; see Chapter 9), are clear.

These developments in Seljuk times particularly cannot be seen apart from the continuous mutual influences between Iran and Byzantium. The authority and prestige of the eastern church created constant pressure to keep circulated religious manuscripts in classical rather than vernacular Greek, and partly as a result of this textual discipline, literacy among Byzantines is believed to have been widespread. It is clear that a rich vernacular literature appeared early in Byzantine history and became more elaborate from about the tenth century on. This was partly achieved by a blurring of the line between secular and religious literature; plots and themes from classical Greek literature could be woven into Christian hagiography, and biblical tales and saintly lives could be stretched into popular romantic epics and satirical comedies. Byzantine influences on the literary life of Alexandria was continuous and sometimes strong through the Fatimid, Ayyubid, and early Mamluk periods, creating continuing complexity in the cultural life of Egypt and reflecting Egyptian trends in monasticism and mysticism back to Byzantium. The connections to the Levant and Anatolia were also strong, as a high number of Byzantine authors—perhaps the majority of active Byzantine authors before the twelfth century—were natives of these areas. The tendency toward demotic language is evident not only in surviving texts but also in the steady efforts of church and state authorities to edit and criticize texts written in vernacular forms. Well into the times of the Ottoman patriarchy, the Orthodox Church was in a steady, low-grade war against vernacularization—and regionalization—of historical chronicles and didactic religious works, which only stimulated the development of popular vernacular romantic writings in both Greek and Persian.

The Balkans, subject to Byzantine and Turkic influence from Avar to Ottoman times, was a rich center of teahouse and public entertainments. By the fourteenth century, Bulgaria's ninth-century vernacular Bible translation and hagiographies developed into poetic epics, story cycles, and early novels. Themes were often inspired by Greek histories, Alexander stories, legends of Troy, or love stories from Abbasid or Seljuk poetry (sometimes refractions of Indian themes). Nearby Bohemia was influenced not only by Balkan trends toward vernacularization but also chivalric ballads from Germany, with which Bohemia retained strong cultural exchange into the modern period (see also Chapter 9). In this context of rapidly developing vernacular religious and popular literature, the first Latin–Czech dictionary was produced in the fourteenth century as a significant volume of ecclesiastical, biblical, and historical work was being translated from Latin to Czech (see also Chapter 9). Finally, in the Caucasus, rich and continuous historiographical developments from the eleventh century on, increasingly in both Georgian and Armenian languages, continued under the Mongols and into the Ottoman era. It is possible that the authority of the body of work by the fifteenth century was a consideration in the early Ottoman recognition of an Armenian patriarchate—perhaps based not only on the history of the Armenian Church but also on the fact that the Armenians, like the Byzantines, had an impressive body of literature in their own language.

In eastern Eurasia, Mongol myths, ballads, poetry, and history were orally transmitted and not written in Mongolian until the adoption of the syllabic Uighur script in the early thirteenth century. The cycles were similar to Turkic epics, with the addition after the twelfth century of the Tibetan epic of Geser of Khrom (i.e., "Ceasar of Rome"). Mongol nobles who were not engaged in battle, horse racing, wrestling, or polo hired singers and actors to entertain them. Partly because of this traditional taste, the Mongol courts in West Asia, Russia, and China tended to privilege the spoken local languages over the classical languages of the scholars and bureaucrats. The result was the encouragement of vernacular styles and native languages during this period and national literatures thereafter. Many Yuan nobles, like their Turkic predecessors in China, were patrons of the arts, with a particular attachment to musical theater. As early as the fourth century, when small Turkic and Xiongnu dynasties were ruling North China, dance and music performed with masks and stringed instruments are first documented. They were simple in form, really a kind of comic dialogue between actors. In the Tang period, they took on elaborate plots (many of them based on folktales or romanticized historical fables) and large casts. This demanded a certain level of sponsorship by the court and nobility, which continued through the Song period. The Yuan court also stepped up to support theater but with a difference: the performances were not to be in the stilted classical Chinese used to that point but rather in colloquial, local Chinese, which could be understood by all in attendance. They patronized a number of dramatists who are well known today—for instance, Guan Hanqing (1241–1320), whose subsidies allowed him to complete at least 60 plays. The Yuan court preference was for revenge plots, stories of chicanery by cunning women, and confused purposes among villagers. In contrast to earlier opera, which featured a soloist narrating the action, Yuan-period dramas featured entire singing casts, with plentiful acrobatics and orchestral music. Theatrical performances, tuned to the tastes of Mongol sponsors, may have been a conduit of the pronounced influence of Mongolian language upon the traditional dialect of Beijing.

The appeal of melodrama in theater and song was paralleled by an emergence of popular writing (probably drawn from well-known story cycles of the time) and the appearance of the first novels in Chinese. In the case of the best known, such as *Water Margin* (*Shuihu zhuan*) and *Romance of the Three Kingdoms* (*Sanguo yanyi*), authorship is obscure, and even the historicity of credited authors is not unquestioned. The texts were much amended in the Ming period and, later, which rendered early modern products with unclear stylistic resemblance to Yuan-period originals. But the Yuan provenance is itself obvious. *Water Margin* is a tale of Song-period robbers and rebels that could have been written only in the Yuan period, and its origins in oral storyteller performance is another mark of its Yuan provenance. Both works are among the first in vernacular Chinese (*baihua*), and both are closely intertwined with medieval theater, which frequently adapted their episodes for musical performance. In Korea, folk music—still heavily influenced by shamanic songs—was appreciated at the Goryeo court and, because of that, was also known in Dadu. The period saw diminished influence in Korean song and theater arts from classical Chinese poetry, and the flourishing of a genre of folk songs carrying the narrative of story cycles, often accompanied by stringed instruments played by women. The same plots and often the same music could also be seen in puppet shows and short plays with actors in colorful masks. The content was, as in the case of Chinese theater, full of action, tragedy, and passion. And while Europe had its own nascent theatrical tradition from ancient Greece and medieval mystery plays, the Yuan also may have had an influence on some aspects of European entertainment: Marco Polo's rendition of his reported adventures at the court of Kublai Khan was first a profitable theatrical production in Venice, where its themes and techniques may have drawn color from the Yuan performances Polo witnessed in China.

The overall effect of post-nomadic rule across Eurasia from the tenth to the fifteenth centuries was encouragement of vernacular speech and some movement toward its standardization in popular performance as well as the theatrical and literary genres derived from these vernacular interventions. The contents and the media worked together to promote local identification with individual languages and access to popular performance regardless of degree of literacy—and in a few venues, regardless of social class. They also provided the platform for development of popular—and eventually printed—literature in the fourteenth and fifteenth centuries.

THE PAINTED WORD

There are episodic indications that writing and particularly printing had always been an interesting feature of sedentary religion to nomads. Shamanism was granular, and there were no theoretical arguments or lofty pronouncements to be carried in writing from community to community. Nothing (with the possible exception of genealogies) was written that was not ritually destroyed by fire. The idea of writing and transmitting spiritual information of great power was clearly intriguing to the Turks. Regimes of Turkic legacy frequently featured in their dynastic histories specific moments in which their founders had invented, amended, or commanded the use of scripts suitable for the dynastic language. The fascination with writing may have contributed to the enthusiasm of the Ilkhans, Timurids, and Mughals for illuminated manuscripts as well as Timur's famous ring that supposedly was incised with the entire Quran—microscopic, but still infused with the ineffable power of the book. The concept of the "peoples of the book" in Islam may have itself resonated comfortably with nomadic attitudes toward scriptural religion.

Turkic and Mongol nobles showed a variety of attitudes toward the literate elites of their conquered territories. Those who were willing to offer their skills and loyalties should be privileged, and those who resisted should be eradicated. The result was the selective survival of traditional elites and the culture they represented: classicized and universalistic languages, elaborate poetic forms, and rarified social rituals. In both China and Iran, landholding elites who resisted Mongol rule were displaced (and usually eliminated) and their lands given to collaborators. The Chinese examination system was whittled away to virtually nothing, and officials were selected from only approved families. Sponsorship of philosophers was obviated by the endorsement of a simple orthodoxy (based on the commentaries of Zhu Xi, 1130–1200; see Chapter 9), and imperial favor was shown to painters specializing in landscapes and animals. Throughout western Eurasia, the legacy of earlier Turkic regimes like the Seljuks was used by later Turkic regimes like the Timurids and Ottomans to promote poetry, autobiography, and philosophy in Persian and Turkic vernaculars rather than Arabic. The result was that, in a century and a half, the preferences of the nomadic regimes for popular endorsement and local culture had changed, though in varying degrees, the common written standards and artistic tastes of virtually all classes across Eurasia.

Religious proselytizing, as suggested in previous chapters, was a longstanding vehicle for the development of medieval literatures in vernacular languages long before the direct effects of the nomadic regimes. In a sense, the Bible was an example of repeated vernacularization, since the Old Testament had been translated into vernacular Greek before the beginning of the first millennium CE and the New Testament had been translated from Greek to Latin at the instruction of the Roman emperors after Constantine. But in these instances, the intention was to produce a new standard that would be used for universal instruction of priests, who would in turn lecture the communities of believers in local dialects even while using Latin for the liturgy. In Christianity, surviving incomplete translations of the New Testament—such as the first-century Coptic, second-century Syriac, fourth-century Gothic, sixth-century Makurian, and seventh-century Chinese and Anglo-Saxon—were aids to clergy who needed standard translations of the universal text while preaching to local listeners. Charlemagne ordered a similar but more extensive project for Frankish in the eighth century.

A slightly different turn was represented by the translation of the entire New Testament into Bulgarian as well as hagiographies of the saints in the ninth century (see Chapters 4 and 5) and the Abbasid-era translation of the entire Bible into Arabic, which made complete texts available to local readers. A marked change in use of scripture was evident, though not at all uniquely, in the Cathars, who demanded the entire Bible in their own language for direct reading. Religious dissidence became a new and vigorous motor of vernacular writing and reading, as critics of the Roman Catholic Church produced the Bible in English, Czech, and German for their believers to read for themselves. As vernacular scripture and religious dissidence became inseparable, the opposition of both the papacy in Rome and the Orthodox patriarchate in Konstantiniyye became more unbending, at least through the fifteenth century. Afterward, the church in Rome changed its policies in order to find new believers to offset the departure of dissidents into Protestantism and Anabaptism: they authorized the translation of the Bible into Chinese and Malay, a new Arabic edition, and some teaching materials in Japanese and native North American languages. In the case of the patriarchate, we have seen above that modifications in the system of community recognition allowed the use of many local vernaculars to be endorsed by the later Ottoman government, which implicitly or explicitly permitted the development of additional Christian religious authorities outside the patriarchate.

The number of readers to whom these texts were directed is unknown. Vernacular materials produced under the aegis of the Roman Catholic Church were in most cases intended to spread the word orally—regardless not only of local speech but also local literacy levels—and to offer vernacular renditions of teaching materials whether or not they were requested. In contrast, the demand of dissident and reform movements from the Cathars and later to not only have the texts in their own languages but also to read and interpret them for themselves bespeaks confidence in a significant level of reading ability, at least in the immediate community. Jan Hus deliberately transferred his activities from lecturing and preaching to published writing, producing a medium for private study and contemplation that he thought would exceed the number of listeners he could address directly. But the popular demand for mass production of religious literature is difficult to assess.

The Islamic world was an interesting contrast. Historians identify the Abbasid caliphate as having the greatest diffusion of literacy of any medieval society. As part of the dynamics of the Islamic conquests of the seventh and eighth centuries, popular languages such as Aramaic had been sublimated or eliminated by Arabic throughout Syria/Palestine, the Arab Peninsula, and North Africa. The result was sustained diglossia, in coexistence of hybridized local dialects with standard Arabic writing and a liturgical language that was commonly intelligible. In Iran and Central Asia, though successive Turkic regimes had promoted the development of the first Persian literature and the writing in their own Turkic dialects, literacy in Arabic was always a requirement for participation in religious life. Unlike Christianity, Islam had put a high value on the reading of scripture, and young men, as in the traditions of Rabbinic Judaism, were expected to be able to make their way through portions of sacred text. The language was important not only for religious life but also for the law, which developed a rich tradition of precedent drawn from the Quran and the commentary of judges across the caliphate. Christians as well as Muslims could read scripture in Arabic, and the Abbasid state supported constant translation projects from Greek into Arabic, promoting the professional study of Arabic even among those for whom it was not a native language. In short, the high demands for literacy in Arabic provided a matrix for literacy that did not have a correspondence in medieval Europe.

In East Asia, Mahayana Buddhism was based on an early translation of Buddhist texts—whether the sayings of Buddha himself or his students—from Pali into Sanskrit, and wherever Mahayana missionaries went across Eurasia, they worked to have the texts or significant portions of them translated into local written languages. This was facilitated by the spread across the Turkic world of phonetic scripts developed from second-century Aramaic, including Syriac, Manichaean, Armenian, and Uighur. Many of these texts, some of them hundreds of years old at the time, were sealed in caves near the overland trade settlement of Dunhuang (in Gansu Province of China) in the eleventh century. They encompass a huge assortment of Buddhist texts along with a few texts relating to Manichaeanism, Daoism, and Central Asian Christianity. Translation of religious texts into Chinese—also well represented at Dunhuang—was powerful in ways that were not possible with phonetic or syllabic scripts like Latin, Arabic, or Uighur. Because of its relative independence from sound, written Chinese of the early medieval period could carry the message of Buddhism not only through China but also to what are now Vietnam, Korea, and Japan. In those societies, elite men were literate in classical Chinese from at least the seventh century. If this had been the only written medium, however, access to the texts would have been restricted to a small number of aristocrats, government officials, and other literati. In China, this may have remained the case for a few centuries, but by the twelfth century Tibetan was being written in a revised South Asian script, and long texts relating to the Tibetan school of Buddhism were being produced and read by a large clerical population. In the later middle ages, Japan, Vietnam, Korea, and the Kitan and Jurchen empires all developed independent syllabaries from the Chinese script, which allowed them to annotate Chinese texts in their own languages. In the cases of Vietnam, Japan, and Korea, these syllabaries became full writing systems, bringing elite women, merchants, and lower-ranking government officials into the ranks of the functionally literate; some went on to become authors of poetry, letters, and autobiography. East Asia never had the Islamic world's consensus that boys and young men of the professional and merchant classes should be literate in a standard text, though a selection of philosophical classics were known by memory to a select male elite. Chinese writing was a universal medium in which a few fairly short texts were regarded as essential, producing regional diglossia and facilitating widespread functional literacy in the medieval period.

The Timurids and Ottomans extended the use of Turkish to military administration (one of the few salary-paying dimensions of government). Ottoman bureaucrats spoke and wrote in Persian except in North Africa, Iraq, Syria, and the Arab Peninsula, where the standard administrative medium, as for the entire religious sphere, was Arabic. The styles encouraged by the court (through sponsorship of already existing trends in elite or popular use) ran from the intensely disciplined "divan poetry" to saga-like dramas of love and war. Beyond the court, communities used their own speech in daily life but, for trade and many administrative tasks, used Ottoman Turkish. In the Timurid empire, the Chaghatay Turkish language, which became the standard of the Timurid court, was part of the eastern branch of Turkic languages. The Sartic majority of their agricultural zone all spoke a Persian dialect (which the Timurid rulers, like their Chaghatay and Ilkhan predecessors, called "Tajik"), and like the Ghaznavids, Seljuks, and Ilkhans, the Chaghataids and then the Timurids institutionalized it as the working language of their Persian and Transoxianan administrators. From Seljuk and Ghaznavid times to the end of the Timurids, as Chaghatay borrowed literary forms and vocabulary from Persian (and Persian continually imported Turkish words), it became a broadly appealing reference for Mamluk Kipchak and Ottoman Oguz as they attempted to develop their own literary standards. The Mamluks were actively promoting their Kipchak Turkish as the identity language of Mamluk elites regardless of their ancestry. By the middle fifteenth century, Ottoman Turkish was independent enough to break away from any reliance on Chaghatay as an administrative and literary medium. But in Central Asia and the Mughal courts in India, Chaghatay remained a sophisticated literary language in its own right. Not only poetry but also philosophical works, religious didactic texts, and legal commentary were written in the language, and in the fourteenth century the Quran was translated into Chaghatay.

Virtually everywhere across medieval Eurasia, scribing—particularly in legal or government matters—was a profession, whether full or part time. The need in certain situations for highly technical language and legible handwriting or Latin, Quranic Arabic, or classical Chinese would require the employment of such individuals, just as today we often require the aid of a lawyer to handle certain documents whether or not we can read; the ubiquity and profitability of scribing is not in itself evidence for a low rate of literacy. By the end of the fourteenth century, it is reasonable to conclude that most of Eurasia was educated enough and had access to the necessary writing technologies to support more vernacular texts than we can now ascertain were available. The time-consuming manuscript was still the most common mode of textual production. We know that everywhere in Eurasia, the production, transport, and sale of books were all profitable by the late twelfth century. Universities concentrated thousands of scholars and students in a single location. They were served by hostels, public houses, and tailors but also by booksellers, indoors or out, who at least in Europe, worked under license from the universities, which kept large facilities for scribes and bookbinders busily producing work. Monasteries and religious colleges also were centers of scribal activity.

Across the Turkic spectrum of the late medieval and early modern period, painting was an important narrative complement to prose sagas and poetry. It had a special role in religious traditions (so long as God and Muhammad were not be represented) possibly as a legacy of the Manichaeans, whose sacred texts were said to have been illustrated by Mani himself. The Ilkhanid period had been critical for its embrace of painting styles and techniques from China, Iran, and Byzantium. Written adventure stories and histories were illustrated or, in some cases, displaced altogether by series of vivid paintings, often with landscapes recalling China or Mongolia and figures acting out scenes from the Quran, Iranian myths, or ancient fables such as the Alexander Romance. After the Ilkhans, the Timurids and small, local dynasties in Iran sponsored the production of these "miniatures," which by the fifteenth century could be mass-produced by woodblock and were often bound in books consisting entirely of a visual rather than textual narrative, or accompanying text in particularly elegant books.

In both the Ilkhan and Timurid periods, Iran and Azerbaijan were the sites of extraordinary illuminated manuscript production, which had started in sixth-century Europe and spread throughout the Muslim world. Both the illuminated manuscript and woodblock-illustrated book represented the cultural agenda of transmitting highly literate content to audiences ranging from the illiterate (including children) to the pre-literate, to the functionally literate. In the Turkic Muslim domains, some of the best illustrated books were dedicated to dynastic or national epics. They featured silk backgrounds and gold thread, vivid colors, and integrated text and figures in a continuous narrative field. The illuminated manuscript—a culture in its own right, uniting scholars, scribes, painters, papermakers, and bookbinders with patrons and distributors—was also not strictly delimited in geography. The Ilkhan court was renowned for sponsoring manuscripts of the highest artistic quality, but Bulgaria was also known for its manuscripts in Old Church Slavonic (best known, the *Gospels of Tsar Ivan Alexander* in the fourteenth century), and about the same time, Hungarian workshops contributed the gold-painted pictorial chronicle of the kings of Hungary in Latin. As a counterpart to the illuminated manuscripts of the Islamic world, the Russian churches of the

Jochid period were adorned with narrative wall art and iconographic carving, the most famous examples of which were in Novgorod and Moscow.

China and Korea in the twelfth century already had a vigorous transnational book trade, thanks to the competition for the examinations and the thriving development of speculative "neo-Confucian" philosophy (see Chapter 9). The Yuan period saw several changes. The Yuan government encouraged the printing of Confucian classics to show its patronage of Chinese culture but did not give money or tax allowances for the publication of traditional poetry in the ornate, allusive style that had previously distinguished elite writing. Many literati displaced from government service concentrated on their land and others entered commerce. But a considerable number took up painting and new styles of poetry, which could be combined in many works. Yuan court preferences pushed the development of painting in this period. Portraits and tableaux of horses and landscapes that combined the Mongol love of simplicity with the subtlety of Buddhist esthetics were highly valued, and the great painters of the period all capitalized on these qualities. Zhao Mengfu (1254–1322), Guan Daosheng (Zhao's wife, 1262–1319), and Ni Zan (1301–1374) were among those honored for their distinctive and often moody monochrome works.

Zhao was a grown man when the Song dynasty was defeated and he was introduced to the elderly Kublai. Later Yuan emperors appointed Zhao to sinecures that allowed him to establish the characteristic Yuan style. Guan Daosheng also became well-known for her rather ghostly studies of plants. Ni Zan came from a "Confucian" family of wealth and education, suffered through the disorders of the middle fourteenth century, and saw the transition to the Ming. During the troubled times of his early adulthood, he gave away his possessions and lived for a time on a barge. His inimitable ink paintings were, according to him, done with no interest in realism but were intended only to manifest his feelings. These combinations of directness, simplicity, and unapologetic emotional self-expression became characteristic of all the popular arts of the Yuan period. Changes in the popular tastes and marketed products of China and Korea had an impact upon Japan at a time when its main island was undergoing significant political centralization, partly in response to two attempted Mongol invasions and the possibility of more. The Mongol threat had helped consolidate control of the state by a military elite, whose tastes in turn dictated a new culture of simplicity, spirituality, and veneration of heroism in war. Many governors were patrons of the arts, with a decided preference for theater over poetry. This is the period in which the theatrical art of No arose. Its greatest playwright and theorist, Zeami, an intimate of the shogun of his day, died in 1443. Not only in theater but also in popular storytelling and painting, a taste for the epic cycle was pronounced, and a favorite was the *Tale of the Heike* (*Heike monogatari*), based on a twelfth-century civil war. It is possible that the thirteenth-century work was written expressly for performance by lute-playing mendicants; in any case, the material immediately became the subject of theatrical performances.

THE REPLICATED WORD

The introduction of printing should be seen as a slow and relatively late response to what was probably a long-standing, largely unmet demand for texts. The trends in vernacular history and fiction; the propagation of regional and near-national narratives, the rise of religious dissident communities demanding scripture in their own tongues, and popular entertainment in many media created pockets across Eurasia where a hunger for reading material could no longer be satisfied with the scribal and printing capacities of the thirteenth and fourteenth centuries. Ink was easily made from ash, animal by-products, and plant dyes and was common across Eurasia from the classical period on. Brushes and styli were also well-known. What changed during the middle ages were the writing surfaces. In the fifth century, for instance, the Chinese were writing on paper made from rice or wood pulp, Central Asians were writing on local paper made of cotton pulp or imported from China, and Europeans were writing on parchment of various qualities. Paper, whether from cotton, rice, or wood pulp, was much easier to make and transport than parchment and also easier to bind, making the circulation of writing a bit cheaper and easier in Central Asia and East Asia than in Europe. The gradual distribution of paper from the Islamic world to Europe laid the groundwork for the explosion of mechanical printing in the fifteenth century.

In China, the carving of wooden plates to print on paper had probably started before the fall of the Han empire in the third century, when the same method also began to be used to pattern textiles. But weak demand for a large number of copies of the same text prevented woodblock printing from becoming a profitable industry. Before the ninth century, philosophical texts used to prepare officials for government service were not yet standardized and tended to circulate in manuscript among the estates of the elites. It was Buddhism that made the demand for woodblock prints rise. It required a large number of standard texts and often with illustrations included for teaching groups who could not read or afford books of their own. Woodblock printing of Buddhist texts became an important industry in medieval China and Korea. In Song times, printing became even more profitable because the growth of the examination system in China (which in a smaller and different form was also used in Korea) had produced a partly standardized syllabus; degree candidates wanted their own copies of the sayings of Confucius and the writings of Mencius.

Conditions for the development of woodblock printing were widespread in Buddhist Central Asia, but the Islamic world and Europe were not heavy participants. They all had access to proper paper—wood and rice pulp paper or linen, hemp, and cotton pulp in the Central Asian style, which had spread to France from Andalusia. But in the Abbasid caliphate, wood was expensive. It was used before the Ilkhan period, but infrequently. Equally influential were differences in understanding the spiritual impact of the written or printed word. In the Buddhist world (possibly under the influence of Turkic Central Asian attitudes toward written scripture), the existence of a religious text was the essence of its power, and how it was produced was incidental. The printed page could work spiritually very much like the writing on a spinning prayer wheel: the printed word has a power of its own, a sort of perpetual prayer independent of the human voice, a powerful companion to the sick or dead. But in western Eurasia, an old value—possibly inherited from Hinduism—equated careful hand copying of texts with prayer; the production of the text, not its final perpetuity, was its power. Europeans were nevertheless willing to use an efficient press machine—unique to them—for rolling paper and binding leather covers to books. With adaptations it could be used to produce woodblock prints, which were often used for book illustrations. The earliest surviving printed version of Quran materials dates to the early fourteenth century, from the Mamluk territories. There is evidence that woodblock printing was used widely (if not as commonly as in East Asia) in the Islamic world for commercial documents as well as the production of Jewish and Christian scripture. It was used after Abbasid times by the Ilkhans for reproducing their best illuminated manuscripts, most famously the *Shahnameh*. But Islamic religious authorities strongly discouraged the production of woodblock printed religious texts, and European institutions tended to protect the authority and profitability of their scriptoriums. By the early fifteenth century copperplate printing on paper was used for a few books but more often for art. For centuries the use of woodblock and copperplate printing for the reproduction of art would thrive in equal portion to textual printing techniques, with the first multicolor woodblock prints appearing in China in the sixteenth century.

Things changed with the introduction of movable type, which had a halting start in eleventh-century China, where printers experimented with exchangeable individual characters in a page-sized frame of wood or metal. At first, the characters were carved from wood; they were later mass-cast in ceramic or brass, but the characters tended to shift in the setting, leaving the texts fuzzy and unattractive to well-heeled customers. Movable type had spread by this time to Korea and Xixia, and it was Koreans who figured out that using beeswax to settle the characters in the frames made them stable and still removable; they produced a collection of Buddhist teaching texts in movable type before the end of the Goryeo period. Not only were the esthetics of the type improved but the process made possible the high-volume, accurate reproduction of many pages in rapid succession. Korea afterward became a major exporter of books to China, where demand had shot up in the Song period as increased wealth and education made the examination system more competitive. After the Yuan declaration of orthodox philosophy and revival of the examination system, demand for more inexpensive editions of a more limited number of texts soared. By the time the Mongol trade systems made Bukhara, Samarkand, Karakorum, and Dadu familiar to European merchants and missionaries, movable type in China, Japan, and Korea was approaching maturity.

Between about 1250 and 1450, Europeans knew of woodblock type from many sources—Muslim communities in Italy, Sicily, and Spain; printed money in Yuan China, Jochid Russia, and Ilkhan Iran; and playing cards, which were widely used in reasonably standard patterns from China to western Europe—and were using forms of it for image reproduction. But they had probably rarely, if ever, seen their own languages in print. Laurens Coster (1370–1440) in Haarlem claimed that the idea of printing came to him "in a flash of light" when he noticed that words he had carved in wood could leave an impression in the sand. Perhaps there were really Europeans as out of touch as all that (a little unlikely since the basic process he invoked could as easily have described some incidental printing techniques used in ancient Mesopotamia). In any case, Coster seems to have started some printing with wooden characters in a frame, later substituting superior metal casts, which would have approximated the process used across eastern Eurasia at the time. He may have run a successful small business for a few years before his death. The local narrative says that his equipment was taken to Mainz. If true (there being virtually no evidence), this would put the Coster equipment in the ambit of Johannes Gutenberg (c. 1394–1468), who labored through the 1430s, 1440s, and early 1450s to invent a stable and efficient printing machine. It was likely an adaptation of the press machines used for various purposes across Europe, but he added a spectacular innovation: a metallurgical breakthrough that permitted mass production of individual letter casts. He had also perfected a new ink that was not smudged by the process of rapid, mass production of printed pages.

Gutenberg's first productions are not definitely known. One of them might have been his own narrative of how he invented the press. In 1455, he printed a complete Bible in Latin with German blackletter type and, a few years later, a Latin psalter in the same format but with a printer's mark. By that time, he had lost his original press—and the rights to the Bible—to one of his creditors and had an instant competitor. The speed with which the printing industry and book sales expanded is vivid evidence of the depth of reading demand in Europe (see Map 10.1). The first book printed in Czech was a history of Troy, probably in 1470. The medieval Hungarian chronicle was printed in 1473 in Buda. The first book was published in Spanish (part of a poetry contest held in recently reconquered Valencia) in 1474. In 1492, an entire language course in Castilian was published to celebrate the recovery of Andalusia and the coronation of Isabella and Ferdinand of Aragon as monarchs of a united Spain. The first printing operation in Russia seems to have been established in 1552 for the Muscovite tsar Ivan IV as a favor from the king of Denmark. As Gutenberg's machine plans spread westward, the production and consumption snowballed. By 1550, it is probable that three million books were printed a year, more than European scribes could produce in a century. European cities with major printing operations in the sixteenth century were growing in wealth exponentially compared to cities with no major printing companies. By the beginning of the seventeenth century, printing, papermaking, and ink production were all profitable industries in the Netherlands (where the greatest proportional number of European readers lived), Germany, Austria, France, Italy, and Switzerland.

Latin Bibles were profitable, as Gutenberg had guessed, but they were being rapidly overshadowed by demand for the New Testament and the whole Bible in local languages, which increased the opportunities for printers. Several manuscript German translations of the entire Bible had been completed before Gutenberg, and one of them quickly came into print by 1466. The first Italian translation was printed in 1471. The first printed Czech Bible, based partly on the work of Hus, appeared in 1488. In ensuing decades, translations in German dialects were also printed; Martin Luther's Bible, printed in 1534, was a relatively late addition. Productions of the fifteenth and sixteenth centuries were sometimes from the Greek or Latin text, but others were translations of translations purely for the purpose of producing the Bible in a regional language and selling it. Both Swedish and Dutch translations of the whole Bible were printed in 1524. The first translation into French by the Anabaptist dissident Jacques Lefèvre d'Étaples was printed (in Belgium) in 1530. The first English translation of the New Testament came out in 1526, and the first entire Roman Catholic printed Bible in English in 1582. The first proven translation of the entire Bible (and Apocrypha) in Welsh was printed in London in 1588. In 1602, the Bible was printed in Irish in Ireland by the Protestant colonial authorities eager to discredit Catholicism.

The profitability and regional diversity of sixteenth-century European printing was provided additional markets—and sustaining profits—by demand for Bibles in Arabic and Turkish as well as Torahs from non-Muslim religious communities across the Ottoman world. In contrast to the challenges of constantly differentiating texts of the Bible in Europe, the Ottoman markets were for single editions of texts in Hebrew and Arabic. The Torah was quickly set into print, most often in Italy—the wealthiest European country of the time and the one with the strongest ties to the Ottoman empire and the Eurasian trade networks—but also in Thessaloniki, within the Ottoman borders. The first Italian edition appeared before 1492 and the expulsion of Jews from Spain. Thereafter, publishing operations in Hebrew and Ladino were supported by Jewish populations in Konstantiniyye and Ottoman Anatolia, especially after their communities were enlarged by refugees from Spain. The first prayer text for Arabic-speaking Christians was produced by papal authorities sometime around 1500; Francis I of France (see epilogue) commissioned printing (at the same facility in Italy mentioned above) of the Book of Psalms in Arabic and Syriac for the same audience. Also in Italy, the first Quran was printed in 1530, though the precise market intended is unknown; some Arabic characters were incorrectly printed, and Ottoman authorities forbade the importation of printed Qurans to their territories. In 1643, also in Italy, learned commentaries written by Islamic scholars of the Seljuk and Ottoman periods were printed, certainly for the use of Europeans studying Islamic language and religion and possibly also for the Ottoman market. The only serious competition was in Konstantiniyye, where printing presses for religious texts, commentaries, and newsletters in Arabic for Christians and in Hebrew and Ladino for Jews were in operation before the end of the fifteenth century.

William Caxton (1422–1491), the first known English printer, made it a point to translate and print some popular French works for the business he started in London in 1471. He found instant commercial success with fabulous and romantic tales, many drawn from medieval French ballads and epic poems. In 1476, he produced an edition of Geoffrey Chaucer's hundred-year-old *Canterbury Tales*, with inset woodblock illustrations; it was an instant success. He followed it in 1485 with *Le Morte Darthur* by Thomas Malory (who was either a vicious criminal implicated in a series of capital crimes or an unfortunate with the same name as said criminal). A book in a similar spirit was Marco Polo's *Travels*, which also started out in Old French. An Italian publisher produced an ostensibly definitive edition (claimed to be based upon a Latin original, which is almost impossible) and printed it in 1559 in Venice, where it quickly became the equivalent of a best seller. By that time, tales of travels among sultans and khans had become a profitable genre. One of the best examples was by "John Mandeville" (not a real person), whose story of travels depended on the inspiration and a little bit on the text of Polo's *Travels*. The book was circulating as an elaborate illustrated manuscript in French (its original language) and English well before the fifteenth century, and it was brought into print in several forms by 1550. It also helped inspire a fanatical readership of romantic tales of knights and courtly women, most directly inspired by the centuries of mounted warfare to drive the Muslim rulers from Spain. The entire genre was pilloried by Miguel Cervantes (who had spent five years in Muslim North Africa and made the metafictional claim that the story was translated from an Arabic memoir) in his *El Ingenioso Hidalgo de la Mancha*—Don Quixote—published in Spanish in two parts, in 1605 and 1615 (the second part a novel about the veracity

Map 10.1. The growth of markets for printed literature, c. 1480–1600. *Note*: Important early cities with printing industries are marked. Patterned regions are domestic markets for publications in regional vernaculars. Straight lines indicate the destinations (but not the transport routes) for works produced before 1600 in Hebrew and Arabic for diasporal communities and proselytizing missions.

of the first part). The work, part of the process of establishing a standard written Spanish, was in its first printing more widely read in Peru than in Spain. Subsequent printings made it a hit in Spain, so much so that pirated editions deprived Cervantes and his publisher of most of their profits.

It is not a coincidence that the emergence of the printing press and national vernaculars was at every stage so intimately connected to the Turkic-ruled, post-nomadic Muslim world—whether as a profitable market or as commercial hook for promoting sales. The latent engagement of Eurasia that broadly powered early print in Europe was noticed by authorities who condemned the world of secular diversions and cosmopolitan associations. In 1497, Girolamo Savonarola ordered the burnings of "vanities" on bonfires—objects of diversion (like stringed instruments, including the Muslim lute), fancy Eurasian fabrics like silk and damask, Arabic and Greek manuscripts, and profane literature of the travel romance sort. But he only got himself excommunicated and, a bit later, executed. By his time, the Vatican was running one of the biggest printing operations in the world, busily planning to convert Ottoman Muslims and pagans from far Asia with their powerful new tool.

THE PAST AS A FOREIGN PEOPLE

When Rashid al-Din was beheaded in 1318, the Ilkhan regime was on the cusp of the transition from a cautiously equivocal, internationally pragmatic to a more rigid and less resourceful order. Rashid al-Din had fulfilled many roles in the reigns of Gazan and Uljeitu, but the best remembered today is as the author of the remarkable illustrated text, *Compendium of Chronicles* (*Jami al-tawarikh*). The book has remained a major source of Mongol history because of Rashid al-Din's access to Gazan's perspective as a great-grandson of Chinggis. Rashid al-Din and Bolad Chingsang (see Chapter 7) epitomized a cosmopolitan, synthesizing, self-consciously civilizing state project. Their consultations had provided Rashid al-Din some detailed knowledge of Mongol documents, which he could supplement with his knowledge of the court lore of the Ilkhans. But Rashid al-Din's enterprise was much vaster—he intended to literally write a history of the world, with the narrative culminating in the glory of the Toluid empires. His was not the first history of the world. Encyclopedias appeared from time to time in the classical world, and in Byzantium, a few compendia of chronicles and histories combined with topical works were produced starting in the sixth century.

Abu al-Hasan al-Masudi (893–956) of Baghdad was the author of two remarkable world histories (as well as numerous other works) in which he combined the knowledge gained from his travels as a merchant with his personal reading of Greek, Roman, Coptic, Syrian, Indian, and Islamic historians to write interwoven narratives of economic, political, and cultural developments from the beginning of the world to his own era. Al-Masudi was not a court historian (in fact, he is usually read today as a Shi'i author), and he chose to accompany his historical narratives with his own commentary, citations from the Quran, and even comments he had heard from others. Rashid al-Din may also have been influenced by *Great Mirror* (*Speculum Maius*) of Vincent of Beauvais (1190–1264), who seems to have spent most of his life in Paris and nearby. *Mirror* was divided into three parts, the first two of which (on nature and religious doctrine) were apparent influences and sources for Roger Bacon (see also Chapter 9), and a third, which was a composite history. It was clearly drawn from European sources (most important, the *Chronicon* of Helinand of Froidmont, who died sometime after 1229) and freely mixed romantic legend with credible history. The resemblances to al-Masudi (who had not been translated into Latin) were also noteworthy: like al-Masudi, Vincent started history at the beginning of time, covered ancient Egypt, and accompanied his narrative with commentary and extensive quotes from the classics. Vincent takes the story all the way up to his own time, concluding with the campaigns of Louis IX against the Mamluks.

Rashid al-Din had access to all these authors and to their own sources. His method was to write topical chapters, some of them folded into larger chapters of the work. They included accounts of the Turks and Mongols, drawn from a translation of Chinggisid history, interviews with Gazan and his family, and materials from Bolad and from Juvayni's history (see Chapter 11); Iran (drawn from Islamic histories of the Abbasid period and from *Shahnameh*); a history of China (largely based on materials supplied by Bolad); a history of the Franks (basically, Europe, drawn from medieval histories, including Einhard's biography of Charlemagne); and the Jews and early prophets, based on the Torah and the Quran. It is itself an expression of the high arts of medieval Iran, featuring exquisite calligraphy and vivid painting defining the art of the "Persian miniature." Editions for popular distribution were manufactured by woodblock-printing processes.

After the Ilkhans, the Akkoyunlu and Timurids ruled Iran and then were succeeded by the Safavids. The Ottomans remained in Anatolia and absorbed the former Mamluk territories. As a consequence, there was no clear date at which government by Turkic conquerors, or their history, ended; these regions entered the early modern period with Turkic or post-Turkic rulers who sought ideological vehicles for grafting their dynastic histories onto the regional cultures whose expression they had encouraged. This blending of the cultural attitudes of the eras of Turkic rule with succeeding popular cultures was also evident in regions with subsequent, self-consciously hostile attitudes toward Turks and Mongols. This was a contrast to other parts of Eurasia where Turkic rule ended and successor states quickly moved to elide nomad domination from their histories by constructing deep, legitimating connections of themselves to ancient rulers. At the same time, the native historians upon whom they relied often sought a further distinction, clearly marking themselves and their cultures from the long and still-threatening history of barbarity.

In Russia, nomadic rule receded gradually as the power of the Muscovite state waxed, gradually absorbing many Jochid-era institutions. Like the post-nomadic rulerships of the Caucasus, the Muscovite and Romanov rulers of the sixteenth and seventeenth centuries represented themselves as descendants of biblical and classical Greek figures, resting their legitimacy on their non-nomadic origins even as they relied on nomadic-era instruments of rule (see Chapter 11). In Eastern Europe, post-nomadic attitudes could be sharper, particularly when aggravated by continuing tension with the Ottomans. In Hungary, for instance, the medieval historical classic was defaced by scratching Attila out of its illustrations. In East Asia, the end of Mongol rule came to a clear end—with Zhu Yuanzhang's conquest of Dadu in 1368 (see Chapter 7). In Korea, the attachment of the Goryeo court to the Yuan empire was so strong that the Goryeo ruler decided not to recognize the new Ming dynasty in China, though Goryeo also refused to join the Northern Yuan—with whom they shared descent from Chinggis—in war against Ming.

The issue of Goryeo's relationship to China and Mongolia was resolved when Goryeo was succeeded by the Joseon dynasty in 1392, which in fundamental ways modeled itself on the government of the Ming. This included a strong condemnation of Mongol-style cosmopolitanism. Instead, the Joseon court mandated both an adherence to rigid Confucian political and social principles as well as a focus on new literature in the Korean language. But the Mongol era taste for scientific knowledge and contact with philosophical communities remained strong, and manuals on calendrical sciences, meteorology, and agronomy were disseminated through the powerful publishing abilities of the new government. Joseon dynasty militarism was primarily directed against the Jurchens (who used Mongolian in their written communications and, in the Korean language, were often referred to in the same terms as the Mongols), who were living in the north of the Korean peninsula. The drive to push Korean borders northward to the Yalu was an organizing force in early Joseon politics.

It had been during the Mongol period that Goryeo historians had begun for the first time to recount the entire history of the Korean peninsula and to search for the ancestral roots of the Korean people. They produced two classics of lasting influence, the *Chronicles of the Three Kingdoms* (*Samguk sagi*) in the twelfth century and the *Miscellany of the Three Kingdoms* (*Samguk yusa*) in the thirteenth. They combined specific information from early Chinese chronicles of the fourth to twelfth centuries with Korean folklore, traditions of Buddhist (in this case, Zen) adepts, and poetry. They were written in classical Chinese, with few indications of intrusion by Korean grammar or style. Under Joseon court patronage, the great fourteenth-century dynastic saga, *Songs of Flying Dragons* (*Yongbi ocheon'ga*), introduced a new theme: it recounted the mission of the Joseon rulers to defeat northern barbarians in order to protect an archly Confucian culture. Apace with campaigns to expel or enslave the Jurchens, court historiographical efforts were combined with a new interest in finding a way to write in Korean rather than Chinese. One result was the invention of the Korean syllabary in 1446, aided by perfection of movable-type printing. The Joseon court vigorously promoted the development of a literature in the native language. A result was the growth of a popular literature based on historical romance and fantasies of saving civilization by fighting off barbarian Mongols and Jurchens.

Ming historicization of Yuan is a critical moment in the story being examined here. The custom in China was for each dynasty to commission a history of the previous dynasty, based on review and redaction (and eventually, partial or complete destruction) of that dynasty's own documentation. This was a fundamental element in the new dynasty's legitimacy. In its time, the Yuan court had dutifully commissioned histories of the Song, the Kitan Liao, and the Jurchen Jin empires, all nominally edited by the Mongol scholar Toghto (f. circa 1350). They refused to do a history of Xixia, possibly because of a standing Chinggisid policy of eradicating Xixia as both a political and historical entity (see Chapter 6). As the Yuan imperial government had taken shape in China, the keeping of records in Chinese and Mongolian had proceeded apace. Surviving copies of what must have been voluminous Mongolian–Chinese interlinear judicial documents indicate that a good deal of Yuan administration was done bilingually, but no originals survive. Immediately after the Ming founding in 1368, a history of the Yuan was commissioned and dashed off in about a year. The language of the history is terse and dispassionate and appeared to be based on the Chinese documents exclusively. This was one of the first Ming acts of historical authorship: to obliterate the legacy of Mongolian documentation and the viewpoint expressed in it. As a poet–official wrote for the Yongzheng emperor, "Barbarian destiny is ended forever."

Ming founder Zhu Yuanzhang (1328–1398) was particularly vehement in his denunciation of Mongols and Mongol domination of China. He established his capital at Nanjing, where the Mongols had never had a capital; he attempted to sever China's engagement in continental Eurasian trade, which he saw as a Mongol imposition; and he considered dropping the state prescription of Zhu Xi Confucian orthodoxy (see Chapter 9) that the Yuan had instituted. Even in his artistic tastes, he promoted the theatrical work of Gao Ming (1306–1370), whose plots (*The Tale of the Pipa* is well-known today) dwelt upon agonizing hardships of the Mongol period, and scholars of the early Ming pointed to the particular paintings of Zhao Mengfu and Ni Zan in which animals and even the natural landscape seemed to be suffering from harsh conditions and purposeful deprivation. Nevertheless, whether by force of circumstance or as a product of deliberation, the Ming government preserved most of the structural features of Yuan civil and military organization and some of its specifics, including the research academies (staffed in part by Muslim and Mongol scholars) and the court's special relations with Muslim communities. These ambiguities in the Ming relationship to its Yuan predecessor came to a spectacular and disturbing climax with the conflict between the historian Fang Xiaoru (1357–1402) and the Ming Yongle emperor, Zhu Di (1360–1424, r. 1403–1424; also see Chapter 11).

Fang—the son and student of officials who had been executed in one of Zhu Yuanzhang's many paranoid rages—emerged in the late 1370s as a critic of the new dynasty's failure to warmly and exclusively embrace Confucian principles of government. He denounced Ming perpetuation of Yuan government practices and accommodation of the cultures of Mongols, Turks, and Muslims in China. He insisted that such groups—to whom he referred with Chinese words normally translated as "barbarian"—had no true comprehension of law or social propriety but could appear acceptable as rulers or even as neighbors only if they mimicked Chinese rituals, dress, or language. True assimilation, he argued, had been achieved among the native populations of south China over 2,000 years of thorough cultural contact and suasion. But the northern natives had had their cultural eccentricities enhanced instead of attenuated through the periods of northern domination of China, whether by Kitans, Jurchens, or Mongols. In Fang's view, the Ming government was disastrously compromising with the moral deficiencies of barbarians remaining in China. While Fang was becoming recognized throughout scholarly circles of central China for these critiques, the government itself was afflicted by ambiguities in resolution of basic power issues. A coup of 1402 (see Chapter 11) displaced and resulted in the death of Fang's imperial patron. Fang refused to acknowledge the new emperor. He was tortured, mutilated, and threatened with the execution of all members of his family to the ninth degree of relationship (a traditional punishment for treason), in response to which he was reported to have used his own blood to write an invitation to the emperor to kill the Fang kin to the tenth degree. Fang was killed in an unspeakable fashion, and the massacre of Fang consanguines ensued (with nearly 900 deaths reported). The conflict between the new emperor and Fang (and hundreds of other officials) was political in the small sense: Fang saw himself obliged to remain loyal to the late emperor and refused to accept the new regime—or the demise of Fang's state program for re-Confucianization that would be inevitably result. But it was entwined with much larger political and ideological issues that would be in conflict for centuries. Not surprisingly, the legend grew (and was fictionalized more than once) that the emperor was in fact a Mongol, sneaked at birth into a Ming imperial cradle but growing up to be the gaudy barbarian that Kublai was in retrospect regarded as being—and that Fang Xiaoru had foreseen.

Fang's proposition that civilization was in essence inaccessible to Turkic conquerors and their ancient forebears (in his belief, all authoritatively represented in the Chinese histories of the pre-imperial age) was an argument that such peoples could not be assimilated and, far less, accepted as rulers. This was not an ancient belief among Chinese philosophers and historians but was a newly widening axiom of the Ming period and later. Over the course of two centuries, Fang's principles of civilization and barbarity would be taken up and developed by historians as an inflexible code running through Chinese historical narrative from its beginnings. In their interpretation, all of Chinese history taught the lesson of a necessary superiority of China over its neighboring peoples as a corollary of the necessary superiority of civilization over barbarity. The ideology converged with a strong turn toward materialist philosophy in the early seventeenth century (repudiating the idealist metaphysics of Lu Xiangshan and Wang Yangming; see Chapter 9) when the human body was read as a code in which identity was indelibly inscribed. This line of reasoning reached a peak of intensity and danger in the mid-seventeenth century, when Fang Xiaoru's intellectual descendants lived through and attempted to reject the conquest of China by the Qing empire, which had originated among the large, remaining Jurchen populations of Manchuria.

READING NOTES: INTIMATIONS OF NATIONALITY

Much of the vision of this chapter was influenced by the remarkable essay by Simon Leys (Pierre Ryckmans), "The Imitation of Our Lord Don Quixote," *New York Review of Books* 45, no. 10 (Jun 1998), http://www.nybooks.com/articles/1998/06/11/the-imitation-of-our-lord-don-quixote/. See also John M. Hobson, "Countering the Eurocentric Myth of the Pristine West: Discovering the Oriental West," in *The Eastern Origins of Western Civilisation* (Cambridge UP, 2004), 1–31. For more general background on the themes of this chapter, see Mona Baker and Gabriela Saldanha, *Routledge Encyclopedia of Translation Studies* (Routledge, 2009), and Max Roser, "Books," OurWorldInData.org , https://ourworldindata.org/books/, for data on the volume of publishing in the late sixteenth century. On the relationship of fixed-text copyrights and religious differentiation in sixteenth- and seventeenth-century Europe, see Thomas F. Cotter, "Gutenberg's Legacy: Copyright, Censorship, and Religious Pluralism," *California Law Review* 91, no. 2 (Mar 2003): 324–392. On medieval travel fantasy literature, see John Mandeville, *The Travels of Sir John Mandeville* (Penguin, 2005) and Marco Polo, *The Travels of Marco Polo: The Illustrated Edition*, ed. and trans. Henry Yule (Sterling Signature, 2012).

Regarding paper, ink, print, literature, and popular culture, the following have been useful for this chapter: Joseph Needham et alia, eds., *Science and Civilisation in China: Volume 5, Paper and Printing* (Cambridge UP, 1985); Jonathan Bloom, *Paper before Print: The History and Impact of Paper on the Islamic World* (Yale UP, 2001); Thomas T. Allsen, "Printing," in *Culture and Conquest in Mongol Eurasia* (Chapter 7 reading notes), 176–188; Hang Lin, "Printing and Book Culture in Middle Period and Early Modern China: Rethinking the Chinese Experience with European Comparisons," *Crossroads* 10 (2014): 123–153; T. H. Barrett, "The Woman Who Invented Notepaper: Towards a Comparative Historiography of Paper and Print," *Journal of the Royal Asiatic Society* 21, no. 2/3 (2011): 199–210; Elizabeth Eisenstein, *The Printing Press as an Agent of Change: Communications and Cultural Transformations in Early-Modern Europe* (Cambridge UP, 1979); Mark Kurlansky, *Paper: Paging through History* (Norton, 2016), esp. 48–75.

On translation and printing of bibles, see Richard Griffiths, *The Bible in the Renaissance: Essays on Biblical Commentary and Translation in the Fifteenth and Sixteenth Centuries* (Routledge, 2017). On the economic impact in Europe of early printing, see Jeremiah Dittmar, "Information Technology and Economic Change: The Impact of the Printing Press," *The Quarterly Journal of Economics* 126, no. 3 (Aug 2011): 1133–1172. These publications are the source of Map 10.1 of this book.

On literacy and printing in the Islamic world (including the early modern period after the focus of this book), see Maurtis H. Van den Boogert, "The Sultan's Answer to the Medici Press? Ibrahim Muteferrika's Printing House in Istanbul," in *The Republic of Letters and the Levant*, ed. Alistair Hamilton et alia (Brill, 2005); Yasemin Gencer, "Ibrahim Muteferrika and the Age of the Printed Manuscript," in *The Islamic Manuscript Tradition*, ed. Christiane Gruber (Indiana UP, 2010); and James Clyde Allen Redman, "The Evolution of Ottoman Printing Technologies: From Scribal Authority to Print-Capitalism," in *The Ottomans and Europe: Travel, Encounter and Interaction: From the Early Classical Period until the end of the 18th Century*, ed. Seyfi Kenan (ISAM, 2010). See also Geoffrey Roper, "Muslim Printing before Guttenberg," Muslim Heritage, http://www.muslimheritage.com/article/muslim-printing-gutenberg.

There are also important websites on the development of the Quran, from manuscript to print. Among them are "The Quran in East and West: Manuscript and Printed Books," Columbia University Libraries, https://exhibitions.cul.columbia.edu/exhibits/show/quran/qurans/printed; "Smithsonian Collection of Qur'anic Manuscripts," Islamic-arts.org, http://islamic-arts.org/2011/quran-folios-at-the-smithsonians-museums-of-asian-art/; and "Mamluk Qur'an," British Library Online Gallery of Sacred Texts, http://www.bl.uk/onlinegallery/sacredtexts/mamlukquran.html; "Early Western Korans Online," Brill Online Primary Sources, http://primarysources.brillonline.com/browse/early-western-korans. On the mutual stimulation of early modern printing between Venice and the Muslim world, see "East Meets West in Venice," Muslim Heritage, http://www.muslimheritage.com/article/east-meets-west-venice/gallery/1029.

For background on cultural change in Seljuk, Ilkhan, and Ottoman western Eurasia, see Kumiko Yamamoto, *The Oral Background of the Persian Epics: Storytelling and Poetry* (Brill, 2003); Jan Rypka, "Poets and Prose Writers of the Late Saljuq and Mongol Periods," in *The Cambridge History of Iran, Volume 5: The Saljuq and Mongol Periods*, ed. J. A. Boyle (Cambridge UP, 2008), 550–625; Erich Trapp, "Learned and Vernacular Literature in Byzantium: Dichotomy or Symbiosis?" *Dumbarton Oaks Papers* 47 (1993): 115–129; Stefano Carboni and Linda Komaroff, eds. *The Legacy of Genghis Khan: Courtly Art and Culture in Western Asia, 1256–1353* (Metropolitan Museum of Art, 2002); Robert Hillenbrand, ed., *Iranian Painting from the Mongols to the Qajars: Studies in Honour of Basil W. Robinson* (I. B. Tauris, 2000); Donald N. Wilber, *The Architecture of Islamic Iran: The Il Khanid Period* (Princeton UP, 1955); Reem Saud AlRudainy, "The Role of Women in the Būyid and Saljūq Periods of the Abbasid Caliphate (339–447/ 950–1055 to 447–547/1055–1152): The Case of Iraq" (PhD diss., University of Exeter, 2014).

For the *Shahnameh*, see Chapter 11 reading notes.

On cultural change in eastern Eurasia, see Wilt I. Idema and Stephen H. West, *Chinese Theater, 1100-1450: A Source Book* (Steiner, 1982); Jiang, Tsui-fen, "Gender Reversal: Women in Chinese Drama under Mongol Rule (1234-1368)" (PhD diss., University of Washington, 1991); Walther Heissig, "Tracing Some Mongol Oral Motifs in a Chinese Prosimetric Ming Novel of 1478," *Asian Folklore Studies* 53 (1994): 227–254; Paul J. Smith, "Fear of Gynarchy in an Age of Chaos: Kong Qi's Reflections on Life in South China under Mongol Rule," *Journal of Economic and Social History of the Orient* 41 (1998): 1–95; and Susan Naquin, *Peking: Temples and City Life, 1400-1900* (U California P, 2000). On a famous play by Guan Hanqing, see "Bao Thrice Investigates the Butterfly Dream," in *Monks, Bandits, Lovers, and Immortals: Eleven Early Chinese Plays*, ed. Stephen H. West and W. L. Idema (Hackett, 2010); Morris Rossabi, "The Mongol Empire and Its Impact on the Arts of China," in *Nomads as Agents of Cultural Change: The Mongols and Their Eurasian Predecessors*, ed. Reuven Amitai and Michael Biran (U Hawaii P, 2014); and Ivan Morris, *The World of the Shining Prince: Court Life in Ancient Japan* (Penguin Books, 1979); Joseph S. C. Lam. "'There Is No Music in Chinese Music History': Five Court Tunes from the Yuan Dynasty (AD 1271–1368)," *Journal of the Royal Musical Association* 119, no. 2 (1994): 165–188. On whether or not the *Heike monogatari* was composed for immediate performance, see Hasegawa Tadashi, "The Early Stages of the Heike Monogatari," *Monumenta Nipponica* 22, no. 1/2 (1967): 65–81.

For the *Secret History of the Mongols*, see Chapter 6 reading notes.

On differentiation of identities in the late medieval and early modern period, see particularly Ehud R. Toledano, *As If Silent and Absent: Bonds of Enslavement in the Islamic Middle East* (Yale UP, 2007) and Kecia Ali, *Marriage and Slavery in Early Islam* (Harvard UP, 2010). My quote regarding the end of "barbarian" destiny is my translation of a line from Zeng Qi's *Ying zhi fu ping hu yue*, the original quoted in David M. Robinson, "Justifying Ming Rulership on a Eurasian Stage," in *Ming China: Courts and Contacts 1400–1450*, ed. Craig Clunas, Jessica Harrison-Hall, and Luk Yu-ping (The British Museum, 2016), 8–16. For development of Fang Xiaoru's discourse of essential identities, see Pamela Kyle Crossley, "Trial by Identity," in *A Translucent Mirror: History and Identity in Qing Imperial Ideology* (U California P), 57–88. For further exploration of themes in differentiation, see

C. E. Bosworth, "The Imperial Policy of the Ghaznawids," *Islamic Studies: Journal of the Central Institute of Islamic Research* 1, no. 3 (1962): 59–74 and Thomas Allsen, "Ever Closer Encounters: The Appropriation of Culture and the Apportionment of Peoples in the Mongol Empire," *Journal of Early Modern History* 1, no. 1 (1997): 2–23. On *millah* in reference to the Muslim community or cultural sphere, see Ibrahim Mohamed Zein (Zain), "'Relevantization' of Ulum al-Millah and Its Contribution to Islamization of Human Knowledge," *Revelation and Science* 2, no. 2 (2012): 67–83; and Olivia Remie Constable, *To Live Like a Moor: Christian Perceptions of Muslim Identity in Medieval and Early Modern Spain* (U Pennsylvania P, 2017).

On the differentiation of Muslims in China in particular, see Ch'ên Yüan (Chen Yuan), *Western and Central Asians in China under the Mongols* (U California P, 1966); Jonathan N. Lipman, *Familiar Strangers: A History of Muslims in Northwest China* (U Washington P, 1998); Michael Dillon, *China's Muslim Hui Community: Migration, Settlement and Sects* (Curzon P, 1999); Zvi Ben-Dor Benite, *The Dao of Muhammad: A Cultural History of Muslims in Late Imperial China* (Harvard UP, 2005); Maria Jaschok and Jingjun Shui, *The History of Women's Mosques in Chinese Islam: A Mosque of Their Own* (Psychology P, 2000); Tan Ta Sen (Chen Dasheng), *Cheng Ho and Islam in Southeast Asia* (Institute of Southeast Asian Studies, 2000); Michael Brose, "Central Asians in Mongol China: Experiencing the 'Other' from Two Perspectives," *The Medieval History Journal* 5 (2002): 267.

In Romanov times, Muslim differentiation and objectification were part of the process of the general distillation of "Russians" from non-Christians. For background, see the following works by Michael Khodarovsky: "Ignoble Savages and Unfaithful Subjects: Concerning Non-Christian Identities in Early Modern Russia," in *Russia's Orient: Imperial Borderlands and Peoples, 1700-1917*, ed. Daniel R. Brower and Edward J. Lazzerini (Indiana UP, 1997), 9–26; "Four Degrees of Separation: Constructing Non-Christian Identities in Muscovy," in *Culture and Identity in Muscovy, 1359-1584*, ed. Ann Kliemora and Gail Lenhoff (UCLA Slavic Studies, 1997), 248–266; *Russia's Steppe Frontier: The Making of a Colonial Empire, 1500-1800* (Indiana UP, 2002); and *Where Two Worlds Met: The Russian State and the Kalmyk Nomads, 1600-1771* (Cornell UP, 2006). See also Matthew P. Romaniello, *The Elusive Empire: Kazan and the Creation of Russia, 1552–1671* (U Wisconsin P, 2012). While the *soslovie* of Romanov times are too late to be a feature of this discussion, their roots in Muscovy social categories heavily influenced by Jochid identity regulations is evident. See Khodarovsky, *op. cit.*, and Gregory L. Freeze, "The *Soslovie* (Estate) Paradigm and Russian Social History," *The American Historical Review* 91, no. 1 (Feb 1986): 11–36 and Alison K. Smith, *For the Common Good and Their Own Well-Being: Social Estates in Imperial Russia* (Oxford UP, 2014).

On the role of popular epics in early definitions of national affiliation, see Victor Mair, "Perso-Turkic Bakshi-Mandarin Po-shih: Learned Doctor," *Journal of Turkish Studies* 16 (1992): 117–127; Michael E. Meeker, "The Dede Korkut Ethic," *International Journal of Middle East Studies* 24, no. 3 (Aug 1992): 395–417; and Rinchindorgi, "Mongolian-Turkic Epics: Typological Formation and Development," *Oral Traditions* 16, no. 2 (2001): 381–401. For the title "ceasar" and the Tibetan hero Geser of Khrom or Geser of Ling (an actual place in present-day Tibet), see J. Luvsandorji, "The Question of the Origin of the Geser and Janggammaar Epics," *Archiv orientální* 48 (1980): 122; Chao Gejin, "Mongolian Oral Epic Poetry: An Overview," *Oral Tradition* 12, no. 2 (1997): 322–336; and Igor de Rachewiltz and Narangoa Li, *Joro's Youth: The First Part of the Mongolian Epic of Geser Khan* (Australian National UP, 2017). Those seriously interested in this should also read Katharina U. Kőhalmi, "Geser Khan in Tungusischen Märchen," *Acta Orientalia Academiae Scientiarum Hungaricae* 34, no. 1/3 (1980): 75–83; and Ida Zeitlin, *Gessar Khan* (George H. Doran, 1927).

On historiographical dimensions of cultural differentiation in this period, see Charles J. Halperin, "The Missing Golden Horde Chronicles and Historiography in the Mongol Empire," *Mongolian Studies* 23 (2000): 1–15; Elliott Sperling, "Tibetan Buddhism, Perceived and Imagined, along the Ming-Era Sino-Tibetan Frontier," in *Buddhism between Tibet and China*, ed. Matthew T. Kapstein (Wisdom, 2009), 155–180; Peter K. Bol, "The Rise of Local History: History, Geography, and Culture in Southern Song and Yuan Wuzhou," *Harvard Journal of Asiatic Studies* 61, no. 1 (Jun 2001): 37–76; S. M. Grupper, "A Barulas Family Narrative in the *Yuan-shih*: Some Neglected Prosopographical and Institutional Sources on Timurid Origins," *Archivum Eurasiae Medii Aevi* VIII (1992–1994): 11–98l; Nurlan Kenzheakhmet, "The Qazaq Khanate as Documented in Ming Dynasty Sources," *Crossroads* 8 (2013), http://www.eacrh.net/ojs/index.php/crossroads/article/view/41/Vol8_Kenzheakhmet_html; and Peter Lee, *Songs of Flying Dragons: A Critical Reading* (Harvard UP, 1975).

Byzantine influence on Kievan historiography and its recession during the Jochid period is explored in some of the following English language scholarship: Konstantin Sheiko, *Nationalist Imaginings of the Russian Past: Anatolii Fomenko and the Rise of Alternative History in Post-Communist Russia* (Ibedem, 2012), 99–116, especially its discussion of the "Primary Chronicle" (*Povest vremennykh*), which is late Jochid in composition but may be mid-Kievan in narrative 16; Paul Magdalino, *The Perception of the Past in 12th Century Europe* (Bloomsbury, 2010), 162–164; and Sean Griffin, "Byzantine Liturgy and the Primary Chronicle" (PhD diss., UCLA, 2014).

For the history of Eastern European and Armenian historiography and identity building, see C. A. Macartney, *The Medieval Hungarian Historians: A Critical and Analytical Guide* (Cambridge UP, 1953); James R. Payton Jr.,

"Imagined Communities: The Ottoman Balkans," *Occasional Papers on Religion in Eastern Europe* 35 (2015): 1–16; Francis Woodman Cleaves, "The Mongolian Names and Terms in the History of the Nation of the Archers by Grigor of Akanc'," *Harvard Journal of Asiatic Studies* 12, no. 4 (1949): 400–443; and Robert P. Blake, *History of the Nation of the Archers, the Armenian Text Edited with an English Translation and Notes by Robert P. Blake and Richard N. Frye* (Harvard UP, 1954).

Chapter Eleven

Ruling in Place

One bitter irony of the demise of Fang Xiaoru and his lineage is that the Mongolisms he despised in the Ming government were in the coming years personified by his tormenter—the Yongle emperor, Zhu Di. He was one of a set of rulers in the interstices between Eurasian medievality and modernity who dismantled the old structures of elite control of historiography and religious legitimation of state power, replacing them with fluid popular cultures and fairly consistent, state-controlled narratives. In some ways, they encouraged modern forms of culture and political authority; in other ways, they stimulated—sometimes by hostile reaction—new patterns of centralization, militarization, and conquest. In the fourteenth through sixteenth centuries, wars spread across Eurasia as new conquest states continued the patterns of centralization and militarization that were rooted in the eras of Turkic and Mongol domination. They extended mining, added industrial facilities to manufacture firearms and artillery, and, in some cases, added labor gained from colonial ventures or from better financing provided by spreading commercialization. These centuries forged not only the early modern processes of conquest, international law, and boundary marking in all its cartographic and diplomatic splendors but also the qualities of rulership of the early modern period: self-legitimating, identity generating, and inscribing itself in public discourse and memory through printing and mass education.

NEW CONQUEST STATES

Ming founder Zhu Yuanzhang had designated his eldest son as heir apparent, but when that son predeceased him, Zhu made up a rule to be followed in perpetuam that the new heir must be selected from the line of the designated heir and not from a collateral line—an apparent wish to avoid the practice,

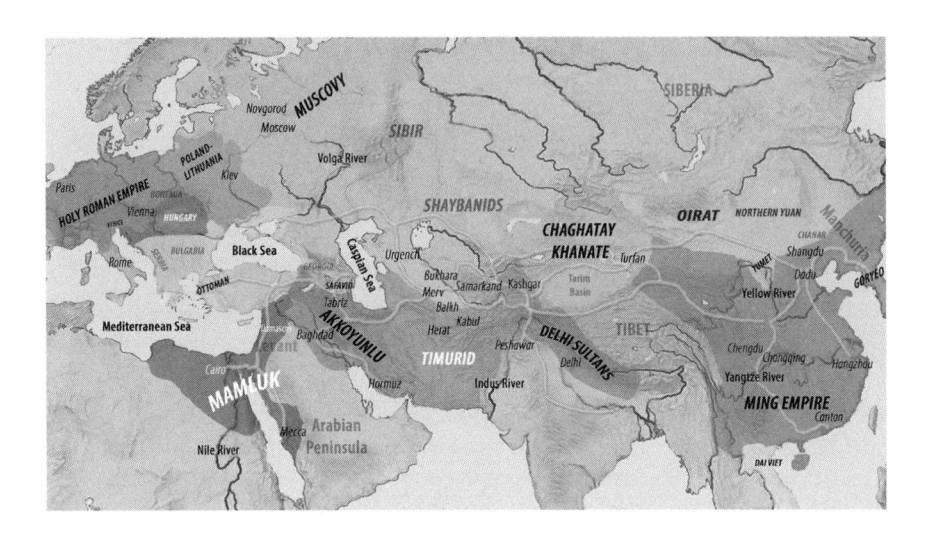

Map 11.1. Ottoman-Ming Eurasia, c. 1500.

which he scribed to the Mongols, of making all adult sons eligible as successors. This meant that Zhu was succeeded by his grandson; several of his adult sons never reconciled to their disenfranchisement. Sporadic rebellions or threatened rebellions ensued, as the young emperor relied heavily upon a set of officials, including Fang Xiaoru, to curtail the privileges of the nobility and enhance the reach of the bureaucracy. This led to the circumstances that crushed Fang Xiaoru: In 1402, Zhu Yuanzhang's fourth son, Zhu Di, overthrew the young emperor, installed himself as the Yongle emperor, and presented a body as proof of his imperial nephew's death. The Fang family were a fraction of the victims of a massive purge of the bureaucracy in the first years of Zhu Di's reign, as the emperor used execution, torture, and rigorous surveillance in an attempt to turn the government back to the smaller, more compliant apparatus of the sort that the Yuan had operated. Though the examination system was re-established as the avenue to government appointments and the Ming civil bureaucracy dwarfed the absolute size of the Yuan civil bureaucracy, it never approached the scale of the Song government relative to the space and population it claimed. As with the Yuan, delegation of significant government responsibility and power to the aristocracy continued as a feature of the Ming government, leading to episodes of court intrigue and low-grade civil war.

When Zhu Di was still a prince, his lands had been in the province that surrounded Beijing (the former Dadu), and his personal capital had been in the city. As emperor, he intended to rule from Beijing and replicated there the government installations that the first two sitting Ming emperors had created in Nanjing. The "Forbidden City" of today reflects closely the immense building project of the Yongle period (1403–1424), in which the palace grounds used by Mongols, Jurchens, and Kitans were expanded, surrounded with vermilion walls, studded with golden-roofed palaces, all decorated with gardens, artificial streams, and lakes crossed by alabaster bridges. The emperor's ambitions in building were clearly modeled on those of Kublai, but it is unlikely that was his sole inspiration. Zhu Di was in a contentious relationship with Timur (then, in the last years of his life), who had replaced Kublai's old rivals, the Chaghatay khans, from much of Central Asia. Like the Timurids, Zhu Di had a taste for building on a grand scale— palaces, tombs, and hunting grounds. Parts of the Great Wall were rebuilt in his time from an intermittent, crumbling, unprepossessing ruin to what one sees today. The emperor also decided to become a cultural patron in the style of Kublai and Gazan by sponsoring a compilation of all known knowledge. He commissioned a flock of eager scholars to comb Chinese manuscripts and archival documents, classify the information, and produce essays on every topic. The concept owed quite a bit to the traditional genre of Chinese historical compilation and to Song fashions in technical manuals, but also clearly drew inspiration from at least refracted knowledge of the Eurasian traditions of universalist compendia, from al-Masudi and Vincent of Beauvais to Rashid al-Din (see Chapter 10). As it happened, the encyclopedia (written in five years, impressive if we consider the intended scope) could not be published. The treasury had run out of funds and could not commission the carving of woodblocks for the nearly 23,000 volumes. Today, a fragment of the collection exists, and it is impossible to assess how much information there was or what its sources were. It could have been a grand culminating Eurasian masterpiece which, if published might have sparked a transformation of popular discourse and scientific exploration; or it could have been a parochial, repetitive literary monument that even if published would have interested few. Its ambition is all we can be sure of.

Well after these other projects were underway, the emperor added the enterprise for which he is best known today: the voyages of Zheng He, between 1403 and 1433, made use of Song-period but still-superior seagoing technologies, including immense, buoyant, and steady ships and waterproof compasses. The Chinese ocean ship, the "junk" (from a Javanese term), was not a new design. Their distinctive curved sails, suspended on bamboo frames, had been seen throughout the Indian Ocean for hundreds of years. Their particular buoyancy permitted them to become very large, transporting good and humans on a new scale. The great size of Zheng's ships has often been noted, but on balance it appears that the Yuan had used ships of the same size, or larger, as Marco Polo reported sailing in them from China to Iran in 1292 (see reading notes). The voyages were emphatically not explorations. Zheng was familiar with the geography of getting to the Straits of

Hormuz by land or by sea, and many of the Chinese Muslims in his entourage had made the pilgrimage to Mecca themselves. If he was in doubt, he had detailed navigation manuals to show him around the Indian Ocean; on subsequent voyages, he reached Hormuz and sailed along the entire southern coast of the Arabian Peninsula and the northeast coast of Africa, reaching south of Mogadishu. Zheng carried with him a statement that he delivered when he made port in South Asia, the Persian Gulf, and East Africa: the glorious and universal lord, the emperor of China, was announcing that his country was fully open to commerce (in case they had heard of the closing of trade by the first Ming emperor; see Chapter 7), and all countries were invited to dispatch ambassadors, present samples of their wares, and receive trading patents. Many complied, their samples including zebras, lions, rhinoceroses, and the giraffes, the latter of which a ruler of what is now part of Kenya sent repeatedly. In exchange, they were left samples of China's spectacular, hygienic, and durable white and blue porcelain as well as enticing amounts of Chinese coins.

The emperor had also charged Zheng with visiting Chinese merchant communities in Southeast Asia to affirm their allegiance to the Ming, demand taxes from them, and pressure rulers of states in what are now the Philippines and Indonesia to send tribute to the Ming court. If Chinese settlers resisted, as did a community on Sumatra, they were subject to severe military punishment from Zheng He's marines. The decades of voyages and land expeditions may have been an important factor in establishing lucrative trade relationships with West Asia and East Africa. Not long after the voyages started, the emperor changed the currency system, which had been manipulated a few times in the interests of stabilization. While only silver and printed money were used for domestic trade, the emperor authorized the minting of more traditional copper money for purchases from abroad. Steadily, Ming became the world's leading manufacturing economy, its greatest single exporter and the site of markets highly desired by merchants and producers around the world. But in 1433—well after the death of the Zhu Di and in the year that Zheng He died—officials of the Ming court ordered the ships to be burned and all state voyaging to cease. Their given reason was that the expense of the program had emptied the treasury. The emperor's grand sea campaign in peace was as ruinous as Kublai's grand sea campaigns had been against Japan and Java. Like Kublai the emperor had partly relied upon paper money to finance the sea projects, resulting in not only crippling of the treasury but also inflation. Indeed, the emperor's style was altogether a replication of Kublai's and did not as closely resemble any Ming emperor before or after him.

Certainly, of the grand projects of the Yongle period, the fortified palace complex at Beijing could not be abandoned nor the Great Wall dismantled; aborting the encyclopedia and ending the voyages were the primary steps that could be taken to save the empire's finances and allocate money to its pressing military affairs. Ming defense requirements were high from the beginning, growing larger through the entire dynastic period (to 1644), but defense and conquest expenditures were frequently indistinguishable. In response to the relief from Yuan pressure, new conquest states arose across eastern Eurasia. Ming was one of them. Its attempts to expand or defend its boundaries led to military conflicts in virtually all directions, including sea conflicts with Sri Lanka, Japan (as part of a larger late-sixteenth-century land conflict in Korea), and Portugal, which was then establishing its colonial hold in East Asia. Its expenditures and the political complications of these border conflicts led to financial and factional difficulties that worsened over the Ming era.

Kublai's on-and-off war against Japan had caused him disinterest in trade along the coast, which could not have rivaled the huge profits generated by the overland trade. Grain and tribute from south China could be moved to Dadu along his Grand Canal, legal trade with Japan was discontinued, and the coast left largely unsurveilled. As a result, an entire pirate world between Japan and the Philippines, touching the coasts of Korea and China and engulfing Okinawa and Taiwan, was seeded in the Yuan period and in the early Ming was flourishing. The Ming policy of closely monitoring the distribution of trade licenses (usually linked to enrollment among the states who performed the prostration rituals at the Ming court) stimulated a profitable trade in illegally obtained or forged licenses. Pirate communities mixing Japanese with the native peoples and later with large numbers of Chinese-speaking immigrants, developed. These multilingual, extralegal settlements thrived off the sea trade and commerce with native inhabitants. In later centuries, they also absorbed the languages and religions of the earliest European colonialist arrivals in East Asia—the Portuguese, the Spanish, and the Dutch. Pirate colonies in the region were independent of the legal states and sometimes militarily formidable. In the Yongle period, a set of Ming coastal fortifications was planned, but the development was modest in comparison to enlargement of the Great Wall.

The earliest and most pressing Ming strategic problem was the formation of the "Northern Yuan" state, founded by descendants of Kublai who had fled Beijing and some provincial capitals at the time of the fall of the Yuan in 1368. They retained the Yuan laws and rituals and the seal of Chinggis, which had once been enshrined at Karakorum (where they briefly attempted to establish their own capital), and for periods they used the same name of Great Mongol State (*yeke mongghol ulus*), favored from Chinggis to Mongge. They adhered strictly to the Chinggisid principle in their selections of khaghan and relied even more strongly than the Yuan court in China had upon Tibetan clergy for their legitimation (and transmission of the consciousness of Chinggis to their own khaghans). They were an influential state in eastern Mongolia but rapidly catalyzed the centralization of other federations who opposed them, particularly the Oyirods (Oirats, later Junghars) in the west. In the late sixteenth century, the old Onggut (see Chapter 6) territories on the Mongolian side of the Great Wall produced the Tumet federation, whose leader seized the initiative in competitive patronage of Tibetan Buddhism when he invited the first known Dalai Lama (reported to be the third actual Dalai Lama, the first two being occulted) to his capital, the ancestor of modern Huhhot, in 1578. All three Mongol federations—particularly the Junghars—grew to be formidable conquest states in Ming times, and from an early point, the Ming pursued two strategies with them. One was to use the rewards of the embassy system and trading licenses to keep them in competition with each other. The second was to muster sufficient military strength along the northern border to contain and when possible invade the Mongols. The Yongle period was an especially aggressive one, as the emperor was sure that he could force the submission of the Northern Yuan. Like Kublai, he led some of the campaigns himself; he was returning from one of them when he died in 1424. The campaigns were serial failures and emboldened the Mongols in repeated incursions south of the Great Wall, on at least one occasion surrounding Beijing.

In these conflicts the Ming were constantly demanding horses from the relatively unorganized, mixed Mongol and Jurchen populations of southwest Manchuria. In the Yuan period, the peoples of the area—farmers of wheat and sorghum; horse, dog, and falcon breeders; textile producers; and sellers of gathered delicacies, such as ginseng and pine nuts—had been subjugated early and their headmen given Yuan titles and insignia. After the fall of the Yuan, such symbols and Yuan political vocabulary suggested some degree of political centralization, usually based on commercial wealth and landholding. The early Ming state executed a number of successful military campaigns in this area to eradicate residual Mongol holdouts, and the Yongle emperor imposed upon the region a set of notional "commandaries," which corresponded to the influence range of the leading lineages, giving their leaders new recognition, importance in his campaigns against the Mongols, and access to Beijing. The result was the emergence of a small conquest state with fuzzy beginnings in the fifteenth and sixteenth centuries but coalescing as the Qing empire (1636–1912) that would eventually rule Manchuria, China, Mongolia, Tibet, and parts of Central Asia.

To their west, the early Ming were in repeated hostilities with the surviving Turkic khanate in Turfan and with the Timurids. In the early Yongle years, Ming forces successfully reduced the Turfan holdings, but progress was interfered with by the Oyirods (now the Junghar federation), who were moving in to acquire territory of their own. The Ming were weakly aided for a time by the last Chaghataid khan of the area, but he was eventually captured by the Junghars; afterward, the Ming attempted to create a princely fief in the area. The continuing war with the Junghars was inconclusive, but the Ming did manage to expel remaining Uighurs from Gansu and block the overland trade through Turfan and Hami, constricting economic development for large regions of northwestern China. The conflict, in combination with the early rivalry between Timur and Zhu Yuanzhang and between Shahrukh and Zhu Di, contributed to an ideological battle between the Ming and the Timurids over not only Turfan but all of Central Asia (see below). Tibet was a related but comparatively simple issue for the Ming since they continued the Yuan practice of regarding it as a distinct entity governed by religious hierarchs with a unique reporting relationship to the empire based in China. A far greater problem was neighboring Yunnan, which had been a Yuan province but had broken away and become virtually independent again—this time under Mongol aristocrats—by the time the Yuan fell. Zhu Yuanzhang had literally no sooner established his capital at Nanjing than he sent an emissary to Yunnan stating that Ming intended to control the territory. By the middle 1380s, Yunnan had been absorbed and, as it had been for Kublai, was regarded by Zhu Di as a likely launching point for campaigns against the many small kingdoms of the Southeast Asian peninsula. In most cases, rulers were required to acknowledge the suzerainty of Ming and allow their territories to be redrawn and administered from Yunnan. The supply to Ming of lumber, gold, silver, horses (from Tibet), tea, and spices was an important element in the Ming economy, so when Southeast Asian rulers resisted Ming demands in the mid-fifteenth century, the empire mobilized large expeditions to subdue them and further divide their domains.

But a century of Mongol pressure had created states capable of resistance and expansion. One of the best-organized states of Southeast Asia, Dai Viet (an ancestor state of Vietnam), had had its capital at Hanoi briefly occupied three times by Mongol troops just after the fall of the Song in 1279. Dai Viet had agreed to pay tribute and to allow Mongol armies to pass southward to invade its neighbor Champa in 1283, which also came to an agreement for tribute. The two kingdoms remained intact through the Mongol era, but when they went to war against each other in 1400, Ming forces occupied Hanoi and installed a puppet government. In 1428, Dai Viet leaders drove the Ming armies out, and the conflict ended with Ming enrolling Dai Viet as an embassy state, otherwise leaving it alone. In a series of ruthless campaigns, Dai Viet armies systematically annexed the territories of Champa. By 1500, the process was nearly complete. Champa disappeared except for a small remnant state in the far south. At roughly the same time, the Khmer empire, based at Angkor (perhaps the largest city in the world at the time), which had escaped harassment by the Yuan and Ming armies, was destroyed by its neighbor Ayutthaya, which emerged as a conquest state in its own right in the fourteenth and fifteenth centuries by absorbing states weakened by the Mongol assaults upon the state of Bagan and its clients (see Chapter 7).

Korea and Japan were linked in some ways for the Ming as they had been for the Yuan: the former was regarded as a gateway to the latter. Achieving the conquest of Korea was for Kublai the key to outfitting and launching expeditions to Japan, which was less than 600 miles across the Tsushima Straits. The Goryeo royal family became close enough to the Yuan court to identify with them and refuse to acknowledge the advent of the Ming. But the early Ming needed horses—tens of thousands of them—from Goryeo for its campaigns against the Mongols, and in its final year, Goryeo was forced to acknowledge the Ming. By then, a dangerous dispute had broken out between one Goryeo court faction arguing that the fall of Yuan created an opportunity to invade Manchuria and another arguing that such a move would mean war with Ming. The former group was victorious, and its leading general created a new dynasty, Joseon, which ironically became distinguished for its devotion to Ming and stereotypical Confucian culture. One factor consolidating the relationship between Joseon and Ming was that Joseon, like Dai Viet, had become a conquest state. It was led by militarists and was overtly expansionist, consolidating control over the Jurchen areas south of the Yalu River and enlarging a slave class made up in significant part of conquered Jurchens. Joseon generals were also innovators in military technology. The formula for destructive gunpowder was kept from the Koreans by both the Yuan and the Ming, but Korean officials acquired the information by subterfuge. In the later fourteenth century, they had mounted cannons on their patrol ships. They used gunpowder-driven arrow launchers against enemy personnel directly or to propel fire arrows into the riggings of enemy ships. In combination with the Korean skill in armoring their ships, these techniques made the Joseon navy, though small, one of the most formidable defense forces of the fifteenth century. The years of Korea supplying grain, cotton, horses, and soldiers to the Yuan armies had created pools of expertise in military organizing, quartermastering, weapons technology, and naval warfare, leaving Joseon eager to leap at the opportunities offered by recession of Mongol power. Over the decades, Ming and Joseon were able to coordinate their trade and military policies to keep as much wealth as possible out of the hands of the Jurchens of southern Manchuria, to keep them politically disunited and militarily intimidated, for as long as possible.

The Ming–Joseon alliance had a tragic test when Japan invaded Korea in 1582. The attempted Mongol invasions of Japan had made a deep impression and hastened the changes in Japan that were already occurring in the social and political structure. In the Kamakura period (1185–1333), Japan was organized under a shogun, a supreme military leader who protected the emperor at Kyoto and administered the affairs of state. This shogun would in turn distribute land and privileges to his followers, who would render him tribute and supply him with soldiers. Lords in the north and east of Japan were remote from those in the south and west, and beyond a declared devotion to the emperor and the shogun, there was little unity in the country. The Mongol threat helped change this because it was not only alien and terrifying but also prolonged. Part of the preparation against the Mongols included strengthening the position of middle-level military officials. The civil code that had been created under Kamakura was frequently ignored in the interests of increasing the powers of military commanders. Remaining members of the old aristocracy in Kyoto lost political ground to the shogun and his high-ranking followers after a civil war of 1477 massively replaced traditional aristocrats with new militarists.

As this happened, the shogun somewhat centralized his military government and methods of communication. Warlords of the south and west, who were closest to the expected point of Mongol attack, rose in influence. A second aspect of the preparation was an attempt to imitate what had been observed of Mongol war tactics, including a retraining of the warriors and an attempt to outfit for defense against the cavalry and the advanced weaponry of the attackers. Finally, the entire realm was involved in attempts to construct defense works at Hakata Bay and other points along the Kyushu shore. This demanded a national system to transfer resources from other parts of the Japanese islands to Kyushu and other southern points for the mutual defense. The shoguns continued to actively plan defenses well into the fourteenth century and through the Ashikaga period (1336–1573), which contributed to the consolidation of the position of the warrior elite and their culture. The result was the emergence of another conquest state, as generals with increasing power and wealth fought each other in the late sixteenth century to unify the country and become the next shogun. During his wars to expand his own domain, the leading general, Toyotomi Hideyoshi (1537–1598), invaded resource-rich Korea, with the possible plan of invading China afterward. The massive (in regional terms) force of more than 150,000 warriors arrived in 1582. Ming was caught off guard and took months to begin to roll its huge cannons and large cavalry into the fray. The Ming–Joseon alliance fought the invaders to a standstill twice, discrediting Hideyoshi in his struggle to become shogun. But the invasion ended only when Hideyoshi died after an illness in 1598. Japan was unified by the Tokugawa shoguns instead of Hideyoshi, Korea was as materially and financially devastated as it had been by the Mongol onslaught of the fourteenth century, and Ming was strategically distracted and financially stressed.

Under similar dynamics, and in the same period, a series of West Eurasian conquest states arose. Jochid rule was eventually whittled down to the so-called White Horde of Tokhtamyish (d. 1406) and to the Khanate of Crimea (see below). The disintegration was due to a variety of forces—including invasions by the Chaghatay and the Timurids—but a new power emerged that was one of the most imposing conquest states of the early modern period: Muscovy. The family of Alexander Nevskii had ingratiated themselves with the Jochids and quickly became a leading power among the former Kievan nobles (see Chapter 8). Moscow had not only a Nevskii princeship but also a favored riverine position between the Jochid seat and the Kievan plain, allowing them to be named as the first among the princes and the primary agents of Jochid rule. Kiev, which had been a large and wealthy city before the Mongols, lost prestige, population, and wealth to Moscow over the Jochid period. The role of Muscovite troops in suppressing an anti-Mongol rebellion in 1327 at Tver left Moscow without rivals. Its prince was given special lawmaking powers and a monopoly on tax collecting. The Nevskii descendant Ivan established a dynasty at Moscow by declaring that his sons and not his brothers would be his successors. This broke with a Kiev tradition that went back at least to the period of Khazar tutelage and perhaps earlier, and anticipated the same reforms by the founder of the Ming 50 years later.

In the late fourteenth century and early fifteenth centuries, Moscow exercised its military power to intervene in the conflicts sparked by Jochid disintegration. They attacked Kazan repeatedly, successfully defeated Jochid aristocrats challenging their augmentation of territory, and deliberately or not aided the Timurids in dismembering Jochid authority. Moscow continued to build its centralization and military power. In 1478, it achieved the signal success of capturing Novgorod and, in 1485, absorbed Tver. The prince of Moscow at the time, Ivan III (Ivan the Great, 1440–1505), declared himself a ruler of "all the Rus" (*vseya Rusi*, that is, all the princedoms and khanates of the Kievan and Jochid world, a phrase that had already been used in the title of church patriarchs). The state had no particularly consistent name but was often called after Ivan's title of "the ruler of Moscow." As Moscow's independence evolved, so did its adaptation of Mongol institutions and political values. Access to political office and landholding status was controlled by state identity regulations based on ancestry. The expanding Muscovy empire was united by an overland courier system based on the existing Jochid roads, bridges, and stations. A census was instituted that was in essence the cadastral surveys of the Jochid years. And the Muscovy aristocracy was constituted in part by Jochids or Kipchak descendants (now, all generally referred to as "Tartars") who had married Russians, or moved to Moscow after converting to Christianity, or lived in Moscow for generations as liaisons to the Muscovites. Rapid expansion eastward, including virtually the entire Volga River basin, was made possible by the gradual fragmentation of Mongol and Turkic khanates. But on the west, things were challenging, largely due to another new conquest state.

Lithuania had had a complex relationship with the changes in the region as a result of the Mongol assaults of the 1230s. In the face of the danger, it united at just that time and, in ensuing decades, formed a kingdom. Lithuania is considered to be the last part of Europe to be made Christian—or it was at least the last part of Europe to be subjected to an anti-pagan crusade. In the later thirteenth century, it was set upon by the Teutonic Knights, whom the Nevskii family were trying (with the help of the Jochids) to keep from encroaching on their domains. In the three-way fighting, Lithuania was actually able to expand its holdings to former Kievan territories. When the Mongols did not come back to Europe after 1241, Lithuania became one of the largest eastern European domains, and in the late fourteenth century, it absorbed Poland. When Moscow was in the process of expanding in the fourteenth century, Lithuania was its primary challenger. In 1399, the Lithuanians gave safe haven to a disenfranchised Chinggisid prince and then joined his fight against the Jochids in expectation of acquiring more former Kievan territory. When they lost, several Kievan cities already under Lithuanian rule rebelled, and Lithuania concentrated on a final defeat of the Teutonic Knights. In a series of wars between 1492 and 1582—punctuated by periods of peace in which Lithuania respected Muscovy claims to sovereignty over former Kievan lands—Lithuania and Muscovy fought over and traded territory, to Lithuania's gradual disadvantage. In the process, the Lithuanian and Polish aristocrats worked out a system of mutual recognition, legal and linguistic plurality, and religious accommodation (between Catholicism and Eastern Orthodox faiths). They also began electing their shared kings. However, their union decreased in strength because of factionalism, and the empire was eventually destroyed by an invasion by Sweden in the seventeenth century.

Lithuania had been pressed by another conquest neighbor, Hungary, where centralization had begun in wars against the Kipchaks in the eleventh century. From an early point, Hungarian expansion included ambitions in the Balkans, part of which—Croatia—was absorbed in the very early twelfth century. Inconclusive struggles against Mongol invasions and unsuccessful alliances with the Kievan princes helped to discredit the native Hungarian dynasty and allowed the Angevins (based in Sicily; see Chapter 8) to claim the kingship. In the fourteenth century, Angevin ambitions helped map the expansion of the Hungarian conquest state that battled for territory against Lithuania, Albania, and the former Hohenstaufen lands in southern Italy. In the process, Hungary helped weaken the Byzantine empire before its fall to the Ottomans in 1453. It was the Ottomans themselves who blocked further Hungarian ambitions in the Balkans, signaled by the Battle of Nicopolis in 1396 (see Chapter 8) but continually reinforced for almost two centuries of war afterward. The Ottomans eventually captured Buda and occupied part of Hungary until the early eighteenth century. Control of non-Ottoman Hungary passed to the Hapsburgs, who used part of it for resettling their own displaced Balkan populations.

With its rivals distracted by border wars and dynastic transitions, Muscovy became not only the undisputed sovereign over the former Kievan lands but also a center of international trade. The first joint-stock company in England (predecessor of the English Levant and East India Companies) was given its monopoly on the trade with Muscovy in 1555. It had been an English strategy for some time to try to get through the Arctic to China (the "northeast passage") because the Portuguese and the Spanish already controlled the routes through the Indian Ocean. A number of deaths of English mariners ensued, until one crew stopped at Archangel and was afterward conducted to Moscow. There they met Ivan IV ("the Terrible," 1530–1584), who while expanding Muscovy territory into Siberia, was also adapting Danish printing technology to start his own publishing house, which within ten years had a varied list of religious and secular titles, all in Russian. Ivan was polite when learning from the castaways that the English planned to flood Moscow with textiles, but he was most interested in the possibility of acquiring English firearms, ostensibly for the ongoing wars against Lithuania–Poland. Word of Ivan's request got out, and the elites of Lithuania–Poland and Sweden began communications with Elizabeth demanding that she ban any such trade, which she did (and made serious attempts to enforce). Nevertheless, the belief that English merchants were supplying Ivan with advanced weapons (perhaps acquired in Germany) became widespread. It is possible that Elizabeth considered a formal alliance with Muscovy; while she told Ivan firmly that she would not marry him (as he had proposed), she offered that he could come to England if he had to escape his political enemies. In fact, the profitability of the London–Moscow trade (on which the company lost its monopoly in the later sixteenth century) was based on nonmilitary goods, mostly cotton and wool from London and mostly fur, animal skins, flax, hemp, and wax from Moscow. Of those, furs were the most profitable, as worldwide demand was exploding. From recently acquired Siberia, Muscovy was importing furs of animals from polar bears to squirrels (the latter primarily for people who could not afford sable). The trade would continue to enrich the Muscovite state and then, in the seventeenth century, its Romanov successor, for about a century—that is, until they depleted Siberia of its furs and were surpassed in the trade by Qing China and British North America.

To Muscovy's south, the Ottomans survived the period of post-nomadic conquest states largely through their diplomatic arts and—for a time—unparalleled military technologies. During the fourteenth through sixteenth centuries, they strengthened their hold on Greece, the Balkans, North Africa, and the Levant and extended their naval reach through the Mediterranean. In the sixteenth century, they moved into Iraq. Defeat of the Mamluks added part of the Arabian Peninsula to the empire, though the Ottomans permitted Mamluk officials and military forces to do the direct governing. On their eastern flank, the Ottomans combined forbearance, diplomacy, and opportunism. Babur's branch of the Timurids were building their new base in India as the

Mughals and the Ulugh Beg branch restricted their northern interests to Central Asia, where they were still vexing the Ming. The Turkic states of Akkoyunlu and Karakoyunlu, who had displaced the Timurids from Iran, were still fighting over it until the demise of Karakoyunlu at the end of the fifteenth century. The chaos in Iran deepened, as the struggle between the two Koyunlus had permitted the rise of independent quasi-states under the control of religious orders, primarily the Sufis—including the Hurufis, whom the Ottomans had been deporting to the Balkans and to Azerbaijan—and they began to undermine the Akkoyunlu victory. At the very beginning of the sixteenth century, one of these Sufi states gained control of all of Azerbaijan and declared itself the Safavid dynasty (see Map 11.1). The Ottomans attempted to negotiate with the Safavids—whose conquests spread quickly across Iran—to stabilize the border between them and backed up their demands with military force when necessary. Open conflict in the early seventeenth century was resolved with the Ottomans acquiring their first Caucasus territory, part of modern Georgia, but losing Baghdad.

At about the same time, Muscovy began expanding its tendrils toward the Georgian states of the Caucasus. In a situation that will sound familiar—because it parallels in superficial ways the war that broke out over the Caucasus between the Jochids and the Ilkhans in 1262—ambitions from a state based in Russia stimulated the Ottomans to make their own attempts to control all the Caucasus. It did not succeed, but from the sixteenth century on, the Ottomans were obliged to be as vigilant about their eastern flank as they had previously been about the Balkans and the Levant. In the late fifteenth century they had installed a Chinggisid refugee as khan of the Crimean Tatars. Subsequently, Crimea became an ally of the Ottomans and an enemy of Muscovy. It was not until the later sixteenth century that Muscovy and Crimea fought their first brief war, the first of several in which Russia and the Ottoman clients—or the Ottomans themselves—clashed over control of the Black Sea. The Russian court paid an annual tribute to the Ottoman client state in Crimea until 1700, adumbrating two centuries of hostility between the Russian empire and the Ottomans.

TRANSCENDENT RULERSHIPS AND SOVEREIGN NARRATIVES

Within a century of the recession of the Mongol regimes of Eurasia, the continent was dominated by vigorous conquest states all arising from the effects of conquest and occupation by Mongol states of one kind or another. Defenders, rivals, and successors came out of the centuries well armed and highly centralized. Their commercializing economies and developing structures of finance and credit underwrote military expansion. Rising capacities for popular literacy, military conscription, and some new forms of popular education permitted conquest rulerships to float new narratives legitimating their rule. From the time of the earliest Turkic federations of Eurasia, the rulers—whether khans, khaghans, shahs, or sultans—had tended to keep the religious rituals of their courts closed to the public and to keep their own relations with founded or hierarchical religion along the lines of cordial disinterest or tenuous patronage. Over the course of the medieval period, various Turkic groups moved into systems in which religious hierarchs legitimated rulers or incorporated a ruling persona as caliph, and the response of most Turkic leaders was to assume the role of military protector and advocate—legitimating themselves in such systems by their functions, more than by their own personal conviction. Certainly, the spectrum of religious devotion by Turkic and Mongol rulers was wide, perhaps best demonstrated by the deep animosity of both the Mamluks and the Jochids toward the Ilkhans, whom they regarded as insufficiently sincere in their service to Muslim orthodoxy.

Nevertheless, the disjuncture between Turkic rulers and the religious hierarchs of the regions they ruled was always present and had been continuous from the early claims of Turkic Orkhon rulers—who may themselves have been drawing on a few centuries of khanal ideology—that the khaghan or khan's legitimacy came from nothing but Blue Heaven itself, was manifest in the history of conquest, and could not be delimited or overridden by any human religious authority. Rulership was, in short, a charismatic office in its own right. When European kings were relying upon popes or patriarchs to interpret God's endorsement of them and East Asian emperors and kings were looking to officials and tutors to affirm their Confucian virtues, Turkic and Mongol rulers were already relying on manifest legitimacy not subject to interpretation by anybody but the ruler himself. It is not difficult to see a reflection of such attitudes (or to explain them) in the cases of Frederick II, Manfred, Ivan the Great, or Zhu Di, all affected contemporaneously or retrospectively by the Turkic and Mongol conquest ideologies.

In virtually every instance (with qualifications for the Mamluks and Delhi sultans), personal worthiness was regarded as translatable to dynastic worthiness. This was often expressed in traditional epics, some of which were eventually committed to writing. *The Secret History of the Mongols* (see also Chapter 6 reading notes), for instance, while narrating the rise of Chinggis adopted the point of view of the Borjigin lineage, which was regarded after Chinggis's time as corporately carrying the charge of Heaven's approval. It has a long introduction relating to the supernatural origins of the Mongols (from the union of a wolf and a doe) and 22 generations of Borjigins who formed and led the Mongol federation. There are copious details relating to the kidnapping of the young woman who would be Chinggis's mother from the Merkits by Chinggis's father, the murder of Chinggis's father, the struggle of boy Chinggis to survive, and the conflicts between Chinggis and the head shaman, and between Chinggis and Jamukha, all leading to Chinggis's victory and revelation of Heaven's will. Its themes are classic in the heroic literature of Eurasia, from the fictional Alexander to the Turkic epics: a valiant hero struggles against duplicitous enemies but wins through, thanks to the endorsement of Heaven. The *Secret History*'s last sections belabor the loyalty, bravery, and self-sacrifice of Tolui (who in the account appears to die by offering himself to Heaven in place of the ailing Ogedei in 1232)—enough that it seems clear that Kublai would have put some resources into having it written and preserved. Mongol discretion might have argued against the *Secret History* being published and distributed since the histories of the Borjigin and Chinggis might have been as closely held a matter as was the shamanic life of the lineage (to which it was related). On at least one occasion, in 1331, a Chinese scholar was ordered by the emperor to consult the *Secret History* in order to compile a collection of edifying government precedents, but Mongol keepers of the text refused access to it. Nevertheless, it was followed by or contemporaneous with more than a dozen accounts in Mongolian written in the thirteenth century. Among the accounts of this period was the "Golden History" (*Altan Debter*), which Rashid al-Din acknowledged as a source (thanks to Bolad's translations) for the *Compendium of Chronicles* (see Chapter 10), but the contents are lost and its relationship, if any, to the *Secret History* cannot now be definitively assessed.

The early Ming court not only wrote its own history of the Yuan (see Chapter 10) but also sought to co-opt the legitimacy of Kublai by claiming to have inherited his legitimacy. Their theory, first enunciated in the time of the founder Zhu Yuanzhang, was partly drawn from the long-standing traditional Chinese theory that obliged them to write the Yuan history in the first place: each dynasty actually drew its legitimacy from the Zhou dynasty endorsement by Heaven (*tian*; see Chapter 2), transmitted through the intervening dynasties between Zhou and the present. That is, they drew upon the model of righteous rule by which the Zhou had earned that endorsement but also literal inheritance of the endorsement itself. The purpose of history writing was to review the ways in which fallible last emperors of one dynasty had lost the endorsement to the first emperors of a successor dynasty. In this way, the Ming historians demonstrated (and this is the way each imperial history opens) that Kublai had found the previous empire in disarray, "set the ritual vessels upright," and recaptured legitimacy. And since Kublai had been legitimate, the restoration of order after the inevitable decline into error of the Yuan made Zhu Yuanzhang legitimate too.

Dynastic narratives with a similarly artful intention to combine the elision of the Mongols from their origins with a claim to inherit their transcendent legitimacy issued from the court of Muscovy. Bits of history written by churchmen in the Jochid period survived and were probably first collated under court sponsorship in 1520 (see reading notes). The earliest dynastic narrative in the Muscovy period was *The Book of Ascension* (*Stepnayya kniga*), a combined genealogy and law code (in some ways resembling a similar combination in *The Secret History of the Mongols*) written under commission from Ivan IV and probably completed in 1583. It was a celebration of the descent of the rulers of Moscow from the Roman emperor Augustus and the Rus king Rurik. The church is not absent from the legitimation of the succession of rulers, who are by the late sixteenth century are not submissive faithful nor warriors for the church but are saints in their own right, complete with miracles—which were, like military victories, objective signs of endorsement by God, needing no interpretation by the church.

Probably the most elaborate and complex sovereign narrative of the late middle ages was the *Shahnameh* (see also Chapter 10). The relationship between Firdawsi and the Ghaznavid sultan who sponsored the work seems to have been up and down, resulting in a few passages in the epic that do not cast the sultan in the most flattering light. But there was a more complicated issue for the Turkic Ghaznavids and, later, for the Seljuks and the Ilkhans. Firdawsi had incorporated the Avesta (see Chapter 2) account of the Turanians, hostile to the ancient Iranians. They were reported to be nomadic and lived to the east of the Iranians, and although some Turanians were Zoroastrian, others still adhered to some unnamed ancient religion. It is obvious to modern readers that the Turanians could not possibly be Turks because the Avesta refers to a period when Central Asia was populated by speakers of Indo-European (mostly Iranian or Tocharian), before the arrival of significant numbers of Turkic speakers. But by Sasanian times, "Turan" was a common reference to the origins of Avars, Huns, and Gokturks (see Chapter 3). The Iran/Turan dichotomy remained in the political rhetoric of the Abbasid and Samanid courts. The Ghaznavids, Seljuks, and Ilkhans had to decide what their position was with respect to the Iran/Turan dichotomy.

They decided that the greater theme of the *Shahnameh*—the emergence of righteous rulership over all the peoples of Iran—was more important than some troubling but ambiguous references to the Turan. Firdawsi had provided a genealogy of rulership and carried it up to the Turkic Ghaznavid court, his sponsors. The long history of Central Asian rulerships that had so many ritual, terminological, and institutional origins in Achaemenid and Sasanian Iran was for the first time given a direct pedigree and linked to Turkic rule in Iran. Of these many imperial editions of the original and the Arabic and Turkish translations, the most outstanding and best known version was that produced by the Ilkhans in the fourteenth century, and it remains the standard by which the *Shahnameh* is known today. In the interval between Firdawsi's completion of the manuscript and the early 1300s, copying and recopying of the text had produced many variations in length, content, and style. Gazan commissioned a group of scholars (perhaps headed by the son of

Rashid al-Din) to compare the existing manuscripts and arrive at an authoritative text. Painters in the imperial workshop were put to work on color illustrations (about 190, if the number in the published work is representative). Like Rashid al-Din's illustrated *Compendium of Chronicles*, it was published as a huge, two-volume, illustrated work. Woodblock printing (see Chapter 10)—and printers—imported from China were employed to produce an edition with inset monochrome illustrations.

The power of *Shahnameh* as a literary work and the appeal of its encomia to rulership made it sponsored by a wide range of Turkic regimes before and after the Ilkhans. The Seljuks invoked the *Shahnameh* for the reign names of their sultans. The Ayyubids of Egypt had the work translated into Arabic in the 1220s for the edification of their Kurdish and *mamluk* officials and soldiers. While the Ilkhans were producing their magnificent edition, the work was also partly translated into Ottoman Turkish and, in the fifteenth century, into Kipchak Turkish under the sponsorship of the Mamluk sultans. The Akkoyunlu (and their Karakoyunlu enemies) ordered copies for themselves and their princes, and the Delhi sultans did an illustrated edition. The Turkic Safavids, who took control of most of Iran in the sixteenth century, commissioned a fresh, illustrated edition, intended to surpass the glories of the Ilkhan production (and it actually had more illustrations). The logic was reenacted many times: rulers who sponsored their own editions of the *Shahnameh* made it implicitly a book about their own legitimacy. At about the same time, the Timurids sponsored a new edition of the original Persian text, and Timurid princes competed to see who could commission the most eye-catching personal edition. Partial translations into Chaghatay were undertaken at various points, and *nameh* came to be an instant reference to written narratives of military victory and endorsement by God.

Rashid al-Din's *Compendium of Chronicles* incorporated a great deal of the *Shahnameh* narrative of rulership and combined it with other imperial narratives relating to Iran—most important, the work left by Ata-Malek Juvayni. The Juvayni family were exemplary of the Sartic population: Persian-speaking officials who had served under the Khwarazmians and later under the Mongol empire in Karakorum, which Ata-Malek Juvayni visited in 1252. He accompanied Hulagu in the attacks on the Ismaili state, then in the siege of Baghdad, and then served as governor of Baghdad while his brother became the leading financial official of the Ilkhanate. Juvayni remained a participant in Mongol political consultations in Karakorum and then at the Ilkhan court for the rest of his life. He transmuted his access to the documents of the Ilkhanate into a historical narrative—*History of the World Conqueror* (*Tarikh-i Jahan-gusha*), a major source and conceptual influence in our modern understanding of Chinggis. Today, it is to Juvayni that are attributed the more extravagant inflations of the sizes of Mongol armies and Mongol massacres as well as romanticizing of Chinggis's attributes as a general, but there are details that are valuable—particularly his eye-witness description of the destruction of the Ismaili capital at Mount Alamut and his detailed descriptions of Mongol life in the early thirteenth century. The mark of Hulagu's era was strong on Juvayni's narrative, which was basically an insider's celebration of Chinggis and his legacy, a literate man's translation of Mongol legend and self-celebration into history. The *Shahnameh* and Juvayni materials allowed Rashid al-Din to bring the narrative up to the Ilkhan court (as Firdawsi had brought his up to the Ghaznavids). The scope of *Compendium of Chronicles* was immense enough that it is assumed that it was assembled by a team of writers. This is probable, but if so, it is nevertheless guided by the vision of Rashid al-Din: righteous rulership dating to the ancient Iranians, to Alexander, and to the Sasanians culminating in the Chinggisids and the integration of civilizations under their governance. It is a global narrative but with a clear sovereign intent directed at the Ilkhan government of Iran, making it the most expansive and influential of the late medieval sovereign narratives.

The Ottomans stand out as the court that did not commission a *Shahnameh*, though the text circulated among Ottoman readers. The rulers were instead building a historiographical tradition of their own. Their major focus was the Seljuk sultanate, the last Turkic regime to be recognized by the Abbasid caliphs in Baghdad. They appointed historians to narrate the Seljuk award of regalia of office to the founder Osman and his son, and after the conquest of Konstantiniyye, they combined the legacy of Roman emperorship with that of Turkic *gazi* heritage to broaden the roots of Ottoman legitimacy. They even commissioned from the official Sukrullah (d. 1488) their own global compendium, published in about 1458, which used the basic template of Rashid al-Din's *Compendium of Chronicles*. But it disdained Rashid al-Din's Persian and Ilkhanid particularisms. The ancient rulers of Iran were cast into a general category of pagan potentates of the pre-Islamic era while the Greeks were given a chapter of their own, with Alexander as the model ruler. Where Rashid al-Din's global history was crowned by Ilkhan conquest and the rule of Gazan in particular, Sukrullah's culminated in Ottoman conquest and the rule of Mehmet II in particular. But as in the case of the *Shahnameh* and *Compendium of Chronicles*, the search of the Sukrullah history for outstanding landmarks fixing legitimacy in time and place was meticulous, particularly with the positioning of the Seljuks as legitimate Ottoman predecessors. The Ottomans also consciously continued the Turkic tradition of the heroic dynastic epic, in some ways their own *Shahnameh*. It took its most refined form in a very early-sixteenth-century work, "Chronicle of the House of Osman" (a title shared by several different compositions before the fifteenth century). In one of the best known sequences, Osman encounters a Sufi teacher and afterward experiences a dream in which his body (i.e., his dynasty) becomes a source of sustenance and protection for humanity. It is accompanied by commentary that strongly echoes the ancient

Central Asian ideals of Heaven-endorsed rulership but now rooted in the particulars of the Ottoman empire.

CONQUEST AND SIMULTANEITY

The style of rulership developed under Mehmet II was an elaborate instance of what I have elsewhere called "simultaneous rulership" (see reading notes). This is not the same as the process of synthesis by which all institutions, including rulership, incorporate useful elements from other institutional or cultural systems. Simultaneous rulership is something else: it is the engendering within the rulership of distinct legitimating personae, based upon stereotypical representations of select conquered or allied peoples who can be represented as agents of conquest. These personae are performed in historical narrative, public ritual, and monuments in the languages and orthographies of the peoples (actually their histories) being represented. Such rulership is "simultaneous" in its conceit of imperial utterances that are not actually translated from one language to another, but issue instantaneously—in thought and in pronouncement—in the languages and the ethical systems of the imaginal peoples being represented. It is a technology of conquest that enlists conquered peoples as historical actors in the dynasty's victorious progress. It is central to the concern of this book because it integrates the long history of objectified and administered cultural identities within the Turkic states with a self-legitimating rulership that is post-medieval. And it is a pillar of our modernity because it carries within it the code of discrete national identities that populations across Eurasia accepted—or rejected—as the great land empires dissolved in the nineteenth and early twentieth centuries.

Some elements of simultaneity were old in Eurasia. The use of multiple languages and scripts on monuments or claims of inhabiting two or more rulerships at once could be traced at least as far back as Alexander and perhaps to early Hittite or Sumerian empires. It is fairly easy to discern in virtually any context of overland conquest—in which the ruling dynasty is required to enlist large numbers of supporters from conquered populations and to deal with the incorporation of populous cultural zones. English conquest of Wales in the thirteenth century, for instance, was the cooptation of the last surviving rulership of Wales (which happened to be called "leadership" of Wales, normally translated into English at the time as "prince" of Wales), sponsorship of ostensibly "Arthurian" sites and narratives, and the insertion of a few Welsh-derived mottoes (not necessarily in Welsh) into royal heraldry; English monarchs normally today incorporate the thirteenth century title into their lifetime accumulation of titles. From the third century at the latest, the Turkic empires spreading across Eurasia were inclined to develop simultaneity rapidly in their rulerships and to preserve it to a degree far more substantial than non-Turkic governments at the peripheries of Eurasia. The reasons have already been discussed: the necessity of retaining the loyalty of a conquering caste settled among a much larger and culturally different population, reliance upon local officials and clergy as agents of the hastily constructed state, wariness that the court could become captive to the influence of religious sects or bureaucratic factions, and the acceptance by the courts that cultural and religious discontinuities between the rulers and their populations were normal and probably desirable. In simultaneous ruling systems, any individual apart from the sovereign was restricted to a publicly formulated caste, cultural, religious, or genealogical identity, and the transcendence of the rulership was salient. These mutually enforcing dynamics became widespread and powerful in early modern thinking about national, ethnic, and religious identities.

In China, simultaneous rulership was a feature of post-nomadic or Turkic states from at least the third century, with establishment of the Northern Wei (see Chapter 3). The khaghans/emperors not only performed the emblematic rituals of both their own followers and the Chinese population but also reserved segments of their capitals for these performances (an adumbration of the organization of Ordu-Balikh a couple centuries later). The onslaught of Northern and Central Asian invading conquerors between the third and sixth centuries coincided with the spread of Buddhism to many sectors of society, and Buddhism had its own role—of the chakravartin, or of the Deva-protected ruler, or even of the ruler as *bodhisattva* (see Chapter 4)—to play in complicating simultaneities in rulerships based in China. Such simultaneous complexes continued through the Tang. As the empire reached more deeply into Central Asia, the role of the ruler as khaghan of the Turks was more pronounced and could be as concrete as monuments in the Orkhon Valley with Turkic runes on one side (the voice of the khaghan) and Chinese on the other (the voice of the emperor). But the political troubles of ninth-century China muted simultaneity in the rulership (as the state attempted to mute the identity emblems of Turks and Sogdians in the empire). In the period of disunion after the fall of Tang, simultaneity became a characteristic of the northern dynasties—Xixia, Kitan, and Jurchen Jin—but not a part of the presentation of the Song empire occupying most of China, where cultural discontinuities between ruler and ruled were not regarded as normal or advantageous. As discussed previously, it was from the Kitan and Jin primarily that the Yuan empire in China drew both its identity mechanisms and simultaneity. The simultaneity in Kublai's rulership was frank. He was the khaghan of the Great Mongol Ulus and fought a devastating civil war in Mongolia to prove it. But he was also the emperor of China, and at times worked assiduously to make this credible. It was this aspect of Kublai's simultaneous legitimacy that the early Ming emperors were eager to claim. They had their argument, discussed above, asserting that they had the thread connecting them through Kublai's dynasty to the legitimacy of the Zhou.

But the Ming needed another persona in the rulership to make visible the object they wished to attract: the loyalty of Mongols who were already serving the Ming in the court and the bureaucracy, and the many Mongols of the three federations whom the Ming hoped to attract. They quickly cast themselves in certain contexts as the heirs of Kublai not only in his capacity as a legitimate ruler of China but also in his specific capacity as the universal ruler of the Mongols: "We have received the mandate of Heaven and ascended to the place of Kublai to rule 10,000 places and govern every category of people." It was also in this precise role that the Ming emperors acted as patrons of the Chinese Muslims (see Chapter 7). Subsequent discreditation of Zhu Di (who has been rehabilitated in modern times) and progression of the fiercely racialist polemic that Fang Xiaoru had promoted, obscured this simultaneity in Ming imperial presentation, particularly after the decline of the expansionist ambitions of the mid-fifteenth century and earlier. Simultaneity would return to rulership in China with the Qing empire in the mid-seventeenth century; rule over the Mongols and continued cultivation of a conquest elite remained critical issues through the eighteenth century.

After a period of competition among the formerly Jochid principalities, Ivan IV in 1547 was the first tsar—that is "caesar," a term used by the Franks, the Bulgars, the Kievans, the Seljuks, the Tibetans in their way (see reading notes), and the Ottomans. The particular form of tsar was first used by Bulgarian rulers in the tenth century (see Chapter 4). When the Rus princes broke away from control of the failing Jochid regime, they reclaimed the term tsar for their ruler, translating it with the Greek *basileus*—ambiguously, "captain," "king," or "emperor." The strong equation of "tsar" with a sovereign ruler was reinforced by the contemporary contrast to the surviving Chinggisid khanate in Crimea. After 1615, the new dynasty of Romanovs retained the title to mean what it had meant in Ivan's time and added to it a list of titles (greatly shortened in the Code of Laws) that show strong marks of simultaneity The emperor was specifically tsar of "all the Russias" but was also tsar of former states where he had succeeded by one means or another to the rulership—including not only Poland, Georgia, and Kiev but also the former khanates (some of them Chinggisid) of Kazan, Astrakhan, and Siberia. On the other hand, where the empire dominated not by successorship or acquisition of ruling insignia but by open conquest, the tsar was a "sovereign" (*gosudar'*), as in Armenia and Turkestan as well as a variety of former Russian principalities that had been outside the empire assumed by Mikhail Romanov in the early seventeenth century.

In the early evolution of Ottoman rulership, there are patterns of multiplying personae that incorporate not only the vast sweep in time and space of preceding Turkic rulerships but also the legacy of Abbasid caliphates, sultanates, and Byzantine emperorship. Ottoman rulers made do with *bey* (*beg*) status until 1383, when Murad was accorded sultan status by the Mamluk-supported caliph in Cairo. In 1453, Mehmet II added *kaysar-i Rum*—caesar of Rome—after he deposed the Byzantines and thereafter was called ruler of "two lands, two seas" (meaning Europe and Asia, and the Black and Mediterranean Seas, all meeting at Konstantiniyye). In 1517, after seizing the Mamluk territories of the Levant and Egypt as well as the holy centers of Mecca and Medina, Selim declared himself caliph and claimed the holy objects of the Prophet's sword and mantle, spectacularly subsuming the traditional legitimating authority of the caliphs and making the Ottoman sultanate–caliphate self-legitimating, in theory as well as in fact. It was after this time, perhaps soon after, that Ottoman rulers were referred to as *padishah* (*padshah*), which in the later Ottoman period became the common term referring to the ruler. This word, meaning highest or greatest among kings, is easily traced to the Sasanians and probably was in use by the Achaemenians. As a term that paralleled khaghan, it was used by the Seljuks and the Ilkhans, where it rather explicitly invoked their endorsement by Heaven preceding any endorsement by earthly religious authorities. Its use by the Timurids generalized it across Eurasia, and it was used by translators for Zhu Di to refer to himself in a letter to Shahrukh. The Mughals later made it their preferred ruler reference, coincident with gestures associating their authority with sources prior to and transcendent over Islam—primarily the sun, spectral light, and practice of *darshan*—the traditional Hindu practice of displaying the ruler to the ruled from a balcony, bestowing blessing upon them in the manner of the sun bestowing its blessings on the crops. The term was understood so universally as an appellation of sovereignty that Nicholas I of Russia insisted it become one of his titles in a peace treaty signed with Ottoman sultan Mahmud II in 1829. Afterward, all European monarchies signing trade and peace accords with the Ottomans insisted that they also be called *padishah*. The bounty of padishahs in the nineteenth century should not obscure the powerful meaning of this term in the Persian and Turkic traditions. It meant a monarch legitimated by God directly, one who transcended any need of religious endorsement.

This is in fact a tiny sampling of the long list of epithets that accrued to Ottoman rulership (which like the accumulating epithets of the Russian tsars included the sovereign titles of many small localities of conquest) but sufficient to demonstrate the explicitness of Ottoman simultaneity and probably indicative of the most fully performed personae within the rulership. It was a simultaneity produced by conquest and reinforced by the state's obligation to legally reify and publicly historicize corresponding divisions within the populace. This correlation between imperial simultaneity and identity ascription was so strong that it became the focus of a running rivalry between the Ottomans and the rulers of Russia. Mehmet II adopted *imparator* after his conquest of Constantinople in 1453. It represented the peculiar authority by which the Ottoman sultan ruled over the former subjects of Byzantium—Jews, Greeks, Armenians, Bulgarians, Serbs, and the many other peoples of Greece and the Balkans. The idea that this new role of the emperor would entail a special curatorship of Greek (and Latin) learning was taken so seriously that Greek scholars who had fled from Ottoman domination began to return.

The capture of Constantinople by the Ottomans had outraged Russian churchmen and evidently stirred new ambitions in the Muscovy tsars. Ivan III had married a niece of the last Byzantine emperor and sponsored the adaptation of a host of Byzantine forms and practices to the bureaucracy and court. The myth of descent from the lineage of Augustus provided the tsars a link to Rome and a claim that Moscow, instead of Konstantiniyye, was the true New Rome. It was not an idea original with Ivan. In the period before and after the Ottoman defeat of allied western and eastern European monarchs at the Battle of Nicopolis in 1396, clergy of the autocephalic churches in Bulgaria and Serbia had sought refuge in Moscow and attempted (unsuccessfully at the time) to draw Muscovy into a battle to prevent the Ottomans from destroying the Byzantine empire. In their arguments for holy war, they had proposed Moscow as the true New Rome. After the actual fall of Constantinople and the subordination of the Orthodox patriarchate to the Ottoman sultans, the polemics of Orthodox churchmen for declaration of Moscow as the New Rome and the tsars as the true emperors intensified. A literary genre of praise poems flourished that specifically identified the city of Moscow with the city of Rome and the Muscovy empire with the Roman empire. Much later, Peter the Great (1672–1725) added to this a new agenda item, which was the reconquest of Konstantiniyye and even more comprehensive war against the Ottomans. The battle over New Rome—as an idea more than a place—was intimately connected to ideologies of simultaneity in both Konstantiniyye and Moscow. The Ottomans, as sultans, had on Muslim principles previously claimed to be protectors of Christians in their realm; after the fall of Byzantium, this became more a function of the Ottoman ruler's role as successor to the Roman and Byzantine emperors. His Christians were a super-province of the empire, scattered over all its regions, but now under his protection and authority in a way that had not pertained when they were merely a people "of the book."

The leaders of the Orthodox church recognized the legitimacy of the Ottomans not explicitly as Muslim conquerors of Constantinople but also as proven successors to the emperors of Byzantium. They seem also to have been impressed by the fact that Mehmet had distant royal Byzantine inheritance of his own. The imperial concept for the Ottomans, even if vague, may have been a mirror image of the *dar al-Islam* (see Chapters 5, 8, and 9). By the seventeenth century, the Ottomans had made *dar al-Islam* a super-province balancing that of Rum—Ottoman Christendom—as they claimed patronage over Muslims living geographically under the protection of the Russia tsars in Kazan, Crimea, Kazakhstan, and Siberia. In his time, Peter the Great responded by claiming to be protector of Christians in the Ottoman lands, setting up a direct existential conflict not only between New Rome but also between true emperors inheriting the mantle of the Romans and the Byzantines. In the late seventeenth century, each ruler declared the right to make holy war on the other.

The workings of simultaneity in reference to New Rome were not lost on the Hapsburgs, who were still running the Holy Roman Empire. They had a genealogical schema of their own, one that cut out both the Byzantines (and by implication Muscovy) and the Ottomans, and traced the inheritance from Augustus to Charlemagne and then on to them. It was not the first sign of specific impacts of Central Asian political dynamics on the central Europeans; the Merovingians' myth of God's favor to Clovis (and his Christianization) demonstrated through military victories showed more than a hint of influence from the Alexander narratives and the Turkic myths of legitimation as they would have been heard throughout Anatolia, the Caucasus, and the Balkans. It was not until the last century of the Hapsburg descendants (i.e., in its Austria–Hungary manifestation) that they began to claim their own empire as the literal New Rome (and in their case, without endorsement from any religious establishment at all), in direct opposition to the Ottoman and Russian imperialism.

RULERSHIP AND THE THRESHOLD OF MODERNITY

Religiously transcendent, self-legitimating rulerships of the fourteenth to seventeenth centuries gradually destroyed both the old patterns of authority and the elites entwined with them across Eurasia. The roots were founded in nomadic political patterns that, when laid over the weighty, complex government and religious traditions of conquered regions, produced segmented governments in which it was both necessary to co-opt networked religious hierarchies as administrators or advisers and to permanently limit their potential to undermine the rulership. The result was governments, as early as the Tang in China, the Bulgars in the Balkans, and the Gokturks in Anatolia, in which the Turkic traditions of superhuman endorsement of the ruler could be indirectly drawn upon to subordinate the clergy and displace, to the extent necessary, traditional elites with new servants of the khan. The pronounced dualist governments of Tibet, the Islamic world, Kiev, and central Europe were progressively weakened by these dynamics as they encountered the influences of the Turkic world on the battlefield, at their imperial courts, in their trade systems, and in their centers of learning.

There is no simple generalization for how this happened. The critical tensions between the Abbasid caliph and the authority of the scholars and judges can hardly be universalized to Europe and eastern Asia in the same period. The sharp political and occasionally military confrontations between the church patriarchs and the Byzantine emperors are not easily suggested by this characterization of medieval dualism. Yet such peculiarities in some ways only suggest the strength of the characterization of these conceptually dualistic polities as "medieval." All occur in the context of unprecedented consolidation of the cultural and political influence of formalized, universalist religion, facilitated by similar changes across Eurasia in the centuries after the Roman, Mauryan, and Han empires. The emergence of formal and distantly connected religious governance not only challenged locally derived political authority but also many local and minority religious communities. The medieval association of the maturation of hierarchs as political legitimators suggests something about the transition to early modern rulership. A novel, universalist rulership could accommodate religious and cultural pluralisms that the medieval style had abhorred or ignored. In meaningful ways, the breakdown of medieval duality opened the way to the enlargement of federations such as the Seljuks, the Mongols, and the Ottomans.

The gradual assault on the powers of traditional elites and religious authorities was reinforced by other changes connected to the nomadic rulers. On the peripheries of the nomadic conquest empires, fear of Mongol conquest changed Japan, Dai Viet, Ayutthaya, Hungary, Poland, and Lithuania. They centralized in unprecedented ways and institutionalized the status of new military elites. Within the Mongol and Turkic domains, similar changes were occurring. Delegation of authority by the Jochids, the Ilkhans, and the Yuan allowed new military powers to form within their domains, unleashing a wave of conquest states when the empires broke apart. The wars of the fourteenth and fifteenth centuries allowed the influence of the age of nomadic rule over populous states to continue to influence centralization and militarization of new states across Eurasia.

Military technology aside, the "modern" aspect of these changes lay in the phenomena that accompanied them: the rise of standardizing local vernaculars in literature and performing arts, state objectification of identities based upon criteria of language, religion and territorial ascription, the spread of modern printing to produce shared texts across language continuums, the enthusiasm of new rulerships for narratives that explained the origins of political legitimacy independent of religious endorsement, and the beginnings of mass education and military conscription to distribute all the above to the edges of newly defined domains. Little or none of these changes could have occurred without the reinforcement of the rise of religious dissidence, and particularly of patterns of folk belief, both of which were encouraged in what is described here as the Turkic model—and by extension, the regimes of Frederick II and Ivan IV as well as the Balkan and eastern European rulerships influenced by them. From the earliest traceable points in Eurasia, the problems of reality and consciousness turned on the continuing influence of the doubters of rationalism, whom the medieval religious authorities universally attempted to occult and whom the post-nomadic rulers of the sedentary world repeatedly freed from their darkness.

READING NOTES: RULING IN PLACE

For general background on this period, see Alfred J. Rieber, *The Struggle for the Eurasian Borderlands from the Rise of Early Modern Empires to the End of the First World War* (Cambridge UP, 2014); Stephen F. Dale, *The Muslim Empires of the Ottomans, Safavids, and Mughals* (Introduction reading notes); David O. Morgan, "The Decline and Fall of the Mongol Empire," *Journal of the Royal Asiatic Society* 19 (2009): 4; Margaret Meserve, *Empires of Islam in Renaissance Historical Thought* (Harvard UP, 2008); Giuseppe Marcocci, "Too Much to Rule: States and Empires across the Early Modern World," *Journal of Early Modern History* 20 (2016): 511–525; Thomas Allsen, "Eurasia after the Mongols," in *Culture and Conquest in Mongol Eurasia* (Chapter 7 reading notes), 159–181; Halil İnalcık, *The Ottoman Empire: The Classical Age 1300-1600* (Phoenix, 1973); Ki-Baik Kim, *A New History of Korea* (Harvard UP, 1984).

On the development of a dynastically or rulership-directed historiography, see Lynette Mitchell and Charles Melville, eds., *Every Inch a King: Comparative Studies on Kings and Kingship in the Ancient and Medieval Worlds* (Brill, 2013). On imperial ideology integrating historiography, religion, architecture, and new ideologies of rule, see Alfred J. Rieber, "Imperial Ideologies: Cultural Practices," in *The Struggle for the Eurasian Borderlands from the Rise of Early Modern Empires to the End of the First World War* (Cambridge UP, 2014); Paul Kléber Mounod, *The Power of Kings: Monarchy and Religion in Europe, 1589-1715* (Yale UP, 1999); Mia Rodriguez-Salgado, *The Changing Face of Empire: Charles V, Philip II and Habsburg Authority 1551-1559* (Cambridge UP, 1988); John Watkins, *Representing Elizabeth in Stuart England: Literature, History, Sovereignty* (Cambridge UP, 2002); and Thomas N. Corns, *The Royal Image: Representations of Charles I.* (Cambridge UP, 1999).

As background to the above and a link to earlier chapters, see Peter Fibiger Bang, "Between Ašoka and Antiochus: An Essay in World History on Universal Kingship and Cosmopolitan Culture in the Hellenistic Ecumene," in *Universal Empire: A Comparative Approach to Imperial Culture and Representation in Eurasian History*, ed. Peter Fibiger Bang and Dariusz Kolodziejczyk (Cambridge UP, 2012), 60–75; Peter B. Golden, "Imperial

Ideology and the Sources of Political Unity amongst the Pre-Činggisid Nomads of Western Eurasia," in *Nomads and Their Neighbours in the Russian Steppe: Turks, Khazars and Qipchaqs* (Aldershot, 2003); Reuven Amitai, "Mongol Imperial Ideology and the Ilkhanid War against the Mamluks," *The Mongol Empire and Its Legacy*, ed. Reuven Amitai-Preiss and David O. Morgan (Brill, 1999); and Pamela Crossley, "The Imaginal Bond of 'Empire' and 'Civilization' in Eurasian History," *VERGE: Studies in Global Asias* 2, no. 2 (Fall 2016): 84–11.

For the Alexander Romance, see Chapter 1 reading notes.

The idea of "simultaneous rulership" was first suggested to me by a reading of Michael Cherniavsky, *Tsar and People: Studies in Russian Myths* (Random House, 1969), who was in turn partly inspired by Ernst Kantorowicz's *The King's Two Bodies: A Study in Medieval Political Theology* (Princeton UP, 1957). Despite the skepticism of many scholars toward aspects of both Kantorowicz's and Cherniavsky's work, their observations (more implied than explicit) regarding the dynamic relationship between the ideological structure of rulership and concepts of popular cultural or "national" identities are important. For reflections of these ideas in the treatment of other early modern monarchs, see Peter Burke, *The Fabrication of Louis XIV* (Yale UP, 1992); M. J. Rodriguez-Salgado, *The Changing Face of Empire* (Cambridge UP, 1988); Gülru Necipoğlu, *Architecture, Ceremonial and Power: The Topkapı Palace in the Fifteenth and Sixteenth Centuries* (MIT P, 1991); Susan Frye, *Elizabeth I: The Competition for Representation* (Oxford UP, 1993); Corns, *op. cit.*; and Watkins, *op. cit.* For simultaneity in particular, see also Andrew J. Newman, *Safavid Iran: Rebirth of a Persian Empire* (I. B. Tauris, 2008).

Many readers will recognize that this chapter and some earlier chapters (particularly 3, 5 and 8) touch on a subject that Marshall Hodgson described as "military patronage"—the tendency of some medieval and early modern states to overtly privilege men of military status, create close communication between a small imperial court and cliques of military elites (many of them of hereditary military slave status), and tightly wrap state finances around military affairs. See particularly, *The Venture of Islam, Volume 3: The Gunpower Empires and Modern Times* (U Chicago P, 1958). Many aspects of Hodgson's work are now regarded as in need of qualification or simply outmoded; my own view is that it contains important observations on the processes of state centralization in the early modern period. For further comment on this particular point, see Pamela Kyle Crossley, "Military Patronage and Hodgson's Genealogy of State Centralization in Early Modern Eurasia," in *Islam and World History: The Ventures of Marshall Hodgson*, ed. Robert Mankin and Edmund Burke, III (U Chicago P, 2018).

On the histories of conquest states in the period discussed in this chapter, for Iran and western Eurasia, see Daniel T. Potts "The Aq-qoyunlu and the

Safavids," *Nomadism in Iran: From Antiquity to the Modern Era* (Oxford UP, 2014), 214–260; Kamran Matin, "Uneven and Combined Development in World History: The International Relations of State-Formation in Premodern Iran," *European Journal of International Relations* 13, no. 3 (2007): 419–447; Rajkai Zsombor Tibor, "The Timurid Empire and the Ming China" (Chapter 8 reading notes).

For Muscovy and early Romanov, see Michael Cherniavsky, "Khan or Basileus: An Aspect of Medieval Political Theory," *Journal of the History of Ideas* 20 (1959): 459–476; Richard Wortman, *Scenarios of Power: Myth and Ceremony in Russian Monarchy* (Princeton UP, 1995, 2000). For Muscovy in particular, see Donald Ostrowski, *Muscovy and the Mongols: Cross-Cultural Influences on the Steppe from 1304-1589* (Cambridge UP, 1998); Andrey Mikhaylovich Kurbsky, *History of Ivan IV*, trans. John L. I. Fennell (Cambridge UP, 1965); Henrik Zim, *England and the Baltic in the Elizabethan Era* (Manchester UP, 1972), 43–44, on Ivan's weapons; Olga Dmitrievca and Tessa Murdoch, *Treasures of the Royal Courts: Tudors, Stuarts and the Russian Tsars* (Victoria and Albert Museum, 2013); Brian Davies, *Warfare, State and Society on the Black Sea Steppe, 1500–1700* (Routledge, 2014); J. Pelenski, "The Contest between Lithuania-Rus' and the Golden Horde in the Fourteenth Century for Supremacy over Eastern Europe," *Archivum Eurasiae Medii Aevi* 2 (1982): 303–320; Michael Khodarkovsky, "Taming the 'Wild Steppe': Muscovy's Southern Frontier, 1480-1600," *Russian History/ Histoire Russe* 26, no. 3 (Fall 1999): 241–297; Bruce W. Lincoln, *The Conquest of a Continent: Siberia and the Russians* (Cornell UP, 2007); and Charles J. Halperin, "Muscovy as a Successor State of the Jochid *Ulus*," *Archivum Eurasiae Medii Aevi* 18 (2011): 5–20; see also Tracey A. Sowerby and Jan Hennings, eds., *Practices of Diplomacy in the Early Modern World, c. 1410–1800* (Routledge, 2017).

Muscovy found some law precedents in the Serbian *Nomokanon*; see the history outlined in Borislav D. Grozdić, "Nomokanon of St. Sava Concerning Murder in the War," *Theoria* 53, no. 4 (1020): 87–104. The Nikonian Chronicle, compiled in the early sixteenth century, has been translated in several volumes (the last two unpublished) by Serge A. Zenkovsky. The published volumes are from Darwin Press, between 1984 and 1989. The translation is purposefully limited to chronicle material and is regarded by some reviewers as problematic; it is nevertheless an important resource in English. See also a series of works by Charles J. Halperin: "Rewriting History: The Nikon Chronicle on Rus' and the Horde," *Archivum Eurasiae Medii Aevi* 17 (2010): 11–23; "Rus' Sources on the History of the Jochid Ulus and Its Successor States," *Archivum Eurasiae Medii Aevi* 18 (2011): 7–34; and "The Missing Golden Horde Chronicles and Historiography in the Mongol Empire," *Mongolian Studies* 23 (2000): 1–15.

On the global fur trade, see Richard Hellie, "Furs in Seventeenth-Century Muscovy," *Russian History* 16, no. 2/4 (1989): 171–196; Timothy Brook, *Vermeer's Hat: The Seventeenth Century and the Dawn of the Global World* (Bloomsbury, 2008); and Jonathan Schlesinger, *A World Trimmed in Fur: Wild Things, Pristine Places, and the Natural Fringes of Qing Rule* (Stanford UP, 2017).

For China through the seventeenth century, see John W. Dardess, *Ming China, 1368-1644: A Concise History of a Resilient Empire* (Rowman & Littlefield, 2012); on imperial simultaneity in China, see Pamela Kyle Crossley, "The Rulerships of China: A Review Article," *American Historical Review* 97, no. 5 (Dec 1992): 1468–1483 and *A Translucent Mirror: History and Identity in Qing Imperial Ideology* (U California P, 1999), 3; Scott Pearce, "A King's Two Bodies: The Northern Wei Emperor Wencheng and Representations of the Power of His Monarchy," *Frontiers of History of China* 7, no. 1 (2012): 90–105. On historiography, see David M. Robinson, ed., *Culture, Courtiers and Competition: The Ming Court (1368-1644)* (Harvard East Asia, 2008) and "Justifying Ming Rulership on a Eurasian Stage" in *Ming China: Courts and Contacts, 1400–1450*, ed. Craig Clunas, Jessica Harrison-Hall, and Luk Yu-ping (The British Museum, 2016), 8–16; Hok-lam Chan, "Chinese Official Historiographies at the Yuan Court: The Composition of the Liao, Chin, and Sung Histories," in *China under Mongol Rule*, ed. John D. Langlois (Princeton UP, 1981), 56–107; and Julia Schneider, "The Jin Revisited: New Assessment of Jurchen Emperors," *Journal of Song-Yuan Studies* 41 (2011): 343–404.

On Chen Cheng's expeditions to Central Asia, see Morris Rossabi, "Two Ming Envoys to Inner Asia," *T'oung Pao* 62, no. 1 (1976): 1–34 and Felicia J. Hecker, "A Fifteenth-Century Chinese Diplomat in Herat," *Journal of the Royal Asiatic Society* 3, no. 1 (Apr 1993): 85–98. For China and eastern Eurasia, see Joseph R. Levenson, ed., *European Expansion and the Counter-Example of Asia, 1300-1600* (Prentice Hall, 1967); John W. Dardess, "From Mongol Empire to Yuan Dynasty: Changing Forms of Imperial Rule in Mongolia and Central Asia," *Monumenta Serica* 30 (1973, 1972): 117–165; Joseph Francis Fletcher Jr., "China and Central Asia, 1368-1884," in *The Chinese World Order: Traditional China's Foreign Relations*, ed. John King Fairbank (Harvard UP, 1968), 206–224; James A. Millward, *Beyond the Pass: Economy, Ethnicity, and Empire in Qing Central Asia, 1759-1864* (Stanford UP, 1968); Pamela Kyle Crossley, "Making Mongols," in *Margins of Empire: Ethnicity in Early Modern China, 1500-1800*, ed. Pamela Kyle Crossley, Helen Siu, and Donald Sutton (U California P, 2005); Elliott Sperling, "The Szechwan-Tibet Frontier in the Fifteenth Century," *Ming Studies* 26 (1988): 37–55; Geoffrey Wade, "Domination in Four Keys: Ming China and Its 15 Southern Neighbours, 1400–1450," in *Ming China: Courts and Contacts, 1400–1450*, ed. Craig Clunas, Jessica Harrison-Hall, and Luk Yu-ping (The British Museum, 2016), 15–24 and "Ming China and Southeast Asia in the 15th Century: A Reappraisal," *Asia Research Institute Working Paper Series No. 28*, Asia Research Institute National University of Singapore, July 2004, http://www.ari.nus.edu.sg/wps/wps04_028.pdf; and Kangying Li, *The Ming Maritime Trade Policy in Transition, 1368 to 1567* (Harrossowitz, 2010) (includes discussion of Zheng He's expedition to Japan). On the size of Yuan ships, see Gang Deng, "The Foreign Staple Trade of China in the Pre-Modern Era," *The International History Review* 19, no. 2 (1997): 253–285.

For the Islamic world in this period, see Anne F. Broadbridge, *Kingship and Ideology in the Islamic and Mongol Worlds* (Cambridge UP, 2008); Stephen F. Dale, "The Legitimacy of Monarchs and the Institutions of Empires," in *The Muslim Empires of the Ottomans, Safavids, and Mughals* (Introduction reading notes), 77–105; Beatrice Forbes Manz, "Tamerlane and the Symbolism of Sovereignty," *Iranian Studies* 21, no. 1-2 (1988): 105–122 and "Tamerlane's Career and Its Uses," *Journal of World History* 13, no. 1 (Spring 2002): 1–25; Newman, (*op. cit.*); Caroline Finkel, "An Imperial Vision," and "Sultan of the Faithful," in *Osman's Dream: The History of the Ottoman Empire* (Perseus, 2007), 48–114; and Necipoğlu, *op. cit.*; On Mehmet II, see John Freely, *The Grand Turk: Sultan Mehmet II: Conqueror of Constantinople and Master of an Empire* (I. B. Tauris, 2009).

The standard edition of Juvayni's history of the Mongol conquests is published under the title *Tarīkh-i Jahān-gushā*, ed. Mirza Muhammad Qazwini, 3 vols. (Leiden and London, 1912–1937). An English translation by John Andrew Boyle, *The History of the World-Conqueror*, was published in 1958 and republished in 1997 (U Manchester P). See also Stefan T. Kamola, "Rashīd al-Dīn and the Making of History in Mongol Iran" (PhD diss., U Washington, 2013); Forbes Manz, "Tamerlane's Career and Its Uses," *op. cit.*, 15; Fatma Sinem Eryılmaz, "From Adam to Süleyman: Visual Representations of Authority and Leadership in 'Ārif's *Şāhnāme-yi Āl-i 'Osmān*" in *Editing the Past, Fashioning the Future* (Indiana UP, 2013); Baki Tezcan, "The Memory of the Mongols in Early Ottoman Historiography," in *Writing History at the Ottoman Court: Editing the Past, Fashioning the Future*, ed. H. Erdem Çıpa and Ermine Fetvacı (Indiana UP, 2013); Gottfried Hagen and Ethan L. Menchinger, "Ottoman Historical Thought," in *A Companion to Global Historical Thought*, ed. Prasenjit Duara, Viren Murthy, and Andrew Sartori (John Wiley and Sons, 2014); Gottfried Hagen, "World Order and Legitimacy," in *Legitimizing the Order: Ottoman Rhetoric of State Power*, ed. Maurus Reinkowski and Hakan Karateke (Brill, 2005), 55–83; and Cemal Kafadar, *Between Two Worlds: The Construction of the Ottoman State* (U California P, 1995).

On the *Shahnameh*, including as an ideological vehicle, Abolqasem Ferdowsi, *Shahnameh: The Persian Book of Kings*, trans. Dick Davis (Penguin,

2006; original, 1997); F. Abdullaeva and Charles Melville, *The Persian Book of Kings: Ibrahim Sultan's Shahnama* (Oxford Bodleian Library, 2008); Barbara Brend and Charles Melville, *Epic of the Persian Kings: The Art of Ferdowsi's Shahnameh* (I. B. Tauris, 2010); and the Smithsonian online exhibition, "A Thousand Years of the Persian Book: The Epic of *Shahnameh*," Library of Congress, https://www.loc.gov/exhibits/thousand-years-of-the-persian-book/epic-of-shahnameh.html. On later reflections of the *Shahnameh*, see Stephen F. Dale, *The Garden of the Eight Paradises* (Brill, 2004) and "Autobiography and Biography: The Turco-Mongol Case: Babur, Haidar Mirza, Gulbadan Begim and Jahangir," in *The Rhetoric of Biography: Narrating Lives in Persianate Societies*, ed. Louise Marlowe (Harvard UP, 2011).

Regarding the "Eurasian" school of Russian historiography, see Nicholas Riasanovsky, "The Emergence of Eurasianism," *California Slavic Studies* IV (1967), 39–72; Charles J. Halperin, "George Vernadsky, Eurasianism, the Mongols, and Russia," *Slavic Review* 41, no. 3 (Autumn 1982): 477–493 and *The Tatar Yoke: The Image of the Mongols in Medieval Russia* (Slavica Publishers, 2009); and Marlene Laruelle., *Russian Eurasianism: An Ideology of Empire* (Johns Hopkins UP, 2008).

For historical background the emergence of Muscovy, see Robert O. Crummey, *The Formation of Muscovy: 1304-1613* (Routledge, 2014; reissue of Longman original, 1987); Donald Ostrowski, *Muscovy and the Mongols: Cross-Cultural Influences on the Steppe Frontier, 1304-1589* (Cambridge UP, 2002); C. A. Macartney, *Hungary: From Ninth Century Origins to the 1956 Uprising* (Routledge, 2017); and John V. A. Fine Jr., *The Late Medieval Balkans: A Critical Survey from the Late Twelfth Century to the Ottoman Conquest* (U Michigan P, 1994).

Epilogue

The period of European history that we used to objectify as the "Renaissance" roughly corresponds to the twilight of Eurasian perspective in Europe and the emergence of bristling parochiality, including a rewriting of the heritage of the Greeks as proprietary and "classical" to Europe. Very recent scholarship on Niccolo Machiavelli (1469–1527) effectively places him in the last century of European writers purposefully participating in a Eurasian literary ecumene. As a Florentine, he was a native of the continuum of communications, trade, and cultural influence, from Italy on the west through Mamluk, Ottoman, and Safavid lands to the overland trade network on the east. In his youth, European interest and competence in Greek language was intensifying, and Machiavelli had some interest in Greek philosophy. Aristotle's *Politics* and Xenophon's *Education of Cyrus* were clearly inspirations, but his larger literary framework was drawn from the Islamic world, where the genre of political advisory works for rulers was well established. *The Book of the Secret of Secrets* (*Kitāb sirr al-asrār*) appeared in Arabic in the tenth century, with a preface claiming that it was a letter from Aristotle to Alexander that had been translated into Arabic in Syria in the ninth century. It was a combination of information and political admonitions, with the encyclopedic portions drawn from early medieval Arabic works (such enclosures may have promoted a certain confusion with a similarly named work on alchemy that circulated at roughly the same time). The political commentaries were translated into Latin as early as 1120 and were widely circulated. In ensuing centuries, it was translated again into Latin and later into most European vernaculars. It was one of those works that was as well-known in Christian Europe as in the Muslim world. It inspired Vincent Beauvais and probably Roger Bacon. Machiavelli had ready access to *Secret of Secrets*, though he was unlikely to have been aware of works in Persian that circulated most commonly in the eastern Ottoman, Safavid, and Timurid zones and had not been translated into Latin. The Ghaznavid–Seljuk vizier Nizam al-Mulk contributed one of the best known examples in his "Book of Government" (*Siyasatnameh*) in the late eleventh century. And the genre would continue after Machiavelli, perhaps most famously in the *Mingyi daifang lu* ("Waiting for the Dawn" but usually translated as "Advice for the Prince") by the late Ming (and early Qing) author Huang Zongxi (1610–1695). It is likely that Huang's nearest inspiration was Eurasian, and perhaps directly Chinese, in the Song-period author Sima Guang (1019–1086). But it is not impossible that Machiavelli was an indirect influence; well informed Jesuits had been in China since 1600, and Jesuits were among the most detailed and vigorous in denouncing Machiavelli not only in Europe but also in the widening world of their "counterreformation."

Machiavelli was aware that the Persianate world was primed to appreciate books in the mode of *The Prince* (*Il Principe*), which first appeared with a Latin title that was quickly converted to Italian, a language spoken in merchant communities throughout the Muslim world. When completed in 1513, the book circulated through the trade centers of the Ottoman and Safavid territories and was quickly translated into both Arabic and Persian. An acquaintance of Machiavelli from Florence (who was also a relative of Amerigo Vespucci) took the book to the early Mughal court, and afterward, the efforts of Jesuits, merchants, and ambassadors carried the text farther afield in Asia. The popularity of *Il Principe* in the Muslim world may have been connected to its themes and perhaps particularly (at least in the Ottoman lands) to the author's understanding of the Ottoman empire as a model for Europe. In both *The Prince* and *Discourses on Livy* (*Discorsi sopra la prima deca di Tito Livio*), Machiavelli gave a well informed representation of the Ottoman empire. He credited the sultans with using techniques of displacement of regional elites and control of religious identities to achieve a centralization of power that France and England had not gained in his time. He saw the entrenched hereditary feudal elites of Europe as impeding the sort of control that the Ottoman sultans had achieved by taming the aristocracy (occasionally through execution of contenders). More important, he thought that the Ottomans, because they placed themselves above legitimation by religious elites, had gained security that eluded Italian princes who were still attempting to gain the approval and cooperation of the popes. And most important, Machiavelli saw the Ottomans as the most formidable military power of the day due to the discipline and professionalism of the Janissaries. The Ottoman priorities of spending lavishly on the military and schools—while granting modestly and only when politically necessary to religious institutions—appeared to Machiavelli the proper economic management of a modern polity. It was an additional gift of the Ottomans in Machiavelli's view that Ottoman sultans in their persons had anticipated the model of the richly and secularly educated prince—a patron of the arts, a shrewd interpreter of economics, a lawyer, a strategist. Both in their persons and their style of rule, Machiavelli pronounced the Ottomans more genuine heirs of the Romans than were the leading noble families of Europe.

In Machiavelli's time, Italy, Sicily, the Alps, the Balkans, Bohemia, and Hungary were attenuating their remaining indirect connections with the cultural and political currents of Central Asia. The beliefs and vernacular cultures of these areas were subsequently overwritten by Angevin and Hapsburg political narratives, cementing their "European" particularisms and alienating their fundamental continuities with the histories of Turkic Eurasia. Eastern and western Europe were retrospectively welded together as a medieval and early modern story, and the hypostatized "Europe" was orphaned from its Eurasian historical context. In the process, Machiavelli became a harbinger of European modernity (mostly meaning secular rulership, of the sort he believed the Ottomans had achieved in practice) instead of the theorist of Eurasian conquest and empire that he had been in life.

This representational curtain parting "Europe" from "Asia" did not fall all of a sudden. European historical terminology back to Herodotus and perhaps earlier—when Greek writers marked off Anatolia and Iran from their own world—referred to the land to the east as "Asia." West–East dichotomies remained established in many European traditions but with unstable denotations: sometimes, the Greek-speaking world was the "East" and the Latin world was the "West," and sometimes, the Urals, the Balkans, or Anatolia were the frontage of a putative "East." The medieval European tendency to reify "Aristotle" and "Plato" as reason and mysticism (see Chapter 9) was directly ancestral to the dichotomy, with Europe given instant Aristotelian persona and the "east," suitably Platonic. Over time, demarcations of fundamental religion were draped over the framework, and even economy and society—the "West" became by early modern times, a place of no eunuchs, no slavery (in theory), and no nomads. But it was only after Machiavelli that the Ottomans and the Safavids became the crystalized "East" or "Orient," a literary and philosophical foil to an ideal "West" that was on the march to "Enlightenment." There was no counterpart of this thinking in the Islamic world or in East Asia. Sultans and their courts distinguished between the world of accomplished Islamic rule and the wider world of pagans and infidels yet to be incorporated. East Asian rulers before the late sixteenth century tended to see a horizonless "all under Heaven" of neighbors, strangers, and enemies, incidentally but not irremediably separated by differences of language, culture, and economic life.

The West–East ideology that conditions our reading of Machiavelli today has often been identified as a characteristic of early modern European literature, partly emblemized by the excision of Constantinople from the European landscape, the decline of overland trade connections, and the coterminous rise of exotic fantasy literature—in the style of "John Mandeville"—depicting Asia as outlandish not only in character but also in its limits of reality. Mandevillian fantasy was brought into the early modern period by Antoine Galland (1646–1715) in his *Mille et une nuits* (in two volumes, 1704 and 1717), drawing on medieval story collections in Persian and Arabic (and with parts originating in ancient Indian tales). The "Thousand and One Nights" image of despotic sultans as the fomenters of romantic intrigue continued to animate the European imagination for more than two centuries. The fact that "Thousand and One Nights" and its derivatives were vehicles for the reintroduction of plots long known across Eurasia—including from Aesop and the Alexander Romance—under a new guise of "oriental" fantasy was appreciated by scholars of folklore at the time it was happening but little noted by the general audiences of educated Europeans busily buttressing the new walls between Europe and Asia.

This indifference to the connected histories behind some literary trends may have been reinforced by the utility to political commentators of the artificial contrast that was used with great effect by sixteenth- and seventeenth-century writers constructing an imaginary "Persian" (which might variously be a reference to things Turkic, Persian, or Central Asian) perspective illuminating the emerging critical themes of despotism, humanism, and nationality in Europe. The cynosure of such literature is *Lettres persanes* (1721) by Charles de Secondat (Montesquieu; 1689–1755), but a more interesting example for purposes of this book was earlier: the play *Tamburlaine the Great* by Christopher Marlowe (1564–1593), noted for its stylistic impact upon the thriving theater industry of London. It was published in two parts in 1590, roughly coinciding with the time that Marlowe may have begun to encounter troubles from censors objecting to religious content in his plays (objections that may or may not have been connected to Marlowe's murder). The play no doubt was popular for its torrent of tortures, murders, and suicides, but it was also noted for its theme that even the greatest conqueror is subject to the forces of debilitation and death—an obvious enough cultural legacy of Eurasia, deeply embedded in the Alexander Romance and echoed in the Quran, the *Shahnameh*, and the Arthurian story cycles. The lurid story includes some actual historical referents. Tamburlaine has a humble origin as a "Skythian" shepherd (clearly inspired by Turkic origins of the real Timur), living under Persian rule, who eventually effects a coup that makes him ruler of Persia (a parallel to the real Timur's coup against the Chaghatay khans but here transposed as the conquest of a populous settled civilization by a lawless nomad). He becomes an enemy of the "Turks," capturing their ruler and eventually driving him to suicide (a possible allusion to the Timurid campaigns that drove the Ottomans to refuge in Edirne). The real Timur's conquest of Baghdad becomes Tamburlaine's destructions of Damascus and Babylon. And like the ostensible "world conquerors," Chinggis and the historical Timur, Tamburlaine can find no ultimate purpose in his conquests other than perpetuating them through his sons. He is the personification of an insatiable quest for power as the enemy of love, honor, and, above all, religion. Marlowe's translation of apprehension over rising militarism, despotism, and imperialism in Europe to an "oriental" venue was a convention by the time of Montesquieu, but it had an interesting companion—and repeatedly refreshed inspiration—in the development of relatively factual and sober reporting from the Muslim and particularly the Ottoman and Safavid worlds.

Machiavelli made a reference in *The Prince* to relying upon such reports, but published books of commentary in significant numbers awaited the development of the commercial print industry. The French court of Francis I (1494–1547) received steady information about the Ottomans from high sources—including a son of Mehmet II who fled to the protection of the Mamluks and then various European courts after a failed attempt to gain the Ottoman rulership, and then sojourned in France while attempting to find backing for another coup. Francis, who was himself a monarch strongly resembling the model of an Ottoman sultan—a soldier, a scholar, an arts patron, an advocate of vernacular literature, and an enemy of the Hapsburgs and the papacy—struck a formal alliance with Suleiman the Magnificent in 1536. It was in part a transfer of an earlier protocol between Francis and the Mamluks (now subjects of the Ottomans) that permitted French trade and residence across North Africa and the Levant, but now translated Francis as implied protector of all Christians resident in Ottoman territories. Francis's goal was to gain an ally against the Hapsburgs, and the Ottoman navy proved a critical ally in engagements in the Adriatic and the coast of North Africa.

The relationship between France and Ottoman developed steadily in ensuing centuries, with the establishment of permanent embassies, frequently updated trade and residence agreements, and mutual military aid—the Ottomans fighting the Hapsburgs in the Balkans and the French providing intelligence to the Ottomans in the latter's wars against the Safavids. The alliance between Francis and Suleiman was part of the framework of a developing French fixation on the Ottomans and the Safavids. In the late 1600s, Jean-Baptiste Chardin (1643–1713), a jeweler from Paris, was traveling the Levant, Iraq, Iran, and India. He got an agreement making him the exclusive importer of European jewelry to Shah Abbas II of the Safavids in 1666, and he learned standard written Persian from a Safavid aristocrat. According to his 10-volume account, published in Paris in 1671, Chardin had various adventures and near-escapes during sojourns in Konstantiniyye, the Caucasus, Crimea, Iran, and India before making a fortune and returning to France. His mesmerizing book contributed to the deepening European exoticization of the Ottomans and points east and, at the same time, helped stimulate genuine scholarship in the languages and religions of the Levant, Iran, India, and China. But what was useful intelligence in earlier times became a touchstone of European objectification of Ottoman alterity in the early modern period; Montesquieu based his construction of a political foil in *Lettres persanes* upon both the popular narratives of Chardin and earnest scholarship, a significant turn from the equally informed but Eurasia-oriented Machiavelli.

In England, the court of Henry VIII, who died in 1547, had a long fascination with the Ottomans, partly excited by the French success in gaining commercial and military advantages from the sultans. Henry thought on and off of working out an alliance of his own with the Ottomans against the Hapsburgs and expected that his rejection of the Roman Catholic Church in 1534 would help him in such an endeavor, as it had helped Francis, who had been an avid promoter of Protestantism. Henry showed up for palace events dressed as an Ottoman sultan more than once, a small speck in the late sixteenth- and seventeenth-century European elite fashion for adopting the draping clothing and particularly the rich textiles of the Ottomans. Though an alliance between England and Ottoman was never realized, an English merchant was given license by Suleiman to trade, and the business of the Moscow Company (see Chapter 10) was rapidly expanded to Konstantiniyye and later to Tehran. In 1581, after Henry's daughter Elizabeth and the Ottoman sultan Murad III (1546–1595) agreed upon protocols for the treatment of English mercenaries, merchants, and pirates who fell into Ottoman hands, the government built on the Moscow Company model to create the joint-stock Turkey Company (which in 1592, would combine with the Venice Company to form the Levant Company). England was not a trading power of great significance at the time, and its access to Ottoman and Safavid textiles and jewels was largely through the Dutch; as the volume of Ottoman trade with England rose, so did the profits of English merchants, who were increasingly willing to move to North Africa or the Levant to pursue new wealth. The company provided some oversight of the community needs of resident English families, including domestic help, education, and religious service. English trade could not be separated from the military interests of the English crown and its allies, since containment of the Spanish, Portuguese, and Venetian empires depended upon a steady and profitable flow of money into the coffers of Elizabeth. From its inception, the company, like its Moscow predecessor and East Asian successor, was as deeply involved in information about local governments as it was in actual trade and as likely to manage the flow of weapons as the flow of spices.

In her missives to the Ottoman court, Elizabeth described herself as a kind of female English sultan, "the most invincible and most mighty defender of the Christian faith against all kinds of idolatries," a clear reference to the Roman affinities of the Hapsburgs. She continued to search the reports of Englishmen in the Levant for useful news. They repeatedly raised the theme of religious plurality and accommodation. In 1590, William Biddulph, an Anglican clergyman serving the Levant Company merchants in Aleppo, gave his account of Mehmet II's occupation of Constantinople a century and a half before:

> And instead of the great number of the people that were there slain and carried away as prisoners he caused to be brought thither, out of all the provinces and cities by him conquered, a certain number of men, women and children, with their faculties and riches, whom he permitted there to live according to the institutions and precepts of such religion as it pleased them to observe, and to exercise with all safety their handicrafts and merchandises; which ministered an occasion unto an infinite number of Jews and Maranes, driven out of Spain, to come and dwell there; by means whereof, in very short time the city began to increase in traffic, riches, and abundance of people.

Biddulph had also attempted to describe the cosmological ideas of the Sufis and commented on the remaining popularity of the Greek-derived scientific ideas of Nasir al-Din Tusi. Another informant to the throne, William Harborne (d. 1617), carried what might have been the first reply from the Ottoman court to Elizabeth in 1577. In 1582, he was appointed English ambassador to the court of Murad III, where he claimed that he was energetic in promoting the reputation of his home country. The satirist Thomas Nashe (1567–1601) noted that, to hear Harborne tell it, he "hath echoing noised the name of our island and of Yarmouth [Harborne's hometown] so tritonly, that not an infant of the cur-tailed, skin-clipping Pagans, but talk of London as frequently as of their Prophet's tomb at Mecca." More important, Harborne was a major conduit to England of a view (clearly not persuasive to Nashe) of the Ottomans as rationally mercantile, flexibly diplomatic, and militarily formidable, all of which became important elements of Elizabeth's Mediterranean strategic concepts, as they had long been part of the thinking of states in Italy, Germany, and the Balkans.

From the middle seventeenth century, the prestige of the Ottomans and the enthusiasm for Ottoman models in strategy, political practice, and trade waned. The Ottomans were defeated on the sea by Spain, and the Ottoman reputation for fearsome war-making became an object of European revulsion. The impression of English merchants and clergymen, even in the age of Elizabeth, was based upon a deep horror incited by tales of Ottoman slaughter of Christians across the Balkans and Central Europe, the reported torture and annihilation of the Byzantine court women after the fall of Constantinople, and the gruesome examples made of English merchant crews who refused to pay the Ottoman tolls for passage through the Bosphorus. Both the Ottomans and the Safavids in Persia—who were at war with each other for most of the period between 1603 and 1640—were popularly regarded as monarchs of ignorance and cruelty, riding despotically over populations controlled by fear and superstition. The "Turks" and "Persians" became objects of contempt and gradually sank in European estimation as Jesuit reports of the Ming and, after 1644, the Qing courts in China began to play the former Ottoman role of rational, secular, erudite rulership—indeed, Voltaire based his model of the "philosopher king" on such reports, most likely the biography written by the Jesuit Joachim Bouvet on the Kangxi emperor (1654–1722). The European search for models of rational, secular, impartial emperors would rest with the Qing until English attempts to rewrite China's trade regulations led to the embarrassment of George Macartney in 1793. Thereafter, British newspapers and political candidates would steadily vilify both the Qing empire and the British East Asia company, eventually attempting to ruin both in the Opium War of 1839–1842.

European mathematicians and natural philosophers were perhaps the last to lose sight of the Eurasian legacy. How Descartes's *cogito ergo sum* could have been influenced by Ibn Sina's floating man thought experiment (Chapter 9) has been a pretty problem in philosophical studies. The imagery and the logic of the two philosophers on this point are similar enough that partisans of Ibn Sina denounce Descartes for claiming originality, while partisans of Descartes deny any relationship by finding Ibn Sina's concept to have had different foundations and implications from that of Descartes. The tendency is to search out the specific means by which Descartes could have made contact with Ibn Sina's floating man. Such links can be shown in some cases—for instance, Copernicus's knowledge of Nasir al-Din Tusi's astronomical calculations—but our insistence that they be found wherever India, China, or the Islamic world appears to have preceded some seminal breakthrough in European thought reflects a little too predictably our modern isolation of the rational, scientifically oriented, liberalizing "West" from the static, obscurantist, stubbornly mystical "East." Ibn Sina's commentaries on Aristotle's *De Anima* were translated into Latin around 1200 by Michael Scot—the leading European intellectual who lived steeped in Arabic scientific and mathematical erudition because he served at the Sicilian court of Frederick II. Late medieval European universities were permeated by Muslim philosophical discourse by either translation or the mimetic effect of lectures and ale house discussion.

How Descartes or any of his Latin-reading contemporaries would pick up (in reading or in conversation) a striking image and a pithy observation is not mysterious, and the absence of evidence that Descartes was pouring over Scot's translation of Ibn Sina is not an argument for the originality of Descartes's proposition. It is more important to the themes of this book that, while historians of European thought have no difficulty assimilating Ibn Sina to it, it is far less likely that they would perceive him as the Transoxianan conduit through the Abbasid and Seljuk worlds and into the much wider intellectual heritage of networked Eurasia. Whether or not Descartes spontaneously recreated Ibn Sina's floating man conceit, all that would really have been necessary for it to have an effect would have been for him to transfer it from the receding world of Latin scholarship permeated by Arabic sources to the rising world of French readers for whom the Arabic sources were exotic and, more likely, unknown. By Descartes's time, tabloids, novels, and theater were in French; Latin remained mostly as a contrivance of satire. In the law courts, Latin had been displaced by French, and publishing in Latin was rapidly decreasing from the perhaps 70 percent of all books published c. 1500 to 5 percent by the end of the eighteenth century. Descartes himself was influential in ending the use of Latin in scientific and mathematical description (apart from formulae), but he may also have been one of the last conduits of medieval Latin–Arabic scholastic philosophers to the vernacular media. It is not a matter of medieval knowledge passing from the Islamic world to the Christian world by means of specific portals but more a matter of knowledge and concepts percolating from the Eurasian past by innumerable vesicles into diverse aspects of Muslim, Chinese, Indian, and European thought.

More important, surely, is that Descartes gave an early modern wrapping to the oldest debates of medieval Eurasian philosophy regarding whether there are two realms—one of phenomena, and one of ideal forms, or spirit, or mind, or noumenality—or there is a single phenomenal realm perhaps permeated by noumenal elements of intention or causation. His mind–body dichotomies captured well the rationalist approaches over the previous centuries and over the wide networks of Eurasia—whether Abelard, Aquinas, al-Ghazali, or Zhu Xi. They effectively discredited, at least in their immediate academic circles, any remaining idealist elements, but they did not discredit the long and vexed history of dualist speculation in Eurasian thought. That was left to the likes of Gottfried Wilhelm Leibniz (1646–1716), in whose world of the very late seventeenth century "Asia"—and "China" in particular—had shrunk to a distant puppet theater in which language, dress, custom, and political structure were all characterized by irrational superficiality, duplicity, indirectness, and lack of scientific awareness. Leibniz was actually able to "discover" facts about China by assiduous exploration of libraries across Central Europe and, for a time, entertained the idea that Chinese might actually be the direct descendant of an original, universal human language. When French Jesuits joined Italians and Spaniards in China in the late 1600s, Leibniz began a correspondence with them (including Athanasius Kircher, 1602–1680) that allowed him to gain what, for the time, was an exceptional expertise on Chinese culture, history, and current affairs. To Leibniz, it was a great novelty to bring China and Europe into communication. He shared Voltaire's admiration for the Kangxi emperor. He attempted to persuade Peter the Great to make Russia a conduit for regular exchanges between East and West. By the last years of the seventeenth century, he was trying to enlist European merchants, nobles, churchmen, and scholars in a great program of continuous cultural and scientific exchange with China—his great project for "light and wisdom." Though Leibniz's own learning in things Chinese was unsystematic, it was powered by his conviction that there was something ancient and universal in Chinese culture, something that once identified, would illuminate the sources of knowledge and power in all parts of the world.

Leibniz never found the universal keys that he was seeking in exploration of an objectified "China." But in his reading about the *Book of Changes* (*Yijing*), he may have found help with his binary number scheme, and for the rest of his life, he engaged in vigorous debate with European scholars on the meaning of the Chinese philosophical classics. Inspiration from early Chinese philosophy positing a continuous unity of mind and matter—psyche and substance, consciousness and stimulus—reinforced for him the reality and supremacy of mathematics, and provided him a steady bulwark against the Platonic dualism that he felt had haunted medieval European philosophy, whatever its origins. More important, Leibniz, like many of his contemporaries, argued that the example of Kangxi-era China—like the ancient China of Confucius—demonstrated that government and reason could justify themselves quite outside the terms of religion and even tradition. He inspired generations of European "orientalists" studying Chinese, Egyptian, and Sanskrit and joined with other philosophers of his time in asserting that modern states and societies, like that of China, could be founded upon philosophers, reason, and law. He was credited with exploring a realm that, to even the most erudite Europeans, was impenetrable. He deserved the credit, but it might have been accompanied with recognition of the irony that, three centuries previously, the continuous avenues of knowledge from Europe through the Islamic world to China had still been visible and navigable.

By the time of Leibniz's death, most European states had taken on the qualities that Machiavelli had recommended: a priority on military expenditure and organization, a privileging of merchant activity to enrich the central government, regulation of religious identity, and weakening of the aristocracy. The continuities between the broad developments and Machiavelli's insistence that the Ottoman empire had exemplified them raise the question of how European powers—not the Ottomans, Russians, Qing, Safavids, or Mughals—persuasively claimed to have invented modernity and spread it outward. This is where we join the great debates relating to early modern disparities between Europe and "Asia." The reader can follow (see the reading notes) well developed—and inconclusive—lines of argument attributing European preeminence in the eighteenth and nineteenth centuries to fortuitous discoveries of new sources of coal, iron, silver, and labor; to concepts of exchange and investment that piled up the wealth reserves (capital) for Europe to underwrite large-scale mechanization; to patterns of urbanization in western Europe that permitted the emergence of skilled labor markets; or to cultural valorizing of science, profit, and exploration. The arguments are important, but they fall outside the concern of this book, which deals with the period before the explosion of European power. Yet the question itself underscores the theme of this book: that the role of the post-nomadic rulerships at the threshold of modernity must be seen as having both direct and indirect effects, including contrary effects in some cases. Ming, Muscovy, Mughal, Safavid, and Ottoman may all have inherited the established Turkic patterns of political neutralization of religion, vernacular language and rising literacy, military elites, disciplined aristocracies, and scientific and mathematical patronage that would prove in the case of Europe to be essential to creating outsized wealth and power. But they also retained the long-term Turkic preference for tiny government, low taxation, absence of public debt, and provincialization of policy and fiscal decision making. These practices provided stability and steady production of wealth for centuries, but they could not withstand the challenges of massively mechanized products and industrial-scale weaponry produced by the swelling governments and managed public debt of England and the Netherlands. For a short time thereafter—a couple of centuries—Europe's objectification of an alien and pre-modern "Asia" was commonplace. But in the twenty-first century, as deeper and older patterns reassert themselves, the early modern mirages of knowledge and power differentials—and the perception of "Europe" and "Asia" as distinct places— evaporate.

READING NOTES: EPILOGUE

On the questions of a "great divergence" or otherwise continental differential in the early modern period, see Barrington Moore, *Social Origins of Dictatorship and Democracy: Lord and Peasant in the Making of the Modern World* (Beacon Press, 1966); Theda Skocpol, *Social Revolutions in the Modern World* (Cambridge UP, 1994); Immanuel Wallerstein, *The Capitalist World-Economy* (Cambridge UP, 1979); André Gunder Frank, *On Capitalist Underdevelopment* (Oxford UP, 1975) and *ReOrient: Global Economy in the Asian Age* (U California P, 1998); Giovanni Arrighi, *The Long Twentieth Century: Money, Power, and the Origins of Our Times* (Verso, 1994) and *Adam Smith in Beijing: Lineages of the Twenty-First Century* (Verso, 2007); R. Bin Wong, *China Transformed: Historical Change and the Limits of European Experience* (Cornell UP, 2000); Kenneth Pomeranz, *The Great Divergence: China, Europe and the Making of the Modern World Economy* (Princeton UP, 2000); Huri Islamoglu, ed., *Constituting Modernity: Private Property in the East and West* (I. B. Tauris, 2004); Prasannan Partharathi, *Why Europe Grew Rich and Asia Did Not: Global Economic Divergence, 1600-1850* (Cambridge UP, 2011); and J-L Rosenthal and R. B. Wong, *Before and Beyond Divergence: The Politics of Economic Change in China and Europe* (Harvard UP, 2011).

On changes in European readership of the seventeenth century, see Rebecca Barr, P. David Pearson, Michael L. Kamil, and Peter B. Mosenthal, *Handbook of Reading Research*, vol. 2 (Psychology P, 1996), esp. 58–61. On the history of a "Thousand and One Nights," see introduction in *Tales from the Thousand and One Nights*, trans. Nessim J. Dawood (Penguin, 1973).

For European travelers of the sixteenth century, see John Freyers's account of Safavid Iran: "John Fryer: A New Account of East-India and Persia . . . (1698)," in *Early Modern Tales of Orient: A Critical Anthology*, ed. Kenneth Parker (Routledge, 1999), 87, 222–224. On William Harborne, see Thompson Cooper, "Harborne, William," in *Dictionary of National Biography* (includes the quote from Thomas Nashe), https://en.wikisource.org/wiki/Harborne,_William_(DNB00); see also Susan A. Skilliter, *William Harborne and the Trade with Turkey, 1578-1582: A Documentary Study of the First Anglo-Ottoman Relation* (Oxford UP, 1977). For the reverse view of Ottomans in Europe, see Daniel Goffman, *The Ottoman Empire and Early Modern Europe* (Cambridge UP, 2002). For more general coverage, see Sabine Shülting, Lucia Müller, and Raif Hertel, eds., *Early Modern Encounters with the Islamic East: Performing Cultures* (Routledge, 2016). For Elizabeth's description of herself as a defender of Christianity against idolatrous Hapsburgian Catholicism, see Rayme Allison, *A Monarchy of Letters: Royal Correspondence and English Diplomacy in the Reign of Elizabeth I* (Springer, 2012), 137. Emily Kugler expands upon the theme of English associations of Anglicanism with Ottoman Islamic ideology in *The Sway of the Ottoman Empire in English Identity in the Long Eighteenth Century* (Brill, 2012).

On Machiavelli and the Ottoman empire, see Michael Meeker, *A Nation of Empire: The Ottoman Legacy of Turkish Modernity* (U California P, 2001); Sydney Anglo, *Machiavelli—The First Century: Studies in Enthusiasm, Hostility, and Irrelevance* (Oxford UP, 2005) and Lucio Biasiori and Giuseppe Marcocci, *Machiavelli, Islam and the East: Reorienting the Foundations of Modern Political Thought* (Routledge, 2017). For mathematical exchanges and encounters of the early modern period, see Roger Hart, *Imagined Civilizations: China, the West and their First Encounter* (The Johns Hopkins UP, 2013). For Leibniz and China, see Donald F. Lach, "Leibniz and China," *Journal of the History of Ideas* 6, no. 4 (Oct 1945): 436–455; David E. Mungello, *Leibniz and Confucianism: The Search for Accord* (Hawaii UP, 1977); and Franklin Perkins, *Leibniz and China: A Commerce of Light* (Cambridge UP, 2004). On parallels of early modern European thought in Chinese thought of the same period, see Zhang Longxi, *Mighty Opposites: From Dichotomies to Differences in the Comparative Study of China* (Stanford UP, 1998) and William Theodore DeBary's translation of Huang Zongxi, *Waiting for the Dawn: A Plan for the Prince* (Columbia UP, 1993).

After I had finished this book, I became aware of the book in preparation by Mark Koyama and Noel Johnson, *Persecution and Toleration: The Long*

Road to Religious Freedom (described by Koyama in "Ideas Were Not Enough," *Aeon*, https://aeon.co/essays/the-modern-state-not-ideas-brought-about-religious-freedom), which argues that state development in early modern Europe, and particularly the role of law in state legitimation and the military in state finance, was more important than ideas associated with the Reformation or the Enlightenment. If it means that a reexamination of early modern Eurasia outside the terms that Europe established in its own narrative after Machiavelli, I certainly agree. I hope it is clear that I would emphasize Eastern Europe and the long-term role of Eurasia as an exchange network as sources of stimulation for state development.

Index

Abul Abbas (elephant), 73, 83
Abbasids, 9, 52, 55, 56, 59, 69, 70, 71, 72, 73, 74, 75, 76, 79, 80, 85, 88, 89, 90, 91, 93, 95, 96, 104, 111, 115, 118, 122, 125, 127, 135, 136, 139, 140, 147, 149, 151, 158, 159, 167, 168, 169, 173, 181, 182, 183, 188, 192, 203, 209, 214, 216, 222, 237, 239, 245, 246, 247, 250, 251, 256, 263, 290, 293, 297, 312; and China, 9, 52, 55, 72, 76, 79, 80; caliph or caliphate, 52, 55, 58, 68–69, 71, 74, 76, 85, 88, 89, 89–90, 91, 93, 94, 96, 115, 118, 122, 127. *See also* Baghdad; Buyids; Harun al-Rashid; Samanids, Seljuks
Abelard, Peter, 214–216, 216, 313
Abraham, 35
Abrahamic religions, 205, 220, 222. *See also* "peoples of the book"
Achaemenid empire, 11, 34, 49, 117, 210, 288, 293; Darius, 12; Xerxes, 11
Afghanistan, 5, 8, 32, 50, 69, 72, 88, 91, 94, 136, 147, 182, 245; Kabul, 8, 182. *See also* Balkh; Herat
Africa, 3–4, 6, 8, 11, 12, 14. *See also* North Africa; Egypt; Makuria; Somalia
agriculture, 5, 7, 14, 23, 24, 44, 94, 109, 124, 134, 145, 158, 160, 167, 191; farmers, 45, 93, 103, 109, 126, 144, 145, 156, 157, 158–135, 169, 174, 176, 227, 234, 240, 278. *See also* grains, taxation
Akkoyunlu, 182, 244, 263, 284, 289. *See also* Karakoyunlu, Safavids
al-Ghazali, Abu Hamid, 219, 222, 313
al-Masudi, Abu al-Hasan, 262, 275
Alans, xix, 48, 57, 173
Alexander the Great, 11, 12, 13, 59, 181, 205, 245, 289, 291, 305; Bucephalus, 13, 20; Zulqarnain, 198
Alexander Nevskii, 122, 176, 178, 281, 282; Andrei, 122; misuse, xiii. *See also* Moscow; Novgorod, Vladimir of; Jochid khanate
Alexander Romance, 13, 20, 247, 254, 286, 296, 305, 307
Altan Debter, 287
Anatolia, 6, 28, 29, 43, 57, 65, 68, 89–90, 90–91, 93, 96, 101, 120, 147, 148, 172, 183–185, 187, 191, 208, 209, 215, 222, 225, 233; Ankara, 185; Bosphorus, 65, 183, 311; Bursa, 240; Galata, 193; Salarya River, 184. *See also* Byzantine Empire; Ottomans
ancestor worship, 24
angels/messengers, 30, 214
Aquinas, Thomas, 214, 313
Arabia, 30, 68, 69, 147, 172, 185, 236, 237, 242, 275, 284; Mecca, 51, 68, 236, 275, 293, 311
Arabic language or script, xiii, 4, 13, 71, 72, 85, 88, 91, 96, 123, 167, 168, 171,

319

182, 184, 192, 208, 209, 213–214, 216, 220, 250, 251, 253, 259, 288, 289, 305, 306, 307, 312. *See also* translations
Aramaic language or script, 239, 251
archeology, 6, 12, 45, 74, 79, 176
archery, 10, 54, 186, 205. *See also* horses
architecture, 57, 89, 101, 172, 208; Abbasid, 70; Buddhist, 67, 75; Byzantine, 87; Greek, 86; Ilkhan, 151; Kitan, 104; Ming, 235, 274; Mongol, 123, 135, 175; Persian, 112, 147; Russian, 173; Timurid, 182; Ottoman, 192
aristocracy, 4, 9, 46, 52, 59, 75, 242, 250; Armenian, 170; Avar, 58; Balkan, 185; European, 185, 306, 313; Gokturk, 52; Hapsburg, 175; Japan, 280; Khazar, 58; Kitan, 79; Ming, 273; Mongol, 122, 134, 135, 140, 158, 178, 180, 248; nomad, 14, 15; Northern Wei, 54; Ottoman, 306; Russian, 123, 173–174, 238, 281–282; Seljuk, 91; Sui/Tang, 54; Tibet, 76; Timurid, 182; Xiongnu, 46, 47, 58. *See also* ordo
Aristotle, 209, 210, 212, 214–216, 217, 218–219, 220, 221, 305; stereotype for European scientism, 307
Armenia or Armenians, 57, 70, 74, 89, 120, 122, 123, 139, 170, 185, 241, 245, 293, 294; Armenian language, 98, 252; Armenian church, 240, 241, 247
asceticism, 27, 28, 222
Ashina lineage, 51, 52, 57, 58
Ashoka, 27, 67
astronomy or astronomers, 5, 7, 13, 95, 136, 150–151, 182, 193, 210, 213, 217, 227, 235; observatories, 151, 153, 182, 193, 235; Tycho Brahe, 193; Taqi al-Din, 193. *See also* Maragha; Nasir al-Din Tusi; Ulugh Beg
Augustine of Hippo, 29, 209, 215, 226
Auspicious Conjunction, 181; Lord of (*sahib kiran*), 199
Avars, 57–58, 59, 68, 72, 86, 225, 247, 288
Ayyubids,. *See* Egypt; Saladin 168, 169, 171, 208, 247, 289
Azerbaijan, 8, 139, 141, 147, 149, 155, 167, 185, 243, 245, 254, 284; Tabriz, 147, 149, 150, 154, 206. *See also* Maragha

Babur, 182, 284
Bacon, Roger, 217–218, 262, 305
Bagan, 145
Baghdad, 69, 71, 72, 73, 85, 89, 91, 96, 114, 115, 122, 133
Balkans, 3, 12, 43, 57, 59, 68, 73, 86, 87, 96, 122, 181, 184, 185, 187, 191, 207, 209, 241, 247, 283, 284, 285, 295, 296, 307, 309, 311; as refuge of heretics, 87, 223, 225, 228; Macedonia, 87. *See also* Bulgaria; Serbia
Balkh, 114, 216, 222
Baltic, 75, 174
Batu, 120, 122, 124, 127, 134, 172, 174–176, 177
Baybars, 168, 170–171, 172
Beckwith, Christopher, 209, 210, 219, 231
Beijing, 56, 111, 128, 134, 142, 143, 146, 148, 151, 176, 235, 248, 274, 276, 277; Dadu, 134, 141, 145, 146, 148, 149–150, 151, 153–154, 155, 175, 176, 206, 235, 248, 257, 263, 274, 277
Bible, 88, 225, 226, 247, 250, 258–259; New Testament, 35, 250, 259. *See also* translation
Biddulph, William, 310–311
birds (mythical, symoblic, divinatory), 35
Black Sea, 7, 68, 73, 75, 124, 169, 170, 175, 183, 185, 285. *See also* Crimea
blacksmiths or smithing, 4, 7, 14, 15, 16, 123; in myth, 16, 32; in shamanism, 34. *See also* mining; Prometheus; Wayland
Bogomils, 87, 223. *See also* Cathars
Bohemia, 121, 225–226, 227, 228, 247, 307. *See also* Prague
Bolad Chingsang, 153–154, 159, 262, 263, 287. *See also* Kublai; Hulagu; Ilkhanate; Rashid al-Din; Yuan
books, 112, 150, 156, 192, 193, 244, 249, 253–255, 256–260, 262, 287, 289, 305–306, 309, 312, 314; illuminated, 192, 249, 254, 256. *See also* printing
Borjigins, 106, 120, 180, 181
Borte, 116, 119; and the *Secret History*, 286
Bouvet, Joachim, 311

Index

Britain, 59, 65, 71, 74, 141, 184, 185, 195, 206, 283, 306, 310, 311, 314; Scotland, 74; Wales, 291. *See also* Elizabeth, Henry VIII, Ireland
Bronze Age, 6, 7, 12, 24, 35, 46, 243
Bruno, Giordano, 193, 218
Buddhism, 4, 13, 23, 26–27, 28, 29, 30–33, 52, 54, 56, 65, 67, 75–78, 79–80, 89, 91, 94, 105, 109, 111, 112, 118, 123, 124, 137, 139, 152, 156, 177, 180, 205, 206, 209–212, 213, 220, 222, 226, 252, 255, 256, 264, 292; bodhisattva, 27, 76, 80, 214, 292; *chakravartin*, 67, 76, 292; *chan/zen/dhyana*, 211, 264; dharma, 26; Mahayana, 27, 54, 77, 207, 210, 211, 252; Sakya, 137, 145; Siddhartha, 26, 28, 29, 30, 32; Theravada, 27, 32. *See also* Tibet
Bukhara, 8, 9, 52, 112, 114, 151, 182, 204, 208, 216, 222, 257. *See also* Transoxiana; Sart, Khwarazm
Bulgars, 36, 57, 58, 75, 96, 225, 241; Bulgaria, 184, 185, 254; Bulgarian church, 241, 295; Bulgar khanate, 72, 74, 86–88, 96, 173, 174, 207, 293, 296; Bulgarian language, 13, 88, 241, 247, 250; Nikol/Nicopolis, 184
Buyids, 85, 89
Byzantine Empire (Byzantium), 32, 50, 57, 58, 66, 72, 74, 88, 94, 108, 146, 152, 170, 174, 190, 205, 241, 254, 294, 296, 297; as confessional state, 65–68, 71, 80; and Abbasids, 72, 73; and Bulgars, 73, 86, 87; and heresy, 66, 87, 223; and Kievan Rus, 74–75, 173; and Mamluk sultanate, 171; and Muscovy, 295; and Seljuks, 89, 90, 184; and Ottomans, 172, 185, 186, 192, 194, 240, 241, 283, 293, 311; conflicts with Avars, 44–52; conflicts with Franks, 11, 58, 73, 74; conflict with Sasanians, 57, 68, 207; Constantine VI, 73; popular literature, 247–248; terminology, xii; Varangians, 74. *See also* Constantine I; Constantinople; Justinian I; Christianity; Orthodox Christianity

caesar, 65, 73, 86, 183, 293; Geser, 248, 271; kaysar-i Rum, 183, 293; tsar, 293, 295
caliph/caliphate. *See* Abbasids; Umayyads
Canton (city), 8, 149. *See also* China
Caspian Sea, 8, 15, 111, 120, 122, 147, 178
Cathars or Catharism, 223–225, 226, 227, 234. *See also* Bogomils; Waldensians
Catholicism. *See* Christianity
Caucasus, 8, 57, 111, 115, 120, 123, 125, 134, 135, 138, 139, 140, 141, 147, 177, 185, 192, 242, 243, 244, 247, 263, 284–285, 296. *See also* Armenia; Azerbaijan; Georgia
causation, 23, 31, 214; Buddhist, 26; Christian, 215, 226; Hindu, 25; Iluminist, 221; Islamic, 30, 216–217; neo-Confucian, 212; Plato, 30, 214, 221; Zoroastrian, 25. *See also* Descartes; ibn Sina
census, 80, 118, 125, 141, 144, 157, 176, 188, 282; cadastral, 191. *See also* taxation
Cervantes, Miguel, 260, 261; Don Quixote, 260
Chaghatay, 119, 120, 135, 139, 172
Chaghatay khanate, 145, 146, 154, 160, 167, 179–180, 181, 206, 236, 281, 308
Chaghatay language or literature, xii, 182, 253, 274, 289. *See also* Kaidu; Timur; Timurids
Charlemagne, 11, 58, 66, 72, 73, 209, 250, 263, 296; Aachen, 73, 83; and Byzantine Empire, 12, 58, 66, 73, 209; and Harun al-Rashid, 72, 73; Einhard, 263; empire, 72; Merovingians, 296; Pepin (Carloman, of Italy), 73; Pepin the Short, 72; Roncevalles, 72. *See also* Abul Abbas; Franks
Chen Cheng, 236, 301
China, 5, 6, 7, 8, 9, 11, 12, 14, 15, 27, 32, 34, 36, 43, 44, 45, 46, 47, 49–50, 52, 53, 56, 58, 72, 75, 76, 79, 80, 101, 103, 104, 107, 109, 111, 115, 116, 118, 120, 122, 123, 126, 127, 133, 134, 134–135, 136, 137, 141, 143, 144, 145, 146, 148, 150, 151, 152, 153, 155, 156, 160, 176, 181, 188, 192, 193, 204, 205, 211, 212, 215, 216, 217, 219, 233, 235, 236, 243,

248, 250, 252, 254, 255, 256, 257, 263, 264, 265, 266, 275, 278, 281, 283, 292, 305, 309, 312, 313, 314; and Abbasids, 9, 52, 55, 72, 76, 79, 80; and Buddhism, 27, 52, 54, 72, 76, 78–79, 205, 211–212, 252, 255, 256, 292; and Christianity, 52, 77, 141; and Muslims, 49, 78, 236, 265, 275, 293; and Sogdians, 48, 52, 56, 58, 78, 152, 292; and Tagbach, 49; and Tibet, 11, 13, 52, 76, 78–79, 80, 108, 109, 133, 137, 205, 211, 234, 252, 277–278, 296; and Xiongnu, 6, 14, 43, 44, 45, 46–48, 53, 58, 210, 248; and Turks, xx, 9, 14, 34, 43, 52, 58, 78, 78–79, 103–104, 118, 157, 263, 292, 296; Chang'an/Xi'an, 143, 148, 155, 277; Gansu province, 8, 44, 79, 109, 236, 252, 278; Grand Canal, 143; Great Wall, 53, 79, 101, 274, 276, 277, 278; Hangzhou, 138, 146; Kaifeng, 111, 114, 115, 120, 236; Luoyang, 54, 78; Ningxia province, 17, 79, 109; population, 7, 72, 125, 157–158; Shaanxi province, 8, 53, 143; tian, 36. *See also* Beijing; Canton; Confucianism; Hangzhou; porcelain; silk; Zheng He; Shang dynasty; Zhou dynasty; Qin; Han; Northern Wei; Sui; Tang; Kitan; Jin; Song; Yuan; Ming; Qing empires

Charles University, 225. *See also* Prague

Chinese language or script, 4, 5, 13, 27, 36, 44, 49, 53, 54, 80, 151, 243, 248, 250, 252, 264, 265, 277, 313

Chinggis Khan, 13, 16, 43, 101–122, 123, 125, 133, 138, 141–142, 145, 154, 172, 182, 190, 277, 286, 287, 289, 308; and religion, 115, 203, 204–205; as Temujin, 16, 101, 106, 119; spirit, 116, 180, 181, 206. *See also* Borte; Chinggisids; Jamukha; Mongols; *Secret History of the Mongols*

Chinggisids, 120, 122, 125, 126, 127, 134, 135, 146, 153, 159, 160, 172, 176, 180, 194, 263, 264, 282, 285, 289, 293; hatred of Xixia, 264; principle of succession, 277. *See also Altan Debter*; Jochids; Toluids; *Secret History of the Mongols*

chivalry, 169; *furusiyya*, 169

Christianity or Christians, xvii, 4, 23, 28, 28–29, 30, 31, 32, 33, 35, 50, 52, 58, 65–66, 70, 71, 72, 75, 77, 80, 86, 88, 89, 90, 94, 95, 112, 122, 124, 146, 170–171, 184, 185, 188, 192, 205, 207, 209, 211, 212, 213, 215, 220, 223, 226, 228, 247, 250, 256, 295, 296, 305, 311, 312; Anabaptism, xi, 227; Catholicism (Latinate), 58, 72, 73, 80; Coptic, 66, 208; exarchate, 66; heresy, 66, 70, 87, 216, 223; Holy Trinity, 32, 206, 215; in the Islamic world, 71, 73, 112, 139, 140, 144, 150, 170, 186, 190, 208, 215, 216, 222, 234, 239, 240–241, 250, 259, 309; Jesus, 28, 29, 32, 35, 66, 70, 222, 239; Nestorian and/or Central Asian, 77, 80, 89, 96, 105, 141, 206, 207, 220, 241, 252; Orthodox (Greciate), 73–74, 75, 80, 86, 90, 96, 177, 240; patriarchate, 66, 70, 73, 75, 140, 177, 190, 241, 247, 250, 282, 286, 295, 297; Paul, 209; Russia, 173, 177, 238, 282, 295; Thomas., 32, 203. *See also* Augustine of Hippo; Abelard; Bible; Cathars; Crusades; Gnosticism; Greek patriarchate; Hus; John of Plano Carpini; Luther; Makuria; millet; monasticism; predestination; Prester John; Rabban Sauma; Rubruck; popes/papacy; Waldensians; Wycliffe

college (academic), 209, 210, 211, 220, 253. *See also* monasteries

collegial rule (political), 49, 115, 144, 185; khuriltai, 117; Mongol, 116, 205; Ottoman, 190, 242; Russian, 74, 174; Seljuk, 91

Confucianism, 29, 54, 77, 80, 124, 142, 160, 205, 207, 211, 255, 264, 265, 286; neo-Confucianism, 212–213, 255; in Korea, 264, 280

consciousness, 26, 32, 210, 212, 216, 297

Constantine I, 29, 57, 65, 66, 73, 205, 250

Constantinople, 58, 65, 66, 68, 70, 71, 73, 74, 75, 86, 90, 114, 136, 149, 150, 173, 177, 183, 185, 206, 208, 209, 217, 294, 307, 310; academic nexus, 209, 262; as "New Rome", 65, 183, 295–296; Konstantiniyye, 183, 185, 192, 193,

195, 241, 250, 259, 290, 293, 295, 309.
  See also Byzantine Empire
Copernicus, 150, 166, 218, 312
Copts. See Christianity
cosmology, 25, 30, 70, 203, 209, 212, 214,
  215, 216, 220, 222, 228
cotton, 9, 15, 104, 112, 145, 150, 156,
  169–170, 256, 280, 283
Crimea, 154, 178, 185, 190, 194, 281, 285,
  293, 295, 309; Kaffa, 154, 170
Croatia, 87, 283
Crusades or Crusaders, 85; Balkan, 183;
  Baltic, 178, 282; Levantine, 89, 135,
  141, 168, 169, 170, 172, 173, 183, 215,
  239; Cathar, 224; Waldensian, 225

Dai Viet, 137, 145, 146, 211, 252, 279,
  280, 297; Champa, 145, 279
Damascus, 68, 69, 140, 147, 149, 168, 176,
  308. See also Syria
Daoism, 29, 54, 78, 124, 141, 205, 211,
  212, 252
dar al-Islam, 90, 190, 207, 295
dar al-Harb, 90. See also "peoples of the
  book"
darkhan. See taxation
Delhi sultanate, 89, 94, 168, 181, 182, 212,
  286, 289. See also Mughals
demiurge, 25, 34, 87, 222. See also
  gnosticism; Plato; Satan;
  Zoroastrianism Ahriman
Descartes, René, 312–313
divination, 35, 193, 205. See also prophecy
dogs, 15, 134, 154; words for, 4
Druze, 190, 240
Dunhuang, 8, 252

Eastern Europe, 43, 72, 86, 168, 176, 193,
  194, 228, 242, 263; and Bulgars, 72, 86;
  and Byzantine Empire, 73, 86; and
  Charlemagne, 73; and Ottomans, 193,
  193–195; Thirty Years War, 229. See
  also Bohemia; Bulgars; Serbia
Egypt, 6, 12, 30, 32, 34, 46, 57, 66, 69, 70,
  85, 111, 123, 135, 139; Cairo, 140, 168,
  170, 171, 209, 294
Elizabeth, 283, 310, 311
emir/amir or emirate, 69, 72, 74, 209

Eurasia definition, 3–4, 6, 16, 16–17;
  periodization, 17
Eurasian exchange core, 6–7, 10, 34, 205
Europe or Europeans, xvii, 4, 7, 9, 12, 16,
  34, 43, 48, 57, 58, 68, 71, 72, 73, 74,
  80, 85, 193, 195, 203–204, 206, 209,
  214, 216, 217–218, 219, 220, 223, 225,
  226, 227–228, 238, 248, 251, 253, 254,
  256, 258, 259, 261, 262, 263, 277, 282,
  286, 294, 307, 309–310, 311; alienation
  from Eurasia, 305–308, 309, 314; and
  "idea of science", 218–219; Alps, 87,
  225, 226, 228, 307; Danube River, 58,
  67, 121, 122; Muslim, 72, 258, 260;
  periodization, 6, 17, 305. See also
  Britain; Eastern Europe; Ireland;
  France; Germany; religious dissidence;
  Spain; Sweden

Fang Xiaoru, 265–266, 273, 292
finance, 33, 71, 94, 123, 155, 234, 242,
  276, 285, 316; bookkeeping, 96, 150,
  159, 242. See also joint-stock
  companies; merchants; taxation
Finno-Ugric languages and cultures, 34, 73
Firdawsi, 246, 288, 289. See also
  Shahnameh
fire (religious and ideological meaning),
  24, 24–25, 34, 249
France, 59, 74, 141, 184, 194, 195, 205,
  206, 209, 223, 225, 256, 258, 259, 306,
  309; St Denis, 124, 131. See also
  Charlemagne; Francis I; Franks; Louis
  IX; Paris
Francis I, 259, 309
Franks, 9, 58, 66, 68, 72, 73, 74, 80, 86, 87,
  108, 225, 250, 263, 293. See also
  Roman Empire, Frankish
Frederick II, 167, 171, 286, 298, 312
furusiyya. See chivalry

Galland, Antoine, 307
Gandhara, 7, 75, 152, 209, 210, 211, 217
gazi/ghazi, 85, 90, 118, 170, 181, 185, 199,
  290; anachronistic use, xiii
Georgia or Georgians, 89, 111, 120, 122,
  123, 139, 247, 284, 293; kings or
  kingdoms, 111, 122, 123

324 *Index*

Germans or Germany, 8, 184, 205, 229, 247, 250, 258, 283; Mainz, 258; Nuremberg, 225; Saxony, 124. *See also* Charlemagne: Aachen; Frankish empire; Goths
Germanic languages, 4, 13, 247, 258
Ghaznavid sultanate, 85, 88–89, 90, 91, 94, 96, 139, 237, 239, 246, 253, 288, 290, 305. *See also* Firdawsi,Shahnameh
Ghurids, 111, 113
Gibbon, Edward, 180, 203–204, 229
Gibraltar/Calpe, 68
gnosticism, 30–33, 87, 95, 212, 216, 218, 220, 222, 223–224, 225, 229; and Buddhism, 30, 31, 32–33, 212, 222; and Islam, 29–30, 32, 212, 216, 220, 222, 227; and Judaism, 222; Christian, 30–32, 87, 95, 212, 216, 222, 223; Manichean, 32, 215, 222. *See also* Christianity; Manicheanism; Plato; Zoroastrianism
Gokturk empire, 43, 51–52, 54, 55, 57, 58, 89, 102, 244, 288, 296; and Khazars, 58, 89; and Sogdians, 52, 54, 57, 58, 89; and Uighurs, 51, 52, 58, 89, 102
Golden Horde. *See* Jochid khanate
Goryeo, 79, 145, 235, 248, 257, 264, 280. *See also* Korea
Goths or Gothic language, 48, 58, 66, 250; Ostrogoths, 66; Visigoths, 68
grain, 4, 6, 15, 45, 93, 125, 126, 134, 136, 143, 147, 158, 159, 160, 169, 277, 280; millet, 44, 103, 109, 141; sorgham, 109, 278; wheat, 278
Greece or Greeks, 9, 33, 34, 68, 184, 206, 239, 244, 263; and the Ottomans, 185, 187, 190, 191, 192, 193, 208, 241–242, 284, 294; civilization and influence, 4, 13, 20, 31, 47, 50, 52, 91, 182, 243, 248, 290, 305, 307; mathematics or science, 7, 13, 71, 95, 136, 150, 151, 193, 217, 219, 311; patriarchate, 66, 70, 75, 140, 190, 241, 250, 295; philosophy, 28, 71, 136, 208, 209–210, 213, 216, 219. *See also* Alexander the Great; Alexander Romance; Aristotle; Byzantine Empire; Christianity: Orthodox; Plato

Greek language or script, xviii, 4, 30, 36, 65, 70, 72, 86, 90–91, 171, 185, 208, 238, 243, 245, 247, 251, 259, 261, 262, 293
Guan Hanqing, 248
Gumilev, Lev, 82
Guo Shoujing, 151
Gupta empire, 50. *See also* India
Guyuk, 120, 120–122, 123, 124–125, 126, 133, 135

hagiography, 88, 247, 250
halo, 31
Han empire, 4, 11, 12, 44, 45, 46, 47, 53, 54, 65, 211, 235, 256, 297
han (identity), xiii, 233, 234, 237
Hanafite legal school, 90, 190, 208, 216; Abu Hanifa, 90. *See also* dar al-Islam
Hapsburg dynasty, 175, 193, 194, 195, 227, 283, 307, 309–310. *See also* Balkans; Holy Roman Empire; Hungary
Harun al-Rashid, 72, 73
Heaven, 35–36, 51, 115, 122, 148, 170, 286–287, 290, 293, 307; as the sky, 35–36, 204; Blue Heaven, xix; mandate of Heaven, 293. *See also* tngri
Hebrews or Hebrew language, 30, 34, 35, 239, 259
Henry VIII, 310
Hephthalites, 49, 50, 51–52, 57, 89; language, 50; Var, 50; White Huns, 50
Herat, 8, 69, 114, 182, 236, 275
heresy, 29, 32, 33, 66, 67, 70, 87, 88, 203, 206, 214, 215, 221, 224, 225, 226. *See also* Abelard; Bruno; Cathars; ibn Sina; Suhrawardi
Herodotus, 47, 307
Hideyoshi, 281
Himalayas, 6, 8, 76, 133
Hindu Kush, 13
Hinduism, 23, 24, 26, 31, 50, 67, 226, 256; Agni, 24; Indra, 24, 31; Vedas, 24, 32
Hodgson, Marshall, 299
Holy Roman Empire, 172, 175, 185, 227, 296; and Thirty Years' War 227–228
horses, 6, 9–13, 15, 16, 24, 35, 44, 45, 47, 50, 56, 93, 109, 113, 114, 115, 117, 123, 125, 138, 141, 146, 148, 149, 152,

153, 156, 158, 169, 182, 185, 204, 205, 243, 278; and art, 93, 255; and China, 6, 9, 11–12, 14, 15, 44, 45, 47, 48, 50, 54, 56, 109, 115, 125, 137, 138, 146, 148, 149, 152, 153, 156, 158, 205, 243, 248, 255, 278, 279; and Mongolia, 4, 9, 12, 14, 44, 45, 47, 50, 54, 56, 109, 115, 123, 137, 146, 148, 243, 278; and Korea, 115, 280; and myth or religion, 12–13, 24; and nomads, xix, 9, 11–12, 14, 19, 44, 47, 156, 243; and Tibet, 11, 109, 278; and war, 4, 10, 12–13, 45, 47, 93, 137, 138, 141, 148, 153, 280; breeds, 10–12, 15, 278; carts, xx, 4, 6, 103; cavalry, 12, 16, 44, 58, 123, 135, 137, 138, 148, 281; chariot, 10, 12, 36, 38; equids, 4, 10; riding or racing, 54, 135, 205, 239, 248; shooting arrows from horseback, 10, 57, 148, 186; words for, 4. *See also* Alexander the Great; chivalry; Indo-Europeans; trade roads

Hungary, 57, 121, 122, 174, 176, 184, 185, 225, 254, 263, 283, 296, 297, 307; and Mongols, xv, 121, 122, 174, 176, 258, 283, 297; and Ottomans, 184–185, 263, 283, 296, 307; Magyars, 57, 71, 73, 74, 86, 225

Huns, 16, 48, 57, 66, 71, 173; Attila, 48, 263. *See also* Hephthalites:White Huns

Hus, Jan, 226–227, 251, 259

ibn Fadlan, 74
ibn Rushd (Averroes), 181, 214, 217, 220
ibn Sina (Avicenna), 216–217, 219, 220–221, 246, 312
idealism, 28, 212, 214, 215, 217, 218, 220, 222, 224, 225, 226, 226–227, 228, 266, 313; as used in this book, xi, 227. *See also* Augustine of Hippo; ibn Sina; Komensky; Lu Xiangshan; Plato; Suhrawardi; Wang Yangming

Ilkhanate, 57, 136, 138–141, 146, 147, 149, 151, 153, 154, 155, 157, 158–160, 167, 169, 170, 177, 180, 181, 182, 185, 190, 192, 193, 207–208, 213, 221, 222, 223, 238, 239, 240, 244, 249, 253, 254, 256, 258, 262, 263, 285, 288, 289, 290, 293, 297; and Chaghataids, 139, 146, 154, 160, 167, 179–180, 180, 182, 206, 253, 289; and France, 141, 206; and Jochids, 138, 140, 146, 160, 167, 170, 177, 179, 185, 206, 258, 285, 297; and Mamluks, 139, 140–141, 147, 160, 167, 169, 170, 185, 190, 206, 208, 238, 239, 253, 256, 263, 285, 289, 293; and *Shahnameh*, 288–290; and Timurids, 57, 141, 180, 182, 185, 192, 193, 223, 249, 253, 254, 263, 289, 293

"ilkhan", 138, 162. *See also* Bolad Chingsang; Gazan; Hulagu; Nasir al-Din Tusi; Rashid al-Din; Sauma; Toluids

illuminationism, 220–221, 222. *See also* ibn Sina; Suhrawardi

Inalcik, Halil, 199

India or Indians, 7, 8, 12, 13, 24, 26, 27, 28, 29, 31, 32, 33, 43, 50, 52, 67, 71, 76, 77, 85, 89, 90, 94, 107, 111, 113, 120, 136, 137, 139, 147, 148, 151, 182, 191, 209, 210, 213, 216, 217, 218, 219, 245, 247, 253, 284, 307, 309, 312; and Hephthalites, 50, 89; artistic, literary, or political influence, 50, 139, 209, 216, 247, 312; Ganges, 89; Jainism, 24; Kerala, 29; mathematics, astronomy, science, logic, philosophy, 151, 209, 210, 213, 216, 306. *See also* Buddhism; Delhi sultanate; Eurasian exchange core; Ghurids; Hindu Kush; Hinduism; Mauryan; Mughals; Pakistan; *rajputs*

Indo-European groups or languages, 6, 10, 24, 35, 36, 43, 49, 288

Indo-Iranian groups or languages, 28, 36, 91

Innocent III, 29, 34, 224

Iran, 4, 6, 8, 9, 11, 13, 25, 27, 28, 29, 31, 32, 35, 46, 66, 68, 69, 71, 79, 85, 89, 91, 94, 104, 111, 118, 120, 125, 133, 135, 136, 138, 139, 140, 144, 146, 147, 149, 150, 155–157, 158–159, 160, 167, 172, 176, 181, 182, 185, 190, 192, 195, 205, 207, 209, 219, 222, 240, 241, 243, 244, 245, 246, 247, 250, 251, 254, 263, 275, 284, 288–290, 307, 309; and Azerbaijan, 139, 149, 155, 167, 185, 243, 245, 284; and Mongol invasions, 135–136, 157; and Transoxiana, 13, 52,

69, 70, 94, 111, 118, 120, 133, 135, 139, 150, 167, 175, 182, 222, 245, 246; influence over Central Asia, 46, 52, 57, 79, 88; Mt. Alamut/ Alburz range, 135, 150, 220, 289; Nishapur, 69, 222; Pars, 57. *See also* Abbasids; Achaemenids; Afghanistan; Baghdad; Khwarazm; padishah; Safavids; Sasanians; Sart; Seljuks; shah; shahanshah; Sogdian people or languages; Tabriz; Transoxiana; Zoroastrianism

Iranian languages or cultures, xix, 4, 7, 11, 13, 28, 30, 34, 43, 47, 49, 52, 57, 58, 70, 71, 91, 101, 102, 112, 117, 157, 175, 246, 254, 288, 289. *See also* Alans; Kurds; Persian language and culture; Sarmatians; Sogdians; Tajiks

Iraq, 9, 27, 68, 89, 104, 120, 138, 139, 144, 147, 155, 157, 160, 167, 185, 207, 209, 219, 222, 240, 245, 253, 284, 309. *See also* Baghdad; Iran

Ireland, 46, 259

irgen, 107–108. *See also ulus*

Iron Age, 6–7, 46

ironworking, 7, 10, 16, 52, 93, 123. *See also* blacksmiths or smithing; mining

Islam, xix, 4, 11, 13, 23, 29–30, 31, 32, 58, 65, 68, 70, 71, 77, 78, 80, 85, 88, 89, 90, 91, 94, 96, 105, 111, 123, 139–140, 150, 151, 160, 170, 171, 177, 180, 181, 186, 188, 190, 193, 205, 206, 208, 209, 210, 211, 212, 213, 214, 215, 216, 219, 220, 221–222, 226, 227, 228, 236, 237, 238, 239–240, 245, 246, 249, 250, 251, 252, 255, 256, 259, 263, 290, 295, 296, 305, 307, 312, 314; and gnosticism, xi, 32, 212, 216, 221, 222, 227; *djinn*, 35, 214; Ismailis, 127, 133, 135, 150, 190, 208, 220, 289; Shi'ism, 68, 69–70, 71, 85, 90, 95, 139–140, 170, 190, 208, 220, 240, 262; Sunnism, 68, 69, 71, 80, 85, 88, 89, 90, 92, 94–96, 118, 139–140, 144, 170, 179, 181, 185, 190, 207, 239. *See also* dar al-Islam; gazi; Muhammad; Quran; Sufism

Istanbul. *See* Constantinople: Konstantiniyye

Italian language, 13, 171, 206, 260, 306, 313

Italy or Italian people, 59, 171, 172, 259; Muslims, 171. *See also* Polo; Machiavelli; Rome; Sicily; Venetian empire

Ivan I, 178

Ivan III, 282, 286, 295

Ivan IV, 283, 287, 293, 297

Jalal al-Dim Rumi, 96, 222, 245, 246

Jamukha, 106, 286

Janissaries. *See* Ottomans

Japan, 17, 27, 75, 79, 145, 153, 211, 212, 250, 251, 255, 257, 276, 277, 280, 281, 297; Shinto, 76; threatened by Mongols, 145, 153, 280–281, 297. *See also* Hideyoshi; Shotoku

Jerusalem, 65, 171

Jin (Jurchen) empire, 79, 104, 105, 106, 109, 111, 113, 115, 118, 119, 120, 126, 138, 141, 143, 148, 151, 234–235, 263, 264, 292. *See also* China

Jochi, 116, 119, 172

Jochid khanate, 127, 135, 138, 140, 141, 146, 154, 160, 170, 172, 175–178, 179, 181, 185, 194, 206–207, 238, 243, 254, 258, 281–282, 285, 287, 293, 297; "Mongol yoke", 176. *See also* Alexander Nevskii; Batu; Berke; Moscow; Sarai

John of Plano Carpini, 122, 124

joint-stock companies, 283, 310; East India, 283; Levant, 283; Moscow, 283, 310; Turkey, 310; Venice, 310

Joseon, xx, 154, 235, 264, 280–281. *See also* Korea

Judaism or Jews, xi, 28, 30, 31, 33, 58, 69, 71, 80, 89, 118, 124, 160, 208, 211, 222, 225, 226, 236, 239, 257, 259; Ladinos, 192, 259. *See also* Khazars; Torah

Jurchens, 79, 104, 105, 108, 234–235, 264, 265, 275, 280. *See also* Jin empire; Qing empire

Justinian, 30, 66

Juvayni, Ata-Malik, 136, 263, 289; family, 289

Kaidu, 179–180

Kalka River (battle), 111, 174

Kangxi Emperor of China (Xuanye), 311, 313, 314
Kara Kitai, 80, 105, 106, 109–111, 111, 113, 115, 118, 139, 172, 182, 205, 207; Balasagun, 111. *See also* Kitan; Kuchluk
Karakhanids, 80, 85, 88, 109, 111, 112, 113, 115, 118, 172, 182, 238, 245, 258; Karluks, 53, 55, 237, 245
Karakorum, 123–125, 134, 134–135, 146, 147, 148, 173, 175, 176, 179, 205, 206, 209, 277, 289; compared to St Denis,; Erdene Zuu, 135; Ordu-Balikh, 102–103, 105, 123, 147, 292; silver fountain, 131. *See also* Ordu-Balikh
Karakoyunlu, 284, 289
Kashgar, 8, 55, 112
Kashgari, Mahmud, 245
Kazakhs, 106
Kazakhstan, 8, 90, 101, 295; steppe, xii
khaghan, 49–51, 52, 54, 58, 59, 68, 73, 75, 89, 108, 119, 122, 123, 124, 125, 126, 127, 133, 134, 135, 138, 141, 144, 148, 154, 174, 176, 285–286, 292, 293; Avar, 58, 59, 68, 72; Bulgar, 58, 59, 73, 174, 207, 241; Gokturk, 52, 54; Hephthalite, 50, 51; Khazar, 75, 174; Mongol, 143, 205; Northern Yuan, 277; Ottoman, 183; Rouran, 49; Tagbach, 49; Tang, 54; Uighur, 51, 52, 56; Yuan, 134, 138, 141, 143, 144, 145, 146, 154, 277, 292. *See also* Guyuk; khan; Kublai; Mongge; Ogedei
Khan-Balikh—. *See* Beijing: Dadu
Khazars, 58–59, 73–75, 80, 86, 89, 174, 175, 207, 282; and Judaism, 58, 80, 89, 207; influence on the Rus, 73, 74–75, 83
Khwarazm or Khwarazmians, 87, 91, 101–111, 112, 113–114, 115, 116, 118, 119, 120, 123, 133, 136, 179, 236, 237, 289
Khwarazm shah, 91, 112, 113, 118, 237; Jalal al-Din, 120. *See also* Sart, Bukhara, Samarkand
Kiev (city), 59, 74, 111, 121, 124, 136, 173–174
Kievan federation, 59, 74, 75, 111, 121, 122, 173, 174, 176–178, 281, 293, 296; grand prince, 74. *See also* Novgorod; Rus; Russia; Ukraine
Kipchak Horde. See Jochid khanate
Kipchak/Cuman, 71, 111, 121, 167, 170, 172, 173, 174, 181, 253, 282, 283; steppe, xii. *See also* Jochids; Mamluks
Kipchak language or literature, 253, 289
Kircher, Athanasius, 313
Kirghiz, 103, 111, 113
Kirghizstan, 111
Kitan (Liao) empire, 79, 80, 104, 105, 107, 109, 118, 143, 148, 246–247, 252, 264, 265; Kitans, 78–79, 104, 109, 113, 116, 141. *See also* Kara Kitai; Yelu Chucai
Kitan language or script, 141, 252
Komensky, Jan (Comenius),– 227
Korea or Koreans, 9, 13, 27, 75, 79, 108, 115, 120, 122, 123, 127, 133, 134, 137, 138, 145–146, 150, 151, 205, 211, 234–235, 252, 255, 263, 276, 277, 280, 281; and the Yuan, 134, 145, 146, 151, 234–235, 248, 255, 263, 277, 280; printing, 150, 255, 256, 256–257. *See also* Goryeo; Joseon; Confucianism
Korean language or literature, 49, 243, 248, 264; *Samguk sagi*, 264; *Yeongbi ocheonga*, 264
Kubadiyan (Tajikistan), 50
Kublai, 126–127, 133–138, 138, 141–146, 148, 151, 153–154, 159, 179, 188, 193, 204, 205–206, 248, 255, 265, 274, 276, 277, 279, 280, 286, 287, 292, 293. *See also* Beijing: Dadu; Bolad Chingsang; Hulagu; Mongolia: Shangdu; Toluids; Yuan
Kuchluk, 109, 111, 118, 205, 206. *See also* Naimans; Kara Kitai
Kurds, xix, 57, 208, 289

Ladino. *See* Judaism
Latin language, 4, 13, 30, 36, 43, 66, 68, 70, 71, 74, 171, 206, 208, 214, 217, 225, 227, 247, 250, 252. *See also* Bible; translation
Leibniz, Gottfried Wilhelm, 313–314
Levant, 28, 29, 31, 33, 35, 57, 65, 68, 70, 80, 82, 85, 89, 141, 146, 167, 168, 169, 170–171, 172, 209, 220, 227, 233, 239, 242, 247, 283, 284, 285, 293, 309, 310;

Tyre, 8. *See also* Jerusalem; Palestine; Syria
Liao empire. *See* Kitan
Lindner, Rudi Paul, 199
literacy, 5, 49, 80, 247, 249, 251, 285, 314; in Arabic, 251–252; in Chinese, 49, 213; in Greek, 247
Lithuania, 277, 297
Liu Bingzhong, 142, 144
Lu Xiangshan, 212, 221, 222, 267
Luther, Martin, 226, 259

Machiavelli, Niccolo, xx, 305–307, 309–310, 314; *Discourses on Livy*, 306; *The Prince*, 306, 309
Mackinder, Halford, 3
Magyar. *See* Hungary
Makuria, 170, 250
Mamluk sultanate, 167–172, 185, 190, 191, 193, 194, 206, 208, 219, 237, 239, 245, 247, 253, 256, 271, 284, 286, 293, 305, 309; and Sicily, 171–172; Circassian sultans, 168; Mongol sultans, 168; usage in this book, xii, 135. *See also* Baybars; Crusades: Levantine; Kipchak Turks
mamluk (status), 85, 88–90, 93, 94, 111, 139, 140–141, 147, 160, 289; usage in this book, xii. *See also* Delhi Sultanate; Mamluk sultanate
Manchuria, xii, 48, 49, 79, 101, 104, 106, 109, 126, 141, 235, 266
Manfred, 172, 286
Manicheanism, 23, 29, 32, 33, 50, 52, 56, 59, 69, 77, 80, 94, 105, 112, 207, 215, 222, 239, 252, 254; Mani, 29–30, 33, 254. *See also* gnosticism; Islam; Sufism
maps/cartography, 151, 208, 235, 273
Marlowe, Christopher, 180, 308
mathematics, 7, 13, 71, 95, 96, 136, 150, 182, 193, 208, 209, 210, 213, 214, 217, 219, 222, 312, 314; Abbasid or Seljuk, 95, 136, 150, 182, 217, 222; Chinese, 150, 151, 265; Greek, 13, 95, 193; Indian, 71, 213; Transoxiana, 71, 136, 150. *See also* Descartes; Guo Shoujing; Omar Khayyam; Nasir al-Din Tusi
Mauryan empire, 4, 27, 65, 67, 68, 297. *See also* India

medicine, 5, 71, 116, 144, 147, 151, 187, 243; pharmacology, 7, 151, 217, 219
meditation, 26, 28, 30, 33, 114, 211, 222
Mediterranean Sea, 3, 6, 8, 29, 50, 57, 68, 154, 172, 183, 185, 194, 233, 284; Adriatic Sea, 72–73
Mehmet I, 185
Mehmet II, 183, 185, 190, 193, 208, 223, 240, 290, 291, 293, 309, 311; as simultaneous ruler, 291, 293
mercenaries, 57, 58, 74, 80, 85, 88, 89, 168, 310
merchants, 9, 13, 71, 77, 94, 96, 109, 113, 115, 124, 125, 145, 146, 149, 155, 157, 160, 169, 192, 195, 208, 252, 257, 262, 276, 284, 306, 310, 311, 313, 314; Sartic, 115, 149, 155. *See also* finance; joint-stock companies
Merkit, 105, 106–108, 119, 286
Mesopotamia, 25, 36, 258; Assyria, 49; Hittites, 291; Sumer or Sumerians, 36, 291; Gilgamesh, 36
metallurgy, 5, 6, 7, 153; bronze, 6; steel, 109. *See also* ironworking
migration, 6, 15, 35, 43, 87, 157, 168, 233, 244
millet (*millah*, doctrinal community), 239, 240–242, 243
Ming empire, xx, 120, 135, 141, 146, 151, 160, 179, 181, 212, 213, 234–237, 248, 255, 263–264, 264–266, 273–281, 282, 284, 287, 292–293, 305, 311, 315; and Japan, 255, 276, 277, 280–281; and Korea, xx, 235, 255, 264, 277, 280, 281; and Mongols, 146, 235, 264, 265, 273, 277–280, 293; and Jurchens (Manchus), 235, 264, 265, 266, 278, 280; and Vietnam, 279–280; Muslims, 142, 235–237, 265, 293; trade, 146, 235–237, 255, 265, 275, 277, 278. *See also* Chen Cheng; Huang Zongxi; Wang Yangming; Zheng He; Zhu Di
mining, 16, 34, 45, 109, 153, 273. *See also* blacksmiths
Mithraism, 29, 33, 65, 91
monasteries or monasticism, 33, 56, 67, 76, 77, 78, 88, 124, 135, 209, 211, 215, 218, 238, 247, 253; Buddhist, 33, 56, 67, 76, 77, 211; Christian, 33, 77, 88,

124, 209, 211, 214, 238, 247. *See also* colleges
Mongge (Mongke), xii, 120, 122, 124, 127, 133, 134, 138, 140, 151, 162, 204, 205, 209, 224; spelling, xii
Mongolia, 9, 12, 14, 16, 27, 43, 44, 45, 47, 48, 50, 51–52, 52, 54, 56, 79, 80, 101, 102, 103–104, 105, 106, 109, 111, 116, 119, 120, 124, 125, 136, 243, 254, 264, 277; Awarga, 111; Gobi Desert, 101, 105; Khentii mountains, 14, 116; Kherlen River, 43, 111, 116; Onon River, 14, 43; Orkhon Valley, 45, 52, 102, 103, 105, 123, 286, 292; Otuken, 34; Selengge River, 14; Shangdu, 134, 142, 148, 176, 205, 206. *See also* Gokturk; Karakorum; Kitan; Merkit; Naiman; Tatars; Uighur
Mongols, xix, xx, 5–6, 8, 14, 15, 16, 27, 43, 80, 90, 133–160, 168, 173, 174, 174–176, 176, 177, 178, 179, 181, 182, 185, 188, 191, 195, 240, 243, 250, 255, 257, 262, 263, 264, 265, 273, 274, 277, 278, 279, 280, 281, 282, 283, 285–286, 288, 289, 292, 297; conquests,– 101, 127; Great Mongol *Ulus* (State), 277; Uriangkhad, 108. *See also* Chinggisids; Ilkans; Jochids; Merkit; Naimans; Ongguts; Tatars; Toluids; Yuan
Mongolian language or script, 4, 36, 48, 49, 79, 108, 109, 112, 172, 203, 204, 205, 206, 207, 208, 213, 234, 235, 236, 247, 248, 264
Montesquieu (Charles de Secondat), 308, 309
Moscow, 149, 176, 182–183, 194, 238, 254, 281–282, 282, 283, 287, 295, 310. *See also* Alexander Nevskii,Ivan I, Ivan II, Ivan III, Jochids, Muscovy
Mughals, 112, 179, 181, 182, 192, 207, 213, 223, 237, 249, 253, 284, 293, 306, 314; Shah Jahan, 181. *See also* Babur; Timurids
Muhammad, 30, 35, 68, 69, 85, 204, 239, 254
Muscovy, 281–285, 287, 295, 296, 315
music and theater, 5, 52, 54, 134, 144, 150, 155, 172, 192, 193, 222, 243, 248, 249
Myanmar, 145

mythology, 12, 13, 25, 28, 34, 35, 51, 141, 217, 244, 248, 254, 295, 296; chthonic deities, 23. *See also* ancestor worship

Naimans, 105, 107, 108. *See also* Kuchluk
Nasr al-Din Tusi, 139, 150, 220, 246, 311, 312. *See also* astronomy, Hulagu, Ptolemy
Nepal, 76, 123
Newton, Isaac, 218, 227
Nizam al-Mulk, 90; *Siyasatnameh* (Book of Government), 305
nomads, xviii–xx, 6, 14, 15–16, 34, 36, 44, 47, 57, 79, 104, 156, 169, 179, 207, 239, 249, 312; nomadism, xviii, 14, 158; "nomad algorithm", 6, 18; nomadology, xviii, xxi; pastoralism, 7, 10, 12, 14, 43, 44, 45, 47, 57, 103, 104, 106, 109, 158, 181, 233
North Africa, 6, 11, 12, 68, 70, 73, 74, 85, 90, 96, 136, 167, 169, 171, 192, 195, 207, 209, 220, 233, 242, 251, 253, 260, 284, 309, 310; Fez, 69, 209; Mogadishu, 236, 275; Tunisia, 69, 170, 185. *See also* Egypt
North America, 6, 14, 283
Northern Wei empire, 49, 54, 79, 80, 192, 292; Yuwen lineage, 54. *See also* Tagbach; Sarbi
novels, 247, 248, 312. *See also* music and theater

Ogedei, 116–122, 122, 123, 125–126
Ogedeid dynasty, 125, 127, 133, 179, 180. *See also* Kaidu
Oguz Turks, 13, 58, 89, 91, 111, 168, 184, 186, 244–245. *See also* Akkoyunlu; Seljuks; Ottomans
Oguz language or script, 253
Omar Khayyam, 95, 222, 246
Ongguts, 105, 108, 277. *See also* Shatuo Turks
Onogurs, 58
optics, 193, 214, 217, 219
ordo (estate), 47, 51, 79, 102, 104, 107, 116, 134, 233; soslovie, 238. *See also* *ulus*
Ottomans or Ottoman empire, xix, xx, 5, 43, 57, 85, 112, 167, 181, 184–195,

208, 223, 225, 237, 240–242, 243, 247, 253, 293, 294, 297, 315; and Balkans, 184, 185, 186, 247, 311; and Byzantine Empire, 183–185, 283, 293, 294–295; and Crimea, 194, 295; and England, 195, 310; and France, 194, 309; and Greece, 184, 187, 190, 191, 241, 242, 284, 294; and Hungary, 283; and Jochids, 194; and Levant, 172, 242, 284, 285, 293, 309, 310; and Machiavelli, 305, 306–307, 314; and Mamluks, 172, 185, 194, 263; and Muscovy, 194, 284, 285, 295; and North Africa, 185, 192, 195, 242, 253, 284, 309; and Safavids, 194, 263, 284, 311; and Timurids, 172, 308; and Venice, 172, 184, 185, 194; cities, 192; Edirne, 308; enmity with Hapsburgs, 193–195, 283, 296, 309–310; fratricide, 190; gunpowder weapons, 185; historiography, 290; Janissaries, 186, 187, 190, 192, 306; *kanun*, 190; militancy, 85, 185; music, 192–193; printing or sales of printed books, 259; trade, 191–192, 194, 310, 311. *See also* architecture; astronomy; Christianity: in Muslim lands; Christianity:patriarchate; dar al-Islam; Mehmet I; Mehmet II; millet; Oguz; Sufism; Suleiman I; Turkish language or script

padishah/padshah, 91, 170, 182, 183, 293
Pakistan, 50
Paleolithic, 23, 24, 102
Palestine. See Levant
Paris, 124, 174, 206, 209, 214, 215, 217, 218, 225, 262, 309
Pecheneg, 71, 73, 75
"peoples of the Book" (ahl al-dhimmi), 69, 90, 93, 207, 238, 249, 295
Persian Gulf, 29, 149, 155, 157, 185
Persian language and culture, 34, 57, 69, 70, 85, 88, 89, 90–91, 93, 96, 109, 112–113, 115, 118, 122, 135, 138, 139, 142, 147, 147–150, 155, 181, 182, 185, 192, 206, 216, 217, 220–221, 222, 237, 240, 245–247, 250, 251, 253, 289, 290, 293, 305–306, 307–308, 309; "Persian miniature", 263; use in this book, xii

Peter the Great, 295, 313
Phags-pa, 137
Philo Judaeus, 28
plague, 135, 154, 157, 170, 178
Plato, 28–29, 31, 209, 210, 212, 214, 215, 217, 218, 220, 221, 307; stereotype for Oriental scientism, 29, 307. *See also* Aristotle; ib Sina; Platonism
Platonism, xi, 30, 31; neo-Platonism, 214, 215, 222
Ptolemy, 149, 150, 193, 216
Poland, xv, 121, 122, 174, 225, 227, 282, 283, 293, 297
Polo, Marco, 13, 146, 148, 248, 260; *Il Milione* (Travels), 13, 260
popes/papacy, 66, 68, 70, 73, 122, 123, 124, 135, 141, 146, 170, 172, 184, 195, 206, 214, 224, 225, 226, 227, 286, 306
popular religion, xix, 29, 95, 223. *See also* Gnosticism; heresy; Sufism
porcelain, 109, 275
Portugal, 68, 185, 194, 276
Prague, 193, 225
predestination, 31, 32, 226
Prester John, 80, 141
printing, 5, 71, 75, 193, 249, 255, 256–261, 264, 273, 283, 288, 309; woodblock, 71, 150, 255, 256, 263, 288; mechanical/movable type, 193, 233, 256, 257–261, 264, 273, 283, 297, 309
Priscus, 48
prophecy or prophets, 29, 30, 34, 68, 181, 204, 213, 222, 227, 239, 263. *See also* Jesus; Mani; Muhammad; Sufism
Pyrenees, 209

Qin empire, 44, 46, 54
Qing empire, 213, 266, 278, 283, 293, 305, 311, 314
Quran, 30, 32, 90, 220, 221, 239, 249, 251, 254, 256, 259, 262, 263, 308; printed, 256, 259; translation, 253

rajputs, 89, 94
Rashid ad-Din, 139, 147, 154, 159, 160, 262–263, 286, 288, 289–290; *Jami al-tawarikh* (*Compendium of Chronicles*), 262, 286, 289–291. *See also* Bolad Chingsang; Gazan; Juvayni

rationalism, xvii, 95, 212–215, 216, 219, 220, 222, 223, 226, 227, 297, 311, 313; as used in this book, xi; See also idealism
religious conversion, 67, 69, 72, 73, 75, 86, 88, 89, 91, 93, 122, 140, 160, 177, 181, 185, 187, 206, 208, 216, 236, 237, 238, 239, 261
religious dissidence, 208, 212, 216, 227, 238, 250, 297
Roman empire, 4, 8, 47, 48, 57–58, 89, 108, 190, 248, 295; eastern, 65–66; Frankish, 66, 74; Holy, 172, 175, 184, 227, 296
Rome, 65–66, 73, 74, 124, 135, 141, 146, 150, 185, 193, 206, 209, 218, 225, 250, 293; "New Rome", 65–66, 183, 295–296
Romanovs, 263, 283, 293
Rouran, 14, 48, 49–52; language, 49
Russia or Russians, xx, 6, 10, 58, 108, 119, 125, 128, 140, 141, 167, 172, 173, 174, 176, 177, 178, 179, 181, 190, 192, 203, 205, 238, 243, 248, 258, 263, 282, 285, 293–296, 313, 314; "all the Rus", 282, 293; Rurik, 287; Rus, 58, 70, 73–75, 111, 115, 122, 123, 172, 173, 174–178, 238, 287, 293; Suzdal, 176; Tver, 176, 178, 282. *See also* Christianity: Russia; Kiev; Moscow; Muscovy; Novgorod; Romanovs; Ukraine; Volga River
Russian language or literature, 4, 49, 176, 178, 238, 283

Safavids, 147, 172, 182, 185, 190, 193, 241, 263, 284, 289, 305, 306, 307, 308, 309, 310, 311, 314; and Ottomans, 289, 305–307, 308–311, 314
Saladin, 168
Samanids, 85, 88, 216, 237, 246
Samarkand, 8, 9, 52, 114, 176, 182, 193, 257. *See also* Transoxiana; Sart
Sanskrit language or script, 4, 27, 36, 205, 211, 213, 252; Pali, 27, 252
"Saracen" meaning and allusions, xii, 167, 220
Sarbi language, 48–49, 54, 62, 211. *See also* Tagbach; Northern Wei empire
Sarmatian, xix, 48, 57

Sart, 112, 113–115, 120, 122, 126, 129, 143, 149, 151, 153, 155, 180, 191, 216, 235, 236, 246, 253, 289; Sartaghul, 112, 129. *See also* Tajik
Sasanian empire, 4, 50, 57, 58, 68, 70, 71, 157, 190, 205, 207, 246, 288, 289, 293; and "Persian", 57. *See also Shahnameh*
Satan, 25, 31, 203, 215, 222, 227
Sauma, Rabban, 141, 206, 209, 215, 217
Scandinavia, 12, 34, 74, 75, 173, 174; Denmark, 193, 258; Sweden, 282, 283. *See also* Varangians; Vikings; Russia: Rus
science. *See* astronomy; mathematics; medicine; optics
Secret History of the Mongols, 128, 286, 287
Seleucid empire, 4, 13, 70, 91, 205, 243, 245
Seljuk dynasty, individuals or period, 57, 89–91, 94–96, 111, 122, 136, 139, 168, 190, 225, 244, 244–245, 246, 247, 250, 253, 259, 288, 289, 290, 305, 312
Sejuk sultanate, 57, 89, 90, 94, 139, 150, 180, 182, 192, 193, 194, 207, 208, 214, 216, 222, 237, 238, 239, 240, 241, 243, 253, 288, 290, 293, 297
Seljuks of Rum, 94–96, 101, 120, 123, 147, 183, 184, 215, 225; Alp Arslan, 89; battle of Manzikert, 89. *See also* Oguz Turks; Omar Khayyam; Sufism
Serbia, 184, 241, 295; *Nomokanon*, 300
shahanshah, 49, 91. *See also padishah*
Shahnameh, 246, 288–289, 308
Shahrukh, 293
shamanism, 24, 34, 35, 52, 59, 76, 80, 87, 95, 96, 116, 117, 177, 180, 206–207, 220, 223, 240, 248, 249, 286; and Sufism, 96, 98, 223, 229
Shams ad-Din, 236
Shang dynasty, 12, 36
Shatuo Turks, 55–56, 78, 79, 104, 105. *See also* Ongguts
sheep, 6, 14, 106
Shotoku, 75
Siberia, 14, 16, 23, 34, 35, 43, 47, 79, 101, 134, 141, 143, 283, 293, 295
silk, 8, 9, 15, 53, 56, 71, 75, 111, 126, 141, 143, 145, 156, 170, 173, 245, 254, 261

"Silk Road(s)". *See* trade roads
Sima Guang, 305
Skythians, xix, 12, 47–48, 91, 173, 308; Saka, 47
slavery, 6, 9, 14–15, 24, 47, 51, 52, 56, 72, 75, 85, 93, 103, 111, 114, 133, 158, 159, 173, 187–188, 205, 206, 233, 235, 237, 264, 280, 307. *See also mamluk*
Slavic people or languages, 58, 75, 86, 87–88, 173, 185, 207, 241. *See also* Bulgars; Russia; Serbia
Sneath, David, xxii
Socrates, 28
Sogdians or Sogdian culture, 48, 52, 54, 56, 75, 89, 152; language and script, 52
Solomon, 36
Song empire, 79, 104, 107, 109, 115, 120, 122, 127, 133, 134, 135, 137, 138, 141, 143–144, 151, 152, 153, 154, 155, 157, 212, 213, 235, 243, 248, 255, 256, 257, 264, 273, 274, 279, 292, 305; and Kitan, 79, 80, 104, 109, 143, 265, 274, 292; and Xixia, 79, 80, 109, 115, 143, 264, 292; wars against Jin, 104, 109, 115, 120, 138, 143, 292; wars against Mongols, 79, 104, 107, 109, 115, 120, 122, 127, 133–134, 135–138, 143–144, 153. *See also* Confucianism: neo-Confucianism
Spain or Spaniards, 11, 68, 73, 170, 185, 194, 209, 241, 258, 259, 260, 261, 310, 311; inquisition, 192; Muslim, 69, 72, 73, 171, 209
Spanish language or literature, 259, 261. *See also* Cervantes
statuary, 13, 50, 75, 78, 102; Greek influence hypothesis, 20
Stepnayya kniga, 287
Sufism or Sufists, 30, 95–96, 97, 140, 190, 208, 222–223, 225, 245, 284, 290, 311. *See also* illuminism; Islam; Omar Khayyam; Rumi; Suhrawardi
Suhrawardi, 221–222
Sui empire, 54, 143, 192–193, 211
Suleiman I, 309, 310
sultan (title), 85, 89, 93, 139, 179, 184–185
Syria, 13, 32, 66, 68, 69, 70, 74, 85, 139, 140, 147, 168, 169, 170, 172, 184, 185, 219, 221, 237, 240; Aleppo, 8, 310; Antioch, 4, 170. *See also* Levanr; Mamluks; Ottomans
Syriac language or script, 52, 250, 252, 259

Tagbach, 48, 48–49, 52, 54, 79; as "China", 49. *See also* Sarbi; Northern Wei
Tajik. *See* Sart
Takla Makan
Tang empire, 9, 11, 16, 52, 54, 56, 58, 71, 72, 76–79, 80, 105, 106, 109, 117, 118, 143, 148, 149, 153, 192, 205, 211, 212, 244, 248, 292, 296; and Abbasids, 9, 52, 55, 59, 71–72, 76, 79, 80; and Buddhism, 9, 52, 54, 56, 75, 76–78, 79, 80, 105, 205, 211, 212, 292; and Tibet, 11, 52, 55, 72, 76, 78, 79, 80, 211, 248, 296; and Uighurs, 52, 54–56, 58, 72, 78, 105; civil war, 55–56, 72, 77–78. *See also* Tang Taizong Wu Zetian
Tang Taizong/Li Shimin
Tanggut. *See* Xixia
Tatars, 104, 106, 108, 238, 285
taxation, 5, 47, 52, 69, 73, 77, 80, 88, 90, 93, 94, 107, 117, 118, 125–126, 134, 139, 140, 141, 144, 149, 155, 156, 157, 158, 159, 160, 169, 170, 176, 178, 188, 190, 192, 205, 207, 215, 233, 234, 236, 238, 239, 242, 255, 281, 298, 314; darkhan, 52, 65, 117, 178; tax farming, 126, 155, 158
teahouses, 243, 245, 247; samovar/*authepsa*, 243; tea, 9, 56, 243, 278
Theodosius, 66
Tibet or Tibetans, 11, 52, 55, 72, 76, 78, 79, 80, 108, 109, 133, 137, 145, 218, 234, 235, 248, 277, 279, 296; Buddhism, 76, 206, 211, 252, 277, 293. *See also* Kublai; Phags-pa; Talas; Tang; Yuan; Xixia
Tibetan language or scripts, 13, 80, 205
Timur, 175, 178, 180–182, 185, 190, 193, 223, 236, 274, 278, 289, 308. *See also* Auspicious Conjunction; Marlowe; Timurids
Timurids, xix, 57, 141, 172, 179–182, 185, 192–194, 207, 208, 213, 223, 236, 249, 250, 253, 254, 263, 274, 278, 281–282, 284, 289, 293, 305, 308. *See also*

Babur, Chaghataids, Mughals, Shahrukh, Timur, Ulugh Beg
tngr, 36
Tolui, 116, 134
Toluids, 122, 133–160, 167, 169, 175, 177, 178, 206; and agriculture, 156–160; and other Chinggisids, 146, 172, 179; civil war, 134; historiography, 262, 286; information exchange, 134, 149, 153–154; interests in Tibet, 137; trade, 146, 149, 154. *See also* Chinggisids; Ilkhans; Jochids; *Secret History of the Mongols*; Timurids; Yuan
Torah, 30, 259, 263
trade roads, 7, 8–9, 33, 44, 48, 57, 77, 103, 105, 109–111, 113, 120, 124, 134, 146, 149, 155–156, 170, 175, 236, 236–237, 252, 277, 278, 282; camels, xx, 9, 109; caravans, 9, 14, 53, 94, 105, 112, 123, 147, 148, 149, 154. *See also yam*
translation, 13, 27, 250, 252, 259, 291, 312; Arabic to Chaghatay, 253; Arabic to Greek, 214; Arabic to Latin, 214, 217, 262, 305, 312; Greek to Turkish, 193; Greek to Arabic, 71, 214, 251, 305; Persian to Greek, 150; Chinese to Mongolian, 153; Italian to Persian, 306; Korean to Mongolian, 145; Latin to Bulgarian, 247; Latin to Czech, 247; Latin to English, 226; Latin to French, 225; Mongolian to Persian, 263, 286; Persian to Arabic, 288, 289, 305; Persian to Chaghatay, 289; Persian to Turkish, 288; Sanskrit to Chinese, 211
Transoxiana, 8, 13, 52, 55, 69, 70, 76, 89, 94, 96, 106, 109, 118, 120, 125, 133, 134, 139, 150, 167, 172, 175, 179, 181, 182, 207, 222, 245, 246, 253, 312; Amu Darya, 8; Syr Darya, 8, 89; Tashkent, 9, 52; Urgench (Konye-Urgench), 112, 114. *See also* Bukhara; Samarkand; Sart
Tulunids, 168
Tungusic peoples or languages, 34, 49
Turan, xx, 34, 288. *See also* Shahnameh
Turfan (Turpan), 9, 103, 120, 136, 139, 273, 278
Turkestan, 104, 233, 293. *See also* Kazakhstan, Xinjiang province

Turkey, 43, 185, 188, 208, 310. *See also* Anatolia
Turkic languages or scripts, xii, 36, 43, 44, 48, 49, 51, 58, 71, 80, 87, 88, 244, 245, 249, 253. *See also* Chaghatay language; Karluk; Kashgari; Kipchak; Oguz; Turan
"Turkic" as historical role of diverse people, xii, xix, 4, 6, 47, 182
Turkish language, xii, 168, 183, 188, 240, 253, 259, 288, 289
Turkmenistan: Marv, 9, 69. *See also* Transocxiana
Turks. *See* Chaghatai khanate; Gokturk; Kipchaks; Oguz; Shatuo; Uzbeks; Yakuts

Uighurs, 52, 58, 103, 104, 112, 115, 122, 151, 278
Uighur empire (khaghanate), 51–52, 55–56, 72, 78, 87, 102, 105. *See also* Abbasid; Gokturk; Talas; Tang; Tibet
Uighur language or script, 4, 109, 128, 129, 206, 252
Ukraine, 68, 74, 77, 122, 173, 176, 184
Ulugh Beg, 182, 193, 284
ulus (patrimony, empire, state), 107–108, 116, 148, 158, 172, 179, 277. *See also irgen*; *ordo*
Umayyads, 55, 68–69, 73, 91; caliph, 69, 205, 239; Cordoba, 72, 209; North Africa, 73, 209
Urgench (Konye-Urgench). *See* Transoxiana
Uzbeks, 154
Uzbekistan, 8, 112, 182

Varangians and Vikings, 74
Venetian empire, 170, 172, 184, 185, 194
Venice (city), 124, 146, 248, 260; ghetto, 131
Volga River, 59, 75, 172, 175, 178, 282

Waldensians, 225, 226, 226–227
William Rubruck, 124, 154, 205, 209, 217; dates, 131
writing, 4, 36, 49, 96, 109, 233, 242, 245, 249, 252, 253, 256; chancelleries, 109, 143; words for, 49

Wu Zetian, 54, 77
Wycliffe, John, 226–227

Xinjiang
Xiongnu, xix, 11, 12, 14, 44–48, 49, 50, 51–52, 52, 53, 57, 58, 102, 107, 211, 248; economy and population, 44, 45, 46; shanyu/chanyu, 46, 61. *See also* Ashina; Huns
Xixia (Western Xia, Tanggut), 79, 80, 105, 109, 111, 113, 115, 118, 143, 257, 292; and Chinggis, 109, 111, 113, 115, 264; and Song, 79, 80, 109, 115, 143; Buddhism, 80; pastoralism, 109; pluralism, 118, 233–234
Xu Heng, 213

Yakuts, 43
yam (communications system), 117
yasa, 107, 117, 118
Yelu Chucai, 141–143, 144; and talking beast, 164
Yongle. *See* Zhu Di
Yuan dynasty, 138, 141–144, 146, 147, 149–153, 153–154, 155–157, 158–159, 160, 180, 181, 190, 193, 205, 234, 235–236, 236, 237, 240, 263, 264–265, 273, 275, 277–280, 287, 292, 297; and Tibetan Buddhism, 222; Confucian orthodoxy, 213, 255; identity policies, 234–235; popular arts, 248–249, 255–258. *See also* Beijing; Bolad; Chaghatay khanate; Goryeo; Japan; Kublai; *Secret History*; Tibet
yurt, xix, 48, 103, 107, 148

Zheng He, 236, 275, 276
Zhou dynasty, 36, 46, 49, 287, 293
Zhu Di (Yongle emperor), 265, 273, 273–274, 276, 278, 286, 293, 294. *See also* Zheng He
Zhu Xi, 213, 250, 265, 313
Zhu Yuanzhang, 263, 265, 273, 278, 287
Zoroastrianism or Zoroastrians, 23, 25, 29, 30, 50, 91, 112, 207, 215, 221, 222, 239, 246; Ahriman, 25, 31; Ahura Mazda, 25; amesha spenta, 27; Angra Mainyu, 25; Avesta, 25, 32, 246, 288; mainyu, 28; Mitra, 25, 29, 31; Spenta Mainyu, 25; Zoroaster/Zarathustra, 25, 26, 29. *See also* Indo-Iranian groups or languages